A BRANCH
TO REST ON

A BRANCH TO REST ON

THE AUTOBIOGRAPHY OF GEORGE WRIGHT

Edited by

ELIZABETH CADIZ TOPP
ANTHONY LUENGO
LISE WINER

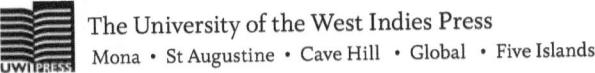

The University of the West Indies Press
Mona • St Augustine • Cave Hill • Global • Five Islands

The University of the West Indies Press
7A Gibraltar Hall Road,
Mona, Kingston 7, Jamaica
www.uwipress.com

© 2025 edited by Elizabeth Cadiz Topp, Anthony Luengo, and Lise Winer

All rights reserved. Published 2025.

A catalogue record of this book is available from the National Library of Jamaica.

ISBN: 978-976-658-040-7 (hardback)
978-976-658-041-4 (paper)
978-976-658-042-1 (ePub)

Cover image: Detail of a painting by John Cadiz, *The Family Tree*, 2021, reproduced courtesy of the artist.

Cover and book design by Robert Harris
Set in Scala 11.3/15.3 x 24.

Printed in the United States of America

CONTENTS

Foreword by Dr Noble Philip.................................... VII
Introduction by Elizabeth Cadiz Topp, Anthony Luengo, and
Lise Winer.. IX

THE AUTOBIOGRAPHY 1

Preface by George Wright.. 3

PART ONE (CHAPTERS 1–8) 1–65

On market day in Sans Souci, George is given away to Uncle Bishop and Tanty, who feed him, clothe him, and send him to school. He experiences a village Christmas, a village wake, and the obeah and bush medicine that fail to save his doomed friend Alvin. Tanty beats him hard and often, and he runs away to Port of Spain to save his life.

PART TWO (CHAPTERS 9–18) 67–165

George learns how to be a yard boy and is hired and fired. He packs a punch and packs biscuits; sleeps in a tree, in a lumber shed and in a rented room in Belmont. He opens an account with the Penny Bank and moves in with his brothers. He lands a job as a labourer and enjoys Aunt Bertrice's cooking.

PART THREE (CHAPTERS 19–39) 167–392

George falls in and out of love, until Philomena captures his heart forever. He works on a bauxite barge and experiences for the first time a new country on a new continent – Suriname. He builds a house in Laventille for his growing family, and after many adventures and mishaps, he finally meets the man who believes in him. He becomes George Wright, the man of business.

CONTENTS

Postscript by Sandra Wright 393

Glossary 395

FOREWORD

I met George Wright in the late 1970s. I was introduced to him by his daughter, Vinneth. We became good friends as he attended a Sunday school class I taught at a church near his home. In the mid-1980s, together with some of my university friends, I engaged in developing a recently purchased abandoned estate in L'Anse Noir, Toco. This adventure necessitated my going on a two-hour trip each way on Saturdays. Mr Wright learned of this project and decided that he would accompany me.

That decision created a bond between us. He was from the Toco area and still knew folk who lived there. He also had the talent for interestingly telling tales infused with great detail. I was getting a free education about life in rural Trinidad in an age when residents needed to contrive a means of living.

George was a family man. His advice always concluded with words about preparing a way forward for my young children. (I had three young ones who were all under six.) He urged me to work hard while I was young. He was pleased that I owned my home. For him, home ownership was essential once you had children. He had constructed much of his own home.

He believed that working hard and building solid relationships were the means of successful living. To support this position, George provided hilarious but true stories about his time with Charles McEnearney and Co. The stories were designed to inform me of the need for a focused and resilient approach to life. At the time, I was a recent University of the West Indies business graduate and a lover of history.

FOREWORD

Given the recency of the 1970 Black Power movement marches, I was also curious about interactions between the social classes. His insights about his life, as they related to this subject, were valuable. George lived in Laventille, the intellectual home of the movement.

On one of our trips, he disclosed that he had written about his life. I was intrigued since I had no idea that a self-made man of his time would find the resources to record his experiences. He gave me a copy to read, and I was blown away by his attention to detail. His book describes his work life and social networks and helps one appreciate an older man's view of life pre-Independence. His work can be described as a contribution to the social history of Trinidad.

I believe this book is an incredible contribution to understanding life in Trinidad. The book is helpful for historians and non-academic persons who seek to acquire principles for good living. I feel honoured to be asked to write this foreword. I strongly recommend it to all. We will all learn from reading it.

Dr Noble Philip, Trinidad. W.I.

INTRODUCTION

In his adult years, George Wright (1920–2001) lived in Laventille, a hilly, densely populated area of east Port of Spain, Trinidad. This is where he spent his retirement writing the story of his life. His large, cursive script fills three heavily bound, lined, legal-sized volumes. They sat on a table in the sitting room of his self-built house, where they attracted the attention of Elizabeth Topp. A Trinidadian now residing in Toronto, she was accompanying her cousin Patricia McEnearney on a social visit to George and his wife, Petronilla. Patricia had known George for many years; he had been employed by her father, Burton McEnearney, an American/Trinidadian entrepreneur. There was a framed photograph of Burton, George's mentor, wearing a World War II US soldier's uniform, in a prominent place in the sitting room, and one of his sons was named after him. Burton was an important man in George's life.

Elizabeth asked if she could read a few pages of the autobiography and was immediately engaged by it. With George's permission, she took the books (comprising in total 550 pages) to a local photocopy shop so that she could read them in their entirety on her return to Toronto. A combination of circumstances and the unplanned vagaries of life meant, however, that the photocopy, once read, was placed on a shelf and not looked at again until 2020. A pandemic was raging, regular life had come to a halt, the calendar was empty, and the time was ripe for once again re-reading George's autobiography, and embarking finally on the long road to getting it published. At this juncture, Anthony Luengo, an

INTRODUCTION

editor with a lifetime of experience in textbook publishing, and Lise Winer, lexicographer and scholar of the English Creole of Trinidad and Tobago, joined Elizabeth on this project.

It is the story of a life recorded in arresting detail, of George's hardscrabble boyhood in the remote fishing village of Sans Souci, the escape from childhood abuse by running away to Port of Spain, and making his way in the big city alone and with no resources. Living in a tree, working as a yard boy, and working aboard a barge headed for Suriname, it is a life filled with picaresque adventures, with false starts and mistakes, hobbled by a minimal education and lack of marketable skills, but guided always by a belief in hard work, a strong moral compass, and extraordinary energy and curiosity. It records his conversations, what he wore, what he ate, whom he met, his friendships and love affairs, his meeting with Petronilla, his mixed interactions with the "elites" and "aristocrats", all told against the backdrop of a Trinidad rapidly changing through the years leading up to and beyond World War II.

George loved the act of writing. His daughter, Vinneth, talks of the sheaves of poems and letters that he carried with him in his briefcase, addressed to a host of important people. This aspect of his writing life is described in his foreword. The writing of his autobiography, on the other hand, was not easy for George; there were many times when it was a slog, and he lacked the zeal that inspired his poems and letters. But he persevered, stopping and starting again, with the encouragement and goading of friends and family. He began the project in 1993, and it was finished and signed by him in 1997, four years before he died in 2001 on the second of May. At several points in the autobiography, he makes it clear that he hopes that it would be published in some form, addressing the "Dear Reader" directly; his desire was to keep the reader engaged, by using devices such as invented dialogue, often in Trinidadian Creole, and recounting interactions that he could not possibly have remembered verbatim but which he uses to enliven and entertain.

A few words about the editing process: the earlier section of the

INTRODUCTION

book, dealing with his childhood and early teenage years, is particularly engaging and cogent, and required very little editing. What editing took place was in the interests of clarification: for example, annotating possibly unfamiliar words and references, and translating passages of Creole into standard English. George himself sometimes explains local expressions and words in the text.

In the latter part of the book, we encountered long passages of repetition and descriptions of activities, for example, the process of building his house, which takes several pages and is very detailed. The narrative pace dropped considerably, as he settles down and becomes "a man of business" in Port of Spain. It was important for us to keep the reader engaged by controlling the flow of the narrative, and we felt that we were doing what George would have wanted. In fact, we think that he wrote the manuscript and then transcribed it into the ledgers; in the process, he lost track of where he was in the transcription and, to be on the safe side, re-copied several pages. These we deleted. At no point did we substitute our own words for his. We shortened the manuscript and annotated it, but we did not rewrite. There is a glossary of English Creole words at the end of the book, drawn from Lise Winer's *Dictionary of the English/Creole of Trinidad and Tobago*. As these words appear in the manuscript, they are identified with an asterisk.

George uses a rather formal, old-fashioned English, with sometimes idiosyncratic grammar and sentence structure. He attended school very sporadically, but was highly literate. His reading list is expansive, encompassing the Bible (which he quotes often), William Shakespeare, Charles Dickens, Sir Walter Scott, Charles Kingsley, Dale Carnegie, and even Adolf Hitler. His writing style, we would like to suggest, is influenced by his early absorption of school texts such as the J.O. Cutteridge's *West Indian Readers*, and his later reading of English literature and poetry from the Victorian era. Sentences such as: "Let me just say this of the man who moulded me. I had been an old drift log from Toco whom ... he took clean and shaped into a piece of furniture that could be used," or more prosaically, "I had yet $5.00 as spending money. I had not a watch, so I therefore thought of making myself a

INTRODUCTION

gift of one especially for my new appointment on Monday morning" bring authors like Dickens to mind. And his ability to describe a scene in minute detail is quite remarkable: "There were pipe fittings strewn upon the floor, bolts and nuts of all sizes lying like stones and pebbles, cans of paint disorderly arranged, galvanize and Celotex lying and standing here and there with dents, broken edges and foot marks. To be precise, the only articles that were well stacked were the lumber. 'Oh no,' said I, 'this will not do.'" We made only minimal corrections to his writing, in the interest of clarity.

It is interesting to note as well that to protect the identities of people George did not think particularly well of, he disguised their names, for example, Odelma, Otchins, and Perman. Where he provides full and accurate names, it indicates these people are high in his esteem.

Many memoirs and autobiographies have been written about Caribbean people who have accomplished important things, have been active in public life, and have a degree of celebrity. What makes George's story uniquely important is that it is the only one we know of that addresses the everyday life of a working-class Black man on a Caribbean island, in the middle years of the twentieth century. It gives an especially vivid picture of rural Afro-Trinidadian life on the remote north coast of Trinidad in the 1920s, and then of the social and economic conditions in the rapidly changing city of Port of Spain from the 1930s to the 1970s, all from the perspective of someone starting off at the very bottom rung of the ladder.

George's life story lends itself to the microhistorical approach which has, over recent decades, illuminated history through the lens of individual cases, lives, and lived experiences.[1] It is our hope that, as such, it will prove a rich resource for scholars of many disciplines, and a book to be read for its own sake, with delight and absorption.

ELIZABETH CADIZ TOPP, ANTHONY LUENGO, and LISE WINER

---

1 See, for example, Istvän M. Szijarto and Sigurður Gylfi Magnusson's *What Is Microhistory? Theory and Practice* (London and New York: Routledge, 2013).

INTRODUCTION

George Wright in his early twenties

THE
AUTOBIOGRAPHY

PREFACE

Now she may not at all welcome how this book has begun, neither may he like its ending. Yet everyone has the given right to his or her own opinion. At this juncture, let me say there are others who may be seeing only its darkness, while to many a radiant beam may be seen which is light. Let us at this stage avoid criticism, as we do know that both darkness and light are needed in this vast firmament.

Although I have written many unpublished poems, in no way have I ever claimed myself to be an author. There were poems directed to prominent officials of governments and industries, those only to relatives and personal friends, many of which were destroyed by fire or stolen, not forgetting through careless storage, the damages done by those little silver-fish. May I say that I was inevitably saddened by these misfortunes because they were all written for my own recreation and enjoyment.

For instance, there was an open competition held for the writing of my country's national anthem, of which Mr Ken Oxley and myself jointly submitted our version. However, this was gracefully won by Mr Patrick Castagne, the author of our beloved "Forged from the Love of Liberty".

May I say that I have written and posted poems to my country's first prime minister, Dr Eric Williams, also our governor general, Sir Solomon Hochoy, which were poems of cheer on our first five years as a nation.

And there were those to mark the visits of Emperor Haile Selassie of Ethiopia, President Kaunda of Zambia and the expected visit of Mrs

PREFACE

Indira Gandhi of India. A poem was also dedicated and sent to the first president of my country, Sir Ellis Clarke, to the family of the late President Kennedy after his assassination, and one to the then-prime minister of Jamaica, after the disaster of Hurricane Gilbert. However, I do believe that due to their busy office at the time no replies were received from them.

Acknowledgements were however received from the following: former Police Commissioner Mr Randolph Burroughs, Mrs Coretta King, the three astronauts who successfully made the first moon landing, Mr Hubert Humphrey, a former vice-president of the United States of America, President Lyndon B. Johnson, also of the USA, and her most Gracious Majesty Queen Elizabeth the Second of Great Britain.

In my venture please allow me to mention the following names of folks who encouraged and morally supported me: Mrs Hazel Perkins Mosca, Messrs Burton and Claude Anne McEnearney, Mr Everard Scott, Dr Steve P. Bennett, Captain E.G. Melville, Mr Horatio Modeste and my dear son, Lincoln A. Wright. With reverence I say thanks.

Many times I have been advised to have some of my work published in the media; this I never did. However, there comes a time when one should bow and listen, as when attention is directed to yeoman's remarks. On the first of November 1988 President Ronald Reagan of the USA used a remark which perhaps may have been overlooked by many. And I quote, "It is not too late to seek a newer world." And so I have now picked up the challenge by presenting a biography of my childhood and youthful life, which associate with that of my adult and working life.

I visited the USA in July 1993. While in Long Island I happened to meet an old friend, Mr Tony Lazare. He read a poem I had recently written in honour of my dear wife (Marm). He said to me, "George, why don't you write a book on your life?" About four hours later that very day I travelled to Ludlow, Massachusetts; there at the home of another friend, Mr Alfred La Riviere, while in conversation he said to me, "George, why don't you write a book?" A week later I was in Canada. While there I visited a very good friend, Mr Britten Bernard,

PREFACE

who said to me, "Georgie, you are wasting precious time, have you ever considered the writing of a book?" I then said to myself this is surely no coincidence. So, lackadaisically, I picked up the challenge when I returned to Trinidad. I worked but lacked the zeal. But in July '95 Alfred called me from his home; while in conversation he enquired how was I getting through with the book. I told him I had not worked on it for the longest while. "That don't sound like George. Come on, man, don't be slothful!" So I again started.

Though humble, yet I make no apology for the following. Few are the Trinidadians who were not born of slaves' descendants or indentured servants. Or may have worked in the domestic services of the upper class. I therefore admonish you, do not be ashamed or be self-deprecatory of your beginnings or status. Just bear in mind that there must be pioneers in the start of every venture. Remember that a slave once became second-in-command to an Egyptian king. Always banish self-pity; it can be self-destructive. May I also advise that the word "menial" be used only with dignity. Silver and gold are good, but the hoarding thereof can breed unhappiness. Be content with your blessings, however small; just use them wisely. Benjamin Franklin once said, "Contentment makes poor men rich, while discontent makes rich men poor."

This book was written with the hope to encourage all saddened, hopeless and down-spirited people who and wherever they are with the hope that they might be inspired to look up and work towards the bright side that there is of life. You can buy or give your copy to someone, but please, I admonish, don't you lend.

I hold but one regret, which is that my sister Hilda Atherley had fallen asleep before it was written.

SIGNED GEORGE WRIGHT, 7-5-97

PART ∙ ONE

Chapter 1

George's early childhood in Sans Souci; evil spirits and malnutrition; on market day George gets new guardians

I was born in the Caribbean island of Trinidad in the County of St David in the northeast ward of Toco in which lies the fishing village of Sans Souci.[1] As I memorize a rough inventory at the time, there were no more than sixty cottages and eighty ajoupas*, along with twenty-five barrack rooms* on lands which were holdings of the Bowen and Gordon Grant Estates. There were two primary schools, one Anglican, the other Roman Catholic. Both schools were also used as churches for Christian worship.

I fell into the category of the unfortunates, those children whose fathers had died when they were an early age. My dad died when I was two years and eighteen days old, leaving as well my baby sister, who was then eighteen days old. We were both born on Christmas Day, she on the twenty-fifth of December 1922, I on the twenty-fifth of December 1920. Dad died on the twelfth of January 1923. My mother then had five children for whom to provide. Unfortunately for her, she was the common-law wife of my father and a mere washer by profession, which made her life a very rough one. Then came an eminent split in the family. My elder sister was taken by our maternal grandmother, and

---

[1] The village of Sans Souci lies seven kilometres east of Toco, the most northeasterly village in Trinidad. As the crow flies, the distance to the capital, Port of Spain, is sixty kilometres.

my eldest brother by our paternal grandmother. Which then left three of us in the care of our mother.

My mother very soon formed an association with another man, the result of which was very terrible. We were taken to live in one of the estate's barrack rooms, and although I was no more than three years, I can clearly remember the following event. Mother went into the village to wash. She took with her my baby sister and my brother. She left me in the care of another barrack-room neighbour. All I had gotten as a meal from that creature for that day was some dissolved sugar in water (a beverage used by peasants and called "sweet-water"*). When my mother came home that evening* these were the kind of words that came from the mouth of that woman: "Plum! Oh, Plum, don't give Crecy" – (a nickname by which I was called) – "no food, ee* belly full, ee well eat today." I was horrified at the given statement, but still hoped that my dinner of cooked bananas in coconut milk and fish (which was the staple meal) would yet be given to me. I, however, was denied it and was instead given a cup of warm herb tea. My kindly brother sneaked me a piece of his cooked banana. Today, well after seventy years, I do remember that event. Dear Reader, please be very careful when choosing nurseries and babysitters, for there are those where saints can dwell, while others are a living hell.

Within that era of my life I suffered desperately from big-guts*. My stepfather said that I had an evil spirit eating with me so he prescribed charcoal to be placed in my every meal. I was a very ravenous eater and, if not closely watched, I would devour the charcoal at times. I also had the ill habit of wetting my bed. For this my stepfather would then hold a frog or toad to my penis as he exclaimed loudly, "Bite ee pigin*, bite ee pigin."² It did instill a fear which I hold for those amphibians up to this day.

I was one day taken to the village and was very much surprised to see so many people. There were lots of grown-ups and children. Pork, fish, ripe bananas, chunks of sugar cane, and vegetables for sale were

---

2   'Bite his penis, bite his penis.'

CHAPTER ONE

displayed under the eaves of a shop. There were big men having strong drinks and ladies dressed in brightly coloured dresses with their heads tied with multi-coloured kerchiefs as they busied themselves among others in and out of the shop. Occasionally, you got the smell of spilled pitch-oil* carried by lads in uncorked bottles. And there was that pleasant aroma coming from the tray of a woman as she lifted the white spread which concealed her ware of cakes, buns and bread. Without segregation, she sells to all who come, but occasionally you may see her curtsy with a smile and bow to others. Yet not too far off there is another woman brightly dressed with a white headband and a red flower tucked to the side as she busied herself over a large basin of souse* as she attends to a boozer. As I greedily glared at those delicacies, right across the street beneath a covered section was my stepfather, beating away on a drum, while a few curious lads and old men looked on. My mother, who was poorly dressed as compared to the other ladies, held my little sister, while my brother joked and laughed with boys of his age. This day was a Saturday or market day.

Suddenly a heavy hand rested upon my shoulder. As I looked up, there was a man who smilingly said to me, "You know me." "No," I replied. "Just now," said he as he darted into the shop. Very quickly he returned with a kaiser ball*. "Here, take this." I ravenously chewed on the candy. He bent down and softly said, "I am your uncle." I looked at him. "I am Uncle Bishop," said he. I then remembered that name being mentioned at home, so I looked at him. "You want to come and live wid me, you go get plenty food." From the mention of the word "food" my heart leapt. "Yes," said I. At that very moment, my brother came running from across the street. With a very quick action he held my mouth. "Is whe you ha dey?"³ With a quick squeeze and jerked action out came my candy, falling to the ground. He quickly picked it up, and with a greedy grin he bit it in two pieces; he pushed into my mouth the smaller of the two and sped off again to his friends without saying a word to Uncle.

---

3   'What do you have there?'

A BRANCH TO REST ON

Market vendor, Trinidad

CHAPTER ONE

Uncle stood up as I took hold of his hand. "Hi, Plum! Plum!" he shouted to my mother, who was speaking to another woman who touched her upon her shoulder and pointed towards us. Mother then looked to our direction with a smile upon her face. She lifted my sister and held her astride upon her hips and walked towards us. "Ah-ah, Bishop, how yuh do? Lang time nah see." "Plum, gal, ar alright, oui*. Ah see yuh bring Crecy out in de village. Wha happen to am – he staunted, he sick or wot?"[4] Before she could have given him an answer, the drumming ceased and quickly came my stepfather from across the street.

Without an introduction, he acted right away as a cunning salesman who had in his possession some bad merchandise and was very anxious to get rid of it. "Yuh want am, Bishop? Tek am nah. Yuh nah ave no pickney. Ee go be good company fo Pet. Jest now ee go grow to help bring water because right now ee does help ee brother pick bois flot* to stuff pillar fo dem to sleep on, an help sweep up de yard." With that brief statement, he looked my mother in the face. "Wha yuh say, Plum?" "Yes," nodded my mother. "Gargie de tell mih sometin jes before he dead," said Uncle. "But hole on, nah go way. Leh me go talk to Pet fuss."[5] My stepfather then took my mother aside with my sister in her arm; they spoke but I heard not what was said. Very quickly Uncle was back, and with a big smile he said to them, "Ah go tek am. Pet say bring am."[6] Alas, my friend, bang! bang! went an unseen gavel, as I was sold not for currency but was bought through pity.

Let me now use my correct name, George, instead of "Crecy," the nickname. My father's name was Raymond Adolphus George Wright. I

---

4   'Hey, Bishop, how are you doing? Long time no see.' 'Plum, girl, I'm really all right. I see that you've brought Crecy into the village. What's the matter with him? Is he stunted, sick or what?'

5   'Do you want him, Bishop? Do take him. You don't have a child. He will be good company for Pet. Soon he will grow up enough to help bring water because right now he helps his brother pick kapok to stuff pillows for them to sleep on, and helps sweep up the yard.' With that brief statement he looked my mother in the face. 'What do you have to say, Plum?' 'Yes,' nodded my mother.
   'Gargie told me something just before he died,' said Uncle. 'But hold on; don't go away. Let me go talk to Pet first.'

6   'I will take him. Pet says to bring him.'

was named Reginald Emmanuel George Wright, but generally answer to George Wright. My paternal grandmother's maiden name was Catherine Paul. She had been married to McLeod, who very shortly became deceased; they had no children. She then met Wright, with whom she had an association; they had one child, who was my father, Raymond Adolphus George, who was then called McLeod by some folks and Wright by others. Wright also died, and she met Lucas and had a relationship with him, which resulted in another boy child, Felix Alexis Bishop,[7] surnamed Lucas. Lucas also became deceased. Without wasting time Catherine became the common-law wife of Morris. They had four children: Samuel, Helen, Camelia and Beaulie (a boy and three girls). Morris also died. Without delay she met Woods, who in six months slept with the others. After which, men ran from her invitation.

My uncle then said, "Come, George, let me lift you up." By then I had already lost all taste of the candy and now welcomed the jolly ride astride his shoulders. Very soon we arrived at his home. He then called aloud, "Pet! Oh, Pet! Ella! Ella!" "Yes, yes," came an answer, as a woman, with all smiles, appeared at the door. She was short and plump with round features and short black hair with plaits stuck out as she laughed with pearly white teeth. Then as if shocked, she looked at me and said, "Poor thing, so this is the boy. George right now must be turning in his grave to see his condition." Then Uncle very gently pushed me towards her and said, "Go, boy, to your Tanty*." From that very moment and through my childhood days she was called Tanty.

Then said Uncle Bishop, "Ella, you know something, I forgot to ask Plum about his clothes." With tear-filled eyes she said, "Don't you worry about that. I have two tight dresses there; I shall rip them and make him some clothes." Very quickly I was taken to the nearby river, bathed, and dressed in one of Uncle's vests. As we got back Tanty said, "Bishop, I made some pauslie with worm grass* and a small piece of bois cano* leaf in it for him. But let him eat first. Tonight before he goes to bed, we shall give him that to drink."

---

7   Possibly Uncle Bishop's father.

CHAPTER ONE

The supper was the very best I had yet experienced. It consisted of boiled rice and vegetables with fried fish stewed in coconut milk coloured with red roo-coo*. It was like Uncle told me under the shop, the food was plenty. Immediately I came to love and trust them both, especially Tanty with her kind smile. That evening before going to bed I was given the herb tea. Although it tasted very nasty, that was however repaid by its sweetness.

Chapter 2

*George hears church bells and sees the sea for the first time;
yams for Christmas, parang and a new madbull kite*

My bed, which was made up of old used clothing and sheeted with a large cocoa bag*, was very soft, and with a cased 'bois flot' pillow under my head I soon fell asleep. The next morning, however, I heard Uncle saying, "Gol, Ella, he wet his bed." To this Tanty made no remark. My heart leapt with fear as I wondered whether I would be scolded with a horrid toad. I lay still and quite scared. But Uncle came and said to me, "You must try not to pee your bed." Tanty then said, "Yuh ent see he bladder weak? However, don't worry wid dat, it go stop after he get some good bush tea*." "OK," said Uncle, "if yuh say so."

I then suddenly heard a strange sound coming from a distance as though many buckets and pans were being moved around together at the same time. My guardians immediately observed that something was wrong and became concerned. "What's the matter, George?" Uncle asked. "I am hearing something," I replied. To this Tanty laughed and said, "That's the church bell ringing reminding people of church." I looked in wonder at her. "Today is Sunday," said she, "and some people go to church and pray. Your father never missed going except if feeling very sick." As the sun became hot that morning, my uncle took me outside and helped me hang my bed clothing to dry. Boy oh boy. I was not switched, neither were any frogs brought to me. (I very soon found that these creatures were numerous due to the neighbouring river.)

CHAPTER TWO

Again may I say the meals were excellent. As evening came Uncle said to me, "Come, let's go and see Grandma and your brother Quildon." I was smartly dressed in a suit Tanty had made from one of her dresses. The distance was about 150 yards around a corner from where we were. As we arrived in the yard, I heard someone say, "What have you brought me?" "Good evening, Mooma," said Uncle. She answered not, but went on to say, "Since yuh tek up wid dat Tobago ooman yuh ent gi me six cents. Ah warn you bout she. Yuh can't say ah didn't because I know dey hands nasty, but yuh a break stick in yuh ears*. Go on, yong man, wen the wost come don't run to me."[1]

Uncle said, "Mooma, look, I have brought George to see you; I took him from Plum yesterday." "Me hear dat aredy. Kate Brebner tell me," she replied. "Go," said he to me, "and tell Grandma good evening." And so he pushed me gently towards her. "Well ah hope yuh behave yuhself a good boy," said she to me without another greeting. I looked at her, and unlike some of the other ladies I had seen, she was a very attractive woman with somewhat straight nose, large white eyes, long features and flowing long black hair, with a command in her voice when she spoke. "Where is Quildon?" asked Uncle. "Ah tink he gone by de bay," she replied. We stood there for a while and not a kind or unkindly word was said. Uncle, then patting me on my shoulder, said, "He wants to see his brother." "Go! Ah tell you he by de bay." "OK," said Uncle, "Come, George, let's go find Quildon." As we were leaving the door, I looked back at her. Yet she said not another word to me or even smiled.

We got on to the beach, and for the first time I saw the huge mass of roaring tumbling waters – waves they were. I was afraid and I held tightly on to Uncle's hand. Timidly I said, "Let's go back home." "You are afraid of those waves?" he asked. "They cannot catch us; they die when they reach the shore. There is your brother," said he, pointing.

---

1 'Since you've taken up with that Tobago woman you haven't given me six cents. I warned you about her. You can't say I didn't because I know their hands are nasty, but you break stick in your ears (don't listen). Go on, young man, when the worst happens don't run to me.'

"Look over there," as he pointed to the way of some shrubs. Uncle yelled and then came Quildon as he ran from some other boys who were seated on a log pounding sea almonds. He came to us with his mouth filled, as he tried to say good evening to Uncle and "Hi, George" to me. "Grandma told me this morning that he came to live with you. Here," said he, poking his hand into his pocket; he pulled out and handed me about eight almonds. "Eat them," said he, "they have no sand." Uncle then told him that it was time to go home to Grandma. Quildon then yelled and waved to his friends as we left the beach.

When we got home, Tanty was busy sewing upon her hand machine. It was an all-steel Singer machine. She raised her head; with a smile she asked, "Did you see Grandma and your brother?" "Yes, Tanty," I replied, and I took the almonds that I hid in my pocket and gave to her. Uncle looked amazed. "I thought you had already eaten those," said he. Tanty then gave me two and shared the others with Uncle and herself.

Then came bedtime. That evening I was again given that nasty-tasting tea, and as I was about to slip into bed, I was stopped by Tanty. "No, no," said she, "don't you pray before going to bed?" I knew not of what she was speaking. Uncle then said to me, "Have you remembered the bell you heard this morning when Tanty said people are going to church to pray?" "Yes, Uncle," said I. "Well, that's what Tanty is now telling you about. One must first pray before going to bed." "Yes," said Tanty, "everyone must pray, even little children." She then said, "Kneel down and let me teach you the Lord's Prayer." This prayer was then taught to me for the first time, and as time passed on I was taught others.

I wore plaits and I could very well remember that they were very much longer than those of Tanty's. She loved combing my hair before combing hers. And when finished she would gather all the loose hairs and place same into a purse-like cloth bag. When this was filled it was sewed and used as a pincushion.

One day I overheard Tanty saying to Uncle, "Boy, Bishop, you know that Christmas is upon us already, as soon as you hear 'ember' look out for December." I knew not of what she was speaking. And so one evening a group of boys and girls came singing some lovely songs at

CHAPTER TWO

our home. Tanty seemed delighted and so she reached upon the shelf for a cloth purse and handed their leader two cents and they left.

Many evenings at sunset Uncle would weed or clean around the yard, filling holes here and there with gravel and sand, while Tanty busied herself sewing. There were curtains, bed sheets, shirts for Uncle, and not for a moment forgetting me with my romper and blouse.

Days sped very quickly, hoarding feelings of excitement. And one evening I heard Uncle saying to Tanty, "Ella, I would be going to zagaya* very early in the morning for the yams. Should Mr Johnson pass, tell him I am ahead of him."

I was awake the next morning when he left and so I darted to the box of ripe bananas. "Stop!" said Tanty to me. "What did I tell you to do when you get up on mornings?" "Pray," said I, "and say good morning to whoever may be around." "Yes, what else?" "Change my sleeping clothes." "And what else?" I was then silent for a moment when I suddenly remembered, "Wash my mouth." "Good boy," said she, "don't let me have to tell you that again." I prayed and hurried to the hibiscus hedge and broke off a small twig and chewed one end of it into a brush as Uncle had showed me. I then scrubbed my teeth and washed my mouth. (Those were the days the average peasant worried not himself to purchase patent toothbrushes and paste, but improvised his own toothbrush as he used salt, soap, or even grounded charcoal as his paste.) I then helped myself to a large banana. Tanty laughed and said, "You may have another."

I then set off for the river. There was a spot on the bank that was my favourite seating place. There I would sit and gaze into the clear waters as I looked at fishes and crawfish swimming leisurely. Occasionally, a horrid-looking eel would quickly dart from between the rocks and grab a crawfish for its breakfast. That morning, however, I had a surprise. A large white bird with very long legs and neck came and perched upon a close-by rock. I remained motionless as I gazed at it. With a quick action down went its head into the stream as it caught a fish and flew off to the nearby trees on the riverbank. I hurried off to Tanty with the news, who said that bird was a gaulin*. She then said to me, "Come and have your tea." As I was eating my last fried bake*, Uncle came with a very stout bag upon his head. "Come, Pet," he shouted, "come and help me down." Tanty then hurried from her washing tray with soap-soaked hands. She helped him down of his burden. "You are back quickly?" "Yes," said he, "Mr Johnson had dug them all yesterday." "But why bring so much?" she asked. "Do you forget this is Christmas week and Mooma and some other people have to get." He then opened the bag. I was very anxious to see its contents. It was a bag of only yams. "By the way, Pet," said Uncle, "did you talk to Mr York about the pork?" "No," said she, "York pork would be too fat. I have spoken to Anderson instead. His pig is more lean."

The next day brother Quildon came to collect the yams for Grandma. With a large smile upon his face, he said to me, "Tomorrow will be Christmas Eve and the next day Christmas. It shall be Georgiana's and your birthday." He then gave me a kindly poke on the side as he said, "Plenty of food, cakes, ginger beer and roast pork." I was very interested in his remark but not with a gluttonous longing, because now I was never hungry. The next day being Christmas Eve as my brother had said, Tanty cooked lots of yams and pork. The yams looked all yellow when cooked. Quildon and one of his friends came and ate. I had my fill, and Tanty sent a large bowl filled for Grandma.

The following day was really Christmas Day. As I got out of bed there was lots of excitement and strange smells in our house. There was the odour of varnish coming from the chairs, blind, and safe*, and also the smell of oil cloth on the table, the appetizing smell of roast pork, and not forgetting that delicious smell of breads and cakes – all filling the house and making one conglomerous smell. In the distance was the ringing of the bells of both churches, Catholic and Anglican, and from a neighbour's house came the most beautiful music and singing. Oh how I wished that they were at our house. I then remembered I had not prayed so I withdrew to my bedside and hurriedly prayed and yelled, "Good morning, Tanty, good morning, Uncle."

The serenaders did eventually come to our house. Their band consisted of a cuatroist*, a guitarist, a violinist, two tambourinists

CHAPTER TWO

and two chac-chac* players, supported by some singing young women. The violinist played with such gusto I heard Uncle saying to him, "Boy, Adolphus, you are playing that violin with such splendour you remind me of a player I heard in a concert in London, England, name Fritz Kreisler,[2] and he made that violin talk in the hall." Except for Tanty, everybody laughed. She busied herself sharing cakes, ginger beer and rum punch, while someone shouted, "Come, man, Bishop, you too smart! Bring the rum! The cacapool*!" These folks stayed at our house a full half hour and then left for another. With a saddened heart I watched them go as they winded their way into a track. As I stood dreaming, Uncle called and said to me, "George, I have a surprise for you." Tanty then came smiling at me as I looked on with wonder. "See here," said Uncle, as he took a very large kite which was hidden behind the safe, "I have made you a madbull*. Come, let's go by the bay to fly it." Boy oh boy, was I happy.

Very quickly, with the sand sinking beneath our feet, we were on the bay with our kite. There we met many men and boys also flying kites, while there were those who just looked on and talked. Very quickly Uncle had our kite up among the others. He was a good kite flyer, and our kite stood out among the best of them. Our kite was in the air fully past an hour when Uncle said to me, "Come, let's get it down quickly, it's going to rain." Very sadly, I watched him pull it down as he wound up the thread. No sooner were we at home than came a shower of rain. By this time Tanty was almost ready with our meats. After which, we three sat down and ate. Then it was that Uncle said to me, "Today you are four years old and Georgiana two." And it was my first known Christmas dinner. Time passed on quickly. And one evening Tanty said to me that tonight is Old Year's Night and we are both going to church. "What about Uncle, is he not coming with us?" "No," said she. "Why not, Tanty?" I asked. With disdain she moved off and muttered, "He goes elsewhere." She then bathed me from a barrel of water, as

---

2   An Austrian-born American violinist and composer, Fritz Kreisler (1875–1962) was one of the most noted violin masters of his day.

she said it was too late for me to go to the river. I was happy about that because at that time the frogs and toads come from their hiding places.

We both got dressed, she in a frock she had made for Christmas and I in a new bodice and rompers. She creamed our feet with coconut oil, slipped on a pair of alpagatas* upon her feet and off we went. Said she to me, "Walk quickly," as the last bell was then ringing. Very soon we entered this large and strange-looking building with its many benches and windows. There we met some strange-looking old men and women. There were also children, a few about my age. I also espied two of the pretty girls who came singing at our home on Christmas morning. In all there were about forty souls. Then from a little room came a bearded man all dressed in a long white gown. He muttered something and everyone stood up as they held books and began singing. Tanty had not a book, but she sang aloud with the others. Their melodies were not new to me for very often I heard them being sung by Tanty. The disguised gent prayed and read from a large book. I saw an old woman sobbing in a corner. The meeting lasted for about an hour, after which we were all dismissed.

As we slowly walked from the churchyard, there was much babbling, especially among the older women. Questions were asked of Tanty about me. Some folks stroked my head, others patted my shoulders, while an old woman pinched my cheek and said, "Ee look just like ee poopa* Garge Wright." "Yuh fine so?" said another, "I fine he resemble Plum."³ I was very happy when we finally headed for home.

The moon shone brightly when we got there as the breeze blew the coconut palm trees to and fro. Tanty then looked up to the skies. With lifted hands she said, "Good Lord, on a night like tonight, where is Bishop?" I then got concerned about Uncle. "Come, chile," said she, "come and drink your tea, for it is more than time that you got into bed." I was then given my herb tea, which was cold. I then prayed, said good night to Tanty, and got into bed. By this time I had learned to get up

---

3   'He looks just like his father, George Wright.' 'You think so?' said another. 'I find he resembles Plum.'

CHAPTER TWO

and urinate during the night, so there was no longer a problem with the wetting of my bed.

The next day was New Year's Day. As Tanty got out of bed that morning, through a window she looked at the rising sun. I then heard her saying, "Praise" and "Thank Poopa Jesus I see the new year." Then appeared Uncle, who said to her, "Happy New Year, Ella." She returned not the compliment but asked, "Where did you go last night, Bishop? You could easily have come to church with us. But, no, you rather go and throw away the few cents. Carry on and see if that will put us anywhere. One thing I will tell you: this is a new year, and no longer will I be taking and putting up with your bad habits. Your mother is already giving me a bad name saying I does tek yuh money and gee obeah* man. But de good Lard will deal wid she. She sit down dey and she don't know how I ave to cut and contrive to make two ends meet. If not, dat mashine ar ded."[4] In my little mind I wondered what she was talking about (the same of which I learned later).

---

4   'Your mother is already giving me a bad name by saying I take your money and give it to the obeah man. But the good Lord will deal with her. She sits down there and she doesn't know how I have to cut and contrive to make two ends meet. If not, that machine is dead.'

Chapter 3

*George loses his plaits and starts school; he learns to read and recite;
he gets licks from Tanty and learns to fight*

Then one Sunday morning as the church bell was ringing, Uncle said, "Well, George, I have to cut your hair today. You are a big boy now, and you would be going to school tomorrow." I felt very sorry to know that I was going to lose my plaits, but I was very much consoled by the news of going to school. Very often I had seen other children hurrying along the street on their way there and wondered when would I join them. I was then taken to the bank of the river where my plaits were shorn by Uncle. Sadly, I watched them being pulled by the swift-flowing stream. Uncle had placed the first plait into his pocket, saying, "This is for Tanty." When we got back to the house there was Tanty looking happy as ever, but yet seemed trying to conceal a disappointed feeling. Uncle handed the plait to her, which she took and placed upon the shelf with her coin purse. She again looked at me and said with a smile, "Now you do look as a* boy. Come and have your tea." It was roasted bake and saltfish*, buljol*, with an enamel cup of homemade chocolate boiled in coconut milk with small dumplings. I had my fill.

I felt a bit awkward without my plaits but very soon became accustomed to losing them. All day Uncle stayed home that Sunday with us. He told me how I must behave myself as a good boy at school. "You are not to give your teacher any trouble. Whenever you want to pee, you must stand up and salute and ask permission. You are at no

CHAPTER THREE

time to talk to anyone in your class. Do not fight nor make faces to anyone. You are at no time to eat in your class. Should you be thirsty, ask Teacher with a salute to allow you to go." And so my uncle went through that exercise over and over that day with me.

The next day I was awakened very early by Tanty. "Come, child, and face the dawn of your happiness or unhappiness," said she. I did well my taught exercise of praying and washing my mouth. "Do not eat any bananas this morning," said Tanty. "It may humbug you at school for your first day." I then went and bathed in the river. When I came back, I was given my breakfast and was made ready for school as my feet were all rubbed with coconut oil. I was then ready for my trek to school.

Uncle had already left for his work. On our way Tanty began to repeat most of what Uncle told me yesterday, as she rehearsed, "Boy, do not talk in your class. Do not give your teacher trouble. Do not fight and play and dirty your clothes." At this a bell rang when we were about half the distance away from the school, which was the very building in which we went to church on Old Year's Night. "Oh me gash!" Tanty exclaimed. "Stand up here; don't move. Ah going back; ah forget yuh recess." While I waited, no one passed by and I was glad for that. Very quickly she rejoined me, with three Haynes sweet biscuits wrapped in a paper. "These are for you to eat when it is recess," said she. We then took a shortcut and arrived at the school with time to spare before another bell rang.

The school was filled with students, boys and girls; about fifty were there with three teachers and one monitor. The classes were opened with a prayer and the singing of the hymn "Loving Shepherd of Thy Sheep". I was placed in the ABC class as I was a beginner. As they sang from hymn books, I was able to sing and called most of the words correctly because Tanty very often sang that song. My class teacher, who was a much bigger woman than Tanty, kept looking at me. She was well dressed, with stockings and shoes upon her feet, and she wore a pleasant smile. There were about fifteen of us in this class. We were taught and sang nursery rhymes, rehearsed the alphabet and counted to ten, all being done in a sing-song manner. A little girl cried very loudly and was made to sit upon a small bench at the doorway. When Tanty came for me that evening she spoke with the teacher. I saw them share a joke. When we got home Uncle was already there; he spoke with Tanty, and they both looked pleasingly at me, I knew not what for.

The next day no one had to take me to school. I went all by myself. In about three weeks I knew almost all the daily hymns and prayers, could count to twenty, and knew all the alphabet by heart. (One of the reasons: whenever I got home, Tanty in her spare time would count to twenty with me, and would also rehearse the alphabet over and over with me.) Whenever Plasticine was given to the class for work, I would always be told that my creation was the best. Again I was helped by my uncle, who would gather the soft mud the crabs took from their holes and form it into objects. I loved playing with the mud balls between my fingers.

Then one morning Teacher said to me, "George, will you like to go to that class over there?" The class was third stage, and it was being taught by the monitor. "Yes, Teacher," said I with a bow. "OK, tell Tanty to come and see me when you get home. You shall go there on Monday." I got home in very high spirits that day. As I broke the news to Tanty she was pleased and said to me, "Tell Uncle when he gets home that Teacher wants him. Say no more than that."

As he came that evening, I told him Teacher wants him. Tanty then added, "You better go now before they close up the school." He then hurried over. On his return he said that the teacher told him I would be transferred from the infants' class to third stage because all my work was very good. He went on to say that the teacher said that I was the brightest child in my class. So he must get me a reading book, pencil and slate, a copybook and lead pencil in readiness for Monday. Then there was a silence. Tanty then said, "So what?" "Ella," said he in despair, "I have no money." Tanty with a disdainful look said, "There is a shilling* on the safe, go and buy the boy books. Pencil and slate will be given to him at school." "I shall rather buy him his own slate," he said.

Before having his supper, he went over to the shop and purchased the items. These were an *Introductory West Indian Reader*, written by

CHAPTER THREE

Captain J.O. Cutteridge, a copybook, a lead pencil, and a metal slate. "What about the change?" said Tanty. He then took from his pocket four candies: there were three extra-strongs* and a lavinee*. At this Tanty laughed. He then had his supper. As he was finished Tanty said, "Bishop, from now on teach him to read that book. My eyes burn. I cannot see the prints clearly, even to thread the needle. I shall have to see if the shopman can get me a pair of spectacles." (These were the days peasants bought their glasses over the counter without advice from an optician.)

Uncle began to teach me that very evening before the dusk. As darkness crept up, Tanty lit the oil lamp, placed it upon the table for us to see, and sat with us. At first I found it to be difficult. But Tanty pointed out to watch the objects and spell the words. To this Uncle readily agreed and so we passed the evening until bedtime. The next day as Uncle left, Tanty again took the book and let me look at the objects and spell the words. And so I got into the feel of it and that she kept on doing secretly from Uncle until Monday morning when I left to appear in my new classroom. At the beginning I was nervous and the challenge seemed a bit tough, but when I observed that I was very much brighter than some bigger children in the class of ten, I quickly began to catch up with the brighter ones. Which was all done in a month's time.

During this period of my life I had never been spanked at home nor at school. But one day I got into trouble with Tanty. At lunchtime I brought a big boy at home with me. Tanty had told me I would not meet her at home at that time because she would be going to another village to visit a sister of hers that was ill. She showed me where the key would be hidden, and, of course, I knew which meal was mine. I shared my lunch with the boy. But somehow along our stay he tricked me, perhaps by sending me outside. However, whatever, it was, he stole some of Uncle's portion. Well, that was it. Tanty was sure mad with me. She switched me so severely with hibiscus stems that my skin became waled*. She used not filthy words, but some remarks she passed surely did hurt. When Uncle came home that evening, I looked forward again for a tanned hide, but when he was told the story, and perhaps seeing my waled skin, he had compassion on me. He flogged me not, but gave me such a scolding that I never again brought that fellow home.

The next day as I sat in class at recess, the chap came and said, "I am coming with you at lunchtime." "No!" said I, "you are a big thief." The news of my accusations spread very quickly in the schoolroom, which did set eyes upon me. So the very next morning at recess a big girl from one of the senior classes approached and said to me, "Runt, you called my brother a thief yesterday?" I looked at her. "No," said I, "I had not to call him; he *is* a thief." The children all laughed. She became more angry and swung a blow at me. "Oh no," said a big boy as he got between us, "you cannot hurt him." "OK," said she, "monkey say cool breeze*, wait until Friday, I will let him beat you up." Now Tanty always said to me, "Don't you ever hit first, but should anyone hit you, burst their head with a stone and run." And so from that evening I began marking crabs and making them my target. As I saw one out of its hole, I would pelt stones at it. In a matter of two days I was a marksman. During this time I made no mention at home of the brewing incident.

My bookbag was made by Tanty; it was really an oversized cloth purse closed by a cord. In it I placed three stones and put my book, slate and pencil in. I tried to escape under a bridge as they waited for me that Friday evening, but a troublemaker saw me and told them. So I was blocked and brought back into the road. A big boy then took off my cap and placed it upon the head of my opponent, who quickly threw it off. At this the children all laughed. I picked it up and put it on again. As I walked off, "No, not so," said another boy, "don't go yet." He then took the boy's cap and placed it upon my head. I also threw it down. And just then he struck me. I felt not the blow for it had no sting, so I kept walking away. The children all laughed. His sister then said, "Hit him hard!" He then sank one in my tummy; it did hurt. I thought about the stones in my bag, but I could not then reach them. So all hell broke loose. It was my first fight and Uncle always said I am not to come home at any time and say anyone of my age or even older beat me up. But here was I now getting the worst of it, then suddenly two of his fingers slipped into my mouth and down sank my teeth into

CHAPTER THREE

them. Nothing then would make me release him as he bawled. At the time his sister was making a drum out of me.

The news of the brawl got to the staffroom, and the headmaster came with his strap. He dealt the girl a few strokes to get her off my back and so I released my victim. The news was also hurried home to Tanty, who came and informed the teacher of what she thought had caused it all. After which I gained full respect from the other children.

Chapter 4

*A new barrack room; George learns to raise chickens;
his friend Alvin comes down with a mysterious illness*

One evening after dinner Uncle and Tanty said to me, "George, we are leaving this house. It is not ours and the owner is coming back from town to live here." "Where are we going?" I asked. "In the barrack," said they. My heart sank as I thought it to be the same place where my mother and stepfather lived. I started to cry. "Why are you crying?" asked Tanty. "I do not want to live at Cousin James (my stepfather) again." "No, no," said she, "we are not going to that barrack, we are going to Valley Estates." I was happy when she said Valley Estates because one of my best classmates lived there. "OK," said I, drying my tears as they both laughed.

That very night they began packing and tying things in large bedsheets, making ready for the next day, which was a Saturday. Early that morning Uncle brought along four friends, and with himself in two trips they moved everything, lock, stock and barrel. Our new home was not as large as the first. Nor was it a house by itself. It was a long apartment building which housed six families. We were in room #2 with one window at the back. The door was horizontally divided. In that way the lower portion was always kept closed, allowing the air to flow freely through the open portion.

The distance from my school was now about four times the journey as compared with that of our previous home. The river was now no longer near to us, although there was a brook which was not very far

CHAPTER FOUR

away. We could no longer hear the great waves splash upon the shore, nor could we now see the ocean as before. But yet, in spite of these disadvantages, I loved our new home.

Now, as I had already mentioned, my best classmate lived here. And although we shared not the same building, we were on the same compound. Their room was room #1, where he lived with two windows and a door. Beyond the apartments were stables which housed two horses, two mules, one donkey, two cows, three sheep, two goats, and a sty with two large sows. Added to this in the yard and around the stables were lots of chicks, hens, roosters, ducks, and drakes all making tumultuous their cries. I spent lots of time as I curiously watched them all. Although this may sound unhealthy, I truly liked the smell of the stables, and if not watched I would sneak over to their stalls with a banana or two and sometimes a piece of bake. Should I be denied, I would gather a handful of grass to share with them. In this way we became friends.

After school I would sometimes be allowed to go to the home of my friend. His name was Alvin Simon. Alvin and I would take our books and go to a nearby plum tree whose limbs were close to the ground. We then would take our fill of its fruits, lie on the grass and learn our lessons. We were both transferred to Standard One. This was all done, to my credit, in the space of six months at school. Again my new book was written by J.O. Cutteridge, a *West Indian Reader, Book 1*. I mastered its contents from cover to cover, and to date I do remember many of its substances.

One day Uncle brought me two chickens. One had absolutely no feathers upon its neck, while the other was fully covered. "Now, George," said he, "you have to mind these chickens, and when they grow big, we shall sell them to buy you your books for school." Boy oh boy, was I thrilled with his gift. For many were the occasions I would sit on our step and gaze at a mother hen and her chicks as she strutted proudly across the yard towards the stable in search of grubs for her young and wished that we had chickens of our own. They came in a Gossage soap box. I asked permission to take them for Alvin to see. "No," said Tanty, "you may trip and fall, and should they get away and go below the house it would be plenty trouble to catch them again. Go and call him to see them."

Alvin and I were both looking at the chicks when Uncle said that they were hungry and should be fed. Tanty came with a piece of bake, which she crumbled and gave to them. It was a pleasure to see them eat, especially the clean-necked chick. As he ate, it was fun to see the food slide down his throat, eating as though its crop would burst. Tanty then brought a sardine tin with water and they both drank. After which Alvin returned to his home.

They were then set under the table. When night fell Uncle brought a jute sack and laid it where they both passed the night. The next morning I put them into the box and cleaned the sack of the droppings. After school that evening Tanty said to me, "George, your chickens shall sleep inside for a while, but in the day they would be left outside, and instead of you feeding Mr Yank's dog with the leftovers, you will now feed the chickens with it and let Bob (the dog) have the bones instead." She then tied two pieces of red cord around their feet to distinguish them. We fed them and set them free among the chickens in the yard. (She also said that they shall find themselves grubs and small insects in the day.)

For the rest of that week after school I ran home very early. I would not even wait for Alvin. The chicks quickly learned my musical tune as I called, "Come, come, come, tay, tay, tay." Wherever they were, they would come racing to me. When they had their fill, the remainder was quickly eaten by their friends. The pair grew quickly and fat. Uncle said that I had a very good hand with fowls. He also said that they were too big to be sleeping in the house, so they would be sold to the shopman. To the latter Tanty disagreed. "Ah, Bishop," she said, "you can easily wattle a portion under de fireside* for dem to sleep." But to this Uncle disagreed and said it was best to sell them and get three more. And so they were sold.

I was now very sad to part with my feathered friends, but what could I do. It was on a market day he took them away. On his return, he handed Tanty three shillings (seventy-two cents). "Oh Gad, Bishop," said she, "dis is all?" He then poked his hand into his hip pocket where

CHAPTER FOUR

he retrieved two kaiser balls. "Here, George," said he, "take one to your friend Alvin." For this I felt so happy that I at once raced to Alvin's home and handed his to him. We then climbed to our favourite branch on the plum tree. At this time there were no fruits. As we chatted, I told him Uncle said that he was getting me three other chickens. He said, "Boy, George, if only we were big we could have gone and cut bamboo for wattle and make a pull-a-ra* for them to sleep, and you won't have to get up on mornings to clean or wash the bag of their too-too*. All you would have to do is throw sand or ashes and clean every Saturday." "Yes, boy," said I, "but we are too small."

It happened that our school gave a concert, and I was given a recitation. These were the lines of my piece:

> Little Tom Tucker sang for his supper,
> What shall he eat – white bread and butter.
> How shall he cut it without a knife?
> How shall he marry without a wife?

My teacher was pleased because I know well my part. However, just a few days away from the concert a big boy from another class was stumbling with his lines. They were a group of six boys who were to recite what they would be at manhood. This boy's recitation was:

> When I am a man, a farmer will I be, if I can
> I will plough the ground, the seeds will I sow
> I will heap the hay, the grass will I mow
> I will bind the sheafs, I will rake the hay
> And pitch it upon the moor away
> When I am a man

My teacher heard me saying it in the classroom and told it to the boys' teacher. They were both amazed and asked Tanty if I could then recite the part with the other boys. "No objection," said she, "as long as no added costume will be involved." I then had two recitations to do, which turned out to be a success.

Alvin was the only child of his parents, Mr and Mrs Simon. They loved him dearly, and he had but little chores to do. He swept or brought water if he wanted. All they demanded of him was that he behaved well and learn his lessons (which he did). It happened thus I went to meet him for school one morning and his mother said to me he was not well; he has fever and will not be going to school that day. "Let me please tell it to our teacher," I said. The next day he became worse ill, and everyone in the barracks became concerned about his illness. Even Mr Hyke, the overseer, and his wife went to their home. Those were the days when doctors could not be easily reached in rural districts, so folks relied on their own medicine, which consisted chiefly of herbs or sea water. In our village a doctor came every fortnight and sometimes found it difficult to come through lack of transportation. He may come on horseback, occasionally a vehicular drive, and there were the times when he even walked the five miles distance. His office was a little hut known as the Dispensary where he dealt chiefly with cases of colds, sores, fever, and hookworms, etc. Poor fellow, he had not even a nurse with him. And in Alvin's case he had made his visit to the village, and it was just three days before, so every bush doctor* had now his own say in the matter.

There was Mr Vest, an old Spanish* gent who came and muttered some prayers, as he prescribed some hot herb tea with a sea bath. There was Papa Joe, who said that the child has family maljo* and must be measured and prayed for. And there were those who said, "That boy has a spirit lash*. Just look at his eyes!" While there were yet the folks who claimed that he was poisoned, "Watch his pee!" The only two individuals to come with a sensible suggestion were Uncle and Mr Worrell, the headmaster of our school, who said it could be a case of yellow fever by the symptoms shown. As preparation was made to take Alvin to Sangre Grande, he died the next day after five days of illness.

Well, now I had lost my friend, and it was my first experience of the death of anyone. A sad moment it was indeed of my little life, and it was also a turning point. Folks wept bitterly, even the teachers. For the funeral service the church bell tolled, hymns were sung, as the reverend preached the sermon with words of comfort to the bereaved parents. The coffin was then borne to the village cemetery for burial.

Chapter 5

Strife between Tanty and Uncle Bishop; George begins to miss school; Mrs Hen hatches twelve chicks, and George experiences a village wake

Alvin's death brought a great change to my lifestyle, both at home and at school. At home Tanty said that the place was cursed and there were evil spirits hovering around. "Just listen to the strange cries of the animals at nights," she said. Uncle said, "Ella, you are following the foolish people. I quite agreed with Mr Worrell on the yellow fever, but if it was not that, I would bet my bottom dollar it was pneumonia." "Bishop," said she, "I am not staying in this place any longer." And so for days there was a constant fight between them. The dividend to this was lack of my school attendance.

Then one morning after Uncle left for work, Tanty said to me, "Boy, ah leaving your uncle today, I am not staying in this place any longer, it is cursed. You can stay with him, he is your uncle." "Oh, no," said I, "Tanty, I coming with you." Shortly after, three men with whom she made arrangements came and moved us to another barrack. The name of this place was Buenos Ayres. And as was expected, the very night Uncle was there.

Reader, please allow me now to use some lingo more freely. "Oh gash so, Pet, yuh lef me and yuh tek almos everything, bed and all, an you tek Crecy wid yuh. Yuh go wock an mine am by yuhself. Me nah go help yuh wid am. Yuh tek every cent we had in the room, even de very fowl money we had dey to buy ee books. Pet, yuh ent have konshens, gol. Yuh mean, yuh hart so hard; wot yuh want me to do eh? Wot yuh want me to do now?"[1]

All through his harangue Tanty said not a word. As she was satisfied that he had nothing more to say, she broke the silence. "Bishop, yuh ent shame. For all dese years ah livin wid yuh, yuh never give me one pin. As consorning Crecy, yuh can tek am right now! Because yuh Mooma say me a mule – me can't have pickney – yuh better go tell she to stap run-in she tong on me. Is true people see yuh going to wock every day but, Bishop, to yuh own kanchance, how much yuh does bring home? Wid de little yuh ge me ah ha to cook wash starch an iron out ar dat to have yuh clean. An before one can say 'Jack Robinson' yuh gane an gamble every cent. If nat dat machine yuh meet me wid, and pulling sand for de road, ah go go naked wid one hand behind and one in front.

"Look, Bishop, please, nah mek me get vex right now, because if ah do ah go reproach yuh. All weh me go tell yuh again please tell yuh Mooma nah call me name wid Kate Brebner dem. She ar say how me ar dis big obeah-woman, ar tie yuh and ar go kill yuh, but leh monkey see fuss de length ar ee own tail before ee talk bout iguana. Becarse ar obeah she bin ar wock, when all dem men weah pass, ar she handed out."

"But Pet, but Pet," he stuttered.

"Wait, wait," said she, "me nah done yet. Furthermore, me nah bin say one word wen you bin ar lamblass me. Yuh bring Crecy, an if me nah see bout am he go go hungry and nasty an fly go mess pan am*. Nowardays yuh too busy to help am wid he lesson. Me bin tell yuh to ask Captain for a piece of lan in Pint Carrat so ah can mek a garden to help meself. To date yuh ent do dat. Why? Becarse too much highwoods to cut down".

"Boy, Bishop, yuh ent shame, de chile mine those fowls. Yuh tek dem

---

[1] "Oh, gosh, Pet, you left me and you took almost everything, bed and all, and you took Crecy with you. You are going to work and mind him by yourself. I'm not going to help you with him. You took every cent we had in the room, even the very fowl money we had there to buy his books. Pet, you don't have any conscience, girl. You mean, your heart is so hard; what do you want me to do, eh? What do you want me to do now?"

CHAPTER FIVE

an sell dem. Yuh tink me en know dat yuh get five shillings for dem. All-yuh* bring home was three shillings for dem. All-yuh bring home was three shillings an, smartie, yuh buy two sweetie for a penny an fool him off. Yuh did not even buy a cent extra-strong for me. Ah fuss yuh angrateful. Dat can never be right, Bishop. Yuh even say yuh go get three more chickens for him. Up to now dem ent hatch yet. Look man all ar go tell yuh, go yuh way an lea me go mine an ah mean dat."[2]

It would seem as though Uncle was defeated by Tanty; he stood in silence. Then said he, "OK, Ella, ah gone, eh." And he left. No sooner had he turned his back, a neighbour who we now lived next to came and knocked at our door and called Tanty. "Oh gash, Pet, gol," said she, laughing, "ah hear yuh, he well deserve all weh yuh tell am. Dem man's too dam advantageous* an ungrateful. Yuh ent see how mine walk off wid dat hore."[3] She then gave Tanty assistance in tidying as

---

2   'Wait, wait, I'm not done yet. Furthermore, I never said one word when you lambasted me. You brought Crecy, and if I didn't see about him he would go hungry and nasty and flies would mess on him. Nowadays you're too busy to help him with his lesssons. I've been telling you to ask Captain for a piece of land in Point Carrat so I can make a garden to help myself. To date you haven't done that. Why? Because there's too much high woods to cut down.'

   'Bishop, aren't you ashamed? For all these years I've been living with you, you have never given me one pin. As to Crecy, you can take him right now! Because your mother says I'm a mule – I can't have a child – you'd better go tell her to stop criticizing me. It's true people see you going to work every day but, Bishop, to your own conscience, how much do you bring home? With the little that you give me I have to cook, wash, starch and iron all that so that you're clean. And before one can say 'Jack Robinson' you've gone and gambled every cent. If it's not that machine that you meet me with, and pulling sand for the road, I'd go naked with one hand behind me and one in front.'

   'Look, Bishop, please, don't make me get vexed right now, because if I do I will reproach you. All that I'm going to tell you again is please tell your mother not to call my name with Kate Brebner and them. She said that I am this big obeah-woman, I tie you and I'm going to kill you, but let the monkey first see the length of his own tail before he talks about iguana. Because she is working obeah, when all those men pass by, she handed out.'

3   'Oh gosh, Pet, girl,' said she, laughing, 'I hear you. He well deserve all that you tell him. These men take too much advantage and are ungrateful. Didn't you see how mine walked off with that whore.'

they chatted. When partly finished she said to Tanty, "Pet, hole on, ar coming back jest now."

She did return in about forty-five minutes. But this time she came not with words but rather with deeds. She had a big pudding pan with the most appetizing-looking fried bake and fish and a jug of unmilked bush tea. "Pet, gal, me nah have no milk," she said, "but yuh an de boy eat dis till ar marning. Gol," said she, "every time ah watch dat chile ah see Georgie, ee poopah." "Oh gash," Tanty said, "Colute, why yuh tek all dis trouble. Thank yuh anyway."⁴ I knew this lady by seeing her in the village, but I knew not her name. However, Tanty put very much milk in the tea, and we three sat at the table and had our fill.

The next morning I heard not the school bell for we now lived much further away. It mattered not, however, because in any case I was not going to school that day. And so after breakfast Tanty took me to a spring in which there were many tadpoles and many millions*. "Here," said she, "yuh will get woter for home every day. Yuh will dip wid de calabash* an fill yuh bocket. Don't play or trow anyting in the spring becarse dat can mek people get sick."⁵

All went well as we both each day cleaned and scrubbed the room and steps. Tanty alone cobwebbed in and out of the room. She did not let me share in this exercise because she said dust would get into my eyes. We both weeded the footpath and around the kitchen, which brought a change to the area. I overheard Miss Colute telling her, "Pet, dat boy could work." And so it happened I did not attend school for all that week.

I was sitting upon the step reading my book one day when Miss Colute called, "Pet, oh Pet, yuh hear who dead?" "No," said Tanty, with concern. "Gal! Punish. Yank now pass an tell meh." "Poor ole man," said Tanty, "he suffer lang enough. Maybe good Lard mek peace wid

---

4 'Pet, girl, I don't have any milk,' she said, 'but you and the boy eat this until the morning. Girl,' said she, 'every time I look at that child I see George, his father.' 'Oh, gosh,' Tanty said, 'Colute, why did you take all this trouble. Thank you, anyway.'

5 'Here,' said she, 'you will get water for home every day. You will dip with the calabash and fill your bucket. Don't play or throw anything in the spring because that can make people sick.'

CHAPTER FIVE

his soul." "Dem a bury am tomorrow," said Miss Colute. "Ah go see wot ah can do," said Tanty. "By de by, Colute, gol, dat a hot bongo* down dey tonight, leh we go nah?" "Yes, Pet, ah wid yuh."[6]

There were two distinct groups at the mourners' home that night. In the yard under a palm-thatched tent there were people playing cards, joking and dancing. Uncle was there; he made a right* to me. Tanty and Miss Colute joined with the folks that were in the house. They were singing hymns and some were even crying. There were also dozens of lit candles all over the house. We were directed by a lady to a bench which looked very much like one of our school benches, and so we sat and joined the mourners. Lots of coffee and biscuits were served, making the surroundings one of joy and sadness. Tanty disappeared. I knew not where she went, so I stayed with Miss Colute and her friends.

About 4:00 a.m. the next morning Tanty showed up and said, "Colute, gal, come leh we go home. We have to get some sleep; dem a bury am today."[7] And so we left for home. I walked in front with a flashlight (a precious commodity in those days). As they brought up the rear speaking in whispers, with occasional laughter, I tried to focus my hearing to their direction but could only get the word "he" which came from Tanty.

They both did leave for the funeral that day about 1:30 p.m. Before leaving Tanty said to me, "Go nowhere, stay at home, take your book and read. If you are hungry, take some food from the pot." Miss Colute also slipped in with her portion: "Yes, boy, hear what Tanty say. We are coming back just now." As they left, I made sure I saw them clear the hill. And so I decided to go out and seek my own adventure.

Alone I went by a mango tree which was much further away from the spring. There I found some lovely fruits upon the ground. As I selected

---

6 'Girl! Punish! Yank just passed by and told me.' 'Poor old man,' said Tanty. 'He has suffered long enough. Maybe the good Lord will make peace with his soul.' 'They will bury him tomorrow,' said Miss Colute. 'I'll see what I can do,' said Tanty. 'By the way, Colute, girl, there's a hot bongo down there tonight. Let's definitely go.' 'Yes, Pet, I'm with you.'

7 'Colute, girl, come let us go home. We have to get some sleep; they are burying him today.'

my fruits, on nearing a dried stump I heard a very strange noise. I immediately backed away. Then, not far from arm's length, there was a long rod lying on the ground. I took it and started beating the bush. I knew for sure the cry was not that of a toad or frog. Then suddenly there was a rush and a loud cackle. It came from a hen that was sitting there upon some eggs. I counted the eggs; twelve were they. I then hurried home with the hope of giving Tanty the news when she got back. To my amazement, there was Tanty, Uncle and Miss Colute sitting upon our step conversing. (I so happened to hear that the dead would not be buried until the next day because they were waiting upon a relative.)

"Good evening, Uncle," said I. "Boy, just a few days I have not seen you, you have grown so much." Tanty gave a disapproval look to me because I had disobeyed her. "Where you get those lovely mangoes?" asked Miss Colute. "Near the spring," I replied. "Near the spring?" said she, "I never knew it have a tree there." "Not too far away," said I. "And do you know something, I saw a large, speckled hen sitting upon some eggs; twelve were they in all. She got frightened and ran off." "Where to?" she asked. "In the bush," said I. "My goodness, that is Mr Drell the overseer's fowl, he missing it for days now and thought maybe it get swallowed by a snake or eaten by mongoose." As I went inside to put my mangoes down, there came Mr Drell. He was given the story, and off we both went to see the nesting place. By this time the hen was back and was quite comfortably settled upon her eggs. I felt myself a young hero when Mr Drell said, "Boy, you are brave to come here by yourself. I'll tell you what, you keep a look whenever you can, and when she hatches I will give you half of whatever is hatched." Here was I now free to visit the mango tree to gather my fruits, also with an incentive.

The good hen hatched all twelve eggs. Needless to say, I visited the area each day gathering my fruits. I arrived just about noon that day, and there was Mrs Hen scratching and feeding her chicks with grubs. She was indeed a very fierce hen with her chicks. And so I went home and took the basket Tanty shopped with and was back on the scene. With some fierce pecks and scratches I managed to secure the

CHAPTER FIVE

Fishing village, Trinidad

chicks in the basket. I scampered through the bush followed hard by Mrs Hen clucking at my heels through the cries of her chicks in the basket.

When I got to Mr Drell's house he had just mounted his horse for the fields. He saw me, dismounted, and came to me with a smile. I saluted and said, "Good evening," as Uncle had taught me. He responded, "I see, young man, you have done it. How many are there?" "Twelve, sir," said I. "Good! Very good. So here I keep my word. Six are yours, take any six." I was shy and could not believe my ears. "Yes, son," said he, "what's your name?" "George, sir." "Go ahead, George, just drop six with the hen." He then came over and helped me with the basket as I nervously gave six chickens down to their mother, who was now no longer fierce as before. And so Mr Drell remained truly a gentleman to his word. I then hurried with my six chickens home to Tanty, while in my little mind I concealed thoughts of great expectations.

During this period I had missed school for about five weeks. Then one morning I went over to the spring for water. On my return Uncle and another man were at home. He had come to reunite his relationship with Tanty, and this man helped him with his belongings. I was not at all surprised because from the very night of the wake when I missed Tanty and as we walked home the morning the secretive manner with which she spoke with Miss Colute, I suspected something was afoot and so it mattered not to me.

Chapter 6

George meets Horace, works in Tanty's vegetable garden and lives through a frightening storm; Tanty practises obeah, and they buy Miss Missy's ajoupa

Now as I have said, from the time we moved into Buenos Ayres I had never heard the school bell nor did I attend school. I read my book when there was no excitement. Because I now found interest in playing with plants, and watching insects especially the ants, or listening to birds sing their tunes, or throwing a watchful eye upon my chicks. One day I was told by a gent who lived in one of the barrack rooms, if I can climb and throw just a little salt on the tail of any bird I will catch it easily. From then Tanty's salt did get into trouble, until she caught me in the act one day. When asked what I was doing, I told her what Mr John had said to me. "Mr John is making a fool of you," she said. It was only then that I realized that he truly was.

It happened thus one Sunday evening there was a visitor to our home. It was Mr Worrell, the headmaster of my school. He came to enquire of my absence. I overheard him telling Tanty and Uncle that there is some good material in me and, through neglect, could be wasted. To this Uncle readily agreed, while Tanty remarked, "Teacher, he can now cipher his own name, and I do hear him reading when he is by himself." "That's not all, Miss Pet," he said, "there are many other subjects he must do to be a good student." Then up came Mr Drell, who asked Mr Worrell over to the big house.

As my guardians reunited, it would seem as though Uncle changed his lifestyle. For now he was more at home, and he weeded all around the kitchen and footpath. He also made a new fireplace and an oven, and he made a lovely chicken house for my six chickens to roost. I was then sent back to school, and life seemed to become streamlined once more.

When I went back to school, I found myself being faced with a problem: a boy who attended the Roman Catholic school was transferred to our school. And it mattered not how hard I tried, I could only be ahead of him in reading, nature study (now science), religious studies and poetry. Now we were not total strangers to each other, for his mother and Tanty claimed to be cousins, and they both washed by the river when I first began school. We kids would then romp on the riverbanks or make sandcastles. He had an agouti* (an Indian rabbit) that burrowed quickly into the sand and so provided us with fun. But never had we the cause to compete in our educational ability. One advantage he had was when I would be absent a few days from school, he was always there. But nevertheless the chap was bright.

Now Horatio, Horace as he was called, filled the gap of my late Alvin, and we became real class chums. Very often when I missed school, he would point out the subject at lunchtime quickly to me, or sometimes on evenings. It was hard, however, for me to accept the fact that he was brighter than I was. Then came the time for our term test. When results were placed on the board, I was first, beating Horace by eight marks into second place. My triumph came through the reciting of the poem "The Lost Doll".[1] Although this may now sound most insignificant, it is a memory which lasted all through my life. A song was taught to the senior classes by Mr Worrell. The title of it was "To the Lords of

---

[1] I once had a sweet little doll, dears,
The prettiest doll in the world;
Her cheeks were so red and white, dears,
And her hair was so charmingly curled.
But I lost my poor little doll, dears,
As I played on the heath one day;
And I cried for her more than a week, dears,
But I never could find where she lay.
This is the first verse of a two-verse poem by Charles Kingsley, published in *The Water-Babies* (Eversley 1862).

CHAPTER SIX

Convention".[2] In one of the verses were these words – I quote: "There are great Donna Wassail three thousand times three." Mr Worrell at this point stopped the singing class and asked how many wassails were there then. To this no one could answer. Horace from our junior class then shouted, "Nine thousand."

At promotion we were both to go to Standard Two, but we were skipped and sent to Three instead. That day as I got home, I presented Tanty my booklist with the news. She was delighted and said Teacher Billy had already informed her. At that very moment in came Uncle. As Tanty broke the news to him, he said that he was not at all surprised because my father was a very bright boy at school. But due to Mr Morris, their stepfather, and his children with Grandma, many days he had to stay at home and babysit.

After dinner that evening, he said, "Ella, I have got some good news for you." (Now I found that he called her Ella whenever he wanted to be in her favour, and should he not, he called her Pet.) "What is it?" she asked. "Well, girl, I got the OK today from the ward officer for the Point Carrat Crown land*. We shall no longer have to ask Captain Smart." Now Captain Smart was a retired English merchant captain who then owned lands on the seacoast of Point Carrat in the Sans Souci outskirts. He was a very kind gentleman, especially to children, and he was the first person I knew in the district to have owned his own private motor car. However, due to the then-narrow roadway, he built his garage about two miles away from his house. Captain Smart could be characterized as a steady old man with a pipe in his mouth, with a polished walking stick in his hand, with a little terrier following at his heels. He would then walk briskly as he hummed a tune on his way home. It was also said that he kept brightly lit lanterns, which he hung on the edge of the cliff as a warning to passing crafts at night. Those were the days when the ferry boat called *Belize* linked the islands of Trinidad and Tobago together. Tobago was then the food basket of Trinidad. From there

---

2 "The Lords of Convention" is a poem by Sir Walter Scott. The lines referred to are:
There are wild Duniewassals three thousand times three
Will cry hoigh! For the bonnet of Bonny Dundee

came an abundance of fruits and vegetables, livestock, molasses (which was then called Tobago sugar), and even corned fish* were harvested. The people of Tobago were hard-working. Many came to Trinidad but settled in Toco, tilling the soil and introducing expert craftsmanship.

As Uncle got the OK for the Crown lands, he wasted no time. He got a few of his friends, and they felled the forest trees, burning charcoal and the land itself in preparation for planting. Tanty did not approve of this. "Bishop," she said, "you do not want to listen to me. Stop breaking stick in your ears. Those gamblers, your best friends, are not helping you for nothing. They have their aim, so be careful."

The land was cleared, and again I was kept away from school for an even longer period. Tanty alone had to plant it. So then I attended school three times, once, or sometimes not at all each week. One good thing: Uncle got the plants, so Tanty had not to worry about that. She truly was a hard-working woman and we did it together. We planted bananas, plantains*, cassava*, tannias*, dasheen* and yams. Pigeon peas* and corn were planted as short crops*. Again I would say that I missed school terribly. At the time I knew not its importance, and was one of the village's best-fed children. I could not then see Tanty left alone with the garden. Uncle was always there at time of harvest. There was one good thing about him: he never let us burden ourselves, we took what we wanted, and at times I think he carried as much load as a donkey.

One Monday evening there was a thunderstorm; it was my first such experience. It started with very black clouds across the mountains, then a strong wind which had all the immortelle* trees dancing as their huge trunks swayed to and fro. Suddenly there was a downpour of rain followed by quick flashes of lightning and a deafening burst of thunder. As winds rustled through the cocoa fields, you could hear the sound of a fallen branch, or an uprooted immortelle tree as it came crashing to the ground. I wondered what was taking place with the cornbirds* as their long nests were tossed to and fro, as they were fixed at the very end of the branches. I also pondered in my mind what was taking place in the heavens. Then the kind hand of Tanty rested upon my shoulder.

CHAPTER SIX

"Come, boy," said she, "you are afraid?" "No," said I. "That is a storm," said she, "coming from the sea. Come and eat."

As I sat at dinner, I remembered my six chickens that were now fully grown. I left the food and rushed out in the rain. "Where yuh going?" shouted Tanty. I pretended not to hear her. She again yelled very much harder. "For my fowls," I replied. I then looked, but they were not in their roost. By this time the place was getting darker. I wondered where could they be then. And behold I espied them very close together at the far end under the house. I did not crawl to get them because my clothes were soaked and dripping, and if I did would then be in a mess. "They are below there," I said to Tanty, pointing. She gave me a kindly look and shook her head as I stood on the step. "Go," said she, "and change those clothes." And as it was now already dark, I slipped into my bed clothing and went back to my dinner.

While I ate, Tanty took a chair and sat at the doorway dreaming as she peered in the darkness. I wondered what could she then be thinking about. Then in came Uncle all drenched. "Ella," said he, "girl, this is weather. It reminds me of an experience we had in Cairo, Egypt." "Go! Take those wet clothes off," said Tanty. I was very sorry that Tanty did not allow him to speak on for I wanted to hear what his experience was. Mr Worrell had been teaching about the pyramids and the amazing length of the River Nile (4,150 miles) of Egypt in General Knowledge, and in Religious Knowledge, how Our Lord Jesus Christ as a babe was taken to Egypt for safety through fear of King Herod.

When he changed his clothes, Tanty set before him a large bowl of the hot vegetable soup, which we both had. As he enjoyed the gourmet meal, I sat by his feet on a small bench. "Uncle," said I, "is there really an Egypt?" "Oh yes," said he, "I was stationed there for over six months." As he ate he spoke. He told me how he went to England as an enlisted soldier in 1914, how he fought against the Turks, who were bravely defeated. They were then sent to Egypt to stave off an attack from the Germans. He also visited the Holy Land. He then stopped speaking as if saddened of some memory. "Can't you tell me more, Uncle?" Tanty then quickly placed her finger upon her lips, which was taught to me as a sign of silence. Uncle then said, "I was a soldier in the War.³ We dug huge trenches to bury the dead. We also slept in holes at times; these holes were known as foxholes. From them we also hid and shot at the enemies." He also told some other stories that seemed somewhat tall to me, but, being my uncle, I believed him. One thing he said that night made me very sad. In Egypt where they were stationed, peasants and their children would come begging. For the children the soldiers would place lots of jam upon slices of bread and give to them, but by the time it got to their mouths, dozens of small flies would alight upon it. The kids would then eat everything, and this was fun for the soldiers, which I thought to be very mean fun.

As I sat and wondered, Tanty said, "So you did not know that Uncle was once a brave soldier?" "No," said I, although I once remembered him speaking of London, England. "Well, that's how he lost his left small toe. It became blistered in his boots as they were in pursuit of a German troop. It could not then be attended to before a week when it took gangrene and had to be amputated." "Ella," said Uncle, "you remembered quite well what I told you." "Is there anyone else in the village that went to war?" I asked. "No," said he, "who could have gone hid themselves." "Can you tell me who are they?" "No," said he, "because you may get yourself into trouble. But from Cumana Village there was one Mr Joseph Stanley who also joined the West India Regiment. He was a very good rifleman. Whenever he said, 'Sniper,' 'Bang!' went his rifle and the German was sure to be dead. Captain A.A. Cipriani loved him. He did not return with the regiment but he stayed in England." The interest of the conversation made me forget all about the weather. But as the lantern flies* criss-crossed in the darkness, you could have heard the gushing waters from the spring cascading down the hill. I prayed and got into my bed that night, no longer thinking about the storm but of Uncle as my hero.

Very early Uncle left home the next morning, but he was back in a jiffy as he spoke with excitement. "Oh, Ella, Ella, you should see outside"

---

3   World War I.

CHAPTER SIX

(he meant the main village). "Here is a flood; the river has overflowed its banks, which has caused water to rise as high as three feet in some yards. Where we first lived, the water is now about one foot deep inside. Two mules, a donkey, pigs, goats, and many fowls and ducks are now washed to sea." He also heard that there were huge landslides blocking the road to Grande Riviere; the roofs of two ajoupas were blown off. Both schools were closed for the day, but both shops were open.

I went to look for my chickens; they were busy scratching themselves a meal below the cocoa trees. And as I looked, to my amazement, all the banana and plantain trees around were uprooted. As I hurried to tell my guardians what I saw, Tanty said, "Come to eat, child." And so before I began my breakfast, I told them of what I had observed. And so I asked what do they think may have happened to our garden. "God is love, child," said Tanty. "Do not let that worry you," said she. To this Uncle said, "Why not let us go down to see how it is?"

On our way down I observed that all the footpaths were all dug up by water that was still gushing from the hills. Here and there were potholes and sand mounds. As we journeyed on, there was a fallen tree here and there blocking the regular path, which caused us to make detours. At last we got to our garden. In my little mind I expected to see great devastation. But when a check was made, our loss was eight banana and six plantain trees. And as Tanty said, four of the plantain trees which fell, had Uncle propped them up three days before when she asked him, they might not have all fallen. Neighbouring planters suffered greater losses. In the entire area we were the most fortunate. Tanty then looked at me and said, "Boy, you poopah spirit really helping, and he with God's help is really taking charge over everything."

At this juncture may I say that my guardians both had their own ideology. My uncle never believed in evil spirits that can bring you harm. Many were the occasions I had heard him saying that there are spirits out there as mentioned in the Bible, but as an individual, one must know how to centre your thoughts. (I then would wonder what he meant.) He held no obeah or voodoo belief, yet he claimed as a child he saw spirits but was never afraid at any time. He would also tell you one gets hurt from what he eats or from the careless handling of his body. Tanty, on the other hand, deeply believed in voodoo and obeah. Oh how I remember the Good Fridays of my childhood days at her home. She would kill a chicken and have it nicely prepared without salt, with a portion of steamed white rice. She would place both dishes upon the table covered with a white napkin. She would then call upon her dead relatives to come and dine. At night, when I thought that they were both asleep, I would get up, and with concealed salt I would have my fill of the chicken. On one occasion, however, I was caught by a swarm of red ants that were there before me in the darkness; my hands and mouth got covered with the insects that gave me stings as a reward.

(Let's now get back again to the garden.) On leaving the garden that day, we burdened ourselves with three bunches of plantains and some uprooted dasheen from the spring. As I had already mentioned, Uncle was a very strong man so he took most of it. Tanty was also very strong in her class. And I always felt that I was the strongest boy of my age group in the village. When we got home Tanty quickly put down what she had to help Uncle down of his load. As he was released, "Ella," said he, "did you see all those manicou crabs* on the way as we came along!" "Yes," said she, "but we could not catch any with our loads." "Look," said he, "I caught two of them." "When did you do that? Had we four more I would have made a good cook tonight." Uncle, turning, said to me, "Let's go and catch some for Tanty." Needless to say, his invitation was welcomed. We did set off and were back in about twenty minutes with twelve lovely crabs. Tanty was all happy. Uncle then said, "Ella, I am dying for a smoke." "Here is six cents," said she (reaching to the shelf), "go out and buy a pack of Anchor cigarettes. I can well do with a puff myself." (They were both smokers.)

It was late when he returned that evening. "Ella, I'm back." "I thought that you were lost or helping the Chinee[4] to roll the cigarettes," said Tanty. "No," said he, "I was…" Just at that very moment Miss Colute came up and said, "Pet, gol, I came three times looking for you this morning

---

4   Now usually considered a pejorative term, this refers to someone from China.

CHAPTER SIX

to find out how you were going. Gal, that weather was something else. I hear plenty damage done in Grande Riviere and Matelot." "Yes, girl, is so I hear. And, Colute, I have some plantains and dasheen here for you." "God bless you, chile. What the storm do to you?" "Well, girl, the good Lord spare us. You remembered He said, 'When I see the blood I would pass over you.' Well maybe there was some blood somewhere." As Tanty made that statement she turned to look at me. "Well, gol," Miss Colute said, "Repelto came here almost in tears, he say everything lay flat in his garden."

As the three chatted, I hurried from the scene to check on my chickens. As I was feeding them from my hand with a cooked plantain, there came Mr Drell. "Little fellow – oh no, I mean George – you are indeed doing quite well with your chickens, for you have yet all six, have you not?" "Yes sir." I dropped the feed that was in my hand and saluted. To this he smiled. "I lost two of mine when following their mother. Probably taken by mongoose or seized by hawks." He then gently stroked me upon my head as he said to me, "Keep up the good work," and he left.

By then Miss Colute had gone to her room. I then sat upon the step and played with my fowls. Yet my thoughts were glued inside to hear what was being said by Uncle and Tanty, because it would appear when Miss Colute came he was just about to say something important to her. There was a lull, and then the silence was broken. I overheard Uncle saying, "Girl, Ella, Abraham and his friend Steward were drinking today. And Abraham told Steward that his mother is selling her ajoupa. When it rained yesterday, it began leaking heavily, and it is difficult for her to get carat to fix it, so she is selling it and would be going to South to live at her eldest daughter." "How much she want for it?" asked Tanty. "Eight dollars," he replied, "but I am sure knowing Miss Missy as I do she would not let six dollars pass if she sees the money." "Well, and what you tell him?" "Tell him, tell him what! First, they were not speaking to me. I just overheard the conversation, and even right now I have not two cents to knock and call a penny." "That is only four farthings," said Tanty jokingly. "But, Ella, you don't have any money?"

"Bishop, is only food I does get from my work money. Look, right now they want to march from his school to Toco on Empire Day. I have to cut and contrive to send him."

"Alright, OK, Pet. I will see what could be done when I get my pay on Friday. I have in three days' work." "That is only $1.20," Tanty said quickly. "Yes, but I had in my day's work yesterday before the storm. I did not work today, but tomorrow and Friday I would be sent to lap trees that fell on the road." "That is another $1.60," said Tanty sharply, "and in all that is $2.80. OK, Bishop, bring me $2.40 and keep forty cents for your cigarettes and bad habit, and I go see what I can do."

As a gentleman Uncle did keep his promise to Tanty. Poor fellow, as he got his pay he brought it all to her, and, of course, she kept her side of the bargain as she handed to him his forty cents and said, "I am going to add the other $5.60." Uncle, who was not himself doing figures, said, "I told you $6.00." "No, no," said Tanty, "I am not robbing anyone. If Miss Missy says $8.00, I am paying $8.00." "But, Ella, are you not first going to look at the place?" "I do know the ajoupa," she replied.

The Saturday morning we three set off for Miss Missy's home. It was on a little hill, and it looked very cosy. Miss Missy was greyed and slightly bent. With a slight hop she came smiling to us. "Pet, Bishop, bless me eye. Wot bring all-yuh here, the storm or wot? Dat is Georgie las boy. Ah always hear he wid all-yuh. Son," (she held my hand) "yuh muss behave yuhself, yuh hear." "Yes, Marm," I bowed. "All-yuh, come in an sit down. Doh use dat chair, Bishop," she said to Uncle, "it is weak. Sit down on dat one dey. I can't get dat vagabond Abraham to do nothin. Look how much busy round de house. All he doing is drinking."[5]

As we sat down, Uncle told her what he overheard, and if it were true, he was willing to purchase it right away for $6.00. "Dat is tough," she

---

5   'Pet, Bishop, bless my eyes. What brought all of you here, the storm or what? That is George's last boy. I always heard he's with you all.' 'Son,' (she held my hand) 'you must behave yourself, you hear.' 'Yes, Marm,' I bowed. 'All of you, come in and sit down. Don't use that chair, Bishop,' she said to Uncle, 'it is weak. Sit down on that one there. I can't get that vagabond Abraham to do anything. Look how much there is to do around the house. All he's doing is drinking.'

CHAPTER SIX

replied. "Yuh can't put another $1.00 on dat?" Tanty said, "Miss Missy, don't mind Bishop, he is pulling your leg. We have walked with the $8.00." Uncle then gave Tanty a hard look and smiled. To this Miss Missy was so happy she lifted her hands into the air praising and thanking God. Uncle then said, "What about a receipt?" "Receipt, Bishop? Boy, shame on yuh. So lang ah know yuh before yuh barn, and de next ting ah can't see good to rite."[6]

At that very moment Mr Abraham, her son, came. He was told by someone that we were there, so he came to see what it was all about. Uncle told him what had transpired, and how he wanted the receipt made. Tanty then corrected, "Not Lucas, let it be Hector.[7] Because should anything happen, his mooma would put me out." To this Miss Missy readily agreed. She even said, "Pet, gol, yuh right, ah know de oman."[8] Neither had Uncle any objection of the receipt being made in Tanty's name. After the receipt was made, Tanty gave me to read it, because her eyes burned also. I read it aloud. "Good," said she, taking it from me. Miss Missy then asked that she be allowed to stay for one week. Tanty then said, "Mam, you can stay for one month." "No, Pet, wot will I be doing in yuh house so lang," and they both laughed.

---

6   'Receipt, Bishop? Boy, shame on you. I knew you so long before you were born, and the next thing is I can't see well enough to write.'

7   Tanty's last name.

8   'Pet, girl, you're right, I know the woman.'

Chapter 7

A guide to the care and feeding of chickens; George learns to use his fists; he receives licks like peas day and night from Tanty

We were back once more living in the village. No more were we in the outskirts, and we were also about three hundred yards from my school as the crow flies. But as the old saying goes, the nearer one may be to the church, the further away one may be from God. We now had a longer distance to trek to our garden that was doing fine. And it could now be ruined through neglect, if not visited. At our new home, water was again taken from an organic spring, which was about the same distance away as the one in Buenos Ayres from where we came. Uncle built a very nice kitchen and a lovely chicken roost. There were two cocks and four hens.

Now unlike Buenos Ayres, where there were lots of grubs to be found under the cocoa trees, or oats grain from the stable sweepings, self-feeding was now a harder task for them. So Tanty made me go up on the hills where there were discarded coconuts; these I gathered and extracted the kernel. This was then diced from ¼" to ½" thickness, and then mixed with half-cooked bananas diced to the same size; green water grass was chopped finely and all were put together with a portion of sand (not dirt). To this, salt would be added with just a little water to dampen it, then everything would be mixed in a large calabash to feed them. Sometimes a few nuts may be chopped in halves and left open for them to peck at the kernel themselves. This was their staple food.

We gathered an average of sixteen eggs each week. Every Sunday

CHAPTER SEVEN

morning Tanty would make an eggnog. The eggs were very large, and should we not use or give them away, they would spoil with the heat. (There were then no cold units.) Occasionally Tanty would say, "I got a bob for eggs today." Eggs were then sold at two cents each. Two hens called to sit, and Uncle made a nesting place at the back of the kitchen. Soon there were chickens running all over our yard. Sometimes they would venture into the house. I liked that and would play with them, but to their entering the house Tanty strongly objected.

We were at the garden one day when there came a downpour of rain. We took shelter under an open shed Uncle had made with a log placed for seating. It was well into lunchtime so Tanty said that we must eat. As we ate, Tanty said, "Boy, you have to start going back to school regularly instead of the irregular visits you are now paying. I saw your teacher Worrell a day in last week, and he spoke not to me but simply bowed, and I know that he is mad at me."

I was sent back to school as Tanty had promised, but on my return I began getting into fights with boys in and out of my class. When I ran out of spar-mates, I began to challenge even bigger boys from the Roman Catholic school who called me names. On one occasion the principal of that school, who was a female teacher and also my godmother, blocked me one day and gave me a real switching. I said not a word at home, but the news did get to them. Benching* became a pastime to me. I did not work hard for tests anymore. I fell back to third and fourth place in my class of eight. I had then few friends in the village. But the friendship between Horace and me continued. They had removed from the village and had gone to live on their own cocoa estate, and had then to walk about 2½ miles to school each day. So daily if we were at home or not, both his younger brothers and himself would leave their lunch in our kitchen, and there they would eat at lunchtime.

In my little world, time sped rapidly, and Tanty seemed to be always quarrelling with Uncle Bishop. She would sometimes say, "Do you think it is fair? You are only harvesting and giving to your friends." "But, Ella," he would say, "when the place was in high woods* and latro* is dem same fellars dat come and help me cut it down, and now ah mus give dem something." "Yes, I do know, Bishop, but not all the time. Next, can you remember when you were bringing those very fellars to help, I warned you to be careful about them. They are gamblers, and they would not be doing it for nothing. They had their aim, and here it is, can't you now see that it is backfiring? And, Bishop, if it has to go on like this, I shall stop working the garden and let George be at school as he should. And I shall tote sand on the road, and with the help of my machine I shall make it by God's grace." There were times that he would stand up and listen to her, while at others he would just steups* and walk off.

Then, lo and behold, one evening there was a big fight, the biggest I had yet seen between them. It almost led to fisted blows. Someone had told her that Uncle had been cheating on her with a younger woman. The result of this was that I began being ill-treated by Tanty. Poor thing, she had then to let out her frustration on someone, and that someone was me. Dear Reader, as Tanty could feel, so could she flog. It was licks like peas*. Our garden was now fully neglected, and she really began toting sand from the riverbank. During that era, sand toting was allotted to women in the villages where they lived. The sand was conveyed in a tray made like a box with two handles nailed to the sides for lifting; they were about 2' x 11½' x 4'. In these, sand was taken from the riverbanks upon the heads of women to the roadsides, where they were formed into mounds to be conveniently taken by motor trucks to repair the roads. Their task was fifty to one hundred trays, according to the distance, and they were paid at thirty cents per task. They worked from Monday to Friday, which brought them $1.50 weekly, but they were paid fortnightly, which was $3.00. I helped Tanty; every two trays of mine was checked as one, although my tray was as filled as anyone else's. According to distance we finished very early, which allowed me half-day at school.

One evening when Uncle came home, Tanty said to him, "Bishop, just because I cannot read and write, you think I am a total fool!" Poor Uncle stood aghast. He looked at me, and then at her in wonder. He then sadly walked from our presence and headed for the street; as he

CHAPTER SEVEN

got lower to the corner he called me. As I got to him, he said, "George, you are a child and I do not have to lie to you. I am now living eleven years wid Tanty. I never for once knew that she could not read or write. She speaks of matters I do not know about, she sings hymns, and knows very much more of the Bible than I do. She counts very much faster than I can. I have seen her helping you wid yuh lessons. And I have never once said to her or told anyone that she cannot read nor write. Why should she now accost me in your presence for this?" With my head lowered I made no comment. He then left me standing and slowly walked off.

Personally I realized very early that Tanty could not read or write, and this is how it happened. There is a picture in the *West Indian Reader, Book 1* which depicts a woman, a lad, and a donkey with a pannier*. Many a time was I told even by the very teachers that there was a very close resemblance of Tanty and myself to both personalities. I showed the picture to Tanty and jokingly said to her, "Look, our names are at the bottom." She looked at it and with a big smile said, "But, yes, look me name in big – P E T." I was astonished and said not another word. For then I recalled that her eyes were always dim, and I must first watch the objects and spell them. Reader, from that day even at school if asked by a teacher or even Horace when my work was good who showed me, I would reply with pride, "Tanty." And although I was now very sorry for Uncle, I do feel that he was a perfect dumb-dumb for not finding it out before it was told to him.

Chapter 8

George escapes from Tanty; fear and suspense on an epic bus journey to Port of Spain

Uncle now sank me into deeper trouble because he began sleeping out from home. The result of this was my skin was now always waled by Tanty, but I was always well fed. Finally, he left one day and never again returned.

One morning I hurriedly passed through a neighbour's yard as I headed for the spring. I was barebacked, as I hoped to take a quick wash. Miss Katie was the woman's name. She stopped me and said, "Good gracious, look at yuh back, chile. Son, yuh Tanty go kill yuh. All dem set a blows, day an nite. Why yuh don't run way and go meet yuh fambly dem at Poter-Spain."[1] I looked at her with surprise. Then said she, "Please no tell any baddy ar tell yuh dat because Pet ar go kill me."[2] "No, no, Miss Katie," I assured her. From that day the thought of freedom came to me. I then began dreaming of joining my brothers and sisters in town. For Hilda, Quildon, Weston and even Georgina, the youngest, had been taken into Port of Spain by senior relatives. We had tests at school, but this was irrelevant to me. I was then promoted to Standard Four. And Mr Worrell was then transferred to Tobago, being

---

1   Port of Spain.
2   'Good gracious. Look at your back, child. Son, your Tanty is going to kill you. All those blows, day and night. Why don't you run away and go meet your family in Port of Spain.' I looked at her with surprise. Then said she, 'Please don't tell anybody that I told you that because Pet will kill me.'

CHAPTER EIGHT

now succeeded by a Mr Kingsley of whom I shall make no comment whatever.

Now preparing myself to run away called for some studious planning. First, I made sure that Tanty was alright fuel-wise by gathering all the wood I could have carried from the nearby hills. It is a fact that she waled my backside. But I knew at times it came not from her heart to do so. For example, here is an episode which took place. As we walked up the street one evening, a woman whose son I had given a sound thrashing stopped her. "Hi, Pet, gol, yuh going home?" "Yes," said Tanty. "Ah, gol, ah hear of all-yuh trials an tribulation wid dat nine-toe man. Ee really ungrateful. Me nah know how yuh put up wid am so lang. Gol, dem is a angrateful generation." As she spoke her eyes were glued upon me. "Ah see dat yuh hole on to dis little vagabon. Nah keep am. Sen am ge ee mooma an James. Let dem mine am. Because ee go do yuh jes like Bishop. Ee go tek ee behine an tell yuh thanks."[3]

One day I said to her, "Tanty, Dr Chase Almanac said that there would be lots of rain from September to December. So we must gather more wood for fuel, what we have here is not enough. I have not heard or seen anyone paying attention to this, so let us now prepare ourselves for that time." "Yes," said she, "but how much can we bring?" "Never mind that, leave it all to me. We shall have all the wood we need for fuel." She looked at me and shook her head, and said, "Alright, do what you can." The next day I began gathering driftwood by the seashore, also wet and discarded branches around the neighbourhood, small greenwood trees from the hills, and finally every scrap of dry wood I could have laid my hands on. An old man (actually he was an uncle of Horace) called me the Woodpecker.

---

3   'Hi, Pet, girl, are you going home?' 'Yes,' said Tanty. 'Ah, girl, I heard about all your trials and tribulations with that nine-toed man. He is really ungrateful. I don't know how you've put up with him for so long. Girl, they are an ungrateful generation.' As she spoke her eyes were glued upon me. 'I see that you're holding on to this little vagabond. Don't keep him. Send him to go to his mother and James. Let them mind him. Because he will deal with you just as Bishop does with you. He will take you from behind and tell you thanks.'

A BRANCH TO REST ON

These were all neatly and tightly packed according to their nature to become dry. I roamed the estates and beach for discarded coconuts (that was no trouble to gather same in those days) for feed for the chickens, for we had then quite a few of them. I cleaned and weeded all around the house. Finally I went to the nearby forest and cut all the carat palm* leaves I could have found as a replacement for those that leaked. As I have said, I had already lost all interest for school.

Tanty happened to have two fortnights' sand money uncollected, so she sent me to Toco to collect same at the Warden's Office. It was an easy trek of five miles in those days. For, as I have said before, automobiles were not many, and travelling as far as Matelot to Toco was done by foot, riding horseback or donkey, or by pirogue* boating. For instance, the first truck that drove into Grande Riviere arrived there only with its chassis. No tray was built on it because of the narrow road and sharp curves. Its chauffeur was one Mr Nathan; you should have seen the heroic welcome he received from the villagers. I was sent to Grande Riviere that very day with a message from Tanty to an uncle of hers.

As I went to collect Tanty's wage that day, I planned then my running away. Tanty had gone to the abandoned garden for some yams. As she left, I hurried to Miss Katie's home and bid her goodbye. She warned me to be careful and that I must behave myself with my family when I got to town. I assured her that I will. As she turned into her house, I took as a reward a salt bag she had then on her oven. I packed all my clothes that I could readily have laid my hands upon in the sack. I was very careful not to enter the press, fearing that I could be blamed for other things. Lucky for me my scout hat and boots were out, so I took them and dressed myself in halfway scout, which, of course, I knew would bring me some recognition and respect.

As I left my village of Sans Souci that day, in my heart I said goodbye. Not to the school but to the hills, river and beach. With my suitcase-sack and boots swung over my shoulder, barefooted as the naughty boy, I trekked towards L'Anse Noire. Just before entering the village I put my boots on. As I left L'Anse Noire they were off again, and I replayed this action at every important point until I got to Toco. At the Warden's

CHAPTER EIGHT

Office, the money was all paid to me – $6.00. There were people there who knew me, and also there were very few rascals living in the villages of Toco. The money was paid to me in this manner.

    3 @ $1 = $3.00
    1 @ $2 = $2.00
    1 half-crown = 60 cents
    1 shilling = 24 cents
    2 – 3 pence = 12 cents
    2 – 1 penny = 4 cents
    ―――――――――
    Total = $6.00

As I received the cash, a woman by the name of Miss Mizpah, a very good friend of Tanty, was there. I gave to her $5.28 to take to Tanty, and asked her to let Tanty know that I had gone to Point Galera to buy coconuts and I shall soon be down. As she and others cleared the scene, I slipped into a nearby parlour* with the seventy-two cents that I had kept. There I bought myself a sweet drink* for three cents, two sweetbreads* for two cents and a one-cent extra-strong. After my snack I placed one of the candies into my mouth. Then slowly but watchfully I walked to the bay where the fishing boats came in with their catch. After taking a survey, I went to a kindly looking fisherman and said, "Sir, I want a fish for six cents. It is to be sent to town." He looked at me with a smile, "Alright, sonny." He then took up a very large carite* fish from the boat. "Do you like this one?" "Yes sir," said I. He then cleaned it and washed it in the sea. He said by having to go so far if it is washed in the river, it would go bad quickly. There was no paper with which to wrap it; I paid him and tucked it into my bag with my belongings.

As I left the bay with my bag swung over my shoulder, I quickly walked to Palm Tree (the village landmark) as though heading really for Point Galera. When I got there, I turned and slowly walked back towards the bus station using up time. I was there at 1:00 p.m. because my bus was supposed to leave at 2:00 p.m. It was the most anxious hour I had spent waiting in all my then life. Finally I saw people entering into the bus. I watched and waited to see if there was anyone from

A BRANCH TO REST ON

Sans Souci. But when there were about ten passengers, I saw no one from my village. I then decided that it was time to board. The name of the bus company was "Within the Time". And they certainly worked that way. As I entered there was a conductor geared in khaki shirt and pants and wearing a black cap with a military look. "Sonny," said he, "is whe yuh going?" "To town, Laventille on the Main Road by the Roman Catholic Church, sir." I spoke out bravely, but deep within I was afraid that he would say no to me. Or may perhaps say the bus would not be taking that route. "OK," said he as my heart leapt joyfully. "Where is yuh money?" "Here, sir," as I nervously handed him the half-crown (sixty cents). "That is a town drop so yuh have to pay de full fare of thirty-six cents." Miss Katie had really said to me the fare would be one shilling and sixpence, which is really thirty-six cents, but I thought it may be a bit more when I kept the half-crown, but she was right.

I chose a seat almost in the centre of the bus. (Those were the days when seats of buses were wooden, like benches, not upholstered as they are today, with streamlined bodies. There were also lathes on the sides with canvas to keep off the weather; the whole housing structure was of wood with neatly covered steel-sheet hoods.) As I was timidly seated, I heard a lady passenger sitting behind me saying, "Look at Mozart, that maco*." I became alert because Mozart was a close relative of Tanty, and one who could now ruin everything. I kept my head bowed, as he seemed to be taking an inventory of everyone in the bus. "Whe yuh going, Crecy?" he concerningly asked. With a flash I replied, "To Sangre Grande at Tanty's aunt who live on Foster Road, and I am coming back with the bus tomorrow." (I tried to speak softly so as not to be heard by the other passengers.) "Oh yes," said he, "cousin Pet did tell me dat yesarday." (I said to myself, what a big liar.) "Wen yuh go don't forget, tell cousin Milly dat Mozart say howdy." As he walked off, he loudly said, "Alright, tek care ar yuhself." I needed not his deep concern but his riddance.

In about five minutes I heard the owner of the bus shouting, "Come on! Come!! What the hell is keeping this bus back. Leave now! Anyone else would have to catch the six o'clock bus." Then three other persons

CHAPTER EIGHT

entered, making an amount of fourteen. I had built up a fear that Miss Mizpah could by now be in Sans Souci, and that Tanty could be now on her way to Toco. "Clang! Clang!" went the bell, the driver started the engine, and we were off, as I bade farewell to Toco. No more blows and cruel treatment. But here I lift my hat to Tanty. I was never starved. As we entered Cumana Village, under a shop two men were fighting. "Heave!*" shouted a small crowd that was gathered around them; some of our passengers also joined in the call of "Heave!" An aged lady shook her head and said that she was sure that it was rum that had them making such fools of themselves. But our bus rolled on as we left the noisy scene.

The roads of Toco were very dangerous for driving in those days. Being a rural district, they were not pitched*, and there were sharp curves associated with numerous landslides with overhanging trees and no road signs of distinction. But the drivers all performed well their duties. That day, as we drove through villages or stopped for an awaiting passenger on the roadway, the conductor would yell: "Come, we go town and mek bassa-bassa*." As we journeyed on, our bus became overcrowded. A big fat mama took my seat and let me sit upon her lap while I held very tightly to my bag. When we arrived at Sangre Grande, many of the passengers, including my mama, set off to catch an awaiting train, which gave those of us who stayed more comfortable seating space. No sooner had we driven off from Sangre Grande, I overheard someone saying that we shall soon be taking the Stretch. This was very interesting news to me. For very often did I hear children who had been fortunate to travel to town speaking quite boastfully how this piece of roadway was as long as the distance from Sans Souci to Toco without a curve and thought it to be impossible. For I could not see how a road could be five miles long without a curve. But I then believed. We very soon reached Valencia, a village that was then very important for its water works.

We used at schools in those days a book called *Little Folks' Trinidad*. It gave a miniature historical, geographical and physical description of the island. And its teaching could be easily memorized. It was through the use of that book as we left Valencia that I knew that we were on our way to Arima. So I was now most interested to see Arima and perhaps a few Carib* people dressed in loincloths with tattooed markings on their faces, holding bows, and arrows slung over their backs. But I was most surprised to see it was somewhat like Sangre Grande. I was most impressed with its clock standing in the middle of the road revealing freely the time of day. It was then 4:30 p.m. As we drove on, a passenger rang the bell and said, "Drop me by the market." And as we drove off there was the huge savannah, all railed. What I was then seeing was the old Arima racetrack. The area seemed to me to be larger than that of Sans Souci village itself laid flat. We then drove through a forested area which looked as though we were on our way headed back for Toco as I fell asleep.

I slept for quite a while and was awakened by a lady who shared the seat with me. She poked me on the side followed by the words, "We is in Sen Wan. Jes now we go meet town." "Ee good far eeself," said another woman who sat behind me. "Becarse ah hear he rag up dat maco Mozart in Toco today."[4] I began rubbing my eyes with the palm of my hands, followed with a wide yawn. "Do not rub your eyes like that, they may hurt," said another lady pleasantly. She was of Oriental descent. "Where are you going?" she asked. Before I could have made a reply, the conductor said, "Oh yes, dat boy. Ah glad you talk, Miss Benard. Ah nearly forget am. Ah know whe to drap am out."[5]

Once more fear and excitement crept over me. (1) Would I find the place? (2) And should I, would they accept me? (3) Suppose they have removed from the area, and if they did, (4) where would I sleep tonight? And so did many other vivid thoughts run through my mind. Suddenly the conductor swung himself upon the footboard. "Go slow, Gurrie," said he, "we have to drop one around here." And so he started looking

---

4   'We are in San Juan. Just now we will arrive in town.' 'He is good for himself,' said another woman who sat behind me. 'Because I heard that he scolded that gossiping Mozart in Toco today.'

5   'Oh, yes, that boy. I'm glad you've raised that, Miss Benard. I nearly forgot him. I know where to drop him off.'

CHAPTER EIGHT

mindfully. "Clang! Clang!" went the bell, as our bus rolled to a stop. The conductor then said, "Come, boy, yuh reach. Look, de church dey, an ar tink dat is the house it have some Toco people living dey."[6]

---

6   'Come, boy, you've reached. Look, the church is there, and I think that is the house where some Toco people live.'

PART TWO

Chapter 9

*George takes refuge with relatives in Laventille
and gets his first job at age twelve; he meets Aunt Bertrice*

It was about 6:30 that evening as darkness overshadowed the surroundings. When I disembarked, the bus drove off. No one said goodbye to me, and to no one did I say goodbye. As I held on tightly to the salt bag, my only possession, I stood wondering what must my next move be. Immediately, a boy much bigger than I came towards a nearby fence. "Hey, boy," I shouted, "can you tell me where Miss Rache Williams live around here?" "Right here," he replied with a grin. "Who are you?" "I am George, her nephew from Toco." Without another word, he quickly ran to the building. I distinctly heard him saying, "Miss Rache! Miss Rache! There is a boy outside the gate who look like your family. Is now asking for you."

Then came Aunt Rache, whom I knew, followed by six children. "Oh my goodness! Look who is here! I cannot believe my eyes. George! George!" said she as she embraced me with a kiss. "Who and you came down? I really heard the bus stop. But knew not that it concerned us. Come," said she, "let's go in. Cecilst, take his bag." As we entered the house, she called aloud, "Willie! Willie! Come, we have a visitor." At this time all my fear and nervousness vanished as I began to feel myself again.

Then came a tall gentleman from across the yard sporting a shirt and tie. "Who is this now?" he asked with a broad smile. "This is George, Tante Plum's last boy with Georgie. He is the one that now live in Toco with Uncle Bishop and Tanty Pet. Quildon do speak of him when he comes here." Then shaking my hand, he said, "Sonny, how are you?" "Well, thanks, sir," I replied with a bow. He then asked Aunt Rache, "Did he alone come down?" "That's what he said," she replied.

Now from the time Aunt Rache met me with the children until then, I said but very little. "OK, let me finish seeing about the horses," said he. "I'll be right back." From the very mention of the word "horses," I felt somewhat happy. Then, one by one, Aunt Rache introduced the children to me. There were three boys and three girls. "This is Bob, who you first spoke to, and his sister Lidia. They both are my stepchildren. These are your cousins Cecilst, Maze, Burt and Merl." They all said, "Hello, George."

Aunt Rache then looked at me, and tears flowed from her eyes. "Boy," said she, "look how strong and healthy you do look. May God bless Miss Pet, for had it not been for her you would have died and gone with your father." She again said, "Should you turn ungrateful to her, God will curse you. You must be kind and always love her as long as you both shall live." Once more my heart leapt in fear, thinking that I would not be accepted in this home.

Then said Maze with a bit of scorn, "I am smelling fish, where is it coming from?" Said I, "It is from my bag." "From your bag?" said they. "Yes," said I nervously. For now my built-up courage had failed after being chided by Aunt Rache with her tongue. Cecilst then emptied the bag, thus separating my belongings from the fish. They all laughed when they saw my toothbrush that was made of coconut stem. "Oh, what a lovely fish," said Aunt Rache. "But we cannot use it for ourselves; it has begun to turn bad. Come take it, Bob, and put it in the icebox. It shall be sound enough to be cooked for the dogs tomorrow."

While I was inwardly contemplating my fate, back came Mr Williams. "Well, well," said he, "what is now taking place? Has he been given something to eat? He ought to be hungry after that long drive." Aunt Rache then said to the children, "Alright, you all may go. For the moment leave George alone with Pappy and I." "Now come on, young man," she said to me, "what brought you into town?" I was now confronted with

CHAPTER NINE

a mammoth question, the answer to which may permit me to stay or not. I looked at them both, and with head downcast I began speaking. Suddenly I remembered Uncle Bishop once said to me, "Don't matter what the situation may be, always look at people when speaking to them." So I looked up and began telling them all of Tanty's goodness to me, and how well she fed me. But when she found out Uncle's unfaithfulness to her, I was ill-treated almost every day under the strain of hazardous work, along with corporal punishment. I now can bear it no longer, so I ran away. "You what! You ran away?" said Aunt Rache. "Yes," I replied. "Did anyone know about this?" "No," said I. (Because I wanted to be loyal to Miss Katie with my word.) "Did you not tell Tante Plum about this?" she asked. "No, no, not at all." "Then how came you to know our address?" asked Mr Williams. "Well, sir, I visited Mother one day, and we were alone so I began to question her about town and the family. She, being unaware of my notion, gave me fully all the information I wanted. After checking them all out in my mind, I thought here would be the easiest place to find and stay if allowed." He smiled. Aunt Rache was then about to say something. "Hold a minute, Rache," said he. So he again continued speaking to me, "You claimed that you got licks almost every day, but yet you have not a scratch. How come?" "Sir, she beats me only on my head, back and buttocks." Mr Williams then gave Aunt Rache an enquiring look and then said to me very calmly, "Then, George, will you please take that shirt off." I did. He then saw the evidence of fresh and dried wounds. "Oh, my God," he exclaimed, holding his head, "Rachel, this woman should be locked up."

I was right away snapped back into the feelings of assurance that I would be allowed to stay and not sent back to Toco. But as he spoke on and I saw a determined look upon his face about how Tanty should be imprisoned, I became frightened and began rehearsing the story about how Uncle Bishop left and we both had to work hard. I could not then attend school regularly, and some of the villagers were encouraging her to ill-treat me as Uncle left home. Aunt Rache then said, "Willie, I do think it was all frustration, which led to cruelty." To this he seemingly agreed.

A BRANCH TO REST ON

Aunt Rache then said, "Do you know something, your brother Anim (Quildon) and cousin Ren were here today showing off a new suit each." I then asked their permission to go and pee. As though I was at school, I made a salute. To this they both laughed and said, "Go ahead." Now as I left for outside, my hearing was glued inside. Aunt Rache asked, "What do you think, Willie?" "Let him stay," he replied. What a joy was that to me. I felt as though floating in the clouds.

I very soon became adjusted to my new home. My cousins and cousins-in-law all seemed fond of me. Here were animals which reminded me of Valley and Buenos Ayres Estate. There were two horses, six pigs, three dogs, and a number of chickens and ducks; there was also enough land space to plant short crops*. Without being overseered, I fell headlong into manual labour. For I knew well the way, and so I found no problems in weeding, cleaning or even washing. As for the handling of animals, when we lived at Valley Estates, Mr Yank the groom showed us (Alvin and I) a few tricks about animals and how to become their friends. He said whenever horses' ears are thrown backwards, be careful, because then they can be very mean. When flung forward, they are friendly. Then give them a banana or a piece of bake, play with them or even scratch their stomachs. Scratch the back and undersides of pigs, they would lie down, and sometimes sleep. Be kind to dogs, you may give a bone sometime. For poultry, that I learned for myself.

Now in Toco, where I lived, horses were used as the chief means of transportation by the police or high officials of large plantation estates, with polished leather saddles and harness, while mules and donkeys were ridden and used generally on the estates by peasants and planters, with crooks* and panniers strapped to their backs for the hauling of cocoa and coffee beans and ground provisions* from rural gardens. But here, in the city, horses were set on racetracks, for military services, and along with mules and donkeys, horse-drawn carts were also pulled.

Working along with my cousins and cousins-in-law was an easy task in many respects. We drew water from a nearby well in the churchyard. This was used for the watering and washing of the animals. About 150 yards away, on the shoulder of the Main Road, there was a standpipe

CHAPTER NINE

from which water was drawn for drinking and other domestic purposes. I outworked the other children in every field of our duties, with the exception of grass cutting for the animals. At this they were very much faster than I was. After cutting theirs, they would help me to cut my quota. The reason for this was back in Toco we used a cutlass* or a swiper*. But in the city or outskirts, scythes or grass knives (sickles) are used. However, Mr Williams, who always seemed amused with my triumph over the others, showed me the art of holding the grass and using my sickle. My opponents were then no match for me. I helped them instead.

It truly was my ambition that I again be sent to school. But most regrettably that could not be. The reason was Aunt Rache had four children of her own, and Mr Williams two. My haphazard arrival meant that there were now nine mouths to be fed, and Mr Williams was the sole breadwinner. He was a carter by profession, and he was the only carter man in the city who sported a shirt and tie, all of which cost money. His only advantage was he owned his own horses.

My brothers and adult sister at the time were in no position to take me. There were other aunts and uncles who cared very little for my welfare (with the exception of one aunt of whom I shall speak later). The others all declined my charge. Again may I mention that, with the exception of meals and shelter, Aunt Rache could not handle the educational side, although she would have loved to do so.

Now ever since the death of my father, I was made to understand that there was an aunt, the sister of my mother, who was very kind to her. To her credit, she was chiefly responsible for my maternal grandmother and my elder sister being in town. Her name was Aunt Bertrice. She also had two children of her own for whom to provide. They were boys for whom she toiled miserably, and this she did even in part of their lives as grown men.

One evening Aunt Rache called me in the presence of Mr Williams. "George," said she, "I am forced to do something that shall hurt us very much. How old were you on Christmas?" "Twelve, Aunt Rache," I replied. "Child," said she, "we are unable to send you back to school." This was no news of disappointment to me because I had already foreseen that. But when she said, "We can no longer mind you," I was shocked, especially with the feelings that I once more would be sent back to Toco. "However," she continued, "you are a big boy, and we shall try to get you a work this coming year." "You will still be able to sleep here," said Mr Williams sadly, "and whatever you work for will be yours and will be spent only on yourself." I was quite in agreement to this. So from then on, a job was in store for me.

That weekend there were quite a few visitors who called at our home. Among them was Uncle Joe, my mother's brother, who willingly would have taken me to Santa Cruz to work on an estate with him. To this Mr Williams said no. Another sister of my mother, whose name was Helen, wanted me to help her in the market, and daily take her grandchildren to school. That would be considered, he said. Aunt Bertrice said, "He can make a very good pay at the club where I work, but there is so much cursing, especially at nights." That was also turned down. Then spoke Anim (Quildon), my eldest brother. He was currently driving for a well-known taxicab company of the day. "Look-k-k," he stuttered, "right now, next door to where I work, Mrs Mudder want someone to take two lunches daily to the pumping station. Let him come and meet me on Monday morning, I will take him over to her." "How much is the pay?" asked Aunt Rache. "I don't know right now. One thing I do know: he will be well fed." Aunt Bertrice said, "Well fed on macafouchette*." However, although not at all happy, yet they decided that I try that job. "What will he be wearing?" asked Aunt Bertrice. "My scout clothes," I quickly answered. "Oh no," said she, "Ren has some clothes ever since he was at school; they were offered to Lou, but he would not wear them. Come with me when I am leaving and I shall give them to you." To this Aunt Rache gave a smile of approval.

There was a bus company at the time which plied from Tunapuna to Port of Spain. Passengers then from San Juan to Port of Spain paid two cents fare. If you could not afford, you would tread the 2½ mile journey, hitch a lift on an animal-drawn cart, or be towed by a cyclist. Aunt Bertrice paid our bus fare of four cents. When we left the bus stand, we got to her home in about ten minutes. It was a large apartment and nicely furnished. I then heard cousin Ren and Lou in an argument.

CHAPTER NINE

Aunt asked what was wrong and were they both fighting again. Ren shouted, "Mother!" "Hold it," said Aunt Bertrice sternly. "I've told you when speaking to me, never lift your voice, have I not?" "Yes, Mother," he calmly said, "I am sorry." "Well, what is it now?" "Mother, Lou wants to go to the cinema with some other boys, but the cinema they have chosen is Gaiety" (nicknamed "Wash Your Foot and Come In"). "I told him that cinema is for vagabonds only and, Mother, you would not like it. He then began jeering at me and calling me names." "Oh no, Mother," said Lou, "he wants me to go at Roxy with him, and I told him that was too far." "So alright," said Aunt Bertrice, "I shall be going to the Globe in an hour's time so you both will join me."

"Hello, George," said Ren, "how are you going?" As he spoke, he rested his hand upon my shoulder. Lou then asked, "Are you spending the night with us?" "No," said Aunt Bertrice. She then turned to Ren and said, "You have some used clothing that Lou never wanted. How about giving them to George?" "Oh yes, Mother, why not?" he replied. That evening I got from him three nice shirts, two lovely pairs of short pants, a T-shirt, and two vests, and he also added two of his own used handkerchiefs. Aunt Bertrice then said, "Come and eat some of this food before you leave."

During this time Lou said not a word to anyone. But he sat gloomily and seemingly disappointed. Ren then wrapped the clothes in some newspaper and gave them to me. Aunt Bertrice then asked, "How are you going back home?" I looked in wonder and said, "How do you mean, Auntie?" She replied, "I mean, how will you travel back home?" "By walking," I replied. "No, no, here is six cents, you can walk back to the bus station and take a bus for a penny or take a cab at the corner for six cents. The choice is yours, you may do what you like," said she. "Many thanks, Auntie," said I. As I left for the door, Lou broke his silence and secretly said to me, "Save your money and walk, boy." If only he knew how well his advice was to me because that was my intention.

The evening was dry, and I walked home very quickly before it became dark. Everyone liked the things I got; even Uncle Joe, who was yet at home, was quite surprised of my prize.

Chapter 10

A fist-fight ends a yard boy job; George packs biscuits instead

Came Monday morning, I travelled to town with Mr Williams. We were there more than on time. When we reached, Mr Williams promptly got a call for a job. He said to me, "Stand by the gate, George, do not move because your brother would be here shortly." I waited there, looking occasionally at the clock upon the wall. At 10:00 a.m. brother Quildon came. Without an apology, "Come quickly," said he, "we are late." He then drove me over to St Vincent Street, to the home of Mrs Mudder. She was a pleasant-looking person, and her build was very much like Tanty Pet's. After speaking with Quildon, she said to me, "You would not have time now to wash the bathroom, nor scrub the drains. When you return from the lunch delivery, you shall do them." I then had not a notion of what she spoke.

I was then handed two food carriers*, one with five lifts, the other three, and was also given a package with cutlery. My brother then said, "Don't you worry. I shall see that things move rightly."

My destination was the pumping station at the western end of Wrightson Road. As we got to Duke and Wrightson Road, he stopped and directed me as to where I must go. My brother said to me, "Walk fast or you would be late. Remember when you get to the building, ask for Mr Jim Passor, the engineer, and deliver it to him, and wait until he is finished." I walked down very quickly, and I arrived all sweating. Mr Passor had apparently come out to see if I had come because someone said to me, "Was it you Mr Passor was looking for? Let me tell him you are here."

CHAPTER TEN

Mr Passor was a sturdy-built man of Spanish descent. He said to me, pointing to a spot, "Wait there under that eave." I was very much amazed to see and hear the commotion that was taking place. There were so many wheels of all sizes suspended from the roof with swift moving belts with deafening hiss of steam and engines working. (As described by the Psalmist, "a noisome pestilence.") The sounds bellowed in my ear as I awaited the return of Mr Passor. Suddenly down came a heavy shower of rain. I then tried to brace myself to the wall to avoid becoming wet. A gent rode up upon a bicycle; he was cloaked. He said to me, "Boy, you will get all drenched there. Come inside and shelter." I followed him in, while I wondered what will Mr Passor say should he see me. "You are waiting on someone?" asked the kindly man. "Yes, sir, Mr Passor." "Oh," said he, "the chief. Does he know that you are here?" "Yes, sir, he told me to stand there, but it was not raining at the time." "OK, you may wait here, and I shall let him know that I bade you in." "Many thanks, sir," I replied.

I learned my discipline from Uncle Bishop, who as we do know was an old soldier, and also from Mr Williams, who was a retired police officer. I have never failed to use it. And I do know that I have many times been helped through its usage.

Then came Mr Passor. "Oh, sonny," said he, "I am sorry. What's your name?" "George, sir." (At this point I clearly remembered Mr Drell, for he had almost the same build and seemed almost as kind.) "Well, George, the foreman now told me that he let you in from the rain. I am so sorry that you got wet." "Not very much, sir," said I, "the mister came just in time to save me." We then walked towards the doorway, and he gave me the empty carriers. By then the rain had ceased, so I hurried back on my way to St Vincent Street.

When I arrived, I was questioned by Mrs Mudder as to how it all went. I gave her a quick rundown of what took place. "Come and have your lunch," said she. "No, Mam, when I came, you said something about the washing of drains and baths." "Oh yes," said she, "I am glad that you have reminded me." She then went to a standing box, which was a rudely made cupboard; from it, she gave me the necessary implements for cleaning. She also showed me the bath and drain, which I did before eating, and I then left for home.

My second and third days at work were done more speedily. I was at home each day by 2:15 p.m. On my fourth day Mrs Mudder said, "George, you would wash the column and the glass windows also at the back today before you leave." "Very well, Mam," I replied. That day, for some reason, the lunch was twenty minutes late. I had then to trot and walk briskly for the pumping station. On my way down, a mule-drawn cart was heading to that direction. I asked the carter for a lift, but he flipped me his whip. I did arrive, however, at 12:03 p.m. by the wall clock. Mr Passor smiled and said, "You are late today, George, by three minutes." "I am sorry, sir," said I without a further explanation. He took both carriers and disappeared as previously. I waited at my usual spot. I had not very long to wait before Mr Passor's son appeared; with his usual smile he handed the containers to me.

As I got back that day, I placed the carriers where I was shown to put them, and proceeded to clean the bath and drain, because I had then some extra to do at the windows and column. I went to the drain. (Now those were the days when plumbing standards were not high in some parts of Port of Spain as they are in the whole city today. Then, all wastewater from baths, sinks and drains flowed from one's premises into the city's sidewalk drains, which then flowed into larger tributaries on their way out.) I began cleaning the drain by hauling the heavy debris on the sides before washing it down. Suddenly a youngster a little taller than I (and perhaps a few pounds heavier) appeared on the scene. I had never seen him before. It happened that where I had the refuse packed to the sides, he threw it in again. I then asked who was he and why was he doing that to me. "I am your boss, and here I can do whatever I like," and at the same time he pulled the broom from my hands and pushed a fair amount of greasy water upon my Raleigh watchicong*. I made no hesitation: between eyes and nose, I sank my right fist, and down went he, because he did not expect it.

Now Uncle Bishop always said to me, should I hit someone and he falls, do not hit him again while he is on the ground because that shows cowardice. Just stand a little way from him. But should he rise and

CHAPTER TEN

attack, then let the fight go on. This was my first fight in the city, and I desired not to lose it. But to my great surprise, the chap got up and ran.

In seconds came Mrs Mudder in a rage to me. I had not time to explain to her what took place when I heard someone calling, "Mrs Mudder! Mrs Mudder!! I was here, and I saw and heard everything." As I looked, there was a lady peering through a window from next door. She then explained to Mrs Mudder the truth, far better than I would have been able to explain. But Mrs Mudder insisted that I should have first come to her and she required no longer my service. She then went inside. On her return she chucked a sixpence (twelve cents) into my hand. "Go home," said she, "I shall speak to your brother. I no longer need you around."

That was then my first experience of being employed and to be sacked by someone. As I walked down the street, I recalled the nursery rhyme: "See Saw Marjorie Daw, Johnny shall have a new master. He shall work for a penny a day because he can't work any faster." Here, in my case, I earned three cents, one cent more than Johnny.

I now hurried to catch Mr Williams. Being Thursday he never stayed late in town, as all groceries were closed at half-day, which slowed his trade. When I got to him, he was just watering the horse. "Well, young fellow" (the way he generally addressed me) "you are very early today." I made no delay but promptly told him the whole story. To this he said not a word, but sadly shook his head. I then began to wonder what will Aunt Rache say when I get home. When we left for home, on our way Mr Williams said not a word to me. However, when we got to turning into the gate, he broke the silence. "George," he said, "say nothing to your aunt, let me speak to her." Strange as it will seem, the children were all at home early that evening. I then related to them my happenings of the day. They were all excited, especially when I spoke of how I dropped the boy with my fist. Cecilst, who later became an amateur boxer, gave me full credit. We four boys then went out to cut grass for the animals. On our return I was summoned by Aunt Rache, who said to me, if it were true what I have said, I was perfectly right in doing what I did. And, furthermore, it was a good thing that my dismissal came in four days because I would have been earning less than one dollar for the month.

About 6:30 p.m. that evening my brother Anim came and said that, although I was somewhat provoked, I had no right to strike the boy. And I must go the next day and make an apology to Mrs Mudder and the lad. Should this be done, I would get my work back. Reader, from Merl, the youngest, to Mr Williams, booed Anim. Aunt Rache, who was his favourite aunt, was so wroth with his statement that she asked him to leave.

The next morning being Friday, Mr Williams said to me, "Bathe and get dressed. You will ride down with me into town, and I shall check for a factory work for you." This indeed was good news; the other children were all happy to hear it. When we got into town, he hitched the cart and animal in its usual spot. "Come with me," he said. I then followed him over to a nearby biscuit company on lower Duncan Street. He spoke to an elderly man, who said that they were all filled. As we walked away, we were called back and asked, "When will he like to start?" Before Mr Williams could have answered, I said, "Now, sir." He looked at me and smiled. "OK," said he to Mr Williams, "he has passed my test. He will be employed this very day."

"Come with me," said he. He took me to a supervisor, who then put me to work with some other boys in the packing of salt biscuits in drums. I later in the day learned that we were doing the weekend run. I then overheard the supervisor saying to the gentleman who took me on, "He is a bit awkward, which generally happens to all beginners." We worked to 5:00 p.m. that day. And on the Saturday, we worked to 1:00 p.m. That Saturday evening I was paid thirty-six cents and was also given a free package of biscuits. I worked for three months with the company and was becoming quite a favourite among the lads. By his mannerism I could have seen that the gent who employed me that Friday was pleased with how I applied myself to the work. The company was none other than the Sunrise Biscuit Company, that is no longer. Due to the smell of the ammonia, however, and being asthmatic, I was forced to leave that work with regret.[1]

---

[1] The cause of George's asthmatic symptoms was an ingredient called Baker's Ammonia, used at the time to make the biscuits extra crispy.

Chapter 11

Yard boy again in elite St Clair; he meets Miss Eva, misunderstands instructions, destroys a lawn, and is fired again

I was once again on the labour beat. Although I tried, I could find nothing that I was capable of doing. Brother Weston came one evening and said there were some people living on Sweet Briar Road who wanted a yard boy and were paying $3.00 a month. What did Aunt Rache think about that? "It is better than to sit idle," said she. Brother Weston said, "Only one thing: you have to start very early at 6:00 a.m." "That's a far distance from here," said she, "how will he get there?" Brother Weston replied, "I shall come to meet him early tomorrow morning and take him to the place." Auntie then looked at me and asked, "What do you think, George?" "I am ready to go," said I. "OK, you can meet him here in the morning," said she.

The next morning Brother Weston was home at 4:00 a.m. We travelled by bus to town. When we got off, he said it was too early for the tramcar. So we walked over to St Vincent Street and walked up to Tragarete Road. As we walked in the early light, he pointed out many landmarks to me that I can follow should I get lost. He also said, "Don't you forget to walk in the direction of the tramline." We arrived before 6:00 a.m. at the house. There was a lady already wetting some hanging baskets of fern. Brother Weston called and said to her that I am applying for the vacancy. "OK," said she with an air of dignity. Brother Weston then left us. As he walked off, he reminded me to follow his directions shown on my way back home.

The lady then said, "Let me take you to the back and tell you one time* what will be your duties here." As we got beneath an eave, she stood and said to me, "You will oil and shine the floors, clean and shine the silvers* and brass, clean the windows, scrub the north porch, clean the bath and toilets, water and weed the plants, trim the hedges, cut the lawn and footpath, sweep the yard, wet the baskets you see me now wetting, scrub the drains, wash the tortoises, bathe Mr Bob (the dog), groom Miss Persia's coat (a Persian cat), or any other thing the Master or Mistress may call upon you to do."

She rehearsed those duties as though she was a poet. I cast my head down and remembered Uncle Bishop's advice to look people full in their face. Our eyes met and she gave a wry twitch at the corner of her lips. "Is something wrong?" she asked. "Yes, Mam," said I. "What is it?" she asked sharply. "How can I do all in one day?" "I never said that you have got to do it all in one day, did I? There are the duties that will have to be performed every day, and there are those you would be told to do as needed."

In this home there were three female domestics: a cook, a housemaid, and the lady who interviewed and instructed me. My first day began with oiling and polishing of the floors up and down stairs. I found it to be great fun, especially when polishing with a twelve-pound polish broom by sliding the broom with one hand and catching it with the next. Then came lunchtime. I was then given a real good lunch of salted codfish and onions with tomatoes soaked in olive oil, dumplings and a lovely drink of mauby*. The lunch was given to me by the cook, a kindly looking old woman in her fifties. I ate and drank everything, it being my first meal for the day. After lunch I swept the yard and cleaned the drains. Before leaving that evening, I was told by the maid (let me call her #1) that the brass and silvers were to be cleaned the next day and also the bathing and grooming of the animals were to be done. She also added, the earlier I came in, it will be the earlier I shall leave.

As the chimes of the nearby Queen's Royal College clock struck six the next morning, I was standing by the gate. When an elderly gentleman came from behind a parked car in the garage with a rag in his hand, he

CHAPTER ELEVEN

said to me, "Good morning, sonny." "Good morning, sir," I replied with a salute. He then smiled and said, "Are you looking for someone?" (He spoke with a Barbadian accent.) "No, sir," said I, "I am working here. I started yesterday, and today I am to clean the silvers and the brass."

"Come with me," he said as he opened the gate. As we neared the kitchen, he called with a low but firm voice (as though he wanted not to disturb someone who may have been asleep), "Eva, Eva." "Yes, John," came an answer. "Look, there is someone here." Then came the kindly cook. "Oh, the yard boy," said she. "Good morning, Mam," said I with a salute. "Good morning, sonny," she replied. Turning then, she said, "John, this is the new boy in Samuel's place. You are here early." "Yes, Mam, the other lady said that I must come early, for the earlier I came, the earlier I shall leave for home."

"Where do you live?" they both asked at the same time. "Success Village, Laventille, by the church on the Eastern Main Road." "Quite a distance," said Mr John. "John," she said, "take him to the storeroom and give him the Brasso, Silvo and rags." When I got back, the cook then showed me wares of brass and cutlery of various shapes, which may have been assembled there from yesterday. "You know how it's to be done?" she asked. "Yes, Mam," said I. (Aunt Rache had two brass bowls and also silver-plated knives, forks and spoons, which we children just loved to clean and shine.)

I quickly found out that Mr John was the chauffeur and that he was out nearly all day driving. "By the way," said Miss Eva (the cook), "had you breakfast?" "No, Mam." "In this place only lunch you are supposed to have. Do you drink coffee?" "No, Mam," I replied. "Then how about some green tea*?" I did not want to say yet another no, fearing I may be rude by so saying. "Thank you, Mam," I replied. In about five minutes, she beckoned me to come. As I went, she lured me to a corner and gave me a large enamel cup with the tasty hot beverage, along with two large hops bread* with herrings in oil. "Stay there and eat that, child," said she. "Don't let that maco see you." At the time I knew not of whom she spoke because Mr John was there when I received the meal. Nevertheless, I had my fill.

At 7:30 a.m., Maid #1 showed up. I had already cleaned half the silvers. Miss Eva whispered something to her; she looked at me and smiled. She then went into an outdoor room similar to the barrack rooms in which I once lived in Toco. In about ten minutes she was out again, smartly attired in a white dress and blue apron as she sported a nurse's cap upon her head, with stockings and flat white sandals upon her feet. Looking at me, she said, "So you did come early," as she glanced at the already cleaned silvers. "Yes, Mam," said I, and she walked towards the main building.

It was at the stroke of 11:00 a.m. by the Queen's Royal College clock when Miss Eva came and said to me, "You are doing a good job, but slow down your hand, because they will pack more work on you." "Thanks, Mam," said I, and so I did. By 12:30 p.m., however, all articles were cleaned and polished. It was 1:30 p.m. when Miss Eva called me to lunch. It was an enamel pie dish filled with pigtail, vegetables and split peas soup. "Eat all and tell me if you want more," said she.

After lunch I scrubbed the tortoises; there were six of them. After a few scratches I got through with the grooming of Miss Persia's coat. I then got into the outside shower where I bathed Mr Bob. He was a black cocker spaniel, and I liked him. I had read a book Mr Williams had on dogs, and this breed of dog was the favourite of the English Sovereign King Charles the Second and his sister Henrietta. So I now thought it a privilege to be bathing one. (As a man I owned two also.) I then hurried and swept the yard and washed the drains. By 3:00 p.m. I was all ready to leave for my home. Then Maid #1 came and said to me, "Tomorrow you will trim the hedge and weed the flower beds. And you will also clean young Massa and Missis bicycles. Madam is pleased about your work so far." "Goodbye, Mam," said I, but as I neared the gate, I remembered I did not tell Miss Eva that I was leaving. So I hurried back and said, "Bye bye, Miss Eva." "Bye bye, honey," said she. "Get home safely."

The next morning, the college clock struck 6:00 a.m. when I was about 50 yards away from the house. As I got to the gate, there was Mr John washing the car. "Good morning, sir," said I. "Good morning,

CHAPTER ELEVEN

sonny," he pleasantly replied. "By the way, what's your name?" "George, sir." "You are a very good worker from what I have seen. Keep it up." "Thank you, sir." I then went and paid my respects to Miss Eva, and was off to the storeroom for my shears. But Miss Eva said that it was too early to start the clipping. "The noise may wake Madam and disturb the neighbours." So I decided to rake up the leaves in the backyard. I had just made the first mound when Miss Eva called and handed a cup of hot cocoa to me along with a large piece of bake with potted meat stuffed in it. As I sat once more in the corner out of the sight of others, Miss Eva asked, "By the way, where are you from?" "Laventille, Mam." She looked at me closely and said, "Were you born there?" "No, Mam, I live there." "Then where were you born?" I was a bit hesitant in my reply to her, and then I drawled the word "T-o-c-o." (My reason for this was after the Mudder's incident, Aunt Rache had said to me, "Don't you go telling people freely that you are from Toco. All town folks do think that Toco people are foolish, and they think it best to take advantage of you.") "Toco!" Her dark brown eyes popped at me with a large grin on her face. "What part?" "Sans Souci, Mam," I now answered her with confidence. "Do you know Mr Fred and Miss Colute?" "Yes, Mam," and so at this point I rested my cup of cocoa on the floor and said, "Miss Colute and I once lived in the same building." "Well, they are my brother and sister." She looked at me again. "Then who are your parents?" she asked. "Miss Pet and Mr Bishop, Mam," I replied. "Yes, I do know them, but I never knew they had children." "No, no, Mam, I am not their child by birth, but they raised me when I was small. Miss Plum is my mother and –" "Stop, stop, stop, child," said she with a sense of remorse. "Don't tell me George Wright that died is your father?" "Yes, Mam," I answered. "Child, from the very first day I saw you, my mind challenge me as though I had met you some place. I told Mr John, 'You can ask him.' The very way you walk and carry yourself reminded me of someone I knew, but I could not call to mind who it was."

"Child," she bitterly exclaimed, "I was to be married to your father, but your grandmother Catherine Paul seemed to want him for herself. She began by saying and doing every imaginable thing to prevent our marriage. Your father had loved church a lot, and so we both went to the reverend asking him to speak to her, but that did not stop her. Then came the last straw: she began to work obeah to break up the wedding. So I said, before she kill me, let me get clear out of the way. Her selfish aim was her boy children could live with any woman but marry none. And so I moved into town. When I heard that Pet was going around with Bishop, I said, 'Whey, papa!* Catherine is not going to allow that relationship to blossom.' But on the other hand, Pet is no damn fool. You see her there. It was a matter of iron cutting iron and steel cutting steel," said Miss Eva with vehemence. I sat in awe and wonder as she spoke.

"Go ahead, child, and do your work," said she as if snapped back into her senses. "We shall talk later." All my work was at my fingertips that day after that self-introductory and pep talk of Miss Eva. I cut the hedge with no difficulty because there was one at home and Mr Williams showed us boys how it must be trimmed. So I got through that very easily. When the real Boss came in at lunchtime, he told me that the hedge looked lovely. (Up to then I knew not my employer's name.) "Thank you, sir," said I with a bow. That was a bit of etiquette Mr Williams taught us boys. I was now so happy I felt not for food through Miss Eva's talk and the Boss's praise of my work.

I was, however, summoned to my lunch by Miss Eva. "Come, child," said she, "come now and eat; you can catch wind" (meaning gas on your stomach). Her kindly voice at that moment set my heart to pulsate back to Tanty. The lunch consisted of stewed tasso* (a hard salted dried meat) in coconut milk, cooked yams, and crushed plantains and callaloo*. As we ate and chatted, I asked Miss Eva if the folks ate the same as we did. "Sh, sh, sh," she placed her finger upon her lips as she muttered softly, "they don't. They eat fancy foods like ham and eggs, chicken and beef steaks, redfish*, Irish potatoes, salads and all those sets of rubbish. But Master P comes here and eats his fill. Look, I have his covered there. Don't you see how strong and healthy he is? All of them do get sick but not him. He is like us," as she gave a social laugh.

She again started talking of the relationship with my father and herself, and went on to say she felt as though I was her own son and

CHAPTER ELEVEN

that she never again fell in love with another man. She came into town, worked and saved her money. She had her own house at St James. Her niece lives there; she keeps one room vacant for when she goes home on weekends. She told me also that she has been working with the Odelmas for twelve years. "They are very good people, but some of us do some very wrong things, which turn some of these folks on the other side, and we will then say wrong things about them."

I was very excited to get home that evening. I decided not to walk through the city, so I took a tramcar. Just before the news broadcast that evening on Radio Trinidad, Aunt Rache and Mr Williams sat themselves in the living room, and Aunt Rache called out, "Come, George, let's hear your news before the news broadcast." The way in which she said it made the children all laugh.

I then related Miss Eva's story to her, plus all that was said and took place that day. Everyone was astonished to hear it all. Mr Williams said, "This is indeed a very small world when you think of it." Aunt Rache said she did remember Miss Eva. She was her senior. Colute and herself were classmates and about the same age bracket. Said Aunt Rache, "I have a vague memory of your father's romance and that woman. But that creature disappeared from the district and was never seen or heard of by anyone that I know up to this day. You are the very first person that I've heard speak about her." Just then the news broadcast began.

The next morning I wanted to be the first in action, so I left home very early. I knew also that I had a very tough day ahead, because Maid #1 had told me the evening before that I had to weed the pavement and lawn grass clean the next day. As I walked up Gray Street to turn into Sweet Briar Road, there was Mr John, who was going to work. We chatted, and I told him how the lady told me that I am to weed the pavement and the lawn grass clean today. "Oh my goodness," said he, "there she goes again." I knew not what he meant and why he spoke that way, neither did I ask him. Just then the college clock struck the half hour of 5:30 a.m. As we got to the gate, he took a key from his hip pocket and opened it. I did not realize that the gate carried a lock and key. "You know something, George," said he, "it will be too early for

you to start the job of weeding. The grass out there is too wet for you to stoop in that cold. Why not clean the children's bicycles for school?"
"That's OK, Mr John," said I.

He bade me follow him. As we got to the storeroom, he opened it with a key that was somewhat secreted on a ledge. He opened the door and gave me a pail, rag, soap and polish. And so I set myself to the task of cleaning the bicycles. When I was finished, Mr John looking at them said they seemed as when they were first bought from Bonanza. He then called Miss Eva, who also agreed that it was a good job. As they left, she whispered something to Mr John; he looked at me and shook his head approvingly. And so I kept shining the boy's bike.

By this time the sun was warm, but the grass was still wet. I said, "Good Lord, help me today, that I may show these people how Toco boys could work." Here was I now with a hoe in my hands. I started on the pavement portion. The grass was soft, and I was strong. In about an hour's time, the pavement was all weeded with mounds made all ready to be cleared. I then went inside and began the lawn. The grass here was very much softer, and with my mind and will with the hoe, I found skill. I had already two mounds made from the weeding of three furrows when Maid #1 came and hastily asked what was I doing. "Weeding the lawn," said I, "as you told me yesterday. Don't you remember you told me to weed the pavement and the lawn this morning? See, I have already done the pavement, and I am now doing the lawn." Without saying a word to me, she looked over the fence. Seemingly frozen, she looked at me, and with haste, she hurried off without saying anything to me. Therefore, I continued with the weeding. In about eight minutes she was back, but not alone. She was accompanied by a lady who I had never met; this woman was the real mistress. By then I was about half the way weeding the fourth furrow.[1]

Mrs Odelma gave such a screech that no two vehicles travelling at 50 miles an hour would have avoided an accident. Her face changed

---

[1] George is understanding the request 'to weed' as meaning 'to clear everything' rather than 'to remove unwanted plants'.

CHAPTER ELEVEN

colours like a chameleon. Very quickly the housemaid, Miss Eva, and a neighbour all appeared on the scene, as I stood wondering where did I go wrong. "Look, looook!" Mrs Odelma screamed, "looook, looook what this Toco fool has done to my lawn and footpath." In a rage she grabbed the hoe from my trembling hands and most probably would have let me have a whack when the neighbour blocked her and said, "Phyllis, don't be stupid." The lady then said to me, "Go to the shed," while Maid #1 came hurrying with a glass of water for Mrs Odelma. Miss Eva and the maid came and asked why did I do such a thing. I told them that Maid #1 told me to do so when I came in today. Miss Eva then said, "Jane, you see this is the same thing I told you. This dam woman is too frontin*. She has but very little to do and is always butting into other people's affairs. She better don't come my way because the first day she should venture, I shall scald her with hot water."

Just then the daughter rode in and heard her mother quarrelling. "Don't you worry about that, Mom," said she, "that grass can be planted back." Then in rode the son. After hearing the story from Miss Eva and Jane the maid, he began laughing and then walked back to the sidewalk and furrows. As he came back to his quarrelling mother, he jokingly said, "Mom, that boy ought to be given a medal for having done so much work in so short a time." "Come, Miss Alice, come, Massa Phillip, lunch is ready. Madam, are you eating now?" asked Maid #1. "No," said Mrs Odelma, gruffly, "I am not eating."

Maid #1 came and said to me to follow her to the kitchen. There was Miss Eva sitting and looking somewhat disgusted. She said to Miss Eva that Madam was firing him and wanted her to be a witness that she has given me the full three dollars for the month. Though sad, yet my heart leapt for joy as I was given the money. I then bade goodbye to Miss Eva and Jane the maid, and asked Miss Eva to let Mr John know I left. Miss Eva then said, whenever I had the time, I must come and pay her a visit. She also handed me a half-crown (sixty cents). Most regrettably, I have never been back to see her.

As I walked out the gate, Master Phillip asked what direction was I heading. "To Marine Square," I replied. "I am going to St Mary's College.

Come," said he, "let me drop you on Park Street," and he did. I did not walk home that day; I took a bus for two cents, and I was there by 1:30 p.m. Strange as it may seem, Mr Williams was at home, being Thursday. I then told them both exactly what had taken place. Mr Williams said that I had been overworked. "No, no," said Aunt Rache, "where in this country can any yard boy work for three dollars under four days? Not even in Government House." She then gave a hearty laugh that only Aunt Rache could have done. "Don't be too sorry about the situation, child, no ill wind blows. You need some clothes and a pair of Raleigh shoes, so this will come in handy." Late in the evening Brother Weston came and said Mrs Odelma said for me to return to work the next day. "No way," said Aunt Rache, "let her keep her work. She now realize she outwit herself with a Toco fool."

Chapter 12

St. Clair to Corbeaux Town, and a new job with the Otchin family;
George meets Miss Laura

The next morning about 4:00 a.m. Bob and I heard knocking and someone calling at the gate. As the dogs were barking, we could not recognize the voice. Bob then said, "Let's go out and see who it is." As we got there, what a surprise it was to see my cousin Vera and her husband. I wondered what brought them here early. We four greeted as Bob led the way back to the house. At this time the barking of the dogs increased, and everyone was awakened.

Aunt Rache then said, "Vera, girl, what brought you both out so early?" "Rache, girl, Bertrice told me that you all are looking for a job for George. I have a friend who works with some people at Charles Street, Corbeaux Town, who need a yard boy right now. Someone was expected to turn up yesterday, but he did not. Why not let him try this morning to see if he would get it? The pay I understand is $2.50 per month. So I asked Tim (her husband) to follow me so that I can let you know." Now Cousin Vera knew nothing of my employment or dismissal with the Odelmas, and no one at this time mentioned anything about it. Aunt Rache then said, "George, will you like to give it a try?" "Yes, Auntie," said I. "Well, get ready to leave with Cousin Vera."

We arrived at Cousin Vera's home at 5:45 a.m. As we got there, a lady was just leaving from her apartment that adjoined Cousin Vera's. "Hi, Laura," said she, "this is the boy of whom I spoke." "Good morning, Mam," I saluted. She looked at me but answered not. Cousin Vera said,

"His name is George." "Well, George," said she, "we must leave now." And so we did. We had not to take any conveyance. As we briskly walked upon the pavement, she said to me, "Your cousin said that you do like addressing ladies as Mam. Please do not address me in that manner. You can call me Miss Laura or Laura, whichever makes you happy." "Very well, Miss," said I.

We arrived at the Charles Street residence at 6:45 a.m. "Good timing," said she. Unlike the Sweet Briar Road house, the gate at this house carried no lock and key but a hook and bolt instead. She opened and we entered. As I looked around, I observed the area was not as nicely built up as the Sweet Briar Road area. The houses here were very much smaller with less land space. This house, however, carried a very large annex at the back, four flower beds, a large lime tree, a very tall coconut tree, and a big pommecythere* (golden apple*) tree. Added to this there was a very enclosed well-kept painted shed. And almost adjoined to this building was a large dismal-looking shed, also enclosed, in which was stored used lumber and other building junks. The kitchen was not attached to the building; neither were its toilets and baths. These were all separate outdoor houses. Miss Laura then came and said to me, "Go over and sit on that bench; the boss will come to you in a moment."

In about twenty minutes, there came a handsome-looking smiling gentleman in his early fifties or thereabouts. "Well, well, good morning," said he to me. I sprang to my feet, saluted, and said, "Good morning, sir," forgetting not my scout and military coaching from Uncle Bishop and Mr Williams. "Laura!" he then called. "Is this the chap?" "Yes, sir," said Miss Laura. "You said that he is from Toco?" "Yes, sir," she replied. He looked at me again; my heart leapt as I wondered whether he may perhaps be thinking I may be too foolish for the job. He then asked me, "What part of Toco are you from?" "Sans Souci, sir." Turning to Miss Laura, who had now joined us, he said to her, "Laura, you are indeed quick on the draw. What's your name?" "George, sir, George Wright." He looked at me and smiled. "OK, George. Just wait a moment," said he. Miss Laura said, "Sir, seems as Madam is calling." He was back to me in about five minutes. He then said, "I have now to leave for my

CHAPTER TWELVE

work. When Madam comes out, she shall tell you what is to be done." "Very well, sir," said I.

My interview with him was taken at the backyard. In about thirty minutes, I was summoned to the front of the house by a most beautiful lady who smiled as she spoke to me. Said she, "Mr Otchin told me to hire you. Do you think you would be able to do the work?" My reply was bold: "It all depends if I am given a chance, but first, what am I to do, Mam?" With a frown, she looked me squarely in the face. "Well," said she, "in this building, you will oil and polish the floor, wash the windows, clean and polish the brass and silvers, scrub the bedroom floor, sweep the yard, wash the drains, scrub the bathroom and toilet, and daily take Mr Otchin's lunch to him. When he gets home, he shall tell you what is to be done next door." "Mam," said I, "are you not forgetting something?" She again fixed me with a look as though I was impertinent, and at the same time as though doubtful of herself. "No," said she, "nothing that I can readily recall." "What about the flower beds, Mam?" "Oh my goodness, thank you," said she. "My roses and cannons.[1] Me oh my," said she. My head was bowed; she looked at me. "Is there anything else that you wish to ask?" said she. "Yes, Mam." "Well, what is it?" "To your instructions, how often must those tasks be done?" "Well, with the exception of the lunch, which must be taken daily from Monday to Friday, the others will be done once a week as necessary." "But how far is the lunch to be taken, Mam?" "At the store where Mr Otchin works on Chacon Street." "Then I see no problem whatever, Mam."

She then took me to the kitchen, and said, "Laura, I will keep him. You said your name is George, is that right?" "Yes, Mam, but spelt W-R-I-G-H-T." They both laughed. Someone called and Mrs Otchin hurriedly left, and Miss Laura followed her with a baby's feeder. Up to then I was not told what must first be done. I then saw an old bass broom* that was badly used, leaning on a galvanize fence. I took it and swept immediately that portion of the yard with fallen lime leaves and

---

1   In this context 'cannons' could refer to 'canna', a type of lily.

banana flowers, which took no more than ten minutes. I then washed the drains which if put together were about seventy yards, using another eight minutes. Standing below the eave were three bicycles, a lady's and two gents', which seemed unwashed for weeks. I looked around for an old rag, but there was none. Then I saw an old pair of pants hanging but partly stuck unto the galvanize fence which separated this property from a neighbour's. I pulled it down and tore it into pieces. I had now more than enough rags, so I began to wash those bicycles. They were not at all done as were the Sweet Briar's cycles, but it was a well-done job. I was just drying the lady's when Miss Laura came from inside. "What are you doing?" she asked. "I am giving these a quick wash," I replied. She looked at me and smiled. As I continued drying the cycle, I heard the dragging of slippers coming, *slip, slop, slip, slop*, then the shuffle of feet behind me. I did not look around. Uncle Bishop had taught me not to look around direct when someone is behind you, but with a slight lean of the head, just using the corner of your eyes. And this I did. I then recognized the form of an old woman, and as the figure crept closer, she stood behind me and said good morning to Miss Laura, who was then at the kitchen window. "Good morning, Mrs Stedy," she replied. "Now, now, who is this one?" "Oh, that's George, the new yard boy," said Miss Laura. "He started just a little while ago." "Well, good morning, George." I stood up and said, "Good morning, Mam" with a salute, as I held the damp rag in my hand. "Well," said she, "I must say it was only yesterday evening I was telling Lloyd about washing his bicycle, and here it is this morning, looking so very nice and clean."

"May, May," she softly called. "Yes, Mother," came a reply, "good morning, good morning, mother." "I have seen that you have got a new yard boy. I hope he keeps to it in the way in which he has started. Under the lime tree is swept clean, and the drains even by me are all washed. He has even done extra to the children's bicycles." "OK, OK, Mother, please say no more." I was astonished of the remark as I stood near to the cycles. Miss Laura then from the kitchen window beckoned me to come. As I went, she told me, "Do not worry with the old lady; she is Madam's mother and she just loves to prattle, yet she means

CHAPTER TWELVE

no harm whatever." Meanwhile Mrs Stedy, with a stick in hand, went back and stood as a sentinel on watch over the bicycles. She was all grey-headed, with flowing long white hair, and slightly bent and well an octogenarian. Miss Laura then said to me, "The children are having their breakfast, and when they have left for school, we shall have ours." "That's alright," I said to her.

The first to take possession of her bicycle was a girl. She looked at all three with wondering eyes as she glanced at her grandmother. "Don't look at me; he" (as she pointed towards me through the kitchen window) "has done it for you. Say thanks to him." She mumbled something and left. Then came two youngsters. "Good morning, Granny," they both said. "Hi," said the bigger boy, "what went on here?" while the smaller looked at Granny. "Don't look at me. It was only yesterday I spoke to you about it, didn't I? It was all done by George, the new yard boy." "Oh thank you, George," said the elder. As they pushed their bicycles out with books strapped to their carriers, I left the kitchen to see them off. On reaching the gate, there was a boy much bigger than I standing there. "Do you want someone?" the elder brother asked. "Yes," said the boy. "Mr Archie Blanc sent me for the yard boy work yesterday, but I could not find the place." "Go back and tell him that we have already hired someone." And they both rode off. They were both QRC (Queen's Royal College) students. This I knew, for while at Sweet Briar Road, boys wearing the said uniform passed that way to school. Inwardly, I was jealous that I could not join them. (Be content with what you have, little be it or much.) As they rode off, the boy who stood at the gate called me, but I pretended not to hear him as I winded my way back.

Without describing it, the breakfast was very good and seemed not to have caste or segregation. After breakfast, Miss Laura said to me she needed pitch-oil for the stove. She handed me a twelve-cent coin and a container. "Go," said she, "to the corner and buy me a gallon." The retailer was a Chinese man who managed the shop. He asked me where was I from, because he had never seen me before. I told him. Then said he, "You must always come and buy here, we have everything." He then called an attendant and said to him, "Fill it right up."

Very quickly I was back. Miss Laura said, "You are back already." She took the tin and said, "Whey, papa, they fill it right up!" Mam was also in the kitchen. I asked her if I can clean the brass and silvers (for up to then she had given me no orders). "No, no," said she, "tomorrow." "Madam," said Miss Laura, "don't you think he should do them today? Tomorrow being Saturday, which is not a whole day for Mr Otchin, he may have something special planned for him to do." "I think you are right, Laura." The articles were then given to me. There were not as many or as ornamental in quality as those of the Odelmas. I did first the silvers. I had just finished my first brass bowl when Miss Laura said, "You better stop now because lunch will be ready shortly." I immediately stopped and washed my hands.

I was now given the directions, this time by Miss Laura. Up Charles Street, down Richmond Street, left into Marine Square unto Chacon Street corner. As I entered the store, a gentleman asked, "Who have you come to?" "Mr Otchin, sir," said I. "Go over there in the shoe department." As he spoke, he gave the direction at the same time. I then saw a wall clock reading 11:55 a.m. Mr Otchin was then fitting a pair of shoes on to a customer. So I stood about six feet away. He turned and saw me standing. "Oh, oh," said he, "you are here. What's your name again?" "George, sir." "Alright," he smiled, "Georgie Porgie*. I will not forget that. Go right up to that corner; there is a little table to rest your carriers and parcel. You can go walking and come back in about an hour."

I said to myself, a whole hour, that's plenty of time to waste. I, however, walked over to Frederick Street and decided to do some window shopping. The street was busy as I walked very slowly, checking on the prices of children's and gent's articles at the show windows. I could not buy, but I satisfied my inward desire. As I got to the corner of Queen and Frederick Street, I turned left and walked towards Chacon Street. As I got there, I remembered I heard Mr Worrell once telling his fifth standard class that Chacon was the very last Spanish governor to have set foot in Trinidad. And Sir Ralph Abercromby was the first British governor. I stood and wondered if they really knew this area. My

CHAPTER TWELVE

Holy Trinity Cathedral, Port of Spain

attention, however, was quickly drawn to the majestic Trinity Cathedral with its steeple clock. The time was then 12:45 p.m. when a porter from the store came and said to me, "Look, boy, Mr Otchin is looking for you." And so I went to him. "OK, Georgie Porgie," said he, "you may take up the dishes and leave."

I was back to the house very quickly. Mam checked the dishes. "Oh," said she, "he ate well today." She then asked me, "Did you find the place easily?" "Yes, Mam," said I. "Laura," said she, "give him his lunch, he is probably hungry." After my lunch, I finished cleaning the brass. I then went on my own to the flower beds and pulled weeds. Then came Mrs Stedy with stick in hand as a fairy's wand. "How long have you been in town?" she asked. "About six months, Mam," I replied. She then hummed a tune which I knew not, then quickly asked, "What work did you in Toco?" With a snap, I said, "Schoolwork, Mam." She scratched her silver-haired head and walked off.

At 4:00 p.m. Mam came and said to me, "George, you may go. I shall see you tomorrow." I went to Miss Laura and told her, "Mam said that

I can leave." "OK," said she, "do you know your way home?" "Yes," said I. Now before leaving home in the morning, Aunt Rache had given me threepence, and I had secreted away the half-crown that had been given to me by Miss Eva. So I had much more than transport money. Yet although it was a very long day, I walked home and was there at 5:15 p.m. When Aunt Rache and Mr. Williams came that evening, I told them everything that went on that day. They both always seem to enjoy my gossips as they listened attentively. Aunt Rache then said, "Child, take in everything. It may be an education for you one day."

The Saturday morning, which was my second day with the Otchins, I was there promptly at 6:00 a.m. Mr Otchin was leaning against the front gate reading his papers, which was then the *Port of Spain Gazette**. "Good morning, sir," said I. He lowered the papers and looked over his glasses in a searching manner. "Good morning," he answered. Then with a quick glance, he said, "Oh, George, it is you. Come in, my lad. I am so glad you have come now. Let me show you what is to be done next door." He then took me to the annex where he slept. It was quite a large place. Both Mrs Stedy (his mother-in-law) and himself shared this building, which was divided into two. The yard was all concreted, except the driveway, which led to the back gate. I have already mentioned about the large painted shed. In it he kept most of his belongings, and running parallel to this clean shed was the horrid-looking used-lumber shed in which area was the coconut palm and golden apple tree.

"Well, George," said he, "Madam said that she is very satisfied with you. I do hope you do not fail us. You had already been instructed as to what must be done at the front house. Well, here at the back, where I sleep and spend most of my leisure time, you will scrub the concrete once a week with white lime to get rid of the moss. Every Saturday, on my side of the building, you would clean and oil the floor, and wash the windows and jealousy flaps* on the doors. Every day, clean and polish my shoes for work. The shed will be cleaned when directed. Scrub the sink every day, rake fallen leaves of the golden apple tree when it is necessary. And any other help that can be given to the home in general." (They had no vehicle.) "You would be paid $2.50

CHAPTER TWELVE

per month. But should your work prove to be good, you would be paid three dollars instead. "Sir, what about that part of the house and yard where the old Mam lives?" "Oh yes, I am very glad you have asked that. I am not responsible for there; her sons control there. Should you at any time have to do anything there, you would be paid a few extra shillings." He looked at me. "Is there anything else?" I lifted my cap and scratched my head. "Sir, what about time off?" "You are smarter than I think," said he. "Oh yes, you would be given every Sunday off. Except if we are having a party. What else?" he smiled. "Sir, can anyone come to me during working hours?" "Yes, only if they are your relatives or someone with a call of emergency. Anything else?" said he with a kind look. "Only one last thing, sir." "What is it? Speak up." "Sir, I did not quite understand when you said the shed would be cleaned when directed or required." "Oh yes, the shed is large as you can see, and it is not fully used. Should I need to have something done in a particular portion, I shall direct you to have there cleaned. Or should I require the shifting or removal of anything, which seldom happens, your services will then be used. But, George, should you of yourself see dirt and grime building up in any portion, don't wait for me to tell you. Go ahead and clean as required." "Thank you, sir," said I with a bow.

As I turned away, he asked, "What are you going to do now?" "I am going for the broom to start sweeping, sir." "Oh no, you must first clean my shoes and wash the sink. After I leave for work, you would be instructed by Madam what must be first done in the annex, and then you shall take full charge of the yard or any other duty assigned to you."

As he left I wondered what must I do. Then came Mrs Otchin and she said, "OK, George, I shall show you in what manner you must handle your chores, but at the moment, come and help me wash these dishes. Someone had supper late last night, and the dishes are all piled in the kitchen sink." The kettle was on the stove, whistling. I reached for it. "What are you doing?" "I am going to pour some hot water upon them, Mam." (Now I had seen Miss Eva doing this at the Sweet Briar Road home.) "No, no, just wash them with soap and water," said she. When I was finished, I swept the yard and began washing the drains, for up to then she instructed me about nothing else. I then realized I had not seen Miss Laura for the morning. Aunt Rache had said to me, "Always try and avoid asking too many questions and much talking. Do it only when necessary." I then heard a squeak from the gate. As I looked, there was Miss Laura heavy-loaded with a basket and handbag, which to me was too much to be carried by a woman. I hurried to her aid. "Miss Laura, how have you been able to bring all of this?" "Well," said she, "I could not bring it all by myself. I paid a penny to a coolie* man who brought it here. Look up the street; nearing the corner, you would see him making his way back." I did, and there was a little man dressed in a loincloth and turban walking briskly up the street. I looked at her inquiringly. "That's what they do for a living," she said. "By the market, you would find many of them. They live and sleep on the pavement there, and by the end of the day, his takings could be thirty-six cents, which is a better wage than we can make."

I took the basket and bag to the kitchen. Then came Mrs Otchin, with a copybook and a lead pencil sticking in her hair as a schoolteacher. "Well, Laura, you are here, how was market today?" "Not bad, Madam," she replied, "with the exception of oranges and avocadoes." They then began counting as they checked each article. And so I went on with the cleaning of the drains.

In about half an hour Miss Laura called me as I went to her. She said, "Come, George, let me show you how to lay the table for breakfast." When this exercise was completed, she rang a small brass bell, and there was the shuffle of feet as five persons came and seated themselves at the table. As I headed for the door, Mrs Otchin called me, "Come, George, I want you to know the children in my presence. There is Mr Yourland, Mr Resford, Miss Marge, and Albert; later you shall see Marlene. Right now she is asleep in her crib." Yourland and Resford smiled and said, "Hello, George." Grace said not a word. As I went back to the kitchen, Miss Laura asked me if I had met the children. "Yes," said I, "except one who is said to be in her crib." "Oh yes, Marlene. She is the baby." Miss Laura went on to say, "You must not forget to address them as Mister and Miss. For even I do that, with the exception of Albert and

CHAPTER TWELVE

Marlene." (I said to myself, I see no harm whatever in that, for at the Odelmas in Sweet Briar Road you called the cat Miss Persia and the dog Mister Bob.)

As I was given my breakfast, Mrs Stedy came over. "Good morning, everybody," said she. The compliment was returned. "Oh, May," said Mrs Stedy, "Orman has forgotten his lights on in his room." "OK, Mother, I will turn them off." "George," said Mrs Otchin, "when you are finished eating, come with me next door. Let me show you what is to be done in Mr Otchin's section of the annex." Needless to say, it was all an easy task for me. By the time Mr Otchin came home at 2:00 p.m. that day, everything was done in and out of doors.

I came to like Mr Otchin very much, for he in many ways reminded me of Mr Worrell, my schoolmaster. They were very much of the same build and stature; they both loved dressing, and kept their hair and fingernails well groomed. These practical habits I have cultivated from these men throughout my life.

Chapter 13

Mrs Archer's mangoes, discord in the family and new sleeping quarters for George in a golden apple tree

I worked hard and honest. The children all grew to like me; even Miss Grace would occasionally poke jokes at me. At the end of that month, I was paid $3.00 instead of $2.50 for which was bargained. With no obligation I also helped Mrs Stedy to clean her place. However, for this, Aunt Rache had warned me never to take any money from the old lady, because she is Mrs Otchin's mother.

Well, for weeks everything worked fine both at home and on the job. At home we boys would go up on the hills late on evenings (because they waited for me when I came home and then the sun would be almost down). We then would cut our grass and help ourselves to nearby fruits. We got along well with many of the neighbours. To some, we were known as "Ambition Boys" (a nickname by which Mr Williams was called because of his shirt and tie outfit). I was a favourite to many of the older folks in the area.

Here is an occasion which amused me for a very long time. One Sunday at noontime, an old woman asked me to pick her some mangoes. The tree carried lots of ants. So the district lads never liked climbing it. For that cause, it kept well its fruits. Hurriedly I climbed, unwarned as to the insects. I picked about seventy-five fruits and was back on the ground. I helped even to gather them. As this job was completed, I looked forward for ten at the very least as my bounty. But instead I was greeted with these words, "Don't you wait for any, because I am expecting my relatives this evening and I have got to share it with them."

CHAPTER THIRTEEN

When I got home, there was a waiting crew of boys who were all looking forward to share in my treasure. But I met them empty-handed. I then told them what the old girl said to me, and they were all hurt. "OK," said Burt, "that's nothing, boy, George, let's clean her out next weekend." "Good idea," we all agreed. The next Sunday evening a watch was set, and as the old woman left for evening mass, we four boys took off to the mango tree. I climbed and picked quickly, while the others gathered. When we got home we feasted and hid the remainder in the barn.

The Monday evening when I came home, there was an angry Aunt Rache awaiting me. "George," said she, "you picked Mrs Archer's mangoes!" "Yes, Auntie, because she is too greedy." I then explained what had happened. Mr Williams, who was there, laughed aloud. She was not now any longer angry with me, but she scolded me by saying, 'Never covet anything that is thy neighbour's' (Ex. 20:17). Someone has said: 'It is better to be lowly born and reign with humble livers in content, than to be packed in glistering heap and wear a golden sorrow.'[1]

One evening as I got home, I sensed that there was something wrong with the entire family. Hardly was anyone speaking with grace to the other. I took the bucket and went over to the well to draw water. I had already made two trips; when drawing the third, Bob came over. I was tempted to ask him what was wrong but held my peace. He then said, "George, have you heard what happen?" "No," said I. "Well, boy, Pappy and Miss Rache had a big quarrel today. Boy, if you hear cuss* for so. She told him that he had another woman. He in turn told her if he had another woman, then she had another man, because she was yet with her children's father. Boy, it was then only left for blows to pass, but the argument met its climax as Bert and Merl began to jeer him and called him names, which got him more upset. Cecilst, Maze, Lidia and myself said nothing. He then told her to leave with her children and he

---

[1] Taken from John Fletcher and William Shakespeare's *Henry VIII*: "Verily, / I swear, 'tis better to be lowly born, / And range with humble livers in content, / Than to be perk'd up in a glistering grief, / And wear a golden sorrow."

wanted none of her relatives around." And so Bob and I went through the evening chores alone.

As we worked together, he said to me, "Boy, George, I am studying you. How would you make out for a shelter?" "Never mind about me, Bob. God never made a bird without growing a branch for it to rest upon." (Really those were words that were generally used by Tanty Pet.) That night before turning into bed, Aunt Rache called me. "Well, George," said she, "by now I suppose you have heard what took place today." I could not lie but truthfully answered, "Yes, Auntie." "Then what are you going to do?" "I do not know," I replied. "Well, I will no longer be here. I shall have to find some place to squeeze with the children, and there may not be enough room for you." Then sadly she looked at me and gently pushed me off sorrowfully.

As I lay in bed that night with thoughts of evacuation, I wondered where must I go. I then thought of Aunt Bertrice, but I said to myself that Aunt Rache may be going there. Hilda at the time was at Aunt Helen's with Georgiana, my younger sister. Quildon and Weston were my best bet. But ever since I made not the apology to the Mudders, Quildon never seemed to care about me, and I knew not where they lived. As these thoughts overwhelmed me, I came upon an idea of asking Mr Otchin to let me sleep in the shed. Again a negative feeling presented itself to me. I then thought of sleeping on the park benches. In those days one could easily have slept there without being molested in any way. For there were no vagrants of today's character. But then where will I keep my clothes and small belongings? Could I not ask Aunt Rache to keep them with her? I knew for sure Cecilst would not interfere with them, but I could not say so of Bert. "Then," said I, "Bob can hide them in the barn." Then came the wild idea of sleeping in the market. For here it was that many people who traded as vendors would sleep for a night or two while selling their produce. In those days there were no electric lamps at the market; vendors used flambeaus*. And there was this 90 per cent chance of my bouncing into someone from Toco, which would certainly hurt my pride.

However, I unknowingly fell asleep. The sleep was sound, and I awoke not before daylight. I could not then walk to work, so I decided to take

CHAPTER THIRTEEN

a bus to town. Then an idea came to me: why not ask Mr Williams if he can drop my trunk of clothes at my work sometime that day. And so I did. "Sure," said he, "what time do you want them?" "Any time that suits you. Just avoid the hours of 11:45 a.m. and 1:15 p.m., sir." "OK, young fellow," said he. When I got to work that morning, it was 7:45 a.m. Mr Otchin was just walking out the gate. "Well," said he, "I thought you were ill." "No, sir, I had a little worry." "Worry! Worry! What worry can you have? Furthermore, don't you know that worries kill," said he, laughing. My mouth then became filled with lies. "When I got home yesterday, sir, someone went into the canister you gave me and took almost all that I had. No one knew how it happened. So I want to ask you if, for a few days, you would allow me to leave it in the toilet where Miss Laura and I change our clothes." "Oh, that's alright with me, George, but you must first ask Madam." Well I knew for sure that Mrs Otchin would not say no to me.

After having done most of my chores that morning, I went to Mrs Otchin and told her of my problem. She right away remembered the canister (which I have up to this day) for she had herself solicited Mr Otchin in letting me get it. She was even more sorry when I said my polished lies about my lost articles. She then said, instead of the toilet, she would ask Mr Otchin to let me put it in the shed. But I told her it will be difficult for me to get anything I needed whenever the shed is locked up in Mr Otchin's absence and I needed something. "OK, suit yourself," said she. "But let us hear what Laura says first when she comes in."

Now the toilet was an old-fashioned one built in the 1920s. It had plenty of space and, if properly arranged, could be turned into a rough sleeping place. Miss Laura, who made mid-week market, did not turn up until 8:30 a.m. that day. While we both were having our breakfast, I truthfully told her what was taking place at home and my now alibi. It was after I told her everything it occurred to me that, in any case, she would have heard the truth from Cousin Vera of the family feud.

Miss Laura was very much concerned, then asked, "Where will you sleep?" "In the square," I promptly replied. "Are you mad! Let me ask your cousin Vera to put you up for a month." "No," said I, "have you forgotten that her husband don't want any of her relatives around? In all fairness, you very well cannot blame him because, as you know, Cousin Vera turned his sister out when she once lived there." "You are right, George." "Don't you worry yourself, Miss Laura," as I then remembered a slogan upon our school wall which read: "I will find a way or make it".

I then went next door to do a bit of cleaning for Mrs Stedy, but with my mind heavily set on a sleeping place. When, behold! I saw the huge fork (or arm) of the golden apple tree. It was the very spot that I would go and relax after eating some of its delicious fruits. "Why not here?" I said to myself. "Right now the weather is dry, and no one ever comes here except for the gathering of fruits, and in any case now there were none. Well, then, what can hinder my sleeping up on that tree. Should there be rain, I can take shelter under the portion of Mrs Stedy's house until it is over." Pronto I congratulated myself for being so smart. I then went back smiling to Miss Laura. "How come you look so happy?" said she. I was just about to tell her my idea when we both heard the cart of Mr Williams outside. He had brought the canister down. "George," he whispered, "I hope you won't hate me for this." "No, no," said I, "actually I will come to see you all on Sunday." "Oh no, not Sunday," he replied, "I shall be taking Bob and Lidia to Marabella on Saturday evening by train to visit my sister. Any other time, you would be most welcome."

I wondered, who will then take care of the animals, but held my peace to that. I took the canister to the toilet. Miss Laura said, "Look what you can do, George. Sit upon the covered toilet bowl and stretch your feet upon the trunk and lean your head against the wall. This will be done in an easy-chair fashion. You can then sleep here until better can be done. Other than this, you can take shelter at the Salvation Army at a penny a night. The only thing I do not like about there, some nasty men do sleep there."

That day when I took Mr Otchin's lunch down, I laid his little table, as I was now fully accustomed with the surroundings at the store. Mr Otchin then sent me to the Ice House Ltd. to purchase a bottle of

CHAPTER THIRTEEN

Ferdi's Rum. He usually bought this alcohol in bottles of three, which was very much cheaper, but should he run out, he would buy an extra bottle for $1.00. When I got back to him, he asked me if I had told Madam about the trunk. I told him yes. "And what did she say?" "She said that will be quite alright." He said to me, "Georgie Porgie, always remember that I told you worries kill." I then took my wares and the bottle of rum back to the house.

Dear Reader, may I say in this short time I was known by the neighbourhood as George Otchin. I was told by a vendor who carried on a charcoal and ground provision depot that I was the first good yard boy to have worked so many months with the Otchins, and I was the most decent and respectful yard boy in the area. But that was not all. She went on to say, when I grow up, she will have me marry her daughter who was yet at school. In her shop she also sold fruits and chunks of sugar cane. Many were the times when I had not anything to do, and I helped her clean and display her merchandise, and of course I had always the privilege to consume, which was an advantage used by me but was never abused. Charcoal in those days was the number one energy in Trinidad used for cooking and ironing because very few people could have afforded the kerosene stove.

Now back to my tense evening. That evening, as I had no home or place to go, I pretended to laze around, listening to a world championship fight between the legend Joe Louis, who was also called the "Brown Bomber", and Primo Carnera, also called the "Man Mountain". This fight was broadcasted through the triangular-shaped speaker of Radio Trinidad. This gadget was affixed to the wall, and from it the news was broadcast from the station. The Otchins were proud owners of such a speaker, and their house was very near to the street, so people gathered themselves to listen. When all attention was drawn to the fight, I did not hesitate. I slipped to the back and was upon my golden apple tree bed, making myself as comfortable as I could.

I was quite fatigued over the thoughts of the past twenty-four hours, so I soon fell asleep. I was awakened by the crowing of cocks from the Sackville Street area. I had not a watch so I knew not what the time was. So I went back to sleep. I was once again awakened by the heavy mule-drawn cart and the repeated sounds of "Gee up, whoa!" followed by the scooping of garbage on the street. I knew for sure that it was around 5:00 a.m. and daylight was not too far off. So cautiously I slid down and went into the toilet to finish off some drowsiness. I may now be asked, why did I not spend the whole night in the toilet as advised by Miss Laura. My reason is short and simple. During the day that toilet is used only by domestics, but at nights it could then be used by anyone.

My being on the premises before 6:00 a.m. could not be challenged because I am usually at work around then. I got busy with my chores, and I also put the kettle on to boil for Mrs Otchin. For she did herself prepare the baby's feed and Mr Otchin's breakfast. "Good morning, George." "Good morning, Mam." "So Joe Louis won the fight?" "Yes, Mam," I sheepishly replied. I then hurried off to next door so as not to be asked any further questions by her. As I got next door, I hoped that I would not now be confronted by anyone else on the matter. Lucky for me, Mr Otchin overslept that morning. I had then to wake him by knocking at his bedroom window with the broom. So he himself made hurry without a conversation on the matter.

I felt relaxed when seeing Miss Laura that morning. On her greeting I knew she was interested to know how my night was spent. I truthfully told her where I slept and why. She fully agreed, but, said she, my health could be endangered by the weather and fallen fruits when in season. I also heard from her the full result of the fight, which was won by Joe Louis in the first round. I was now well prepared to give an answer to anyone on the result of the fight if challenged. I had now to prepare myself for my tree bedroom second night. (1) I had to get two empty sacks, rip and join them together, making a coarse sheet to keep off stings and still the music of mosquitoes and the cold air; (2) I am to have my head covered with a carton for fear of broken limbs or fallen fruits; (3) I am to place the little Big Ben clock in the shed in a position that my hand can reach it through the bars to see the time; (4) I am not to get out of bed before hearing the rumbling of the garbage cart.

I had these all done as I mindfully set to face my second night.

Chapter 14

*George borrows a bicycle and visits his sister; he moves from
the tree to a lumber shed, and then to a room in Belmont*

That evening, after I made sure by telling a member of the family that I was leaving, I slipped into the back between both sheds where I had the articles hidden. About 7:00 p.m. I climbed into my tree bedroom. I took not the carton as planned, but a piece of cardboard instead. I felt now far more comfortable than my first night. My thoughts strayed just a little, but my sleep was good. The next morning I cleaned the children's bicycles. This was always given a jolly welcome by the youngsters, and it was done whenever I felt like so doing. I ran through all of my chores. And as Mrs Otchin left the kitchen, I set to help Miss Laura in preparing lunch. She now always discussed with me what was to be done the next day. I could have then prepared any of the practical dishes, as shown to me by both Mrs Otchin and Miss Laura. When Miss Laura came in that morning, I was dicing some carrots for a salad. She asked how was my night and said how Cousin Vera heard about the home disturbance and is now all worried about me. "She also wanted to know where were you sleeping. I pretended not to know," said Miss Laura, "Come on, George, you have not yet answered my question of how was your night." "Honkey-doh-ray (OK)*," I answered.

It so happened that very day Yourland was given a day off from school. "Boy, George," said he, "you can have my bicycle for the day. But be sure and be here with it by 4:00 p.m. this evening because we have a match against Saints today. And, boy, this evening will be blood and sand. We have to win come what may." "In what position will you be playing?" I asked. "Left wing as usual," he replied.

Now Yourland was an exhibition winner* who ran second in a field of two hundred and fifty in the island. He was sent to St. Mary's College, but for reasons at the time (colonial days), he was transferred to Queen's Royal College. And he had just loved playing against the Saints. Although the weather was partially dry, he had already scored five goals for the season for QRC. May I say also he was a very good cricketer, his lowest score being twenty-one run out. May I also say, by this time, I had grown so familiar with the children that I had no longer to address them as Master and Miss.

I was very glad for the loan of the bicycle that particular day, and so I thought of paying my big sister Hilda a visit when I returned from taking the lunch. Now the start which I rendered in the kitchen that morning was very helpful. For I had been able to take Mr Otchin's lunch and had his table ready by 11:45 a.m.

As I came out of the store, who would I see awaiting me on the pavement? No one but Bob. With a big smile he greeted me. "Hello, George." "Hi, Bob, what brought you here at this time of the day?" I asked. For my heart was gladdened, thinking that he may have been sent by Mr Williams for me to return home. "Well, boy, George," said he, "I break l'ecole biche* this morning to catch you here to find out how things are going with you." "Fine," I told him. Truthfully, I was disappointed with what I thought his mission was. But I was yet glad to know somebody cared. I then asked him to wait for me outside of the Ice House Grocery while I took back the food carriers. To this he agreed.

When I got to the house, Yourland was shadowing around with a football. "Way!" said he. "George, you are back early." I told him his father spared no time in eating because he had an appointment. "Does the deal still stand with the bicycle?" "Sure," said he, "just remember 4:00 p.m. deadline." "I won't forget that," I assured him.

I got back to Bob at 1:15 p.m. He seemed quite surprised to see me with the bicycle. "Well," said I to him, "where do we go from here?"

CHAPTER FOURTEEN

"Up to you, George, anywhere." I said to myself that I would no longer go to see my sister Hilda but would tow* him home instead. On our way he told me Pappy (Mr Williams, his father) was very sorry that I had to go, and that the breaking up of home was now the talk of the neighbourhood. I then stopped by a parlour and bought two sweet drinks, four sweetbread, and two carterman's sponge*, for neither of us had lunch. When we got to his home, it was then 2:15 p.m. Seeing the time, I told him that I shall stay no longer, for I had yet other things to do, promising him that I would come to see them sometime. I then sped off because I intended yet to see Hilda, my sister. (Yourland's bicycle was a Raleigh, also known as the "All Steel" bicycle, the best brand of bicycle in Trinidad at the time. There was then a slogan – "Ride a Raleigh or Walk".)

I did visit my sister Hilda that day. Boy oh boy, was she happy to see me because she heard of the family split. She knew not where was Aunt Rache and the children. How very grieved she looked, for at the time she was in no position to help them. "If only," said she, "I could have won a sweepstake, everybody would be made happy. But that is not to be. Tell me, what about you?" she asked sadly. "Oh, I am fine and quite happy with the Otchins," I told her. Now I saw how burdened she was, and I therefore did not want to add more woes upon her by telling her of my present situation. "Yes, George," said she, "it may be so now. But remember you are growing, and you cannot stay at the Otchins all your life. You are strongly built, but you are so short. Otherwise you could have taken seriously to some real reading, spelling and arithmetic, and, as soon as you get to the age, join the police force." I then looked at a small West Clock she had upon the safe, which read 3:45 p.m. I told her that I could no longer stay as I must deliver the bicycle to Yourland by 4:00 p.m., so I bade her goodbye and left.

When I got to the house, Yourland was just lacing his boots. "Oh boy, George, you are here. I thought maybe you have picked up a puncture." After that day, Yourland never failed to lend me his bicycle. They won the match by one goal that day, very late in the second half, and it was scored by him.

A BRANCH TO REST ON

All went well on my tree bedroom, but one night about 11:00 p.m. Mr Otchin, who was out, came in humming the tune of "Goodbye, Molly, I am leaving". He then turned on every light there was in and out of his apartment and those of the shed. The place became illuminated, and one could have discerned almost anything. A light beam was striking directly to the position on the tree where I was. And should he have come that way and looked up, I would certainly have been seen. I then remembered Tanty had taught me the 23rd Psalm, which she said that I must rehearse silently whenever I am in trouble with my teachers. Not with her, because she taught me and it would not work against her. I then began rehearsing it over and over in my mind. Mr Otchin then came to the side of the shed for his own purpose, but he did not look up. When he was finished, he turned all the lights off again, and I heard his lock click. I was then assured he was inside and nowhere in the now dark yard.

The next day I told Miss Laura of what took place in the night, and how scared I was that I hardly slept the remaining part of the night. She became so very worried about the matter, which caused a dish of cow-heel* that had been prepared for Mr Otchin's lunch that day to be burnt. He was sent Quaker Oats porridge instead, which he welcomed without a fuss.

When I got back from taking the lunch, Mrs Otchin had taken baby Marlene on a visit to a sister of hers who lived at Belmont. Miss Laura looked at the dish and breathed a sigh of relief when she saw it was all consumed. "George," she then said to me, "are you afraid of spooks?" I asked, "Do you mean jumbies*?" "Yes," said she. "Miss Laura," said I, "the only thing that I am afraid of is crapaud*." "Well, that you would not find down here," she said. "Now listen to me," said she as she placed her hand slightly upon her lips, "that old lumber shed you will go there and see…" "Stop! Miss Laura, one cannot see in there even with a light. The only thing that can be seen there is darkness." We both laughed. "That was a good joke," she said. "Now come with me," as she reached for a torchlight up on the kitchen shelf.

As we got to the shed, "Pass here," she said. We then squeezed

CHAPTER FOURTEEN

ourselves through a narrow opening. "I have already been in here," said she, turning on the torchlight. "See, I have broken down all cobwebs that led to that beam." She pointed ahead to a stout beam. "Now listen to me," she softly spoke, "that bag you have for your blanket on the tree, you would convert into a rude hammock. The boys have some ends of rope under the house, the same with which they sometimes play tug of war with their friends. Choose two long pieces, and sew them on to each end of the bag. You then can lash one end to that beam, and the other to that post over there, and you shall then have a perfect bed." "But suppose he should come here to get some old lumber?" "Don't be foolish; should he want a piece of lumber, he would send you for it, and if you are not around, he would much rather face the lumber yard than to come in here by himself. Well, what do you think?" said she. "Good idea," said I. "Well, come on, let's not waste time, for Madam may be back at any moment."

We hurried out, and I chose the two longest and strongest pieces of rope that were there. "Oh, oh," said she, "you will need a bag needle. That's alright, I shall get one." Now Mr Otchin, although he was not himself a tradesman, had all kinds of hand tools. He had a saying, "I would choose them even though I cannot use them. I may have something to do, someone may pass and use them. My work shall all be done, and I'll be proud to have them." This habit I have adopted from him throughout my life.

Mr Otchin gave me a key to the shed for me to clean it every Wednesday, which I gave back to him sometimes. And this was an occasion that it was not returned to him. So I got my needle and twine, and sewed strong my hammock. Miss Laura and I lashed it to the beam and post as she suggested. "Come on now, get in, let's see how it works." I did get in and found it to be quite comfortable except for one thing: it could not be rocked due to the many pieces of junk that blocked the sway of it. "Leave it that way for now," said she. She jokingly got into the hammock herself to see how secure it was. The ropes tightened on both ends with a slow squeak under her weight, which made me double-sure of its make-fast security.

My first night in that lumber shed was very startling. In the pitch darkness came the serenade of crickets. And gradually there were movements coming from the ground and from the far corner of the shed, which increased and spread even beneath my hammock. Suddenly there was a sound as that made by feathered wings, followed by a faint squeak and a seemingly fast flight. Although I could not see yet in the darkness, I sensed the movements. I was not afraid, but deeply concerned as to what was taking place. Then, lo and behold, there was a loud crash upon the roof. This scared the hell out of me. What on earth could that be? Then there was a rolling sound. I only then realized it to be fallen coconuts from the tree. I now kept wondering what would be my next encounter. When a battle in the darkness began, it was that of two rats. So I then summed up everything. The building was infested with rats, and the feathered movements were those of owls, while the squeak could be that of a mouse being caught by an owl. After this I fell asleep without a care of the surrounding sounds.

I experienced one disadvantage, however. I could not then be awakened by the sound of carts, as the building was enclosed and low. I, however, awoke through instinct, as I went to the toilet to finish my sleep. I now fully resided on the premises, known only by God and Miss Laura. I lived there for fully six months. Then one day Miss Laura said to me, "George, something has come to my mind. Suppose, just suppose, the owner of all these properties were to decide to open an entrance from Sackville Street through that lumber shed, what will be your position? Don't you begin to worry right now, but just think of its possibility." The entire block had then belonged to one landlord. As she walked away, I foresaw then it was a concerning matter.

That night as I laid on my back and prayed in the hammock, I again thought about what Miss Laura had said earlier that day. So the very next day, after taking the lunch to Mr Otchin, I decided to go in search of a room somewhere. And so, without telling Miss Laura of my plan, I set out on my venture. First, I clad myself very tidily as though I was going to my vendor friend to make an errand for her, a call I sometimes did. I took with me twelve shillings ($2.88) in my pocket. I said to myself

CHAPTER FOURTEEN

that if only I can get a room for five shillings ($1.20), I would be able to pay my own rent without a strain. So I walked across to Pembroke Street, where there was a house agent. As I entered the office, there were two persons sitting upon a rudely made bench, while a third was being attended to by the agent. "Good afternoon, everybody," said I. It would appear that only the two persons answered. Then, as the agent was through serving his customer, he looked up under a pair of spectacles; with searching eyes he looked towards me. "Good evening, sir," said I again, as I tipped my hat. "Good evening," he replied with a smile. "Come, lad," said he, "what can I do for you?" I pointed at the other two whom I met there, saying that they were there before me. One lady said it was OK, while the other quickly went to the desk. I perceived it was for the payment of rent. As he was finished attending to her, the other lady said to me, "It's alright, sonny, you can go."

Without wasting time, I told the agent of my desire. He seemed doubtful of my need and asked, "Are you sure?" "Yes sir," said I, "the room must not cost more than five shillings a month, and it must be able to hold a cot, a small table and a chair." "Is this room for your mother?" he asked. "No, sir, it is for myself." He then gave me an odd look. "Can you pay the rent?" "Yes, sir," and I quickly pulled from my hip pocket an old wallet that was given to me by Mr Otchin. I took out the note and coins. "Hold it," said he, "let me first see." He then reached for a ledger upon a shelf. As he checked through its pages, "Ah hah," said he, "I have something here, son. It is the only one such room. And it is at Belmont on the Belmont Valley Road. The rent is three shillings a month (seventy-two cents)." "Oh, that will be very good, sir," as I pulled some additional coins from the wallet. "Oh no," said he, "here is the key. Go first and see if you would like it." He then directed me to the place, and off I went.

The room had but one door, which was cut in a horizontal manner as in the barrack rooms of Toco. It had no window and was shouldered by two other rooms. It was also dark inside. I was now accustomed to darkness, so it mattered not. I locked the door and was off again to the agent's office.

A BRANCH TO REST ON

I took a tramcar and quickly was on the corner of Charlotte and Prince Streets. From there I quickly walked across to Pembroke Street to the agent's office. "I have seen the room, sir, and I am taking it." "Young man, you move like Flash Gordon," as he gave a jolly laugh. "OK, son, you always pay first before you live, do you understand that?" "Yes, sir," I replied. (But I really did not know what he meant.) He then wrote me my receipt and handed me again the key. And so I paid my first room rent.

I left the agent's office all excited. I said to myself, "When Miss Laura hears this news, she shall surely be surprised. And surely she shall tell me what the agent meant when he said you first pay and live after."

When I arrived, I received a most uncanny welcome. "Georgeeee! Where have you been? You have people looking all over the place for you. I have even been at the coal shop, and you were not there." Now having seen how angry she was, I could not then explain. But I lied by saying that I heard Mongoose Store in Charlotte Street had some good bargains, so I went over to look at them. "Yes," said she, "I heard of it also, but you just don't walk off like that, young man. You must let someone know whenever you are going out. Here it is Madam wanted you to go at her sister in Belmont, and no way could we find you. Don't you ever do that again." I said to myself, oh my gosh, I am now from Belmont. While I was being scolded, from the corner of my eye I saw a curtain shift in Mrs Otchin's room, and I knew that she was also listening. My heart leapt with fear as I wondered what would she now tell me. But she came and said to my surprise, "OK, OK, Laura, that's enough." Then, turning to me with a smile, "George," she said, "I want you to take this letter to my sister in Belmont. It is very important that she gets it today. It is from our brother who works at the oil fields. You do not have to wait for an answer. Here is four cents for the tramcar." "No, Mam, I will pass through the Savannah and get there quicker than any tramcar can take me." I was then trying to make in some way amends for my error.

So off I went at greyhound speed. As I got to the house, Mrs Jack was just latching her gate to leave. I handed her the letter and was again

CHAPTER FOURTEEN

bounding back. No sooner was I up the street, a thought came to me. Why not go now and look at your room once more? It is now yours with key and receipt. As I gave it deep thought, I had a conviction, "No, George, go back to Charles Street and let Mrs Otchin know that her letter was delivered." And so I continued on my journey.

On my arrival, it would seem as though Mrs Otchin and Miss Laura did not move from where I left them. To the contrary, Mrs Stedy had joined them in conversation. "What happened?" asked Mrs Otchin. "Have you forgotten something?" "No, Mam," said I, "when I got there, Mrs Jack was just closing her gate to go out so I handed the letter to her." "Oh, thank you, George," said she. Mrs Stedy then looked at me. "Go change that shirt," said she, "you are wet, and there is a very bad cold going around." As I turned away, Mrs Otchin said, "By the way, have you eaten?" "No, Mam," I replied. "Well, here is a penny. Buy yourself a sweet drink when you go to eat."

I did not only change my shirt, but I also had a very quick shower before going to purchase my beverage. When I returned, Miss Laura had already heated my meal. I handed the sweet drink to her that she should help herself to some of it. She reluctantly poured a little of it in a cup with a piece of ice.

When all seemed settled, I said, "Miss Laura, I had lied to you a moment ago." I then showed her the key and the receipt, and truly related her the story from A to Z. She was astonished and very pleased as to what I did.

"So when will you be moving in?" she asked. "Tomorrow," said I. "What will you be taking there?" "My canister and my two suits," said I. She laughed softly. "Tell me, George, how big is the room?" I then looked at the interior of the kitchen. "About one third the space of this kitchen or perhaps a little more," said I. "Well, besides your trunk and two suits, what else will you be putting in it?" "I shall like to put a cot, a table and a chair." "Good thinking," said she, "with a folding cot, a small table, a chair, a lamp, and a shelf on which to hang your suits, you cannot go wrong. You would also buy a hasp and staple with a lock and key for the door. Because you do not know whether the last tenant holds a duplicate key for the lock. After this is done, with time you would be able to buy other things. Don't you worry, I shall talk to your cousin tonight, and we shall sum up what must be done. For the meanwhile, keep on sleeping in the lumber shed." "Miss Laura," said I, "one thing I did not quite understand." "What is it?" she asked. "I was told by the mister that I must first pay before I live." To this she smiled. "Yes, George, whenever you are renting, you must pay your rent every month in advance before living. You may find an unusual case where a tenant may first live out the month and then pay. But that is not the right way because many implications can arise when done that way."

That night it was very windy, and it rained very hard; at least four times coconuts fell, and it kept on raining as though it would not cease. It had rained many times before but never had there been a shower like this one. Thank the good Lord, there was no leakage over my hammock. After running my thoughts over what I had done for the day, I fell asleep.

I was awakened by a noise from within the shed. In the dark I opened my eyes and listened. Then there was a splash as though something had fallen in water. I became very concerned. Then there was a flash of lightning which illuminated the dark shed, followed by a peal of thunder. I reached for the torchlight Miss Laura had given me to keep at nights in case I was forced to use it. To my amazement, the floor was covered with water. I then focused the light to the ceiling of the building. The rain was still falling lightly on the roof, and, behold, there were myriads of roaches and other insects making their way to safety. Also, on the dangling end of my hammock rope which was tied to the beam, a big rat was climbing, followed closely by another, in their bid to get to the ceiling in safety. I sat up, and as I focused the light once more, my attention was drawn to two very large centipedes making their way up an old door leaning against the wall. I was confident that I was safe so I went back to sleep once more.

When I woke up, the rain was not falling in a shower, but I could yet have heard the drizzle on the roof. I knew not what time it was, so I decided to make a bid for the toilet. I then also thought of peeping

CHAPTER FOURTEEN

into the "plush" shed to see the time from the clock which I always positioned.

As I stepped off the plank, PLUNK went I into a pool of water that almost reached my knees. I went back to my hammock and took off quickly my wet side of watchicong, fearing of getting a cold. I now lay wondering what must be done. As if spoken to by my inner thoughts, I am not to go out because I do not know what the conditions are like. And in any case, one may not be able to get to work early with weather as it is, so back to sleep I went.

When I awoke, it was daylight. After having slept for over six months in the dark shed, my eyes became accustomed to the darkness and so I could have recognized many objects. I could have seen anyone also on the outside while I could not be seen without a torchlight. I overheard Mr Otchin saying to a neighbour that the water came up with the tide from Sackville Street and flooded the area into Charles Street. And so I decided not to move, as I lay me down in my hammock.

Mr Otchin left for work very late that morning. I then heard Miss Laura speaking to Mrs Stedy. I also heard Mrs Otchin saying, "Poor George, he cannot come out today. Laventille Main Road must be in a mess." I only smiled when I heard this remark, but I could not reveal myself.

It was well after midday, for I heard the Sacred Heart Church bell ring out the midday hour, when I heard Miss Laura call, "George, George, George." "Yes, yes," I answered. "Come and take this quickly." As I went to her, the water had all receded. She handed me a brown paper bag and a sweet drink bottle with fairly hot cocoa. "Eat this," she said, "I shall tell you when to come out." I was very thankful for the bounty, but, strange as it may seem, I was not at all hungry.

In about an hour, she was back with the good news. "Come out now," she said. I quickly headed for the toilet where I stayed for about five minutes. I then came out and greeted everyone as though I had just come in. It would appear that hardly a child in that area went to school that day because the living room was overcrowded. Among them was a guy who always showed me kindness. He had no complex whatever.

On occasions he would bring me reading matter. And unlike the other children, he would join Miss Laura and I occasionally in the kitchen, making jokes or bringing us updates. His name was Donald Bain. He came and said to me, "George, I heard over the radio that the Dry River overflowed its banks, and the playground is beneath water." "Yes, yes," said I, "plenty of water," as I tried to evade the conversation, knowing not just what to say. Just then Mrs Otchin came and said to me, "You should not have come out today in a weather like this." Yourland, who was there, also said, "What happen, George, your bed wet or what?" as Miss Laura laughed almost to tears.

That evening when Mr Otchin came in, he tried to evade passing in the silt that was in his pathway leading to the aristocratic shed. So he decided to take the way of the Old Junk Shed. There was a long steel ship's ladder laying in the pathway with an excess of about four feet. On it, he struck his foot and was all in pain. He hobbled inside saying that the ladder must be removed. But there stands a big question. How? (1) Where was he to put it? (2) It required about eight strong men to move it. (3) It could not be pushed further in or out. So he decided that the excess which blocked the free passage must be cut off. In those days, acetylene and electric torch welding and cutting were not at all commercialized as they are today (the blacksmith yet held the rein in this country). Neither was our little friend, the common everyday hacksaw. So the blacksmith, with his chisel and hammer, was now needed for the job.

The very next day, however, when I took him his lunch, he sent me to a hardware store by the name of Fraser and Company Ltd., a leading hardware store was it at the time. He gave me six cents to buy a three-corner file, as they are called. He said it was for the operation of cutting the ladder. The arm of this ladder was about four inches wide and about an inch and a half in thickness. You had not to cut the treaders, only both the arms.

When I got to the house, I made a rude wooden hilt and anchored my file for cutting. The file being triangular, I had then to make about one quarter of an inch clearance in my cutting task. So I made no delay

CHAPTER FOURTEEN

but started right away. One evening, Yourland, who of the children would anytime make a joke with me, said, "Boy, George, I have read two stories which I really thought to be fictitious, but having seen how honestly you have taken on this job, you are making me feel that there can be some truth in them." "What were they?" I asked. "*Pip and the Convict*,[1] and *The Count of Monte Cristo*,"[2] he replied. "Have you yet those books?" I asked. "Yes," said he. "Then would you lend them to me?" "Yes, George. But what made you give Daddy the assurance anyway that you can file through this ladder?" "Well," said I, "where there is a beginning, there is an ending, except for a perfectly made circle. And your father always uses the remark, 'Tip, tip, tip does little water drop and waste huge stones away.' So, partner, those words give me strength and courage that this can be done." "Look, man, George, do you know something? You just like to work."

It took six weeks using eight files to cut through both arms of the ladder. Needless to say, many nights I would hear both relatives and some of Mr Otchin's good friends tell him outright that he is damn advantageous* whenever they were having drinks in the shed. Mrs Stedy once said openly to my hearing that he was mean and advantageous.

Now the filing of the ladder was done only when I had nothing to do, or if Mr Otchin was at home on a Saturday evening, he would then make me skip some chores for that evening and work on the ladder. When I was finished, it took one of his friends, he himself, and I to remove the piece that was cut off. That evening Mr Otchin gave me four shillings (ninety-six cents). I then added two more shillings to it and paid my agent two more months' rent, for I knew now the meaning of "Paying first before you live." Now although I did not yet occupy the room, occasionally I would go there, sweep, and break down the cobwebs, because I had not yet anything to put in it.

---

1   George is referring to *Great Expectations* by Charles Dickens, in which Pip, the main character, encounters Magwitch, an escaped convict.

2   *The Count of Monte Cristo* is an adventure novel written by French author Alexandre Dumas (père) in 1844.

Chapter 15

George resists temptation, opens his first bank account,
spends Christmas alone and sends money to Tanty

I must at this time say Mr Otchin was a very popular and well-known character to many of the leading citizens. And so his grog table seemed unlimited ("there were none to decline his nectar wine"¹). And so he taught me to make cocktails, rum punch, and puncha crème*, and also souse as an edible. Mr Otchin used an average of twelve bottles of rum each month, and at every twelve empty bottles returned to the Ice House, he collected a full bottle as an incentive, no cash being involved.

On one occasion when I took the empties to the Ice House, I was told to take them to the back store. A porter then said to me, "Way happen, pardner, yuh boss is a big shot or wha? Look so much drink he lef in dem bottles." He then began to drain all the drainings into one bottle; in completion, he had almost a quarter bottle of rum for himself. I was then handed my full bottle, and so I left for the house.

As I walked up Richmond Street, new thoughts were born to my mind. Mr Otchin was a heavy drinker only when he has friends, I being the one to make the cocktails, especially when there were special visitors. And it was also a known fact that I would be sent to buy a bottle of Ferdi's Rum each month from the Ice House. I then thought of becoming an economist. If I can cut short on my serving and use a little more ice, also with the help of the drains from twelve empties, I can at least

---

1   A reference to the poem "Solitude" (1883) by Ella Wheeler Wilcox.

CHAPTER FIFTEEN

make a full bottle every two months. Then that four shillings can be set aside to pay my rent, and by adding two to it, that would always help me to make an advance two-months payment. And so I congratulated myself on being scholarly. Neither will that be in any wise stealing. I then hastened my footsteps to tell Miss Laura of my plans.

Reader, I had not the time to finish telling her my intention when she said with vehemence, "No way!! Don't you ever set your thoughts on such an act. (1) It could be a set-up with the manager and Mr Otchin. (2) He had for years been buying an extra bottle of rum; an inventory could be taken of that, who knows? 3) What has given you the idea that's not stealing? Well, let me tell you, it is crookedness as what that big shot have done in the railway. Blank that idea right now. And don't you ever, ever put your thoughts on anything like that again. You hear what I say?" "Yes, Miss Laura," said I with my head bowed in shame.

"By the way," said she, "after that flood experience the other day, I told your cousin Vera exactly what is going on with your life. She then got in touch with your sister Hilda and Aunt Bertrice, who said that they would together furnish your room for the Christmas. So you would no longer have to worry yourself about that." I was yet so very much ashamed that I began searching my thoughts to arrive at something to amend my error. Then I remembered that I had hidden away in my place of abode (the lumber shed) all my savings in a Raleigh tobacco tin. So I went and fetched it to show her. She counted it, and with a smile of pride, she said to me, "George, you are rich: it is $12.76. But you must not leave it there, for you do not know what can happen and it would all be lost. Tomorrow you must take it all to the Penny Bank*. I shall go with you and pretend that you are my little brother. Otherwise they would want to know how you came by it and a whole set of crap. The Boss Man knows me, so it would be no problem."

At the bank Miss Laura made me make reference to Aunt Bertrice as my proxy and next of kin. "Why don't you stand as proxy, Miss?" asked the manager. "No, sir," she replied. "I am his sister only by the Father. His aunt is more truly blood-connected to him." "OK, if you say so," said he.

When we left the bank, I said to Miss Laura, "You told an untruth." "Did I, George?" she calmly said. "What was it?" "You told the mister that you are my father's daughter." "No, no, I told him that I am your sister only by the Father. Maybe he understood it just as you do, but z'affaire he.² Whenever I make mention of the Father, I mean God who is the Father of us all." Said I to her, "Miss Laura, they can fight you, but they cannot win you." And we both laughed.

My relatives did keep their word about the furnishing of my room for Christmas, even more than I desired. Sister Hilda brought a folding cot with mattress and pillow, a small table and two chairs. Aunt Bertrice brought a double-wick portable oil stove, three drinking glasses, a pair of cups and saucers, one large enamel cup, a small frying pan, a one-gallon enamel cooking pot, two tablespoons, one teaspoon, a camp penknife with many gadgets affixed, and a most beautiful oil lamp with its shade marked "Home Sweet Home". Cousin Vera brought a clothes shelf with its drapes, an oil cloth for a table, an enamel pail, a utensil*, two enamel plates, a small enamel bowl, and a house broom, and they each gave me a shilling to pay January's month rent. They also told me that all the articles were bought at the Mongoose Store on Charlotte Street, and of course they were all transported by the kind-hearted Mr Williams. I was absent then, for Mr Otchin had assigned me to some painting. Being December, the atmosphere was all cramped with work in preparation for Christmas.

One day after returning from taking Mr Otchin's lunch, Miss Laura said to me, "George, you now have a furnished room, so stop sleeping in that shed. The room is now your home. You can leave the hammock, and during the day when there is nothing to be done, you can go there and have a rest." Two evenings after, I decided to take my canister with my belongings to my room. Miss Laura said they would not allow it on the tramcar. "Why not ask your uncle-in-law to drop it for you?" "No," said I. "I shall take it upon my head." She laughed and told me to take out some of the contents and lighten it, which I did.

---

2   "... that's his business."

CHAPTER FIFTEEN

As I have aforesaid, my room was between two other rooms. There was an old Adventist woman at one end and a gent whom I had seen but twice at the other. The first night of my modern life as a bachelor, Sister Hilda, Aunt Bertrice, Cousin Vera and Miss Laura joined them also to see me settle in. Most surprisingly, Miss Laura brought a lovely used curtain for my door, two used sheets for my cot, a new blanket, an enamel flowered ewer and a face basin. Then I saw Aunt Bertrice whispering to Sister Hilda, who then looked to my direction. "George," said Sister Hilda, handing me a penny, "go up the road and buy some ice from the cart."

"There is a parlour just out here," said I. "No," said she, "you always get a larger piece from the handcart." I left, but on my return, the table was laid with glasses, a jug that I did not see before, cakes, soft drinks, sweets and three Revolver stouts. And also seated on one chair was the old Adventist lady, whom they addressed as "Mom". "Surprise!!" they all said. I was really surprised, for I knew not anything, not even from my good friend Miss Laura. We all six had our fill. When we were finished, I was told that they were there earlier, and the goodies were left at Mom's. And so the jug and glasses were Mom's.

When they left, I went to read one of the books Yourland had lent me, and as I became drowsy, I prayed and slumped into my bed. As I recollected the kindness of my relatives and good friends, I fell asleep. At 8:00 p.m. I was awakened by a shower of rain. (I had now my own West Clock, the only article I bought for myself.) That rain beat heavily upon the roof. The room was not sealed so I had the advantage to check for leaks, but there were none. Being very happy about that, I went back to sleep once more. When I awoke, it was 5:00 a.m. I heard the banging of the tramcar wheels and the crowing of neighbourhood cocks, along with loudly speaking pedestrians. I prayed, washed my mouth and was off to work.

When I took the lunch down that day, Mr Otchin sent me to the head porter at the back of the store. "Go," said he, "the porter shall give you a turkey to take home. It is best you take it home first, then come back for the dishes." I was very excited about the matter for I never had a chance of holding a turkey in all my life. I have seen them in yards of the upper classes and have always been fascinated by their struts and cries.

I went to the gent, who showed me a large carton marked "30 lbs. Mr B.O. Otchin". In it was the huge bird, which I took to the house upon my head, and then I returned for the dishes. Mr Otchin then said, "You may free him in the backyard when you get back home." As I got to the house and was about to free the turkey, Mrs Stedy said, "George, I would advise that you first clip one of its wings to prevent it from flying." And so I did. As I freed the bird, Mrs Otchin came and asked, "Did Mr Otchin tell you anything about feeding it?" "No, Mam." "Poor bird," said she, "he is probably hungry. There is nowhere that I can . . ." "Madam," said Miss Laura, "don't you worry yourself. I shall soak some stale bread for him until Mr Otchin comes this evening." Those were the days phones were still counted a luxury and not a necessity, so no communication could be made with Mr Otchin. When Mr Otchin came home, he told Mrs Otchin that he had won the turkey in a one-shilling raffle, and it was for the Christmas table.

Again may I say, as Christmas drew nearer each day, there were added duties to be performed. There was scrubbing, washing, dusting, polishing, painting, carpentry, masonry and plumbing to be done in excess. To get rid of the results of some of these assignments, an old oil drum was converted into a rude incinerator. Mr Otchin knew well how to use his hands at times, and so he made me use mine. I had not now to take him lunch every day because, on some days, he was himself invited out by friends. Whenever this happened, more work could then be done around the house. There were nights I did not go home but would stay and assist of my free will. Whenever this happened, I would unobserved slip into the junk shed and lounge into my hammock for the night.

Then came Christmas Eve. There was baking, roasting, boiling, frying, free eating and drinking, friends coming and leaving. I then recalled my Christmas spent with Aunt Rache and her family. Though good, it was not as elaborate. I stayed up to 8:00 p.m. that evening because it was said that children must be in their beds before midnight

CHAPTER FIFTEEN

were they to receive something from Santa Claus. And so I honestly thought that this guy was really around with the townfolks. There was an extra stocking that remained from the three pairs bought, so I asked Mrs Otchin for it. Smilingly, she handed it to me, saying, "So, George, you are also expecting Santa Claus?" "Yes, Mam," I replied. That evening I was on time to get a crowded tramcar, and I was home by 8:45 p.m. I hung my stocking over my bed, prayed and slept right through to 4:30 a.m. I prayed, and as I looked at the luminous clock in the darkness of the room, I wondered then what could there be in the stocking. I closed my eyes and reached for it. But to my disappointment, it was empty. I sat and stared with irresoluteness, wondering where had I gone wrong. I had not showered that evening, and I wondered if that could have been the reason.

Lackadaisically I walked down to work. I was there by 7:00 a.m. The children were all there looking and remarking on the gifts they received. There were bat and balls, football boots, clothing, a child's drum, a ukulele, and a large teddy bear along with other items. They looked, and they all shouted, "Merry Christmas, George." I responded not in words but smiled. Then Yourland, holding a pair of pants, came and said to me, "I told Daddy I did not want these, but he insisted that I have them. Here, take them, George," and he handed me them. "Thank you, Yourland," said I. But I pondered what did he really mean when he said, "I told Daddy I did not want these"? Then Mrs Otchin, who was next door, came over and said, "Merry Christmas, George." Again I smiled. "What did Father Christmas bring you?" Irresolutely I looked to the ground. "Nothing, Mam," said I. "Perhaps you may have been naughty, George, in some way," said she. "But never mind, he left some things here with me for you." As she spoke, my heart leapt with joy. "OK, go on with your work. But first go over to the shed. It is truly in a mess. It is now somewhat as when he first kept pigeons there." I went over, and truly it was as she exclaimed. Mr Otchin had friends that night, and there was even vomit lying in a corner. I very quickly cleaned and hosed down that portion of the shed.

Mrs Stedy then called me; as I went, she gave me a pair of socks and a handkerchief. Mrs Otchin then came over. "Oh, George," said she, "you are all finished. Mother said Santa Claus did not pass at George's home last night, but he gave me something for him." "Why tell the boy such nonsense," replied Mrs Stedy. Mrs Otchin then fetched a carton that was hidden in a far end of the shed and gave it to me. "Here, take this, it is all yours, George," said she. "Thank you, Mam." Immediately I opened it. In it there were two T-shirts, a pullover, a pair of long pants, a comb and brush set, a toothbrush and Colgate paste package, a jar of scented Vaseline, an Anglican hymn and prayer book, and a piggy bank. As I stared in surprise, "Mam," said I, "are these all for me?" "Yes, George," said she, "you deserve it." I really needed those articles, some of which I was running short of.

I got through all my chores before Miss Laura came in that morning. I then told her of what took place. Shaking her head from side to side, she gave a laughter of joy, sorrow and sympathy that only Miss Laura could. Then said she in earnest, "So tell me, George, you do really believe that there is a Father Christmas?" "Yes," said I. She walked away as she murmured something, but I caught only the word "Toco."

My chores so far seemed completed. It was then I decided to help Miss Laura. She told me that she must leave by 3:00 p.m. to meet her sister, who was coming from San Fernando by train at 3:30 p.m. With most of the special cooking and baking being done on Christmas Eve, there was not much problem. As we hastened to make things right, I heard Mr Otchin call, "George, George! George!!" I had answered to every call, but he did not hear me. As I got to him, he said, "I have seen that you have cleaned the place very nicely. Madam also told me today is your birthday?" "Yes, sir." "How old are you?" "Fifteen years, sir," I replied. "Well, have this for your Christmas and birthday." He then handed me an envelope marked "Happy Birthday" which contained $1.00, and another marked "Merry Christmas" which contained $3.00. "Thank you, sir," said I, as I walked off sheepishly. I quickened my footsteps to the kitchen to show Miss Laura my gifts. "Oh, George," said she, "this would be very nice for the Penny Bank day after tomorrow." "You do know that I have also a piggy bank, Miss Laura," reminding

CHAPTER FIFTEEN

her of it. "George, the Penny Bank is what I said, and you heard me: that's that." I said not another word.

At 1:30 p.m. Donald came with a large paper bag stuffed with used clothing. There were ten children in his family, nine boys and one girl, and there was also some very good clothing in the lot to fit me. I thanked him for them. Miss Laura and I had lengthened the dining table, and it was set with two extra seats should there be a call from an unexpected visitor or two. No one then seemed interested to eat, but by 2:20 p.m., they were all seated at the table. Donald and a young girl from next door also joined them for dinner. Miss Laura at this time waited not for the ending, for, said she, they shall eat at a very slow pace. So she told me whenever they were finished to clear the table and wash the dishes. By 2:50 p.m. Miss Laura was on her way out. When it was 4:30 p.m. everything was over at the table. I cleared and washed the dishes and reset the table for evening tea should anyone have that need. By 6:30 p.m. I set out for home with quite a burden.

When I got home, there was I met with a big surprise awaiting me. Aunt Bertrice and Sister Hilda were speaking to Mom (the Adventist old woman). I knew not her name, so I called her "Mom" as my relatives did. They all greeted me with one accord, "Happy Birthday" and "Merry Christmas." I unlocked the door and bade my visitors in. Aunt Bertrice immediately sprawled upon the cot, while Sister Hilda busied herself in opening two packages on the table. I joined her when opening a third that was resting upon the floor. From it she displayed two pairs of long pants, two shirts, a long tie, two pairs of socks, a lovely cap, two handkerchiefs, two pairs of black shoes, a pair of crepesoles*, some underclothing and a pyjama suit. While from the other two packages came sweet drinks, ginger beer, cakes, bread, ham, and candies. They both then had a good look at the articles I got from the Otchins and my friend Donald. When Aunt Bertrice saw the stocking that still hung to induce Santa, she hugged Sister Hilda and cried.

Along with Mom and ourselves, we had a wonderful time eating and drinking. The old lady was careful not to touch or taste the ham. She otherwise had her fill and left. At 7:00 p.m. Sister Hilda suggested that we now go to Aunt Bertrice's home for about half an hour. "Oh no," said Aunt Bertrice, "not tonight, there are too many drunkards on the road. You eat, drink and sleep your belly full of what is left here. Tomorrow after work, you can come at my home." When they left, I continued with the reading of my loaned book, after which I reached for the hymn book given to me by Mrs Otchin. What was unique about this book was a passage of scripture was quoted, introducing the hymn to be sung, and the name of the writer was also inscribed. I sang two hymns, prayed and got into bed.

The next morning I was up at 5:30 a.m. I prayed, washed my mouth and changed completely into a new attire. I wore underclothing from my relatives, plus the T-shirt, pullover and long pants from Mrs Otchin. I felt smart and so I decided to take a tram ride because I had also some extra pennies. I did not take a transfer ticket from the conductor, but I rode all the way to the corner of Charlotte and Prince Street. As I disembarked and walked along Prince Street west, there was the pleasant aroma of roasted coffee beans. I do not drink coffee, but the smell was good. As I entered Woodford Square, I intended to pass through the Red House into Sackville Street. I heard the nearby Trinity Church bell chiming the melody of the hymn "The Church Is One Foundation". The harmony enchanted me so much that it left an impact on my memory which I have never in my life forgotten.

People were hurrying their way towards the church. Mostly old folks were they, followed here and there by reluctant youngsters. I, however, decided to join in with the worship crew. When we got into the church, the service lasted over half an hour, and then I winded my way to work. When I got there it was 8:05 a.m. I was most astonished to see no one up. Not even Mrs Stedy. I entered the kitchen, for the door and windows were open. As I looked around, I saw that every imaginable piece of ware and drinking glass was used and lying either in the kitchen sink or on the counter. I quickly put the kettle on and hurried off to change my clothes. I then put on Miss Laura's apron and scrubbed the counter, after which I began to wash the mass of utensils, trying my best not to break anything. The kettle began whistling, so I quickly turned it

CHAPTER FIFTEEN

off. Just then there were movements in the backyard, and I heard the shuffle of feet which I quickly recognized to be those of Mrs Stedy.

"Good morning, George." "Good morning, Mrs Stedy." "My goodness, you are all dressed up like Laura. What are you doing?" "Washing the wares, Mam, they are all from yesterday." "Does anyone know that you are here?" I was silent for a moment, as I wondered why must she ask me that. Then I quickly replied, "I do not know, Mam." She looked at what was washed on the counter and peered into the sink and grunted something. The faucet was on, so I heard not what was said. As she walked off, she very quickly turned to me and asked, "Is the water boiled?" "Yes, Mam." "OK, let me go for my teapot." Mrs Stedy was back in about three minutes; she filled her teapot and was off again. I then refilled the kettle, and in about ten minutes, it was whistling again.

It was 10:00 a.m. when Mrs Otchin came out. "George!" said she, with a look of surprise and delight, "what are you doing here? Didn't Mr Otchin tell you yesterday that you are off today?" "No, Mam," I replied. "Neither did Laura say anything to you? Oh my goodness, you both are off today." She looked at the washed receptacles on the counter and peeped into the kitchen sink, seeing it was all cleared. She looked at me with a smile of gratitude. "Thank you, George," said she. She then asked if the water was boiled in the kettle. "Yes, Mam," I assured her. "OK, George," said she, "I will myself make you a good breakfast. You do not fancy tea, neither do you drink coffee, only cocoa. Well, I shall now prepare you some along with a few ham and egg sandwiches," said she, laughing. "Meanwhile, go over to the shed. Mr Otchin may be awake."

I went over to the shed, and there was an unusual number of dirty drinking glasses lying around; they were even upon the ledges. I gathered and washed them all. When I was finished, I mopped the floor. No sooner had I finished was I called by Mrs Otchin for my breakfast. Then came Mr Otchin looking somewhat tired. "Good morning, George," said he. "Good morning, sir," I replied with a salute. Mrs Otchin, who was still in the kitchen, said, "Orman, how come you did not tell George today was his day off?" He then struck his forehead with the palm of his hand. "Me oh my," said he. "I had quite forgotten about that. However," said he, "since the morning is far spent, let him hold on until noon." I was quite happy about his decision, for I was not at all expecting any time off before Sunday. I then swept the yard, for there were peanut shells and palet* wrappers and sticks. It would seem as though the children had a party with their friends.

As I was about to leave, Yourland came and thanked me for washing up, for, said he, that would have been the task of Resford, Grace and himself. "By the way, George," said he, "I have no school or games, not before next month, so you can have my bicycle to take home and ride all over the town, and you don't have to come to work tomorrow," said he, laughing. "Yourland," said his mother, "you can say some silly things at some times, let Daddy hear you." Just then Mr Otchin called, "George!" "Yes, sir," I answered. As I went to him, he said, "Georgie Porgie, you have this place looking 'ship's shape'. When was this done?" I smiled but gave not an answer. Mr Otchin then gave me two shillings. "Thank you, sir," said I, breaking my silence. "OK," said he, "I shall see you tomorrow." As I made my way to the gate, rolling the bicycle, Mrs Otchin also handed me a shilling, and I was off.

Now here was I suddenly born of some importance – dressed in long pants with T-shirt and pullover, new cap, new socks and shoes, with handkerchief showing a bit in my hip pocket, money in my fobs and sporting a Raleigh gent's bicycle. As I rode up the street, someone shouted, "You are looking as the mayor's son!" I continued riding and stopped at my old vendor friend. She was very happy to see me, and I was invited in. I was introduced to her family. I met her daughter, who was about a year older than I was. Many edibles were offered to me, but I refused them all, with the exception of some hazelnuts and dried dates. They all thought that I was bashful. So my old vendor friend packed a paper bag with an assortment of goodies and gave it to me as I left.

When I got to the corner up the street where Donald lived, I looked, but I did not see him. I did not call through reasons of my own. So I stood on the pavement and gently leaned on the bicycle. Then I heard one of his brothers call, "Donald, Donald, look your friend is outside." He quickly came. "Gosh, George," said he, "you are looking smart.

CHAPTER FIFTEEN

Where are you heading?" I then told him in a nutshell of what had taken place. Then two of his brothers joined. We four chatted for a short while, and so I left for Aunt Bertrice's home. I got to her at exactly 1:30 p.m. She was expecting me, but not that early. Ren came and said to me, "George, you are surely looking sharp. Anim should see you now. Tell me, how is the Christmas treating you?" "Very well," I replied. "Boy, Mother told us all about you. Just choose your company and stand clear out of trouble, and you would make it in life." Then in came Lou. "Wow! Wow!" said he. "Look at the big shot. Whose bicycle is that locked on the pavement and leaning against our house? Can I borrow it?" He spoke and asked all in one breath without a pause. I foolishly handed him the key. As he turned for outside again without even asking for his mother, Ren said, "Listen, young man, where are you heading? Be careful with that bicycle. To the contrary, you have no right to borrow it. But seeing that it has been lent to you, see and be back with it within an hour – and I do mean that."

Aunt Bertrice, who was in the kitchen and most probably listening to us, came and said, "Why did you lend him?" But before she could have stopped him, Lou was up the street like Flash Gordon. Regretfully I said to myself, I hope he does not get a puncture. Sister Hilda joined us at 2:30 p.m., accompanied by her fiancé, who was tall and strongly built. "Come, George," said she, "and meet Vic." We shook hands. Boy oh boy, he certainly had a strong grip. "So you came in before us," said Sister Hilda, "and how was your day?" Before I could have made a reply to her question, the door was pushed open and in came Anim, Weston, Cousin Vera and Cecilst. I became a target in the eyes of everyone, they being so very happy to see me. Aunt Bertrice was most delighted to hear that I attended the morning mass, as she called it.

Aunt Bertrice seemed to have expected us all, so she prepared a sumptuous dish of talkari*. We all had our fill with the exception of Lou, who had not returned up to then. Ren and Vic got themselves in a game of cards, as the others spoke on various matters. Then there was a cry from a palet vendor. "P-A-L-E-T, P-A-L-E-T, one for one." I went to the door, and as I got there Ren asked, "Do you want a palet, George?"

"No," said I, as I stopped the cart. I then asked Aunt for a waiter*. I bought fifty of the frozen candies. "Why so many?" asked everyone with the exception of Vic and Cecilst. "Do you want some more?" I then shadowed a false move as though I was again going to stop the cart. "No! No!!" the room sounded, as Vic said loudly, "Class is class."

Aunt Bertrice played the gramophone with records of Christmas carols and some sacred songs. Then it was that my thoughts strayed to Lou and Yourland's bicycle. As I kept thinking seriously on the matter, in came Lou and handed me the key. It was exactly 6:00 p.m. Ren glared at him, but he seemed not the least concerned about Ren and what he thought. I went out to feel the tyres, but was met with a surprise. The bicycle was cleaned, oiled and polished. When I went to the door, he followed me and said, "George, boy, it really riding good. I made a real hit with my friends. I beat them twice around the Savannah." At that time as he spoke, I knew not that the bicycle was cleaned. So personally I felt hurt at his remark. But on seeing the bicycle's condition, I asked, "Where did you get this job done!" "George," said he, "I also paid a visit to Bob and Lidia, and I had it done there." "How is Mr Williams?" I asked. "He is fine. He asked for you, and said you must come and look them up whenever you have some time."

After a lovely evening spent with my relatives that day, I left for home. Being very curious to test the performance of the bicycle, I did myself ride around the Savannah and was satisfied. But as the evening sun was setting, I hurried for my home because I had not a light on the bicycle. When I got home, I leaned it against my room and locked it. The room was now already dark, so I lit my lamp, and as I sat at my table, I reflected over the past day and what lies ahead for the future of my young life.

As I slowly rode to work the next day, one could hear the words of passers-by, compliments of the seasons as folks greeted smilingly. When I got to work, I went right into the kitchen, but there were just a few items to be washed, which I did after I had put the kettle on.

Miss Laura came in at 8:00 a.m. "George," she said to me, "your cousin Vera told me that you worked yesterday. I am so sorry it slipped

CHAPTER FIFTEEN

me to tell you that you were not to. My attention had only been drawn with the meeting of my sister." "I am very glad that you had forgotten, Miss Laura, because the result of that turned out to be a real blessing in disguise." "What do you mean?" asked she with astonishment. I then explained the full matter to her. She was happy not about the washing up but of the results brought through it.

"Well," said she, "since Mr Otchin is not likely to have lunch sent to him today as I now await final word from Madam, we are going to the bank this morning with that $4.00." "No," said I. She then gave me a stern look and said, "What do you mean 'no'?" "Well, Miss Laura, it is like this. Since I came to town, it is now past two years, and I had never been able to send a cent to Tanty or any other thing. It is the first easy cash that I have ever made, and I would like to send it all to her." She then looked surprisingly at me, and with fallen countenance, she said, "George, that is an excellent thought, but by what means will you be sending it to her?" "I will put it into an envelope and post it." "Ah, ah, you would do no such thing because it can all be stolen. Plus, on the other hand, do not send all $4.00. Send her $3.00, and keep $1.00, and that you shall put in the bank for good luck. For putting one dollar in the bank, you need not an adult. Hear what has come through my mind. Take the three dollars to your sister and ask her to go with you to the market. For there I am sure you shall see a vendor who you know. You will then give it to the individual to give Tanty, saying to let Tanty know that you would be up shortly in the New Year." " But I am not going –" "Sh, sh," said she, placing a finger on her lips, "that will be a postal guarantee." I then thought she had made well her say, and said, "Let me ask Mam for the time off." "No, no, you go ahead. I would speak to her, and should push comes to shove that lunch must be taken, I shall take it myself."

I went and deposited the dollar in the Penny Bank, and after, I visited Sister Hilda. She was just about to leave for the grocery. When she heard of my plans she was overjoyed. She told me to hold the money until the next day because the Toco vendors usually come into town on a Thursday. She shall herself go to see if she can find an honest person.

Lunch, however, had to be taken to Mr Otchin on Thursday. When I got back to the house, I told Miss Laura that I am again taking the money to my sister. "OK," said she, "but be careful."

When I got to Sister Hilda, she said to me, "You would be surprised to know who I have seen to take the money up for your Tanty. Just make a guess." I scratched my head: "Mr Worrell, the teacher." "Oh, oh, but no, he no longer teaches there." "Then let me seeee, oh yes, Miss Colute." "Well tried," said Sister Hilda, "but, no, it was Miss Mizpah, the very woman by whom you sent the money from the Warden's Office to your Tanty. Boy, strange, as it would seem we were friends as children in school, but since I moved into Port of Spain, we have never heard or seen each other until this morning. George, George, what is wrong? You don't seem at all interested as to what I am saying." "Yes, Hil, I am, but I am also thinking how would she accept me because that day I lied to her about going to Galera to buy coconuts."

"Oh no, she would not. Because in our conversation this morning, Mizpah told me Miss Pet and her are very good friends, but she had taken mean advantage upon you after the separation of Uncle Bishop and herself. She could not say or do then anything about the matter because Miss Pet can be a very arrogant person if roused and not given her way. She also said that there are villagers to date who talk of children and very often would make reference about you, that a child as you had just been torn away from school." "No, no, Sister Hilda, it was not Tanty's fault, she just could not help it. First, she was ignorant book-wise; next, there were some mean villagers who spurred her to do same."

"Wait, wait, and hear this, George, for this will be very much of a surprise to you. Mizpah said the day you ran away, she was quite aware of the fact. Because the money you kept to buy coconut would have been far too much coconuts for you to tote. And Miss Pet could not use so many coconuts if even she was a baker. Next, the bag you held with your belongings could not hold twelve cents coconuts. Next, you spoke not openly to her, but in a secretive manner from the hearing of others. Those were then sufficient evidence to arouse any suspicion. So when she got to the village, she did not go right away to your Tanty's home,

CHAPTER FIFTEEN

but purposely waited until 4:00 p.m. when she was sure that the bus had left the station and was on its way to town. She then went with the money to your Tanty, who then swore to give you the rawest hiding on your return. So now what do you think, George?"

I shook my head with approval as I now honoured Miss Mizpah's estimation about me.

"Look, George, here she comes." I looked across the busy crowd, and there was Miss Mizpah brightly dressed, as she sported a head-tie of many colours. She came to us all smiling. She hugged and kissed me. "George," said she, "you have grown very big and even stronger." Turning to Sister Hilda, she said, "Girl, this lad was the strongest in his age group in the village. He also surpassed many of his seniors." And smilingly she said, "Make no stupidness* with him because you shall suffer the fate."

Keeping her hand upon my shoulder, she said that sales were very good, for everything she bought was sold, and that she was going back home the very evening with the truck and not the bus that was leaving the next day. She then said to me, "Your sister said that you want to send some money for Miss Pet?" "Yes," said I, dipping my fingers into my fobs, taking out the $3.00 which I handed to Sister Hilda. "No," said she, "give it yourself to Miss Mizpah." Which I did, asking her to kindly give it to Tanty, please. I had not then to use the postal guarantee of Miss Laura. Asking an excuse, I walked across the street to a parlour and bought three sweet drinks, of which we three sat upon a large crate and drank the cold beverage. I then got up and bade Miss Mizpah goodbye, and I left them both chatting.

Chapter 16

*George ruminates on his life and has a
day of mishaps after an unfortunate step*

Time moved on, and I became concerned of what shall be my lot in life. I had a very poor fundamental education, and to make matters worse, I had not a trade, and neither could I then afford to go and learn one. There were old men in the area who worked as yard boys all their lives, changing hands from one family to the other, and also living in yard rooms of their employer until they died or perhaps ended their final days in the Poor House (House of Refuge).

I certainly meant not to be in that grouping. There were also the badjohns* from parts of Belmont and John John. I was strong and could easily have fitted into that group after learning their art. But that would have been shame on Sister Hilda, Ren and many others who always say to me, "George, keep away from bad company." Next must I go back to Toco and work in the plantation fields or – if I am lucky – with the P.W.D. (Public Works Department). For the former, I was fully qualified strength-wise. These were thoughts that haunted me, especially when I laid me down upon my cot at nights.

I then acquired the habit of reading and singing nightly from my hymn and prayer books. For the singing of the hymns I had not a problem, because Tanty had known the melody and the beginning of almost all the popular sung hymns, which I learned from her and comforted me. May I also mention I got myself confirmed at the Trinity Cathedral under an English clergyman whose name was Cooper.

CHAPTER SIXTEEN

I became restless thinking of my future. One morning as I left home, I hurried to catch a tramcar. As I stepped from the pavement, I tread upon a huge lump of excrement. I yelled, "Oh gosh!" A couple that were standing and also awaiting the tram heard me. The man laughed and said, "Boy, that is 'shit'; good luck ah playing whe-whe* today." The woman said, "Nonsense. Look," said she, "there is a standpipe in the corner, go wash your shoe." Boy oh boy, the matter did smell. I lost my tram and decided to walk. I headed for the market because Mrs Otchin had given me twelve cents to buy her some oranges. When I got there, I bargained with a vendor for some lovely ones, only then to discover that I had changed my pants and had not the money for payment.

I hurried off to Aunt Bertrice, who was herself just leaving for work. She gave me the sixpence, but on my return, the vendor had already left. I did get another bargain but not as good as that of the first vendor. I then set off for work. I got there at 7:15 a.m. Mr Otchin was at the gate and seemed not to be in a happy mood, for I said good morning and he grunted. I went into the kitchen where I rested the paper bag of eighteen fruits, which cost six cents. I placed the change next to it. As I went to change my clothes in the toilet, I heard Mrs Otchin saying, "Oh goodie, goodie, George is here, what lovely oranges." It was my first joy for that morning.

After finishing my morning chores, Miss Laura said, "Go buy me some coals*." I hurried to my vendor friend, just to meet her in an argument with a carter who was a wholesaler of coals. Their argument involved the payment for two bags of charcoals that cost two shillings. She claimed that she paid him, while he was claiming that she did not. And so they were butting away at each other like two goats on a narrow ledge. I felt hurt for my friend because of a mean remark he cast at her, and was just about to say something when I espied a partially worn two-shilling almost to the edge of the counter. "Look mister! There is your money," said I with vehemence as I pointed to the coin. The carter then said how sorry he was for he did not realize that he was paid. (But the damage had already been done.) He also commended me on my honesty, saying I could easily have taken up the money and left them with their fight. To this my friend said, "Whom are you talking about? Not this youngster."

Lunchtime came, and I hurried up Charles Street. On nearing Richmond Street corner, I heard someone clapping and calling. As I looked back, there was Miss Laura. I walked back. "Here," said she, "you have forgotten the cutleries." When I got to the store, Mr Otchin sent me to purchase a bottle of Ferdi's Rum; I bought Macaw instead. As I walked off, the cashier called me back for my change. When I presented the change to Mr Otchin, he looked queerly at me and then opened the package, only to discover I had bought the wrong brand of rum.

When I got back to the house that day, I went over to the backyard. I murmured to myself, saying, "George, you have been into far too many mishaps for a day." Mrs Stedy, who was at her window, apparently heard me. She at once said, "Stop speaking to yourself like that." I returned a sheepish look. "Go up to the square," said she, "sit on a bench and relax yourself." This I thought a very good idea. So off I went. When I got there, a game of football was being played among some youngsters. A lad kicked the ball over the rails, and it landed into the street. Two other boys came and impolitely said to me, "Go get the ball." I said, "I did not throw it there, and I am not going for it." Another who joined in poked me in my stomach, I did not fight back, and the others began laughing and called me names and said some very rude things to me. I knew I would have whipped them one by one, but I could not flog them all at one time. A girl of Oriental descent, who apparently was playing with them, said aloud that they had been advantageous. To this they jeered aloud. With the spring of a wild cat, she leapt, apparently being well trained in martial arts. "Leave them to me," she screamed. And boy, did they get a whipping as the non-involved parties stood and laughed.

I then left the square and hurried back towards the house. On my way a young man, who apparently was around at the time, called me names and said to me I should bless my stars that girl was around or those boys would have crippled me. I said, "Maybe they could have, but you cannot." He drew close to me with swearing words and said that

CHAPTER SIXTEEN

with his hands tied to his back, he could cut my – . I looked at him and walked off. He then pulled me back and said, "Stand up, I am talking to you." I did not hesitate to cross a right to his jaw. He fell, and I backed myself to a fenced wall as I recalled Uncle Bishop's instructions. He did get up and sat there on his butt, holding a bleeding jaw. A few people gathered, all with their own opinions. The odds were all against me. Then an old woman came from across the street and said all that she heard and saw. The news very quickly reached the house, and Mrs Otchin and Miss Laura were on the scene. Some bystanders were saying to call the police, while, from the old woman's statement, there were those who strongly objected. Also the presence of Mrs Otchin helped, for no way in those days will a mistress find herself in the midst of a quarrel like this for any servant, especially that of a yard boy.

I spoke for the first time and truthfully said what took place, and I was well supported by the old woman. The guy, who was a very popular character around the neighbourhood, denied not my statement. And so I went back to the house with Mrs Otchin and Miss Laura, all frightened. Mrs Stedy came and said, "Had I not encouraged him to go over to the square, this would not have happened." "No, Mother, don't you think that way, the man is wrong."

That evening, the children all rode in together from school. Little Albert broke the news to them that George was in a fight. Immediately they were in the kitchen, being all anxious to know what took place. I then told them fully of what took place in the square, followed with the incident of the guy and myself. Yourland said, "Boy, George, I am sorry that you have found yourself into such a mess." Resford said, "It is good for that fellow; he is always bullying innocent people around the place." Grace then began laughing. "Don't you all see," said she. "Today is Black Friday and it all fell on George. He is lucky it did not turn itself the other way around," said she, choking herself with laughter.

That evening when I got home, I was all dejected, and as the night shadows fell, I prayed and got into my bed. As I lay me down, I recalled all that took place in my life that day. It began from the moment I stepped into the filth that morning and the man shouted, "Good luck!"

and me having to walk home that evening as I had no money. Amidst those thoughts, I fell asleep.

Well, the story did not end. The Saturday morning, as Mr Otchin left for work, there were two men at the gate. One was the bully with whom I fought and another man. Mrs Stedy, who was there, advised Miss Laura, who had come quite early from the market, to follow me. As we left, Yourland took up the rear. When we got to the gate, there truly was the very guy with whom I had the incident and an older man in his late forties. The elder man said that the young man was his nephew, and his jaw had been dislocated by me yesterday. He was taken to a dentist who said that the dental work that must be done would be approximately in the vicinity of $25.00. And he wanted that sum, or the matter will reach the police and then be taken before the courts. In those days, there was a limb of the law known as Sergeant Major "K". And he was fully respected by the island's lawbreakers. So again, as the police were mentioned, I became frightened. Yourland, who was very hot-tempered, said to the young man, "You are wrong and you know it. Yesterday you did not deny. How come today you have brought your uncle with a different story? Look, man, move from in front of this gate with your nonsense." Miss Laura then said, "Hold it, let George repeat what took place to the mister." And so I did. The gent then looked at the young man and asked was it so it happened. The young man then replied that he was only joking.

Just then Miss Laura excitingly said, "George! Look your family coming." As I looked up the street, there was Sister Hilda and Cousin Vera. A balm of relief came over me, as I wondered how did they know of this. Miss Laura then said that she told it to Cousin Vera when she got home last night. When they both came to the gate, Mrs Otchin said that too many people were then standing at the front gate. She then let me open the back gate and let them in.

Both my relatives now wanted to know what was taking place. I again repeated the whole story, letting them know what was the mission of the two men. Cousin Vera, who was a sturdy 240-pounder, said that the guy was lucky that it was I and not her brother, because I was noble

CHAPTER SIXTEEN

to leave him alone when he fell. But had it been her brother, instead of only a broken jawbone, he would have had some broken ribs also. So let him now count his stars and bless them.

The elder man looked at her and quickly took his eyes off, as he focused them upon my sister, who said to him, "Man, you can take the matter to court if you wish. But I shall first discuss this matter with my uncle Sergeant Major "K" at headquarters. But at the same time, due to a humanitarian point of view, I shall give you part of the money to pay his dentist, although, as you have seen, it was brought up all upon himself. But, nevertheless, I do pity his stupidity."

She then reached into her bosom and retrieved a kerchief wrapped with currency notes, chiefly one-dollar bills they were. She then counted $20.00 and handed it to the fellow's uncle. Mrs Stedy, who had been standing a little way off, on hearing all that had been transpired, said, "Hold it, do not give that money over like that without a receipt and a witness." Resford, who always seemed to like things of this nature, immediately fetched a copybook page and a receipt was made. Mrs Stedy brought a three-penny stamp and had it affixed to it. The gent then asked if anyone there can be a witness. "No," said Mrs Stedy, "you go and get someone of your own to be a witness." The gent then pushed open the gate to see if there was anyone he knew out there. When, lo and behold, a fellow who supported that chap yesterday was just going up the street; he was called to witness same. And so the matter was settled.

I went over to Sister Hilda's home at 4:30 p.m. that evening, only to meet Cousin Vera combing her hair. (1) The reason of my going was to find how was I to pay the money back. (2) How came Sergeant Major "K" to be her uncle? (3) Who was this brother of hers in Port of Spain? However, I was more interested to know about the relationship which joined Sergeant Major "K" and herself. It was something to be proud of, for those were days the highest rank one could attain in the police force was that of sergeant major if you were not Nordic*.

"Well," said Sister Hilda, with head bent as it was being combed. "You owe me not a farthing. I do admire the noble way in which you defended yourself. Had we been living in the United States, the champion Joe

Louis ('The Brown Bomber') could have given you some training." (To this Cousin Vera gave a hearty laughter.) "Next," she said, "we had never a relative in the Force, not even a rural constable. But I spoke in that way to prevent the fellow from thinking court-wise. Let Vera answer you concerning her brother, she is right here."

"Once more, cousin," Vera laughed, and said she, "I have no brother in town, but I saw the old guy looking at me and I sensed that he respected my size." Speaking that way of a brother would have brought some respect, even with fear. I was truly amazed of their wits. That night I again prayed and turned into bed thinking very seriously of my future and what it holds for me. My rental payments were no problem because I was two months' ahead with my payments. I had plenty of clothes. And my stomach could be filled whenever I desired. But was that all to life? How long was I to carry on as a yard boy? Suddenly there was a hard downpour of rain, and I fell asleep.

Chapter 17

A new home with his two brothers; a neighbourly deed leads to the wrath of Mr Otchin; the mystery of the broken canister

Very early I was up the Sunday morning. I never stayed home then on a Sunday when I came to live in my own home, for I had nowhere to go, and should I work, I had free meals. I decided on my way to pass into the Trinity Cathedral and offer a prayer of thanks to the Almighty God for delivering me from my seemingly big trouble with the law.

When I got into the yard, I then remembered that Miss Laura was given a day off. So I busied myself in the kitchen to make the work lighter for Mrs Otchin when she got up. I was at that time a fairly good cook. And Miss Laura, having known she was given the day off, had all meats seasoned and vegetables all in readiness for cooking. So the operation was not at all a tedious one. That day, however, after lunch as I was washing the dishes, my friend Donald came. "Well, George," said he, "I've heard all about it, don't you worry to tell me anything. But I am now here with a big surprise for you." "What is it?" I asked, facing him with the soap suds dripping from my hands. "George, boy, I shall be going out to work from tomorrow." "Waw!" I shouted. "Not so loud," said he, "because I have not yet told it to the Otchins." "I am sorry," said I. "Where would you be going?" I asked, controlling my voice. "At Furness Withy and Company, right down to the corner of my street. Now, bear in mind what once I said to you still stands." "What's that?" I asked. "Have you forgotten?" asked he in amazement. "I once told you, should I get a job, I shall try to get you one there also." "Yes," said I, "but that shall take some time yet. For you shall first have to become a big shot as Mr Otchin or Mr Wilton or one of those rich folks." "No, George," said he, "conditions may work out differently. Let's wait and see."

About four months after Donald was employed, one evening he came to me and said, "George, would you like to work as a labourer? It is plenty of hard work, but the pay is good. You can earn $5.00 a week flat, and with some overtime, you can make $7.00. And I know to this type of work you can fit in quite well because you are not lazy, and you are smart." I said, "But what will the Otchins think about it?" "George," he replied, "you are always bemoaning your future. Well, this now involves your future, and just forget about what anyone may think." "OK," said I, "how and when do I start?" "Just sit tight. I shall soon let you know about that." At that very moment the conversation changed as Miss Laura entered the kitchen.

It happened one evening Mr Emril, Mrs Stedy's elder son, came down from the oil belt, where he was employed, to visit his mother. He also wanted a parcel taken to Mrs Jack, his sister in Belmont. Mrs Otchin called me and said, "Will you take the parcel to Mrs Jack? You do not have to come back, you can go home from there. When Mr Otchin comes, I shall let him know I sent you out." The time was 2:45 p.m. As I delivered the parcel, I went to my home. I had lots of time before nightfall, so I continued the reading of a book Yourland had loaned to me. The title of it was *The Works of William Shakespeare*. I then met a passage which read, "Hence home, you idle creatures, is this a holiday?"[1] I stopped and began thinking. Was it I this passage was written for? Am I to return to Toco, and if so, what for? How will I now be accepted up there? As I dreamed of the passage, slowly the darkness fell, and as my room had but one door for daylight and fresh air, I lit my lamp and sat reading at the table as my thoughts still pondered upon that passage which took a hold of me. I fell asleep.

---

1 A reference to William Shakespeare's *Julius Caesar*, Act 1, Scene 1:
   "Hence! home, you idle creatures get you home:
   Is this a holiday?"

CHAPTER SEVENTEEN

I was awakened by my two brothers, Quildon and Weston, who cautioned me to be careful with the lighted lamp and the breeze blowing constantly. Accidents can take place, which will not leave only me homeless but others can be involved. Quildon was himself sipping a stout. Weston had in his hand two sweet drinks; he handed one to me, asking at the same time for an opener. I said I had not any. Then I quickly remembered that there was one on my combination knife set. As I was about to reach it upon the ledge, "Come," said he, "there is one here." With quick movement, he pressed the head of the bottle against the edge of the tabletop, and with an even quicker movement from a blow of his hand, the cork was off. I was amazed when he gave me back my opened bottle of beverage. I sat upon my bed and let them use the chairs.

Quildon then broke the silence. "Well, boy, George, you going?" "Hunky-dory," I replied (using then Miss Laura's phrase). Weston then said, "Boy, you are always reading something." "Well, partner, there is nothing else that I can do. So, before sitting idle, let me read. It is very much better than wasting time." Meanwhile, in my mind, I was thinking that they were here to tell me of a better job. Perhaps it was in the garage where Quildon works sweeping or washing cars. Where I can then learn to drive. Or perhaps go back home to Toco, as I was thinking earlier.

Quildon again spoke. "How much rent are you paying here?" he asked. "Three shillings," I replied. "This place is hot, and I am sure that it gets dark very quickly. Also scorpion and centipede can bite you here." "Look," said Quildon, "we just got a place, a nice house with electricity and water in the yard. You don't have to go to any standpipe. The house is painted in and out, and it is only $5.00 a month. Why not come and share with us? You won't have to pay anything – we are brothers." Weston then muttered, "What about Stoke?" Quildon gently touched him on the side and said, "That's alright."

I then reached for my copybook, for in it I kept all my notes. I made a calculation. We shall each have to pay $1.67 with a cent to spare was my finding. I then turned to Quildon and said that I would pay $1.66

per month and they both will pay $1.67 each. Quildon then said to me, "George, your mind too big." Now I answered, in that way taking up the challenge, because I said, should Donald get through with the work of which he spoke, I shall be more than able to face that rent. But should he not, I shall be left with $1.34 only after paying my rent monthly.

"When do I have to come with you all?" "Oh, that can be right now, tomorrow, next week, or anytime that suits you," said Quildon. Weston then said, "Don't you forget that the key for here will have to be turned in to your agent with payment of this month's rent." "I am owing nothing," I told him. "How come?" asked Quildon. "I do pay two months in advance." "What!" said he. "You foolish or what? However, you can get back some of that money." I also said, "I will have to speak first with Mr Williams." "Mr Williams! What for? What have he to do with this?" said he sharply. "To remove my things from here." "Oh no, you don't," said he. "There are lots of box-carts that will gladly remove you from here to where we are for two bobs*. Well, when do you want to move?" "Tomorrow, if God spare life," I replied. To this Weston looked at me and shook his head in approval. "At what time?" "At 6:00 p.m.," I replied. "OK," said Quildon. "I shall be here with a box-cart awaiting you. Just make sure and be on time." He then gave me our new home address. As they were leaving, Weston said, "Don't you fall asleep again with that lighted lamp."

When they left, I decided to read no more for the evening, and so I turned into bed. As I lay, all sorts of questions came to my mind. Am I making the right move in joining my brothers? What will be my position should Donald fail with the work? How will I survive on $1.34 monthly? I was consoled, however, with the fact that should I take sick at any time, there would be someone around to relay the message to other relatives.

The next morning I got out of bed, prayed and looked sadly at the room, knowing that I shall no longer be there. When I got outside, there was Mom, my neighbour, just locking her door to go into town. I then told her today will be my last day living here, as I shall be moving into another place tonight. With sadness, she said how sorry she was to hear

CHAPTER SEVENTEEN

that. "For," said she, "I have been living here for twenty-five years, and you have been the most decent person to ever occupy that room. The others were just ragamuffins." She also said to me that I must keep on going that way, and the good Lord will bless me. As we walked from the yard and stepped upon the pavement, my thoughts flashed upon the filth which I had stepped into that Friday morning.

As we walked on, she told me that I must come to the Lord and worship every Saturday. I was indeed flattered by her speech of love and care. But her footsteps were too slow for my pace. I gave her a threepence coin (six cents) to take a tram, bade her goodbye and hastened my speed. That morning I was at work at 7:00 a.m. I did my chores very quickly. And I had enough time to do some cleaning for Mrs Stedy. Every move I made seemed to be just right that morning. When Miss Laura came in, I told her of my plans.

She was somewhat surprised only to hear then of my brothers and their home because she seemed to get the reporter's facts of the entire family from Cousin Vera. She, however, approved of my joining my brothers, with the exception of my having to pay equally the rent. "The very most you should pay is one dollar," said she. "That would be alright," I told her. Because, to date, never had I told her of what Donald suggested to me. As I returned from taking the lunch that day, a Spaniard* who lived next door (this gent's daughter it was that sat at table with the family that first Christmas) came and asked Mrs Otchin if I can assist him in cutting down a guava tree which marred his house. "Surely," said Mrs Otchin, "ask him." Now he once had spoken to me about the tree, but never had he made up his mind to cut it down.

"Georgeeee," said he to me, "will you please come with me to cut the tree?" "Yes, sir," said I, "give me a moment." I then went for the hatchet that was in the shed and hurried to his home. When I got there, "No, no, no," said he, "that will take too long." He then went to his tool room, and I followed him. He unhung a bow-shaped saw and said, "Georgee, this will do the job much faster." We went back to the tree where he demonstrated to me how it must be used. "Sir," said I, "there is a pouyant (sharp, short-hilt cutlass) in your tool room – I saw it. Can I use it?" "Sure," said he, and so he went for it. Very quickly I was at the treetop limbing its branches, while he stood looking up, somewhat amazed. When I was finished, I took the saw and began to cut the trunk. Mr Romian,[2] as he was called, commissioned himself in moving the branches, and it was done with such speed that I wondered what was his hurry. However, by the time I got to the base of the trunk, the branches were all out. "Oh, George," he said, "can you cut those a little shorter for me please? They would be much easier to handle." And so I did as he requested.

He then began to pack the logs at the far end of the fence. Turning to me, he said, "George, you knew quite well how to use that saw." "No, sir," said I, "it is the first time that I have used one." "Wot, boy!" said he. "You ees a genius." He looked at me and somewhat sadly shook his head. "Don't you leave. I am coming right now." As he left, I continued the tossing of the logs where he had left off.

In about fifteen minutes he appeared holding a waiter with a jug and two glasses. "Take this, George," said he, as he handed me a glass. In it he poured a very cold beverage. I looked at him. "No alcohol, sir?" I asked. "No," said he, "it is sweet drink with Nestle condensed milk and a little Angostura bitters." As I held my glass, he said, "Now, you pour for me," holding his glass. "Cheers," said he in his Latin accent, lifting his glass in the same manner that Mr Otchin do when drinking with his friends. I was amazed of his attitude towards me. However, we both had two glasses of the delicious beverage. "Thank you very much, sir," said I. "No, no, I am the one to do the thanking," said he. "Here, take this Georgee," and he handed me a $2.00 note. "No, sir," said I, "I am so happy to do this for you." "George," said he, "happiness is a thing must be shared. Do you believe that?" "Yes, sir," said I. "Well then, if you are happy, let me also be happy by you accepting this. I am not paying you, it is just a token of appreciation." "Thank you, sir," as I timidly took it from him.

When I got back to the house, there was Mrs Stedy speaking to Mrs Otchin. "I was just telling Madam when her father was alive he would

---

2   George refers to this person as both Mr Romian and Mr Romero.

CHAPTER SEVENTEEN

have loved to get someone like you to work on the sugar cane estate. No professional could have done a better job." I laughed and said, "Mam, the tree was green. Had it been dry, it would have been a much tougher job."

I then went to Miss Laura, who was herself busy washing some towels. I told her how nicely I was treated by Mr Romian, and I am going to the shop and have the $2.00 note changed because I am giving $1.00 to her. "George," said she, "don't be foolish, don't you go throwing away money like that. See the good Lord has opened up this way, knowing that you would have to pay that box-cart this evening and also an additional rent to your brothers. Take one day at a time, walk straight, think, and go easy," said she.

I then remembered I had not yet handed in my key to the agent. I hurried and got to the agent's office all sweating and out of breath. He was alone. "Good evening, sir," said I. "Good evening, sonny," he replied with a smile. "What have bring you here at this time?" he asked. "Sir," said I, somewhat dejected, "I am returning the key for my room, for I am leaving tonight to join my brothers." "Oh, I am so sorry," said he. "Then what time are you leaving?" "At six o'clock, sir." "And where are your belongings?" "In the room, sir." "Then, if you should now hand me the key, how would you get in?" I told him how sorry I was to have wasted his time. As I turned to leave, "Hold it," said he, as he reached for a ledger. Slowly he turned the pages. "I have seen here that you do pay two months in advance, and as to date, you are just half of this month. It is not my policy to return money to clients. However, when you come tomorrow, we shall speak." When I returned to the house, I told Miss Laura what a fool I had made of myself. She laughed and said it really did not occur to her, or she would have told it to me. However, it was much better that way because he had been given a day's notice.

That evening when Mr Otchin came home, he called me. "George," he said, "did you cut that tree for Mr Romero?" "Yes, sir," said I. "Now listen, young man," he gruffly said, "you work for me. I do not want you helping anyone around unless I tell you! Do you understand?" "Yes, sir," I replied. He again looked very sternly at me through his glasses and said, "I do mean that."

I had hoped to leave the premises by 5:30 p.m. that evening to meet Quildon at 6:00 p.m. with the box-cart as arranged. But here was I now faced with the mood of Mr Otchin, so I could not. I fixed his tray with drinks in the way I knew he liked it. I then crushed some ice, filling his special aluminium container. I went to Miss Laura, and I told her what was taking place. "OK," said she, "I shall go there now and fool him with some old talk*, he loves to be mamaguy*, and then you can slip away. Hold on a minute," said she, "let me first talk to Madam." She then went and spoke to Mrs Otchin, who came and said, "George, you may leave now."

That evening I was home at 5:50 p.m. by my West Clock, without delay. I had everything placed for the moving. At 6:05 p.m., I heard the rolling of a box-cart. I looked across the street, and there was Quildon walking along and chatting with the carter. He did not see me, so I quickly sat on the step as though I was long awaiting their arrival. As he came, I said, "Did you not say precisely six?" "Yes," said he, "but I am not late, am I?" I made no reply. And so, with the help of the carter, everything was packed on the cart for removal. As I finally locked my door to leave, Mom opened hers. "So you are really going," said she. "I would miss you." As Quildon and the carter made fast the cords on the cart, I slipped a shilling into her hand. "The good Lord shall bless you, son," said she. "May you never be found wanting long for anything." And so I bade her goodbye as the cart was pushed out of the yard.

The journey to my brothers' home was about a half-mile distance away. It was certainly a nice place as described by Quildon. As the items were offloaded from the cart, Quildon said to pay the fellow sixty cents. My heart leapt because last evening he had given me the assurance that the cost will be two shillings. Nevertheless, I now had extra change, so I paid the carter.

In the house there were three beds. I said to myself they had already bought me a bed. My articles were all placed in a corner. I asked no question of him, neither was anything told to me. Shortly after 7:00 p.m. Weston came in. "Well, George, you are here, did Quildon pick you up on time?" "Yes," I replied. He then carelessly said, "Stokes and

CHAPTER SEVENTEEN

I were coming, but you know Stokely. He has to stop by some girl." Quildon only grinned. I then remembered Weston had partly mentioned that very name yesterday evening, when Quildon touched him on the side.

Quildon then said, "Let him put his bed in that corner." And so Weston and I set up my cot. And we left the other articles where they were. Just then in came a tall, well-featured gent, whom Quildon immediately introduced to me as Stokely. Said Quildon to me, "We worked and learned to drive together. And we have been friends, and I do mean very good friends, for years." Then spoke Stokely, "So you are George. I have always heard Quildon and Weston speaking about you as Mr Straight-Forward." To this, they three laughed. Weston then said, "Let us put the shelf up to hang your clothes." I had in my trunk the screwdriver and hammer that I had taken up with me from the Otchins that evening to take it down. And so Stokely, being very tall, helped us, making it an easy job. Stokely then said, "Fellars, we would have to help George to buy some clothes." "Oh no," said Quildon, "he has more than us."

Miss Laura had told me when we were settled that night to bring up afresh the talk of the rent. But before so doing, I must first thank them for letting me share room with them. Then, I must insist on paying my part of $1.66 for the rent. We had then no thought that a fourth party was involved. Next, I knew not the character of the stranger. The house had two bedrooms. Quildon had one, and Stokely the other. There was lots of space in the living room for Weston and myself. Weston finally ran a cord from one portion to the next, and by using some safety pins which he had, he pinned an end of a blanket unto the parallel cord, which brought him some privacy to his bed. I had no problem because I was based in the far corner.

No one wanted to sleep, so we all got engaged in an old talk. Stokely and Weston had a chair each. Quildon brought a stool from under his bed, while I sat upon my cot. When we chatted for about forty-five minutes, Quildon brought a suggestion that a wall radio must be first installed, after which we shall all see about the furnishing of the general house. Stokely thought it a good idea. "From where will we buy them?" said Weston. "From J.T. Johnsons or Salvatori's," said Quildon. "And why not Steels on Charlotte?" said Weston. "I understand they are at present handing out some very good bargains." "Oh yes," said Stokely, "it is on the papers*." He then looked at me and said, "What do you think, George?" Outright I replied, "First of all, how is this rent paid?" "It is already paid," said Quildon, "you don't go worrying yourself about that." I then said, "Fellars, a rent of $5.00 is not easy to be paid by one man. So everyone here must prepare himself to pay his share of the rent, which is $1.25 to his living." Quildon objected, but Weston and Stokely fully agreed with me. I then placed $1.25 upon the table. "As regards the furniture, whenever they are purchased, let me know as to what I have to pay." Stokely looked at me and said, "I do see now the reason why you are referred to as 'Mr Straight-Forward'."

The next day I was promptly at work at 6:00 a.m. I did my regular chores very quickly at the back. Mr Otchin, when he was leaving, said to me, "I did not know when you left yesterday, young man." "Sorry, sir," said I, "but you were speaking to Miss Laura at the time." "OK, OK, but just remember what I told you, understand?" "Eh eh ar eh." I tried to remember and finally I asked, "What was it, sir?" "I told you that you are not to go helping neighbours around unless I told you." "Oh, sir, I won't." And he briskly walked out of the gate.

I then began feeling very unsecured. I went to the front house. I cleaned the children's bicycles; Grace's tyres were soft, so I pumped them. "*Slip, slop, slip, slop*" sounded the slippers of Mrs Stedy. "Good morning, George." "Good morning, Mam," I replied. She then walked to the bathroom door and tapped on it with her stick, which she carried not for support but as a habit. "Yourland," she called, "stop singing and come out of that bathroom. You would be late for school." "OK, Granny," he replied. Yourland, besides sports, had a talented voice as a singer, which he mastered when bathing. Mrs Otchin also had a lovely voice, which I think he inherited through cradle lullaby.

The gate then squeaked; it was Miss Laura who came in. "Good morning to everyone," said she as she walked to the kitchen. I had

CHAPTER SEVENTEEN

already the vegetables for lunch on the stove. Mrs Otchin then came out, followed by the two youngest children, Albert and Marlene. Mrs Stedy then said to me, "George, I have seen the boss wanted to take off your head for cutting that guava tree for Mr Romero." Mrs Otchin promptly took the matter up and asked what it was all about. So I then told her what Mr Otchin said yesterday about the tree and the warning he gave this morning. "Then did you not tell him that you were sent by me to cut it?" "No, Mam." "Well," said she, "George, you are rather silly. However, I shall let him know it was I who sent you when he gets home this afternoon."

It happened that day lunch was sent very early, and I was back at the house by 12:30 p.m.

Miss Laura then asked, "Did you bring the key for the agent?" "Yes," I replied. "Well, why not go now and deliver it to him while you have nothing to do. When you gets back, you can tell me how you likes your new home." And so I set off for the agent. At 1:15 p.m. I was there. "Well, son," said he, "you are here again. I learned that you left our relatives at 6:30 p.m. yesterday." He smiled as he spoke. I wondered how came he to know that. Then, seeing how astonished I was, said he, "You are a very good youngster, and should you at any time need a place to live, don't be hesitant in coming to me, even you have not money." "Thank you, sir." I was yet puzzled to know how he knew about the time of my departure. Then said he to me, "Did you know that the old lady who lived next door is my aunt?" "No, sir." "Well, she has always said how kind you and your relatives are to her. And for that cause, every cent that you have paid in advance rent will be returned to you." He then reached for his ledger and checked.

"Well," said he, "you have paid two months now in advance, which is six shillings ($1.44), and you have lived so far fifteen days out of it. I am entitled to forfeit at least three shillings (seventy-two cents) from it, but with the gentlemanly report I has received of you, I am returning fully back the six shillings to you." "Oh, thank you, sir," said I with a bow, as I bade him goodbye and left. As I walked back to the house, I remembered well Quildon had said I should get back at least a part of the rent money paid in advance, but in no wise had I expected all of it.

Days passed, and one day Miss Laura said, "George, what about those suits and the cardboard cartoon* of clothes you has there? Why not take them to your home? I will go over and ask the shopman to lend you his delivery bicycle after all deliveries are made this afternoon. You can then put everything in the carrier and take them to your home. Only make sure you do not ride between the tramlines because that can rip the tyres off the wheels, and make sure to take back the bicycle early in the morning." "Alright," said I, "should you get the loan of the bicycle, I shall take them up this evening." Very quickly Miss Laura returned with good news from the shopman. He had told her that the bicycle would be loaned to me after the last delivery was made for the evening.

I was indeed very fortunate, for the porter got through with his task by 3:30 p.m. that day. I loaded the articles and was off for my home. When I arrived, it was then I realized that I had not a key for the house. With disgust, I went over to the nearby parlour and asked the lady if she would allow me to leave the articles there until one of my brothers came home. (Stokely was also counted as a brother.) "Sure," said she, "that will be no problem." And so I did.

When it was 4:25 p.m., I returned the bicycle back to the shopman. As I got to the house, Miss Laura, who was yet there, felt very happy to know that I was back and wondered how I came back so quickly. I told her what had happened and where the clothes were left. She told me it is my rights to demand a key. "It is not necessary," said I, "as I am not there during the day." "Don't be foolish," said she. "Look at what has now happened. Suppose, just suppose, you were to go home one night, and there came a sudden downpour. Will you then go to the parlour or ask the nearest neighbour for a shelter? Come on, George, where are your senses?" I bowed my head for she was right. When I got home, it was about 7:00 p.m. I went over to the parlour to collect my items. An elderly gentleman helped me to put the carton upon my head; it was not only cumbersome but it was also weighty, as my suits were also placed upon it while it was on my head.

CHAPTER SEVENTEEN

When I got to our steps, I gently eased it off my head. I had not very long to wait, for up came Stokely. "What are you doing sitting here?" he said. "I am awaiting someone to turn up with a key," I replied. "How come? Have you not a key?" "No," said I. "Look, man," said he, "from the outset, I had three keys cut, for I knew that you were coming to join us. I gave them to Quildon and kept the original. However, come inside," said he, unlocking the door. He helped me with the carton to my corner of the room. In about ten minutes Weston arrived. Stokely then brought up the subject to his notice. As the conversation was on, in came Quildon. Stokely then asked about my key. "Oh," said Quildon, "I gave it not to him because there will always be someone here before he can come in on evenings." "That's not the point," said Weston. "He is paying just as any of us. Look, for instance, he was here at 4:00 p.m. or sometime like that today. He had then to go to the parlour to rest his things. Next, should he come here and it is raining, must he take shelter below the house?" "OK, OK," Quildon stuttered as he took the key from off his key ring and handed it to me.

Several weeks passed by, and one evening I went home just to find the door was locked from inside. I knocked, and there came Stokely sleepily to the door. "Oh, George," said he, "I am so sorry. I came in early to take a nap because I have to hold the night shift for someone." "That's alright," said I, reaching for the *Gazette** that was on the table. There were two very interesting stories that drew my attention. One of an Austrian national who lived in Germany and was a vibrant union leader.[3] The other was that of a Roman Catholic brother in Montreal, Canada, who had also been creating wonderful miracles of healing among the sick; both the rich and poor were cured by his divine healings.[4] I found the stories interesting, more so because it involved two men of different fields.

---

[3] George could be referring here to Adolph Hitler, who was indeed an Austrian national residing in Germany.

[4] Brother André Bessette (canonized in 2010) was known as the "Miracle Man of Montreal"; thousands of miraculous healings were attributed to his intercession.

As it was then quite early, I decided to pay Aunt Bertrice and my cousins a visit. Going to the canister to make a change of my undergarments, I was greeted with a surprise. It was broken into and ransacked. On giving a rough inventory of my loss, I realized that sixteen cents I had in it for the longest while was gone, along with some underclothing. I called Stokely to see what was done. He seemed quite astonished, as he muttered between his teeth, "You mean just like that?"

Neither Stokely nor I made a further issue of it, for we wanted not to create any further unpleasantness among ourselves and relatives. (One thing I know, I have never repaired that trunk. I have kept it all my life, and I now keep special issues of *National Geographic* and manuscript clippings in it.) I mentioned not the incident to Miss Laura, but I at once made up my mind to get a room and get out from among them.

Chapter 18

*A plot succeeds and George starts work as a labourer;
he quits his job with Mr Otchin, who is not pleased*

One evening Donald said, "George, you must be saying that I am a 'Big Mouth'. Well, we are now doing a very big contract at Bishop's. I want you to go there on Monday morning. Don't you come here. You must dress smartly in your doeskin flannel pants and blazer as you often do on Sundays. The reason for this: we are not now hiring anyone else for unskilled labour. You shall see posted a very large sign marked NO HANDS WANTED. Just ignore it, and come in and ask for a timekeeper or a labourer work. You must show no sign whatever that you know me, and I shall do likewise. On your verbal application, you will be told no. As you walk away, I shall call the foreman and other officials who may be there for us to try a practical joke by saying, 'Yes, we can do with a labourer.' Now, here is where your reward will come in. You would then throw off your coat and tie and stand in readiness for work. Everyone will then be taken by surprise – but, of course, not me. You would then be directed to work with the labour gang, who may perhaps be mixing concrete at the time. Now, George, be very sure and be there at 8:30 a.m." "But what about Mr Otchin's lunch?" I asked. "George, don't be a damn fool. This would be a break, a future in your life. You now sound just stupid. Just do as I say and utter not a word of it to anyone. Not even to your best friend Laura. Do you understand?" "Yes, I do," said I.

Then came that memorable Monday morning. I left home for work as usual with thirty-six cents in my pocket, along with four tram tickets. I took a tram heading for Charlotte Street. Now Donald had also said to me make sure and come with a full stomach because there may not be a lunch break. As the tram got to Marine Square, I hurried west to a portion familiarly then called Goats Manor. There was a vendor who traded there, selling the choicest float* and acra*, coffee and bush tea as a speciality. I had my fill of float and acra, followed by two cups of bush tea. When I asked for my bill, I was told, "Twelve cents, sir." It was then 6:00 a.m. Then I saw a few people heading east towards the Roman Catholic Cathedral. I said to myself, a church is a church. And as there was yet sufficient time before 8:30 a.m., which was my appointment, I joined the pilgrims. To my dismay, I could not follow what was being said by the padre.[1] So I prayed in my own Anglican teaching. After spending ten minutes, I once more set off for home.

I hurriedly took a bath and attired myself as instructed by Donald. I felt resolute, as I had long been awaiting this opportunity. Being now quite confident of myself and the time, although I had not a watch, I walked to Bishop's High School, leaving home at 7:50 a.m. As I passed the Colonial Hospital, I heard a clock striking eight as I neared a doctor's villa. I then hurried my way to Gordon Street, occasionally asking the time of a passer-by as though I had forgotten my watch at home. I was on the school's compound at 8:25 a.m. and was pointed the way to the construction by a kindly teacher. I then walked into a shed that was prepared as an office. There was Donald sitting at a desk with a building plan in front of him, flanked by three other gentlemen. They seemingly had been discussing something. Outside was a waiting crew of about a dozen men. "Good morning, gentlemen," said I. Quickly all four at the desk replied, "Good morning, sir, can we help you?" My heart gave a fast beat, then languidly I replied, "I am in search of employment." They seemed disappointed of my request, especially one gent who was dressed in a khaki outfit, including a khaki cork hat*. "We have no vacancy," said he. Said another, "Can't you read? When you go out, just

---

[1] The Catholic Mass was said in Latin until 1962.

CHAPTER EIGHTEEN

check the board." "Hold it," said Donald, "what kind of work are you looking for?" "Anything, sir," said I. "Timekeeper, labourer, once it can bring me an honest shilling." Meanwhile, deep within I prayed that no one of the three would ask, "What's your trade?" "We have nothing," said another. "Thank you, gentlemen," said I, and left.

As I neared the pavement, I heard a clap and someone calling, "Sir! Sir!" As I looked around, it was a workman calling. "You are wanted, sir," said he, "at the office." "Ah," I said to myself, "things are working out as planned." As I went back, I was told by my khaki-dressed friend that he wanted a labourer to join the crew outside. "Many thanks, sir," said I with a bow. The gent who had rudely said to me, "Can't you read," again said in the most sarcastic manner, "They shall be mixing a batch of concrete in the next ten minutes. What will you do?" "Please, gentlemen, can I leave my coat, hat, and tie in here?" Before anyone could have made me a reply, Donald said, "Sure, there are two nails over there on which you can hang them." And so I joined the labourer gang.

There were six of us as labourers. The others seemingly were tradesmen. All eyes were now set upon me. I then observed my uniformed friend speaking to a strongly built labourer as they both gave me a quick glance. We were then summoned to start the barrowing of sand and gravel. The strong guy with whom the gent was speaking said, "You and I will work as partners." "OK," said I. "But," said he, "your clothes will get dirty. Look, I have an old pants over there. I was to take it home to be washed last weekend, but I forgot it. Go take it and put it on." "Thank you," said I, "but I shall work in what I have on." "*Steups, steups*," went he, "suit yourself. I was only trying to help."

The sand was barrowed upon a large wooden platform. My partner, who was very much taller and brawnier than me, was a skilled worker. As we worked on, I realized that we were ahead of the other two pairs. Our mound was made, and we rolled in the necessary drums of cement before they were finished making their mounds. The uniformed gent came and said to them, "Hurry up!" as he looked our way. My partner took a pickaxe and skilfully cut the drums around the rims, opening them quite easily, while I stood watch. When he was through, he said to me, "Open up the material." I knew not what he meant. I said to him, "Alright, but I have a hot piss* that I shall rather first empty." "Go over there," he pointed, "and please be careful. Remember this is a girls' school." I really did not want to do anything, but I knew not the term of "opening the material" as I have aforesaid.

I walked to where he pointed. I did nothing for I had not the desire. When I got back, I found him spreading the sandbank that we had made. And so I fell into the very action, as I learned what was meant of the term "open up the material". When we were finished opening up our material, the other four were just rolling in their cement. In those days cement was chiefly imported from the United Kingdom in drums. But as World War Two[2] raged, steel was then more in demand, but paper sacks, which were far less expensive, were introduced.

We had now to empty our drums of cement upon the material. My partner handled his drum with such skill, as he rolled and emptied at the same time. I carelessly looked on. I ventured to try the same method but was very slow on my performance. I was just about halfway through when he came and took it from me and emptied what was left. Very soon we were both "dry mixing". When this exercise was finished, he bade me bring the water hose. While we were mixing a portion of concrete, the others were pounding away on their drums with a hammer and coal chisel. Then came the gent who asked if I could not read. "What's your name?" he asked. "George Wright, sir." "Well, Wright, you are wanted in the office." I wondered if I had in any way gone wrong. But as I entered there was an English gentleman speaking to Donald and my prospector friend. "How far do you live?" asked the English gent

---

2   The role of Trinidad in World War II is an interesting one. Because German U-boat operations extended to the Gulf of Mexico and the Caribbean, Trinidad, off the coast of Venezuela, became key to protecting South American trade routes and the Panama Canal. A large US naval base, Chaguaramas, was built in the northwest tip of the island, construction starting in 1941. At its peak, there were 135,000 US troops stationed there, and over 10,000 Trinidadian workers were hired for the construction projects. The calypso "Rum and Coca Cola" gives a small indication of the impact of US culture on the island. Naval Base Trinidad was only decommissioned in 1977.

CHAPTER EIGHTEEN

with a drawl. "Belmont, sir," said I. "Can you go home and change and be back here by noon?" "Yes, sir." It was then 10:45 a.m. As I took my coat and other belongings in walking out, from the corner of my eyes I saw a smiling Donald. I got home quickly, changed, had a quick snack in the parlour, and was back again on the job at 11:45 a.m.

My work partner seemed very happy to see me back. One thing he had done wisely was not to let us soak our whole portion with water earlier. Noon then came for lunch break. It was given as we had not to work through. And so we took our several ways. When we returned at 1:00 p.m., my partner said, "We shall continue with our mixing." I held the water hose, as he worked as though he was a human machine. He turned the mixture with great skill, while I soaked on with observance. A mason then came and directed where he would first like the casting to begin. It was to be laid onto a very large floor space. My partner then asked, "Will you like to run the barrow or fill?" As I had changed my clothes, I could now work more freely. So I said it mattered not, but we can both share its exercises. So he began the rolling of the barrow, while I filled. And so we kept on changing position until our mixture was finished.

At the end of the day I was told by the foreman, who was the very prospector who hired my service, that they were all impressed with my performance. And any workman that can keep up with that guy with whom I worked is worth his salt. And as long as there is work, I would be hired. Donald passed by and quickly said to me away from the others' hearing to meet him at his home at 7:00 p.m.

When I got home that evening, I bathed, dressed, ate something from the parlour, and was off for Donald's home. Knowing how punctual I was with regard to the ways of time, I met him standing at their gate. "Well, George," said he with a hearty laugh, "I knew that you can work, but never had I dreamed so well. You can now count for sure that your yard boy days are over. The company for which you now work is one of the largest building and commercial companies in Trinidad. So I will now advise that you go down to the Otchins and let them know that you would be no longer working with them. And it must be told without my name being brought in the picture because a friendship can be ruined." He then asked, "What would you tell them?" I said, "I would frankly tell Mr Otchin that I had realized from the day that I had helped Mr Romero with the hewing of the guava tree, his whole attitude had been changed towards me. I became unsettled in mind, so I began seeking employment elsewhere. I have now gotten one at the Bishop's High School, and I began today." "Good," said Donald. "Also, do not let anyone on the job know that we know each other. Because whenever I can get you a transfer from the site, I shall do so."

I then left for the Otchins' home. As I entered the gate, I overheard Mr Otchin saying angrily, "He is growing out of his shoes of late. When he gets here tomorrow, I shall let him know really who he is." Mrs Otchin said, "Wait first, Orman, don't you get to so hasty a conclusion; he may be ill." Only then did I realize that the conversation was about me. I stood still, as I wondered what must now be done. And so I remembered these words of Uncle Bishop, "Respect everyone, but fear no one."

I then said aloud, "Good night."[3] "Yes!" came an answer from Mr Otchin. Yourland and Grace looked through a window. "Sir," said I, "I have come to let you know from the evening of my cutting down the guava tree for Mr Romero, your attitudes have since been indifferent to me. I then became disturbed in mind and thought it best to get another work, and I have now finally gotten one at the Bishop's High School, where I have started today." "Good for you," said he in a gruff manner. Then, in a most sarcastic way, said he to me, "What subjects are you teaching your class?" I made him no reply, but I simply walked to the toilet where I had a pair of crepesoles given to me by Mr Otchin himself, a short pants and T-shirt. It was there that I had my bank book and some hidden cash in concealment. I tied the shoes by their laces and strung them over my shoulder, roughly balling the clothing into one bundle, which I held under my arm. Yourland and Grace, who were yet by the window, saw when I did this. Grace said, "Here, George,

---

3   Saying 'good night' as 'hello' or 'good evening' is a customary greeting in Trinidad and Tobago.

CHAPTER EIGHTEEN

put them in this hat bag, which I got from my friend Mona today." I wanted to go over to Mrs Stedy so that she may know what was taking place. But on second thoughts I said I better not because there may be questions and answers to be given. And so I walked off. As I got to the gate, Yourland came hurrying to me. "Here, George," said he, poking a coin into my hand. "No thanks, Yourland," said I. "Look," said I, as I clapped my pants pocket. With sad countenance, he looked at me and said, "Don't mind Daddy. Wherever you go, still pass and look us up sometime. And should you want to borrow my bicycle at any time, feel free to come for it." He then gave me a friendly smile as he extended a handshake, and I left.

PART ❧ THREE

Chapter 19

George's eating problem is resolved by Aunt Bertrice; he spends a Sunday exploring Port of Spain, and Theo slips him a note

That night as I walked up Charles Street, I hoped not to be seen by my vendor friend, and I was very fortunate not to. As I made my way, I wondered a hundred times over what will my future be. Many thanks to Miss Laura that I had a little money saved. But what, how and where would I eat? I could not live on float and acra or the parlour relishes. Then suddenly an idea came to me. Why not now go over to Cousin Vera and Miss Laura and let them know what has taken place? And so I did and in time for a hot fish broth from Cousin Vera. Miss Laura and her husband came from their apartment, so I was able to relate my story just once. The foursome listened very attentively while I spoke. I was very careful not to mention Donald's name or that I had at all seen him. Cousin Vera's husband applauded when I made mention of how I had attired myself to get the work, while Miss Laura's husband remarked in no way could he have thought of that plan. As I was leaving, Cousin Vera bade me to wait a little. She then handed me a brown paper bag and said, "Eat that before going to work in the morning." Said she, "I shall pass the news on to Hilda and Aunt Bertrice tomorrow."

That night I got home at 10:00 p.m. I was advised by Cousin Vera to take a tram as it was late. On my arrival, Weston and Stokely were playing a game of cards. "George," said Weston, "I was just finishing this game to come and look for you. What happen? How come you so late? They had a party or what?" Before I could have made a reply, Stokely said with a broad grin, "You pick up or what? Don't be like me for you can be left broke." I then quickly told them of my change, of which they were both happy. I then prayed and slipped into bed, knowing that tomorrow will be that of hard labour.

I worked out the week and became a real favourite of the gang. Everyone wanted me to work as their partner. Occasionally when the architect came on the site, he would say something to me if I was near. Of which I later found was not his custom to the workmen. I was now faced with one problem. It was that of eating. I could not go on daily roughing it out in the parlour or sidewalk. For the work I was now doing, I needed at least one good balanced meal per day to build my energy.

That Saturday I received a pay envelope of $6.50, which was then the largest sum of money that I had ever earned for a week's employment. I hustled down to the Penny Bank and deposited $1.50. Now having $5.00 to spend freely on my own as a bachelor, I had then to think to spend it wisely. I was a non-smoker, a non-alcoholic, a non-friend in my society, a non-limer, a non-feter*, and a non-cinema lover. Now having not those "nons", I had then no major financial worries. My rent being $1.25 per month, I had then a good wardrobe of which I did quite a bit of laundering for myself. My only problem, as I've said before, was my meals. It is a fact that I could myself prepare a good dish, but the storage of groceries could have created a problem. So I therefore decide to get advice from Big Sister Hilda after two weeks. As I recalled for that week, I had over $12.50 free spending money, which was quite a tidy sum.

Sister Hilda and I had not seen each other for quite a few weeks so our meeting was one of gladness. I told her everything in pouring out my problems to her. She listened attentively and said she thinks the matter could be solved. "Tell me," said she, "when last have you seen Aunt Bertrice?" "Oh quite some time," I replied. "Will you now like to pay her a visit?" "Aw, Hil, you do know that I am always happy to meet Aunt Bertrice." "Well then, meet me here tomorrow and we shall go there," said she, laughing. "But can we not go there now?" "OK, just let me hang these clothes out and we shall leave."

CHAPTER NINETEEN

As we walked and talked on our way to Aunt Bertrice, Sister Hilda asked how much was I prepared to spend for meals each week, which will be lunch only. "At the moment," said I, "I can spend $3.00." "Are you crazy!" said she. "You would not be eating at the Queen's Park Hotel." I looked at her inquiringly. "That's too much. Have you forgotten that was your month's pay?" "Well then, how much do you think I should pay?" "Two dollars," said she, "for the very most, and that must include Sundays also." "But where can I get such a bargain," I asked. "That's the reason that I asked you when last have you seen Aunt Bertrice. We are now going there by your request, George, and that subject would be brought up."

We got to Aunt Bertrice's home, and I was greeted with that motherly love. Without hesitation, Sister Hilda placed my problem fully to her. To our surprise, Aunt Bertrice said she had already heard that I had fired my job*. Cousin Vera told her of it a week ago in the market. Said Aunt Bertrice to Sister Hilda, "As far as preparing lunch for him, it will be no problem because I have to prepare lunch for my two sons every day. All I have now to do is add a little more. But how will he get it?" said she. "The distance is so far to ride, and even worse to walk daily."

They were both deliberating on the matter when cousin Ren came in. We greeted each other. He was fully dressed in his police constable uniform, for he had left off teaching and joined the police force. Being well built, he looked well in his military attire. He was then drawn into the conversation. He suggested that I make myself each day some Quaker's Oats porridge or any other porridge that I may like, have my fill, and place some into a tightly corded container. And also that I should buy and eat fruits along with the porridge at lunchtime. He also suggested that every evening after work I should come and have a meal. His suggestions were well taken. As he was about to leave, he said to me, "George, also drink plenty of Libby's evaporated milk, straight or diluted. It is very good." Sister Hilda then said to me, "George, tell Aunt how much do you intend to pay each week." (Sister Hilda did not see when I counted and folded the money into a bit of brown paper. So I had not to tell Aunt Bertrice but rather hand it to her.)

"What's this?" she asked as she opened it. "That's what I can afford to pay," said I. "Boy, George, you are rich, you have plenty of money," said she laughing. Turning to Sister Hilda, she said, "He said I am not to take a farthing from George for his meals as long as he, Ren, was at home and working. And, child, what you have given me here is far too much, had I to take money from you. Child, you work and save your money," said she. "Thank you both," said I shyly, as I nursed the sad feelings deep within of not now being independent.

"Wait," said Aunt, "while you are here, you may have your first meal. Hilda, you may also have a little bite with him, for there is sufficient." "Oh no," said Sister Hilda, but Aunt Bertrice, who would not be denied of her offer, said, "Hilda, girl, I still do cook as Toco people do. Should anyone call, there is always an extra meal that can be served." I was then called to dinner where I was given a packed plate. Hil still took nothing to eat, but they both together had lemonade. I ate, drank, and was satisfied when Sister Hilda and I left.

As we walked and chatted, Sister Hilda said, "George, the good Lord is certainly on your side. Just wait until Vera hears of all this tomorrow." "Yes, Sis, but I am now unhappy by not having been allowed to pay anything." "Ah, don't you worry, little brother, everything will work out." "Work out! How do you mean?" "Listen to me," said she, "here is what can be done. Not every day, but occasionally, you can pass by the market or the shop and buy some goods. And you would not forget their birthdays, whose dates I shall get for you. You may sometimes see something being sold that is nice and inexpensive for her or the home – you can buy it. And, should you do things like that, you would be a happy man."

(Dear Reader, I write the following not in any way seeking praises or glory, God forbid. But as a songwriter puts it, "Weeping may be endured but for a night. Joy cometh with the morning." My joy of gratitude to Aunt Bertrice did come in our later years, when I could render freely certain kindnesses to her. May I say also that the good Lord had blessed me. That for years leading up to the very month she died, I gave her a monthly allowance by cheque.)

CHAPTER NINETEEN

It was a lovely Sunday morning. I bathed, dressed, took my hymn book and was off. I walked the pathway around the Savannah East. As I got to the corner of Dundonald Street, I said to myself it would be a good idea to surprise Mom, my old Adventist friend, who I knew visited the church on that street on Sundays. When I got there, however, the building was closed, and two men were busy sweeping the churchyard. I stood on the pavement gazing towards them. Then the elder of the two saw me. He leaned his broom against the building and came with hastening strides out to me. One of them told me good morning and asked if he could help me. "Yes, can you tell me at what time does your service begin on Sundays?" "Oh, no church today, sir. That was yesterday." "Oh, I am so sorry about that," said I. "I thought there was a service on Sundays also." "No, sir, church services are being kept on Saturdays from 9:00 a.m. On Sunday, however, a special study of the Bible is conducted from 11:30 a.m. until you feel like leaving." "Oh, many thanks," I said to him. "That's alright, sir," said he, "feel free to call on us at any time, for there is always someone here to advise you."

I then decided to take the morning service at Trinity Cathedral. As I neared the church, the hymn "Lead Us Heavenly Father" was chimed with such harmony as a well-tuned steel pan of modern times that it had me wondering. As I walked into the church with a feeling of holiness, I sat in an empty pew. The service had not yet officially begun, for some folks were talking while others knelt in prayer. I was also knelt in prayer when I was shaken on the shoulder by a woman who said, "Young man, would you please get up; this is my pew." I immediately got up, and as I turned to leave, a grey-haired gentleman pointed me to a seat abreast of hers. I sat but with a remorseful feeling. My sacred joy had fled from me.

The service was good. The hymns were loudly sung by both choir and congregation. The minister's sermon was based on Mark 3:4: "Is it lawful to do good on the Sabbath day or evil?" Then came the time of offering. I saw this woman's eyes fixed upon me from the corner of my eyes. I held noticeable a one-dollar bill that could not be seen by other worshippers but could easily be seen by her. (Those were the days that even the elite will place in the offering platter just a half-crown (sixty cents) for the very most and the layman pennies (two cents) and threepence (six cents).) As the sexton came to me, I gracefully placed the dollar in the shining platter. I cared not of what she gave.

As the service was ended, I took a lackadaisical walk towards Frederick and Prince Street corner. I had lots of time. I did not want to call on Sister Hilda or Aunt Bertrice so very early, so I leisurely walked down Frederick Street, doing some window shopping. Then, suddenly, an idea came. Why not pay Bob, Lidia and Mr Williams a visit? So I hastened to the bus station on George Street, boarded a bus, paid three cents – bus fares had then risen to one cent more than to San Juan – and was off to their home.

When I got there, they were all very busy. Mr Williams was cleaning and polishing the hooves of the horses, Bob was scrubbing and washing the floors and walls of the stalls, and Lidia seemed busy in the kitchen. It happened that their cousin Theo came in from Marabella to spend the weekend, so she was occupied with the cleaning of the house. Needless to say, I was given a warm welcome. Mr Williams in particular left off his task to chat with me. I had outfitted myself in my silk three-piece suit when I left home, and certainly I was not now going to fall into any work with them. Yet at the same time I felt odd being around, for it was an atmosphere with work. I then swallowed my pride and asked Bob if he can lend me a change of raiment. He looked at me and laughed. "George," said he, "you leave clothes here when you left. I do not know whether they will now fit you. Come with me." We went to his room, where he pulled from under his bed a carton. Without my trying them on, they were all too small. There was, however, a pair of trousers and a long sleeve shirt that were once given to me by Mr Williams himself that I should wear when going with the boys to cut grass. These now fitted perfectly. I was now barefooted, and in readiness for work.

As we walked towards the stables, Mr Williams said, "Wait a minute, young fella, you came here not to work." "Maybe not, sir," said I, "neither have I come to eat." At once he seemed defeated with my answer. "OK,"

CHAPTER NINETEEN

said he, laughing. He then called to Lidia to fetch me the pair of boots he wears to work daily.

Mr Williams then showed me how to clean, disinfect, trim and polish the horses' hooves. He had already bathed them. So he brushed and rubbed them down with black sage. I then went over to Bob, who had almost finished his chores, and said to him, "Bob, I do know it is not the policy that grass be cut on a Sunday. But let us run up to Corbeaux Alley. I want to see if I have yet the touch of the grass knife*." "That depends on what Pappy would say," said he. He then went on to say, "Personally I would be glad, for that would be an ease up for tomorrow." "OK, leave that to me," said I.

I then went to Mr Williams and laid it on very nicely to him. He did not refuse but said we must first eat. Lidia, however, was not quite finished, so off we went. We chatted on the way, with me doing most of the talking. We at last got to the grassland. "Well, George," said Bob, "this is an open challenge. Let us see today who can cut the fattest and the largest bundle of grass. 1, 2, 3, off we go," said he. At first he led. But unluckily for him he got himself caught with some vines of cowitch*, which had him scratching. And as my hand then got into the feel of the grass knife, I led by sheaves. At the end I shared some small bundles with him, which we bound into two large bundles. I then took the larger of the two, leaving him with his scratches.

When we got back, Mr Williams and Lidia were astonished. Lidia jokingly said, "What happen? Someone had cut that grass and left it, and you both just picked it up." Mr Williams came over and lifted the bundles and approvingly shook his head. We then bathed and had our meals. It was a relish Aunt Rache had taught Lidia to make: cow's cheek, corn coocoo* with crab, and callaloo. As I ate, I wondered what will Aunt Bertrice be saying about the meal which was prepared for me. But I then said to myself, what does it matter? A bird in the cage is far more valuable than nine in the bushes.

It was then fifteen minutes to three by the wall clock and a bright sunny evening. We four just sat idly listening to some songs which sounded boring to us through the wall radio. I broke from the company and joined Mr Williams in the dining room checking some bills. I asked him if he would not mind us going to the Rock Garden. "What time will you all be back?" "Whatever time you would have us back, sir," said I. "Well, you all may go but see and be back here by 6:00 p.m.," said he. I then rejoined and told them what I had done before consulting them. They were overjoyed. Bob said, "George, you are something else." "That will give us a full two hours for ourselves." "Let's change and get ready before someone else should now show up and ruin everything," said Lidia.

Well, I was already half-dressed from when we came from cutting the grass. We were all ready in fifteen minutes. Mr Williams then said that he would take the opportunity to visit Mr Tom, a cousin of his who was ill. "By the way," said Mr Williams, "let me give you all money for the trip." "No, sir, I have got enough to take us all to Toco and back." (We all laughed sharing the joke.) Lidia and Theo were nicely dressed. Bob was attired in shirt and pants with long tie. I left my waistcoat and jacket and was attired like Bob. We then left the house knowing that we must be back in two hours' time.

We took a cab which dropped us at the entrance to the zoo. The driver charged two shillings (forty-eight cents) for the drop. He asked if he should come back for us. Bob said it was a good idea. "Well, pick us up here at 5:30 p.m.," I told him. "OK, sir," he replied. As he drove off, Bob said, "George, I am not able* with you, nah." "That will give us more leisure time without a worry," I said to him. We then covered quite an area as we comfortably walked, looking at the well-kept lawn, flowers and shrubs. The Rock Garden was a place of tranquillity, reclination and romance for some folks, while to others it was an uncovered gallery for a fashion show. The evening was a remarkably hot one. I saw a palet cart and stopped it. We were then at the very point where we were to be picked up by our cab. I told the palet salesman that we were going to eat, and he must do the counting. He can also keep on ringing his bell for the advertisement of his confectionery sales. Theo said, "There shall be no problem in counting, let us all lay our wrappers in one spot." When we had eaten eight, the taxi driver came back for us. The time was then 5:20 p.m. So I bade him to join us. When we were finished, Theo

CHAPTER NINETEEN

counted the wrappings; there were twenty-two in all. I gave the guy a shilling, telling him to keep the change. The cab man then pointed us to a garden tap to wash our hands, and we left.

When we got back, I gave the cab man a dollar because he collected not his first two shillings. The time was then 5:45 p.m. As we sat talking and making jokes, there came Mr Williams at 5:55 p.m. He seemed somewhat surprised. "George," said he, "I knew as long as you were head of the team, you would be all back on time." I then fully attired myself to leave and bade them all goodbye at 6:05 p.m. As I was leaving, Mr Williams said, "George, feel free to come here at any time without an invitation." "Very well, sir," said I. As I made my way to the gate somewhat flanked by the others, Theo sneaked a bit of paper into my hand. "Say nothing," she softly said. I took it unnoticed by anyone. As we stood chatting at the gate, there was the hum of a bus coming from the distance. I then took the bus and waved goodbye to my friends.

I got to Aunt Bertrice's home at 6:30 p.m. Everyone was there, including Sister Hilda. They were expecting me at 1:00 p.m. for the very latest, I was told. And not having seen me then, they became concerned and sent for Sister Hilda. I gave the story from A to Z of my full day's venture. Ren said, "George, at times you do sound superhuman." Lou said, "When next you pay them a visit, come and meet me." "Sure," said I, "as long as you are willing to cut grass on a Sunday." "Are you mad?" said he, "Not even Monday. That's a job for country folks only," said he, laughing.

Sister Hilda then said, "Are you not going to eat?" "Oh no," said I. "As it stands right now, I am filled as an egg." "Is that so," said Aunt Bertrice. "Well then, young man, there is yet space for a bite because an egg is not full. But here is what I shall do. I would pack everything into two carrier bowls. When you get home, go over to your friend in the parlour and ask her to place them near the ice in her icebox. In the morning, take it and hot* same. Put whatever that can hold in your wide-mouth thermos for your lunch. The balance you can use as your tea." Ren at this point jokingly said, "Mother, you ought to be an economist."

I got home at 8:15 p.m. that evening; there was no one at home. So I went over to the parlour as Aunt Bertrice had suggested and asked the lady if I can be obliged the favour. "Surely," said she, and so I left the dishes. I got back home and made tidy, and as I lay on my bed, I began an inventory of my day. As I got to where I was accompanied out by Bob, his sister and cousin, I remembered Theo's slip of paper, which I had tucked away in my waistcoat. I at once reached for it and opened it. First, may I say, it was badly done in penmanship; nevertheless, it could be read. And thus it read: "George, will you please pardon me for this behaviour. I have heard Lidia saying so much of you which I found impossible to believe. But now, having met you for myself, I would certainly think that she has missed half of your sound qualities. George, I have not a boyfriend, for I had never fallen in love. Although I've been approached many times on the subject and think it to be all horse's feathers. Now, George, if you have not a girlfriend, will you consider us being friends? Say this to no one. You may reply to me at the following address in Marabella. No rush for a reply. Theo."

My heart did bubble with excitement as I smoothed and read the note three times. I felt myself important as I kept staring at the open bit of paper. I then reached for my portable looking glass, my comb and hairbrush. Looking at my reflection, I combed and brushed my hair, as I made a large part. There was then a click at the door, and so I knew that someone was about to enter. I quickly tucked the note into my pyjama pocket as I concealed the other articles. Grabbing my book, I stayed still and pretended to be reading. When the door was opened, both Weston and Stokely entered.

"George, you are not yet asleep," said Weston. "But I am going to right now," said I. "Hold it," said he. "I have got some goodies here. You may have some before turning in." "No, no, my good brother, I am filled. Besides, I have already brushed my teeth." Said Stokely, laughing, "I have not yet brushed mine." And so I prayed and got into bed.

Chapter 20

*George gets a promotion; he goes to town to buy new clothes,
visits his family and thinks of Theo*

Came Monday morning, as I went over to the parlour to collect my dishes, there were two fifty-pound blocks of ice lying on the pavement, left there by the ice man who came earlier. I took up a block and carried it into the parlour. "Oh, thank you," said the lady. "Jack was just about to pick them up. Leave the other; he would bring it in." She handed me my dishes. I thanked her as I left with the intent to carry out Aunt Bertrice's instructions.

I hot up and put the food into the thermos. I then had some and was off for work. I was the very first person to be on the site that morning. Within ten minutes came my friend who tried to belittle me the first Monday morning I came there. He greeted me with a warm handshake as he inquired how was my weekend. I was all surprised of this. (I found out later that guy was the timekeeper and field accountant.) By worktime, everyone with the exception of the architect was there.

That day, columns were to be casted, and my partner and I prepared to work once more as we did daily. Then came the foreman (my prospector friend) and said to us, "Oh no, not today, you two are not going to work together and expose the whole gang. Evasily, you come here," calling my partner away from me. He then asked me who in the gang will I like to work with. "Anyone who knows what he is doing," I replied. To my answer, the foreman smiled and asked Evasily the very question which he asked me. "Let me have Vincie," he said. The guy Vincie was a native of St Vincent, a strongly built guy with massive shoulders. "OK," said the foreman, laughing as he called to Vincie, "Come," said he, "you shall work with him today," and he sent him on to join me. He then said to Evasily, "Now you may pick another man for yourself." "Aw, aw," said Evasily, "that's not fair." I wondered at the wisdom of our foreman for in no way would I have thought of picking Vincie.

Together Vincie and I worked quite well, as we worked with the two "S's": strength and skill. When Vincie and I were soaking, Evasily and partner were just opening their drums of cement. We were able to begin casting the foundation of our columns as directed by the mason in charge before they began their mixing. By lunchtime, our three column foundations were filled. Donald then called me at lunchtime and said, "George, the real breakthrough is here, just keep your fingers crossed. Meet me at home after 6:00 p.m. I shall give you the full score."

The gang worked through the lunchtime hour together as a team, and the casting of all columns was completed by 5:00 p.m. The officials all seemed pleased. The architect walked over to the direction of where Evasily and I were both washing our barrows and shovels. I saw him coming from the corner of my eyes and pretended not to see him, so I quickly placed my shovel in the barrow and made my way to the tool shed. Vincie beat me with the hose for a quick wash. I tidied myself and was all ready to leave when I was summoned to the office. I wondered what it was all about, but I quickly remembered Donald had spoken to me. I walked into the office dressed in long khaki pants and a white long-sleeved shirt, sporting a cream armless pullover and wearing my white Raleigh canvas boots. And I had my thermos and work clothes in my handbag. I then stood before three gentlemen: Mr Lenette, the architect; Mr Bain (Donald), manager and company advisor; and Mr Advance, the general foreman. Mr Lenette then asked two other gents who were lazing around to leave.

I stood gazing into space. "What's your name?" asked Mr Lenette. Before I could have replied, "Wright," said Donald. "Oh, Mr Wright, do you think yourself capable of handling a storeroom and delivery clerk's work?" Again, before I could have made an answer, Donald spoke as he fixed me straight in the eyes, "On his performance here among the

CHAPTER TWENTY

working crew, I am sure he can handle that." Mr Advance then said, "I in no way question that. For what I have seen this fellow had been doing up to a short while ago, washing not only his shovel and barrow but that of others. Which is a duty called upon by one to do." I only blushed, for I had not to say a word. Mr Lenette then said, "Gentlemen, from next week Monday I shall be taking Mr Wright to hold the security and do the services of that post." Mr Advance again said, "Have no fear, for from what I have seen of this fellow he is hard-working and without fail. I am sure he can handle that." "Well," said Mr Lenette, "Mr Wright, I shall be giving you a try with two men next week to bring that place as it ought to be. OK, gentlemen, thank you," said he, glancing at his watch, "I have got another site to visit." And so he left.

Mr Advance then said to me, "I am very glad for you," as he closed the office windows. Donald said, "But the man is good." Mr Advance again said, as he rested his hand upon my shoulder, "Tomorrow tell no one, not even the timekeeper, about your new duties next week, understand?" "Yes, sir," I replied. And he jokingly added, "Don't you forget to send me good materials."

Donald then locked the office. Mr Advance, who rode a BSA motorcycle, whizzed off. Donald, who had a small Austin car, said, "George, where are you going from here?" "Nelson Street near the market." "OK," said he. "I shall drop you at the corner of Prince and Frederick Street." "That would be great," said I. As he drove, we chatted. "George," said he, "please don't let me be known. You would not be making any overtime, but your job will be a secured one. I shall try to see if you can at least get $7.00 a week, until better could be done." If I had been told $3.00 a month, I would have been satisfied.

I got off at Frederick and Prince Street corner. It was then raining, so I took shelter under the nearby pharmacy. As I waited, I wondered, "Am I dreaming, can this all be true?" The rain ceased, and so I walked to Nelson Street accompanied by dozens of thoughts. They were like those of fixing Tanty's house, to save a hundred dollars and buy a house of my own one day. To buy my own bicycle to go and see Yourland and his cousin Jack play football at the College. I also thought of buying

Frederick Street, Port of Spain, c. 1950s

some more nice clothes to go up to Toco and show off. By this time, I was standing right in front of Aunt Bertrice's door. I knocked as was my custom. I was welcomed by Aunt, who was at home. "How was your day?" she asked. "Did the food hold out good?" Both her questions were in one breath. "Yes, Auntie," I replied. "You have just missed Hilda. Come and eat." (The menu was stewed kingfish* Toco-style with corn coocoo.) I was tempted to tell her what was going to take place next week. But I then remembered what Mr Advance told me of not telling it to anyone. So I said that "anyone" must also include Sister Hilda and herself until the final moment.

Aunt Bertrice sat at table with me. "Don't feel embarrassed," said she. "No," said I, "I am just looking to see if some can be reserved for my lunch tomorrow." "Don't you worry about that, there is yet in the pots. And Lou do not like fish. I tell you what," said she, "before you leave, I shall heat everything to boiling point and place it in the thermos, so by your lunchtime tomorrow it would still be warm." After I ate and washed, she said to me, "Go lie down on the sofa. The *Gazette* is on the round table. Meanwhile, I shall hot the food for your thermos."

CHAPTER TWENTY

I left at 7:30 p.m. I walked and was at home at 8:10 p.m. When I entered into the house, there were no lights on, and I heard a loud snoring. As I checked, it was Weston. He apparently came home early. I noiselessly made my movements, prayed and got into my bed. I lay upon my back with a somewhat reminiscent feeling of the past day. My thoughts focused on Theo. I began to wonder why and what led her to pick me, an ex-yard boy. Was it the way she saw me spending money? She was a very pretty girl, and I knew for a fact that I was far from being handsome. Two things I knew I had to my advantage: I was very strong and fearless, and I loved to look smart in my attire.

I pondered about seeing her again. And so I decided to have a chat with Bob and Lidia about her whereabouts and to know truthfully whether she had a boyfriend or not. Next, should I write to her? What must I say? And so in my wild thoughts I remembered one day Uncle was having a fight with Tanty, when she remarked, "Bishop, the birds in the air first build themselves a nest before seeking a mate. But man first look for a mate before having a hut." Then I knew not what she meant. But here was I now confronted with her parable. I then turned on my side and fell asleep.

The next day at work Evasily greeted me by saying, "Well, boy, I did not think that I would have seen you here this morning. Because I saw the big wheels grinding with you yesterday evening. Even the timekeeper was concerned. We both waited outside for about ten minutes before leaving." "Evasily," said I, "they want to get some more hard-working men as you are to speed up production. The work is moving much too slow." "Don't come wid dat to me, you too damn smart; it have something in de mortar beside the pestle."

The other days that I worked, all eyes, with the exception of those of Donald and Mr Advance, were set upon me. I worked harder and with more skill because I had then to prepare myself for my own office.

I told Donald that I wanted half-day off on Friday, letting him know why. He agreed. But said he, "George, you can have the day. But as a matter of principle tell it to Mr Advance and let him come to me." I did approach Mr Advance on the subject, who said to me, "Wright, a fellow like you can get a day off with pay, but let me first talk it over with Mr Bain." He then went into the office and was back as he said to me, "OK, OK, Wright, when do you want it, morning or evening?" "Morning, sir." "OK, it is all yours," said he.

The Friday morning, I visited the bank, and for the very first time, I made a withdrawal of $18.00, which was quite a large sum. I went to the very store where Mr Otchin worked. The employees' eyes were all glued upon me. Some showed happiness, others disdain. I was attired in black shoes (once given to me by Mr Otchin himself), black serge pants, white Sea Island long-sleeved cotton shirt (Arrow Brand), a long black tie, and an armless V-cut grey pullover as I sported an Adam hat*.

I went to Mr Otchin. "Good morning, sir," said I. "Yes," he replied without looking at me. "I will like to buy a few things." "As what?" he sharply replied. "Shirts and . . ." Before I could have uttered another word, he said, "Go over there to Mr David." I walked across to Mr David's shirt department. Someone had apparently pointed me out to the proprietor of the store, Mr John, who was an Englishman. He walked seemingly unconcernedly to Mr David's department, but I first got to Mr David. "Good morning, sir," said I with a bow, tipping my hat. "Good morning, sonny," he replied. He remembered me quite well coming with Mr Otchin's lunch. And if there was an occasion that he should speak to me, it was always done in a kindly manner. Mr David was now confronted with Mr John, the owner, and I, a seeming customer. "Go ahead, Mr David," said Mr John, "see what he wants." Mr David now being more relaxed said to me, "Oh, George, you do look smart. I have not seen you here for quite some weeks." "Yes, I do know that, sir," said I. "But I am now here to purchase a few things, sir." (Mr John then turned his back to us, but I knew that he was listening, so I spoke in a manner by which the sound wave could reach him clearly.) I told Mr David that I wanted two pairs of white short pants, two pairs of khaki short pants, two short-sleeved khaki shirts, a long tie nearest to khaki colour, two white ties, one cork hat white, one cork hat khaki, two pairs of high white socks, two pairs of khaki-coloured high socks, one pair of brown boots, one pair of white buff shoes, and three gent's

CHAPTER TWENTY

handkerchiefs in mild colours. (I asked not for white shirts because I already had some.) "Any particular quality?" asked Mr David. "Well, sir, they are for me to work in daily, not the best but at least something that shall look good and lasting." "Oh, I see," said he, "leave it all to me." Mr John then slowly walked to another department without uttering a word to Mr David.

All items were sorted according to my fit from their departments. Mr David then said, "Son, do you have enough money?" "I do believe so, sir," I replied. "First, let me check them for you on a piece of paper before writing the bill." And so he did. "That would be $15.75," said he. "Have you that amount?" "Yes, sir." He then said, "I can give you discount on all items except the footwear and hats. Let me check with Mr Otchin," said he, "to see what he can give you." Very quickly he returned. "Mr Otchin said that prices of those items are already reduced to rock bottom," and he added, "Son, I am so sorry." He again made another check and said, "Son, you would pay $14.57."

As the items were all taken to the counter for payment, Mr John came and said, "Let me see that, Mr David." "Sonny," said Mr John to me, "you have made quite a purchase." He then told the cashier to receive $10.00 for everything as he himself signed the bill. "Thank you very much, sir," said I to Mr John as I bowed and tipped my hat. Mr David showed much delight on his countenance at my gesture. Mr Otchin walked to the counter and looked at the items as they were being parcelled. There were then three other customers awaiting to be dispatched. Mr Otchin then said to me, "Boy, you did not come and collect the part of your monthly wage that I owed you last month. Just see and come for it at the end of this month." He said it to me in a very mean and sarcastic manner which hurt my pride and dignity. This was not because of the store's working staff that were around and hearing him, but because of the three customers that were awaiting to be dispatched. My tongue then became loosened as if it was unfolded by some unseen force. "Sir," said I, "this is no place and time to discuss such domestic matters, and in any case I had no intention of coming to collect a dollar for ten days' work, which I know will make you happy with a bottle of Ferdi's

Rum. Thank you very much, however, for yet being so mindful," said I to him with a smile. I then took my packages, and with a bow I said thanks to Mr David and Mr John and walked out. I was back at home by 10:00 a.m. and rested the packages down, and I was then back on the job by 10:45 a.m.

Mr Advance came and said, "I thought you wanted half-day, young man." "Yes, sir, but I got through with my affairs quickly and easily. So I thought it not fair to laze around." He then said, "Go in and see Mr Bain," while he followed behind me. "Well, you are back," Donald said to me. "Change and fall in with the gang – you may work with anybody you want to." I went and looked at the guys at work, and I joined with the weakest of them. They were completing the casting of a beam. As we were fully in action, Mr Lenette came and said he wanted me at Contract #3 at Centeno with him. "We shall be back," said he, "by 1:30 p.m." I again quickly changed. At this point, I could have seen how happy Donald and Mr Advance were that I had returned.

Mr Lenette was not a careful driver to me. He took wild chances on the road. Occasionally he spoke, but due to his heavy cockney accent, I understood not everything he said. But whatever I understood I tried to make a conversation of it. When we got to Contract #3 site, he showed me the type of material needed for that job next Monday. He also spoke of the tools to be sent and warned that a keen check must be made on replacements. When he had finished the survey of some excavation, he said, "Mr Wright, come, let's get back to town," as he glanced at his watch. We were back at Bishop's at 1:15 p.m. He dropped me at the gate without coming in as he muttered something about lunch. Donald and Mr Advance were very much surprised to see me then. I told them what it was all about. Mr Advance then whispered something to Donald, who said to me, "Don't you worry to change again, you may take the evening off. And remember tomorrow is payday."

I then went over to the shed to collect my thermos and work clothes. Evasily said to the other workers, "Fellars, yuh see wot ah does tell all – yuh now see fuh yuhself, class is class." To this, I only smiled and left for home. I had then $7.00 of my own plus $8.00, the remainder

CHAPTER TWENTY

after spending from my bank withdrawal. When I got home, I decided to catch up with some reading. As I took the book, a thought came to me. Why not go down to the bank and put back at least $10.00 into the damaged account? And so I left. I had intended to walk down, but as I got to the Circular, there came a tram bounding its way for Charlotte Street. I boarded and was quickly set in front of the bank.

On entering I said to myself, "Tomorrow will be payday. Why not put $12.00 instead of $10.00?" Mr Walk, the manager, knew me. I very often referred to him as "Mr Pickwick," a character in Charles Dickens's novel *The Pickwick Papers*, due to a tightly fitted waistcoat that he wore. Mr Walk spoke to his staff authoritatively, "Come on! Come on!" said he. "Someone come and serve this gentleman." I was now no longer treated as a kid but as an adult. Although he barked the order, yet he himself came to me. "Son," said he, smiling. "I have seen that you are back again. What can I do to help you?" A feeling of dignity crept over me. "Well, sir," I replied, "I withdrew $18.00 this morning. I had not to use the whole amount, so I am now depositing back $12.00." "Very good," said he to me in a fatherly manner and also that of a shrewd businessman. "Let me see about it." Those were the days customers had not to queue; one just pushed their way through without any form of discipline. Very quickly, he was back with my deposit book.

I had yet $5.00 as spending money. I had not a watch, so I therefore thought of making myself a gift of one, especially for my new appointment on Monday morning. A little way down Charlotte Street was a very popular watch repair and dealer shop. When I got there, I was shown a very nice luminous wristwatch for $3.00. "Will you take $2.50?" I asked the gent. He looked at me and said, "Make it $2.75." "No," said I and turned away. "OK, OK, $2.50," said he, and so I bought my first wristwatch.

As I winded my way down through the busy street heading for Aunt Bertrice's home, on nearing the market there was a butcher selling beef on a table outside a gateway entrance. "Sir," said he. "Kindly give me a sale; the market will soon be closed for the day. Take some home for your mother." I quickly made a survey of his table. There were heaps of beef stew at six cents each, oxtail cuts for twelve cents. But I got interested in some T-bone steak and roast mixed at eighteen cents. I immediately asked for two heaps, along with two heaps of stew.

I had not a bag, but the butcher wrapped it all up in some white paper which he had under the table. "Please watch for me," said he. And he quickly went across the street to a Chinese shop and was back with a handbag. He then placed everything into this bag. I paid him his two shillings (forty-eight cents) and was off to Aunt Bertrice. On my way, I began wondering if I had not greedily bought too much meat because she had not an icebox. (Fridges were a luxury in those days, and they were owned mainly by the upper classes.) As I got to the house, I knocked. "OK, come in, George." When I entered, there was Aunt Bertrice all in smiles. "From the time I heard that knock, I knew it was you," said she as we exchanged greetings.

"How come you to be so early?" she asked. "I was given time off," said I as I handed her the bag. "What's all this?" said she as she nervously unwrapped the packages. The first was the stew, but when she opened the steak and roast, she looked alarmed. "Where did you get all this beef?" she asked. I told her of my bargain. "Oh yes, from Mr Frank," said she. "I do buy from him; he is quite a gentleman. But, but this is far too much beef," she stuttered. "Oh no, Auntie," said I, "don't you remember the Bible says, 'Meats are for the belly and the belly is for meats'?" said I, laughing. "How come I have not seen that quotation in the Bible?" said she. "Oh," said I, "you would find it in 1 Corinthians 6:13."

Then came Sister Hilda. "Well, folks," said she, "what's going on? What happen here? The beef market move or what? By the way, what are you doing here so early? Why aren't you at work?" Before I could have made a reply to any of her questions, Aunt Bertrice said, "The boss took time off." "What do you mean time off? In his type of work, one is not given time off, don't let him fool you." I still kept back the secret, but I told them of the other matters. At this, Aunt Bertrice said, "Say what you want, but I strongly believe, besides God, your father's spirit is with you." They both finally decided to share the meats, Hilda taking part of her portion to Cousin Vera. I then had my regular meal, taking

CHAPTER TWENTY

no extra portion for the next day, Saturday, when we worked half-day.

Come Saturday morning when I went on the job, I was sent to dig some postholes for the erection of a galvanize fence which divided the property on the southern side. A carpenter was sent with me to lay out the distance between the holes. He told me Mr Advance said I was to dig at least ten holes. Eighteen holes were really required for the complete distance on a ground that was unbaked and tough and I wasted no time as I dug away as an agouti. I timed myself, and at eleven that morning I had dug not only ten holes but fourteen. On my sixteenth hole, Mr Advance came over and said to me, "George, I had quite forgotten that you were here. Who is working with you?" "I am alone, sir," I replied. And he walked in line of the dug holes, looking quite perplexed as he counted. "I can't believe this," he muttered, as he walked back to the office. I continued my digging.

The carpenter then came. "Boy," said he to me, "ah see de big-boots harassing you, whot happen?" "No one is harassing me," said I, "they came to see how the holes were being dug." He looked at the area. "Oh me gosh," said he, "yuh finish all ah dem. I can't believe dat," as he looked at me in amazement. As he stood looking, I went over to the dump and gathered eighteen cement drum covers. I returned and covered the holes from being filled by rain or the scratching of dogs over the weekend.

I went back to the shed shouldering my spade and lushet*. I washed and placed them in the storeroom. May I say also those were the days of labour caste. Very few tradesmen spoke kindly to a labourer on the job. But here in my case everyone wanted to be my friend. It was just past noon when Mr Advance called me and said, "I see that you have covered the holes, that's a very good idea. Go to the paymaster and collect your wage, and you can be off." After I collected my pay, being the first to do so, I got changed and took off. I was paid $7.00, so I had now $9.00. As the bank was yet open, I hurried down and made a deposit of $5.00. I had yet $4.00 with which to play around. I had not now to purchase any groceries, for very little had been used from my first shopping.

Weston and I had spoken of together scrubbing the floor of our home. But I decided to undertake the task all by myself. I bought a cake of blue Gossage's soap for a penny and a pint of disinfectant for three cents. Having got a piece of coconut fibre, I got down on the job. When the task was almost finished, all three guys came in. They were glad that it was done. One of them said, however, that it was late and it will not dry off before sundown. So we slept that night with the doors and windows open. That also helped to control the smell of the disinfectant.

Came Sunday morning, I got up, prayed, bathed, and got dressed into my doeskin flannel pants, blue serge blazer, white buff shoes, and sporting a Panama hat. I again made my way to the Roman Catholic Cathedral to give thanks to God for my new job on Monday. I again could not understand what was said by the priest, so I prayed to God in His way and left. I then went over to Aunt Bertrice. "Boy, you do read people's mind or practice obeah or something. Hilda left just a moment ago. She came to let me know that your Aunt Rache is not at all well and it would be nice if we three could have visited her today, providing that you have no other plan." She also added, "But, George, you do look smart." "Thank you," said I. I then said to her that I had already been to church, and I see it to be no problem following them. "That would be nice," said Aunt Bertrice. "Hilda will be passing again to take that package she left there. So we can then arrange the time."

"Where is Ren?" I asked. "Ren is on duty today," Lou told me. "He was going to the Queen's Park Savannah to watch the horses exercise." I took my coat off, sat and scanned the pages of the *Gazette*. Aunt came by and said, "Take your shoes off and make yourself comfortable on the sofa. I shall wake you up when Hilda comes." I lay with my face towards the wall, as I then thought of my new appointment tomorrow. Then thought I of Theo's wish that I must answer her letter and also of how Tanty was doing in Toco. And so I fell asleep. At 12:10 p.m. I was promptly awakened by Aunt Bertice. "Come now to eat," said she. "Hilda is in the kitchen." And so I went and greeted my smiling sister who was so dear to me. She looked at me and said, "George, you are hiding something from us. But don't you worry yourself, little brother,

CHAPTER TWENTY

let's eat." The roast was prepared like that for a Christmas dinner. And we three had our fill. Hilda, who was already dressed, strung an apron on and washed the dishes. I helped in drying as Aunt busied herself for the trip.

We were on our way to the bus stand when a taxicab man saw us and shouted, "San Juan, Tunapuna." There were two passengers who shared the front seat with him. "No, no," said Aunt. "Yes, sir," I shouted. "Boy," said she to me, "you spend too freely." As we reached the corner of the then newly made Morvant Old Road and Eastern Main Road, we disembarked and made our way to Aunt Rache's home. She was overjoyed to see us. More so, she expressed how happy she was to see me. "Crecy," said she, "every time I hear about you I do feel happy. The fact is you are as ambitious and hard-working as your father Georgie was. You are as good as he was and also just as wicked." Aunt Bertrice at this point said, "Oh no, Georgie was never a wicked man." "Why not shut your mouth," said Aunt Rache. "Can't you remember the time he stewed the tom cat for Ophela, who always wanted 'ready done' wild meat from him for nothing? Come close," said she to me. As I went at her bedside, "Come," said she, "let me kiss you upon your cheek." That kiss turned out to be a very quick but harmless bite. "I had that for you," she laughed.

"Can you remember the very first April day you spent down here with us? You sent me down to the market, saying the children's father sent down some ground provisions by Mr Nathan's truck, and he said that I must come to collect them. When I got there, the man knew nothing of what I was speaking. Only then did I realize it was All Fools' Day." Everyone in the room shared in the joke. "Wait a minute," said she, "that's not all. Mrs Archer, our neighbour, will always call him to weed her yard but will not offer him a penny. She also had a mango doodoos* tree in her yard. Whenever they were full, she would call him to pick some for her to sell and not offer him a single one. For this one night he climbed the tree and cleaned it with Cecilst and Bob. Mrs Archer nearly dead! All-yuh watch him good. Don't you ever think he is easy. Just get him vex you, then will see who he is."

Then in came Cousin Maze, whom I had not seen for quite a while. As the older folks chatted, we held our own conversation. I told Maze a little of how my life was going on. I also mentioned about seeing Theo. "Oh," said she, "that stuck-up. I just don't know who she thinks she is. She just don't like speaking to people. She suffers with a complex. Just imagine she has no friends, neither boy or girl. Only Lidia and some other girl with whom she went to school. Cecilst and Lou went all out to be her friends, but she treated them with disdain. Let her haul herself with her sophisticated high nose. Boy, George, don't you take on them so. By the way, did she speak to you?" "Very little," I replied. But now deep in my heart I concluded that Theo was the friend for me without a doubt.

Maze then said, "George, let me go over to the parlour and get you folks something." "Can I come?" I asked. "Yes," she replied. When we got there, there was no one in sight to attend. Maze then called, "Lin! Lin!" Then came from behind a curtain a smiling Chinese woman. Before Maze could have spoken, "Good day," said I. "Will you please give me six sweet drinks, six sponge cakes*, a penny ice and one tin of Nestle condensed milk." The items were all quickly placed on the counter. "That's all?" asked Lin, inquiringly looking at Maze. "No, nothing else," said she. The attendant then placed everything into a small basket and said to Maze, "You can bring back the basket whenever you have time. Everything will be fifty cents," said she, fixing her eyes upon me. I paid up. As we left, Maze held the basket. "Boy, George, you are something else," said she. "But why buy six? Is only five of us." "The other is should there be another visitor." When we got back to the house, Maze had the drinks all mixed and served. As we chatted, I made no enquiry about her mom's and Mr Williams's lives. Neither did she mention anything about it.

Aunt Bertrice then signalled it was time to leave and so we did at 5:30 p.m. When we got to the Main Road, Hilda said, "Now, young man, no more taxi, we are travelling by bus." And so when a bus came rolling by, we took it and paid nine cents. When we got to Aunt's home, Lou was fast asleep. Ren had left a note saying he was out and will be back

CHAPTER TWENTY

at 7:00 p.m. As we three sat relaxing, Sister Hilda said, "Look out for his big-day surprise tomorrow." By this I was now positive that she knew something of my new appointment the next day. But I still held my peace. She then followed me to catch my tram for home.

There was no one at home when I got there, so I hurriedly undressed and without a bath I prayed and slumped into my bed. Not being overpowered by sleep, I laid on my back trying hard to solve how did Sister Hilda know of my new job. After a while, I arrived at this answer: Donald must have told Mrs Otchin, who passed it on to Miss Laura, who in turn told it to Cousin Vera, who of course told it to Sister Hilda. And I was right.

Chapter 21

George learns to dress smartly and moves to a "plush" bungalow;
Plum, his mother, leaves Toco to live with him

The next day being one of the most important of my life in town, I was up at 5:00 a.m. I asked the good Lord for His blessings and guidance. I then made myself a pot of porridge for breakfast and lunch. I had then a well-deserved bath, after which I attired myself in my new outfit of white. As I was stealing my way out, Stokely got up. "Waw, waw! Don't tell me that you have joined the Marines or something." Quildon and Weston immediately got out of bed. "What happening, boy George?" asked Quildon. "Nothing," said I. "How nothing?" said Weston. "Don't come with that," said he, laughing. "Well, fellars," said I, "I am supposed to start in a new department of my work this morning. I do not know how it will all work out. However, when I get back this evening, God's will, I shall let you all know what happen." I then glanced at my watch, which read 7:05 a.m., and so I left. As I was nearing the parlour, the proprietor began to clear her throat with the teasing sound of "Caehem, caehem". I knew it was an invitation of greetings. "Good morning," said I with a bow. "Good morning," she replied and added, "had I been a younger woman, I certainly would have felt elite being in your company this morning." We exchanged smiles.

I boarded a tramcar bound for St Vincent Street and was on the Bishop's High School compound at 7:35 a.m. Just as I was about to ask a question of someone, Mr Lenette drove in and called me. "I hoped to

CHAPTER TWENTY-ONE

be here before you," said he. "Wright, just let me park my car." When he came back to me, he said, "Wright, you look rather smart. Let me show you to the warehouse." As we got there, two men in their late thirties were standing at the gate. "Good morning, Bass," said they as we passed by; no reply was made from either of us. Mr Lenette then took me to a large wooden building with iron bars upon the door and two large, galvanized padlocks. He held a bunch of keys, and without searching through them, he unlocked both padlocks as the two men came hustling to open the huge wooden doors.

The air was foul, and about a dozen bats flew over our heads. There were many drums of cement, paints and lumber. Mr Lenette then led me to a separate room with all sorts of building materials that were disorderly stored. He then said to the two men who followed us, "Stand here and let no one in." He then walked me to an adjacent building which lay right opposite to the warehouse. As we entered, "Well, Wright," said he, "here is your office." In this office there was a desk, two chairs, a long bench, and at the far corner two very large bottles encased with plaited vines. Upon the desk there were two ledgers, a notebook, a desk calendar, two steel pens, an ink pot, a sheet of blotting paper, a lead pencil, and an eraser. "Well," said he, "Mr Wright, you shall be operating from here. Please be watchful and let no one have access unless with permission from Mr Bain or myself. We are constructing many buildings right now. Written orders will be directed to you for materials and equipment; therefore, at no time must anything be delivered without a signed order. And a delivery note would be made by you," said he, pulling a drawer of the desk and handing me a delivery notebook. "Each contract will be sending you their order with a code, and in making your delivery note, always mention that code before having it signed by the bearer. It is the policy of the department. Also let the bearer have the duplicate copy, never your original. I have my reason for this," said he. "Every noon you would take your delivery notebook with orders to be checked by my secretary. The same exercise must be done at 3:30 p.m., which must be done daily. Should I be out and you should run into any problem that my secretary cannot handle, she would then refer your case to

Mr George Wright" ("your namesake," said he with a smile) "who would give the solution. Do you understand?" "Yes, sir," said I.

As Mr Lenette was leaving, someone came with an order from Contract #4. "Ah," said he, "let me see you attend to this one." (The order called for Celotex, paints, nails and strips.) "Me oh my, I almost forgot to let you know those two men are there to assist you. You do not have to get the materials out for yourself." I went to the storeroom, and I wrote on two slips of paper what I wanted each man to bring out and added, "You may assist each other." From the corner of my eyes I saw Mr Lenette looking at me, but he said nothing. When they had gotten the items out, I rechecked and handed them back the slips, telling them at the end of each day I require that the slips be given to me. I then made out my delivery note and called the clerk to sign and take away the items.

"Oh," said Mr Lenette, "Mr Wright, I've quite forgotten there are animal-drawn carts on the street that do the transportation of same, which is charged to us. Send the clerk or let one of the men go and call one in. To each one destination you enter into the blue-covered ledger and let him sign same, and every Friday evening the ledger you must take to my secretary upstairs for payments." The clerk, knowing the procedure, did not wait, but went and got himself a cart. When the complete delivery was made and as the cart rolled off, Mr Lenette said, "Mr Wright, it will seem as though you have been doing this work for years." As he left for his office, the thought came very quickly that I can bring Mr Williams here to work. I then went and looked on the street. There I counted eight carts all lined up. So I returned to my post with high hopes of bringing Mr Williams here.

I had not very long to wait when two other clerks from Contracts #10 and #5 came in for materials. I had now no problems after having been coached with the order of Contract #4. I took their orders while they verbally rehearsed what they wanted. Once again, I wrote it down on slips and handed it to my attendants. "Go and have your carts lined up, please," said I to the clerks. As they left, I called my attendants. "What's your names?" I asked. "Fred, Mr Wright," said one. "John, Mr

CHAPTER TWENTY-ONE

Wright," said the other. I wondered how did they know my name, but I quickly recalled that they heard Mr Lenette speaking to me. "Let me see your slips again," said I. After looking at them, I observed that #5 had less items. "You both work on this together, never mind #10 was here a little before #5. Let's get rid of the smaller amount first." "Alright, sir," said they, and off they went.

Now I knew nothing of how and where the items were stored. I had then to learn from my attendants without letting them know that I was a complete novice. Very quickly they had the items ready. And so the clerk came up with a mule-drawn cart. "Your items are all out; let me make your delivery note," said I. Meanwhile Fred and John had gone working on the order for #10. I made the delivery note, and we both checked the items. He seemed pleased as I made him sign it. I gave him the copy, keeping the original as instructed. As I turned away, he said to me, "What about loading?" "Oh yes," said I, "as soon as Fred and John are ready with the order that they are now working on." He looked downcast and fully disappointed. He then called to the carter and said, "The load is all ready as you can see, but you would have to hold on as the porters are now working on another order." The carter then said, "Can I not load the items that I can handle alone?" "Yes," said I to him. And so he began while the concerned clerk stood lackadaisically staring into space with folded arms. I thereupon went over to the cart and called to my gentleman friend. "Let's give this fellow a hand," I said to him. "There are two drums of cement to be loaded." He gave a resentful response. But before he could have uttered a word, my hands were on a drum in readiness to load. He gave me a disgruntled look. But somehow the carter seemed to be pleased as we three then loaded the barrels. I then let the carter sign my ledger, and they left.

As the cart jolted off, Fred and John came and asked, "Sir, how did you get that man to work? Don't matter what pressure we may be under, that man would not put a little finger. We were surprised to see him work this morning." Earnestly I listened to them, but I made no comment. I asked, "How are you both getting on with the order?" "It is finished," they replied, "but we are in a bit of a jam with space to roll out the cement."

"How then did you get the two drums out?" "They were at the entrance since last week Friday," said Fred. "OK," said I. Just then the clerk for Contract #10 came up with this cart. "Oh, boy," said he. "Lennox gone already. How my materials moving?" "Yours are finished; it is only the cement to roll out," said John. "Oh goodness," said he, "let me go and stop Mr Antoine, he has gone to give his horse molasses water and bran." Jokingly I said, "You may hurry him but please not the horse." The clerk looked at me and nodded in approval of my remark.

Then came the cart hauled by a steady old chestnut mare. The load was an assortment of cement, galvanize, lumber, steel rods and three wheelbarrows. Having checked and given his delivery note, as he walked off Mr Lenette came. "Please let me see both the order and delivery notes for these materials," said he. Readily I made him his request. Mr Lenette checked not the items on the loaded cart but looked only at written notes. He then said to the clerk, whose name was Ted, "You may leave." I had the carter sign the ledger for the load, and off they went. I then strolled into the warehouse. There was Fred and John in apparent high spirits, talking about Lennox and how he had to work. I yet pretended to throw a deaf ear on what was being said.

"Well, fellows," said I, "this place is in a mess. I am not at all concerned as to who had it this way. But it shall now be kept in my way. It will not all be done at one time, but with a little effort each day, it shall all be done." "Yes, sir," came a ready reply. I then walked through making a survey. There were pipe fittings strewn upon the floor, bolts and nuts of all sizes lying like stones and pebbles, cans of paint disorderly arranged, galvanize and Celotex lying and standing here and there with dents, broken edges, and foot marks. To be precise, the only articles that were well stacked were the lumber. "Oh no," said I, "this will not do. Shelves would be set up for paints and pipe fittings. All articles of its kind will be placed in one area, leaving a free pathway to get at them with a hand barrow. All implements will be properly stored in the room for a quick dispatch. Come on, come on," said I, "this place must be cleaned up." Fred, the elder of the two, said, "Sir, have no fear. We wid yuh," as John supported him in his remark.

CHAPTER TWENTY-ONE

No sooner had I reached my office when a hurried John came to me and said, "Sah, look dey now bring in 'reton'." I knew not of what he spoke. However, I followed him to the direction of an ass-drawn cart which was accompanied by a clerk who said that they were from Contract #7. The cart was packed with an assortment of used and unused building materials.

"Good morning," said I to both clerk and carter. "What have you here?" Now Mr Lenette said nothing to me about returned materials from jobs. So I had then to do some quick thinking. "Where is the slip for these?" I asked. "These are old junks," said the clerk. "So you need no slips." "Well," said I, "if they are old junks, why bring them here? Why not have them taken to the La Basse?" Fred then said, "Bass, all those things are stow way in de back." As the cart was offloaded, I made them call aloud the items that were taken off, and I entered same into the notebook. We were now in the luncheon break and so I sent them off.

At 1:00 p.m. I went to the storeroom only to be greeted with a most wonderful surprise. Fred and John had swept a large portion of the floor and rearranged that section so very nicely; I could not have done a better job. I had in mind to ask Donald for Evasily and Vincie to work with me. But I was now fully satisfied that both these guys were out to pull their weight. I passed the slips to John, who read and passed them on to Fred. Only then did I ask the question, "When was this place cleaned?" "During our lunch break," they replied. Fred said, "We ate our lunch before in order to start cleaning to make it look like something." I told them how very satisfied I was.

At 3:30 p.m. Mr Lenette came. "How did it all go today, Mr Wright?" "Good, sir," I replied. "Did you receive any more orders?" "Yes, sir, one from Bishop's Contract #2." At this he looked at me and smiled. "Also from Contract #7 I received some used materials, a few pieces unused, and some tools." "Me oh my," said he, "what did you do about that?" "I had my helpers stack it in the back, and secured the tools in the shed. I also made the clerk sign a piece of paper for what was brought." I then showed him my notebook and records made in the ledger. "Very good," said he. "However, there is a book upstairs for that record. My secretary will show you how it is to be dealt with." He then went through the delivery notebook with orders received. After which, as I had hoped, he walked into the storeroom. I followed, and he said not a single word as he scratched his crown and left. I was most disappointed.

Having carried out Mr Lenette's instructions, after work that evening I went to see Mr Williams at his home. Lidia had just come in from her sewing classes, also Bob who was now doing joinering trade. They all loved my outfit. I then explained how it all came about. I also asked Mr Williams if he would like to join the rank of waiting carts. "No, George," said he, "over there is too slow, and the carters do not all work as friends." At that very moment a thought came to me. I asked him should he hear of a nice little room or a plot of land to let me know. "Good boy," he said, "I shall work on that." I then bade them good evening, promising to see them for the weekend as I left for Aunt Bertrice.

When I got there, again everyone was happy to see my attire. Aunt said she was growing disturbed not seeing me earlier, for it was now 6:30 p.m. Needless to mention, Sister Hilda was there also. "Well, well," said she, "did I not say that I knew well the big secret!" To this I laughed. "By the way, how come only now you are here?" I then told of my visit to Mr Williams and my idea of the room. "Would you believe this?" said Aunt Bertrice. "I strongly felt so when I did not see you earlier." Ren again said to me, "George, I really do like your outfit." I had my meal, and as it was growing into the late hours of the evening, I said I was leaving because I also wanted to catch up with some reading. Sister Hilda said that she was also leaving. "Why now?" asked Aunt Bertrice. "To let the people see that I am walking with a young respectable handsome gentleman!" To this Lou laughed aloud. "Did you say handsome?" he scoffed. Nevertheless, my sister followed me to catch my tram.

That night I had a very good sleep and was up very early the next morning. I did my chores, bathed, and attired myself in my khaki outfit and left for work. On my arrival, John was already there, followed by Fred fifteen minutes later. We three continued the resetting of the storeroom that morning at 7:10 a.m. At 8:15 Mr Lenette came and openly said he really liked what we were doing. "But let the path to the cement

CHAPTER TWENTY-ONE

be much wider so that the men who pulled the cart would be able to manoeuvre." (In those days there were human-drawn carts from the docks with cement and lumber to take to the leading hardware stores of the city.)

That day, four orders came in and were attended to. At 3:30 p.m. Mr Lenette himself came in. He checked the "D/Ns" (delivery notes) and himself took them upstairs. Now for my own record I used the next ledger. I ruled and made margins and headed it somewhat like what Mr Otchin did in some discarded ledgers where he kept record of his pigeons just before I worked with him. And so I did to every item that arrived or left.

The work flowed well that week, and there was an understanding with Fred, John and myself. We together handled all the heavy manual work, and I let them know my likes and dislikes, putting it to them in this way. "The man who works on the job, I like. The guy who is sick on the job, I dislike. If you are straightforward, I will go with you. For backwards one goes crooked. No slack conversation. By them, others lose you your respect. When one is punctual and mindful of time, jobs are easier to handle." "Sar," said Fred, "yuh is yong but smart."

I gradually began to familiarize myself and be known in the other departments of the company, some of which I had to pay an occasional visit on behalf of my building department. Among them were a sawmill, hardware and building supplies stores, a foundry, a machine shop, a marine and boatbuilding department, an ice factory and cold storage, a lime kiln, and a lawnmower shop that I knew of. With the exception of the lime kiln, these holdings were all housed on one large acreage of land.

Gradually our contracts came to a completion. And due to World War Two that was now raging, we were faced with a business downturn. The Bishop's wing was completed, and Mr Bain (Donald) was now fully in charge of our building department. Quite a lot of renovations were carried out on homes in the elite districts; here and there repairs were done to business places. But then in my small mind of thinking, profits could only be made with big contracts.

A BRANCH TO REST ON

During this period, may I say, I had separated myself from my brothers and their friend. I had taken up residence in a plush little bungalow on Parris Boulevard West in Success Village, Laventille. The good old Mr Williams had gotten it for me. The rent was manageable, but the property was not fenced. I asked Mr Bain if I could have some used materials from renovated buildings. "Sure," said he, "only pay your own cartage." (May I now also mention that I was being paid a tidy salary of $8.00 weekly, from which I saved $4.50 weekly. So I had then no money problem.)

I did get several cartloads of material: used galvanize sheeting, one-inch chicken wire, used wooden posts, boards and laths, and even three old wrought-iron gates. And, to crown it all, I had not even to pay cartage because Mr Antoine, the carter with the old chestnut mare, lived up that very way. And by helping me he found it easy to help himself. Also, without my asking him, he volunteered with two of his friends to help me enclose the property without taking a farthing. With the bulk of used materials I also built a chicken house and a pigsty, as it was my intention to do some backyard farming. When the work was all completed, there were lots of materials lying on the ground. So I shared it with the two guys and one of my neighbours.

One evening after dinner with Aunt Bertrice, my sister Hilda said to me, "George, what I have been hoping for years has finally come to reality." "What's that?" I asked. "Mother has decided to leave Toco and come to live in town." "That's very good," said I. "Yes," said she, "but there is now a problem." "Problem!" said I. "What can that be?" "Well, as you know, I am now married and will be choked for room space." "Well," said I, "Sis, problems are no good." (I then recalled Mr Otchin once told me that worries kill.) "Sis, you may now be married, but I am not. There is more than enough room space at my home to accommodate our mother." "Oh, George," said she, embracing me, "that's why I love you." I then went on to say, "Let Georgiana and herself come and live in the house." (At that time Georgiana lived at Hilda's home.) "I can repair the kitchen in the back and live there." "That's an idea, but it may be too costly. Remember the place right now lacks furniture. And

CHAPTER TWENTY-ONE

it must be furnished with certain accommodations." "That's true, Sis, but it shall all be taken care of. Listen," said I, "how about us meeting here at 5:00 p.m. tomorrow and run this matter over?" Aunt Bertrice, who said not a word during our discussion, responded, "Boy, you do speak like a wise old man." And Sister Hilda readily agreed.

The following evening I was there at 4:50 p.m. Sister Hilda was there also. "Well, boy," said she, "concerning time, you are something else." "Yes," said Aunt Bertrice, "he is like 'Big Ben', you can count on that with him." Without a further conversation, I handed an envelope to Sister Hilda. "What's this?" she asked. "Open and see," said I. She gave me a second look. "Come on, open it. Let's see what is in it." Hilda then tore it open clumsily. A few bills fell to the floor as some remained in her hand. "Oh my gosh," said someone, as I picked up the fallen notes. "Eighty dollars," said Hilda, "what's all this for?" "It is for you to furnish the house." Inquiringly she looked at me. "Boy, you are mad! Half of this will be enough. Should any more be needed, I shall add it," said she. Aunt Bertrice then said, "Hold it, wait a while. Won't you have to get some things for his bachelor's room outside when it is fixed?" "No, Auntie, I have yet my cot, table and two chairs. Plus my shelf wardrobe and trunk. Please keep the money and see what can be done." "OK," said Sister Hilda, "I shall pass in at Mongoose and Little Goose tomorrow and see what bargains I can strike on some second-hand furniture." "In fact, we shall both go," said Aunt Bertrice.

Chapter 22

A household of furniture from a pleasant little lady;
George's love for Theo blossoms

The following evening on my arrival at Aunt Bertrice's, Hilda was there, and they were both in smiles. "Guess what happened," said Sister Hilda to me. "How can I without getting a clue of what it's all about?" I replied. "OK, the furniture," said she. "Oh, then, let me see, 1, 2, 3, you bought them." "Yes," said she, "but not from Mongoose or Little Goose as we had arranged. Boy, Aunt Bertrice and I went into Little Goose, and as we were speaking to a clerk, a little old lady nudged me on the side. I looked, and she smartly beckoned me away. 'If you are looking for a special bargain, I have one,' said she. 'Where?' asked I. 'At Petra Street,' said she. 'Before you do anything, come with me and see it.' I then called Aunt Bertrice, who was yet with the clerk, and we decided to follow the old woman. Boy, George, we went, and although the things are old-fashioned, they are well kept. When I asked her price, 'What do you offer?' she said. I stood and looked around the living room. 'These things are very old-fashioned, and why are you selling them?' 'My daughter lives in Canada and will now like me to join her,' she said. 'I will give you $50.00 cash,' said I. 'Honey,' said she, 'make it $60.00, and take all the pots and pans and other utensils in the bargain.' I gave her $10.00 as a binder of the bargain and told her to hold it and that we would be back to see her later, with the hope that you would go to see them with us." "OK, then," said I, "what are we waiting for?"

CHAPTER TWENTY-TWO

We three then hurried and caught a tramcar going to St James. As we got to the house, we saw a pleasant little old lady rocking alone. "Good evening," said we. "Good evening," she answered as she peered through a pair of glasses at us while we were yet on the pavement. "I am here again," said Hilda. "Oh my goodness, I felt as though you were not coming again. Come in," said she. As we entered, a big pussy cat came purring around my feet. "Will you have a seat?" said this old lady with a smile. "Thank you, Mam." Sister Hilda then told her that I am her brother. "Me oh my, I thought he was your husband." Smilingly she said, "He looks very much like my late husband when we were young," and so she started chatting. "You see, I am Norwegian; my husband was a serviceman in World War One. He originally hailed from the Gold Coast. He was a dentist by profession. After his retrenchment, we both decided to settle in the British West Indies. And so we chose Trinidad. We had three children, two boys and one girl. Our elder son went to the Gold Coast. The other stayed in England and is doing good in the field of law. My only daughter, a nurse, is stationed in Canada in the city of Toronto." And so she kept on prattling as the average old person does in search of solace. "Well, well," she finally said, "what have you decided?" "Aunt and Brother are here, let me hear their opinion." "Oh yes, dear," said she, "you may look around at everything, they will be all yours."

When we were finished with our survey, Aunt said, "Hilda, you are robbing the old woman." "Give her a little more," said I. "How much more?" they both asked. "Let's give her $90.00." "Are you mad!" said Hilda, biting her lips. "A bargain is a bargain." I, then said, "Can I say something?" "That's why you are here with us," said Hilda. "Well, in all fairness, let's give her $80.00." "OK, little brother, we shall settle for that only."

She then called the old lady, who had left us to talk matters over by ourselves. "Well," said Hilda, "Mom, we are going to take them." "Good," said the old lady, "I was wondering whether I would have to return you your $10.00." "No, no, you won't have to," said Sister Hilda. "To the contrary, my brother said you must be paid $80.00." The old dame sat spellbound as she looked at us. And, as if lifted up from the chair by some strange force, she leapt and hugged and kissed us. For me, it was the very first time I had ever been hugged and kissed by a Nordic.

"Come with me," said she, as we followed, "all the drapes and curtains are yours. I had promised a friend some of these sheets and pillows; you go through them and take whatever you want. After, I shall share the others." "But when can we take them?" Hilda asked. "Tonight," she replied. "Then when will you be leaving?" "Next Friday by one of the Lady boats." (Afloat were then the *Lady Nelson*, *Lady Drakes* and *Lady Hawkins*.) "That's risky to sail at this time," said Aunt Bertrice. "I know, but the Lord will protect us all on that boat," she replied with confidence. "Well," said Aunt, "give us a receipt for full possession for, as you know, we are now in full rights."

She left and went into a room and was back in five minutes and handed Hilda a receipt covering all the household articles. Hilda then handed her the remaining $70.00, and the deal was closed. I felt deeply concerned within for the old woman. To remove the furniture and leave her in perfect disarray? "Mam," said I, "when did you say that you were leaving?" "Next week Friday," she replied. "Well, we shall come on Thursday, God's will, to collect them." "Son," said she, "you have truly reminded me of my husband. And now you both seem to have similar ways of thinking. I shall cable my daughter tomorrow and let her know that the furniture has been sold. She did not want them to be given away to the gent who purchased the house." May I say at this juncture that the cat was still purring around me.

On our way to catch our tram, Aunt Bertrice broke the silence with her old saying. "I do know that you do not like to hear me say this," said she. "But I still maintain the thought of God and your father's spirit is helping you in all you do. Just think of all the hell you catch in Toco, and all the hardship and difficulty suffered down here. You are yet getting through victoriously. Will you tell me what is now done is all by chance, is it not a blessing? George, child, you keep on the right road as you are trying to do. Avoid company, for it is difficult to tell the good from the bad nowadays. Always remember all skin teeth not

CHAPTER TWENTY-TWO

laugh."[1] At that remark, Sister Hilda teasingly skinned her teeth at us.

When we boarded the tramcar, Sister Hilda paid and asked the conductor for one transfer to Laventille Playground. We shared the same seat; they made me sit in the middle. "How many carts do you think are needed?" Hilda asked. "That will be too harassing for Mr Williams alone to handle," said Aunt without answering the question. She continued to say, however, "Why not check out Haynes Clark with their mule team wagon?" "Wow! How much will that cost? From Woodbrook to Laventille is quite a run," said Hilda. "By the way," said Aunt, "how about a truck? We may probably get one for twelve dollars." "Aunt, are you crazy?" said Hilda. "No," Auntie replied, "and furthermore, whatever the transport is on, that I will pay." I looked at them both. "Come on, say something," said Hilda. By then our tram was well on its way to the corner of St Vincent and Park Street. And I spoke for the first time. "Mr Williams shall handle everything," said I. Hilda at this point said, "But . . ." "Hold it," said Aunt. "Let him speak." "I shall also get Mr Antoine with his strong horse. Maybe they can pack and move it all in one trip." They both agreed that will be a good idea. "But we must be watchful of the weather," said Aunt. "Don't you worry, they have both tarpaulins," I replied. As our tram stopped, I got off and took my transfer on a waiting tram headed for Laventille Playground and walked home. The next day I spoke to both Mr Williams and Antoine, who gave me the assurance that, should life be spared, they would remove the articles next Thursday at 4:30 p.m.

I told Mr Bain fully of the happenings and what was likely to take place. He said, "George, you can push off at 3:00 p.m. next Thursday." The days fled quickly. The Thursday evening when I got to the house, I was astonished to see the job that the little old lady (Mrs Anna Luguido was the name on the receipt) had done all by herself. The kitchen was completely emptied of its utensils, all packed in cartons. All four beds were dismantled and their parts brought before the doorway. All six dining-room chairs with the table were up front with a couple small

---

1   'What looks like a smile can be deceptive.'

tables and four shelves, a desk, a shoe stand, a clothes basket, and some other fittings of which their names I knew not.

Everything that could be handled by an average hard-working individual was neatly packed to one side. With amazement I watched this creature. "Don't you worry, sonny," said she, smiling. "I do almost everything around here that I can handle. I paint my rooms and outside fence walls, cut my hedge, mow my lawn and tend my plants. Right now it is becoming too expensive to employ a yard boy." (At this juncture, a remorseful feeling crept over me.) As she sadly said, "I shall miss my roses."

At a quarter past four, both carts arrived. They had arranged it that way by themselves and were now overjoyed to see the setting. As we three males were about to take the heavy and bulky items out, I overheard Mam telling Aunt and Hilda, "Come and see your linens, pillows and..." I felt happiness within me as we manned all the heavy and bulky items to the passageway. Everything was then packed upon the carts and neatly covered with the tarpaulins should it rain. We then bade farewell and God's speed to our little old friend, who brought me a vivid memory of Miss Eva. Hilda rode with Mr Williams, who took the lead. Aunt Bertrice sat with Mr Antoine, as I perched myself behind this cart on the lookout for small items should any fall.

We arrived at my gate at 7:30 p.m. that evening without an accident. Both carts were unloaded. All the furniture was placed in places chosen by the women, who then arranged a day on the following weekend to put away* the house. There were many things of which I had no use for, especially being a bachelor. So I told my relatives to help themselves from floor mats to beds. "Boy," said Aunt Bertrice, "you really full of talk. You would leave everything here for your mother."

It was a Tuesday evening when I got to Aunt Bertrice's home for supper. Sister Hilda was there. "Guess what?" said Hilda. Perplexed, I looked at her. "Don't you worry bursting your brains," said she. "Our mother will be down this weekend. So, should life be spared, Aunt Bertrice will join me on Thursday to arrange the house. There is a hitch, however, when she comes." "What is it?" I asked. "I will like very much

CHAPTER TWENTY-TWO

that she spends the first week 'choked up' at me. Will that be alright?"
"Sure, Sis, whatever you say goes."

Now during this period my friendship with Theo blossomed, and we had a date fixed for the Sunday of that very weekend. I looked forward to seeing her. She did come, and we met at the home of her uncle, the usual place of our meeting. We both then decided to be by ourselves. We visited the Gardens, and we also went window shopping. She met Aunt Bertrice for the first time, and there we had a late lunch. They both seemed very fond of each other. Ren came in, and he also met Theo for the first time. While we were fixing some drinks in the kitchen, he said to me, "Boy, George, that girl is most beautiful, she even speaks that way. Believe me, George, you really has good taste." As the three chatted, my thoughts ran back on what Marge had once told me concerning Lou and Cecilst's interest in Theo. And from what Ren had now lavished upon her with his words to me, cowardice and a streak of jealousy crept over me. I then said, "Aunt, we must now leave." She followed us to the door and told Theo she must come again. She then said to me, "It is Sunday, George, so take a nice bus ride up the road." (I knew very well she was hinting to me not to travel by cab.) We boarded a bus which had but half a dozen passengers. So we shared a seat by ourselves. Theo then inquired of me about my new home. I told her just what was about to take place with Mother's arrival from the country. Shyly she said to me, "Can I see it?"

Up to then I can never remember saying "yes" so quickly. We disembarked at the nearest stopping point and made our way to the house. "Oh," said Theo as she looked around, "George, you have a lovely place here. You can plant lots of flowers and vegetables." I told her that I was responsible for the enclosure, and it was her uncle who had gotten it for me.

As we entered, she was honestly overjoyed at how Sister Hilda (who she knew) and Aunt Bertrice had arranged it. Now I was not prepared for a visit like this, so I had not even water in the jug. She peered into both bedrooms with their furnitures*. When in the kitchen (a room was converted for that), she scrutinized every utensil. As we went out to the kitchen that converted as an annex for my stay, she remarked she loved the simplicity. We then went back to the house and lounged ourselves upon the living room couch. It was the very first time that we had complete privacy by ourselves, just being mindful to respect each other as our hearts grew filled with merriment.

CHAPTER 23

Donald and Yourland enlist as World War Two engulfs Trinidad

Mother did come home, and my general lifestyle was changed. First, I went and thanked Aunt Bertrice and Ren for their generosity of having me for meals each day. (Because of that, I was able to make myself quite a respectable bank saving.) "Don't you worry," said Aunt Bertrice, "you are free to call here at any time." She then patted me upon my back and said, "George, you are going to make it. Again let me say you are a young man, but you are carrying an old head upon your shoulders."

Now Sister Hilda had artfully proposed a meeting that we five must attend the first Sunday of Mother being at me: Quildon, Weston, Georgiana, Hilda, and myself. This meeting, she said, was for the sustenance monthly of Mother: Quildon to give $2.50, Weston $2.00, Georgiana 50 cents, Hilda herself $2.50, and I $2.50 plus responsibility. At the meeting Quildon said it was a great day for him, and this has been resting on his mind for many years. And he had hopes of doing so all by himself in the not-too-distant future. And, as a mark of his deep concern, let him be the first to donate his quota. With that short address he promptly gave not only his quota of $2.50 but $5.00 to Mother. (This was the first and last that I knew of his donation.) The others kept their monthly pledge. Georgiana came to live with us. We were happy for I had the outdoor kitchen as my room, which was nicely put away. (It was the best I had as a bachelor.) Mother cooked and washed; all went well.

George and his mother, Plum

But as it is recorded, in the midst of life we are in death. And this goes not only for the physical. World War Two was now raging, and one evening Donald said to me, "George, I am inviting you for the first time to meet my family." I had already known many of his brothers, with one of whom our friendship lasted till he became deceased. But I had never met his mother and only sister. When we got to his home that evening, here was the introduction: "Mother and Sis, this is George, my friend and co-worker. You would not meet a more good, hard-working and honest person. And should he at any time call to see me, I would like to know the same courtesy shown to others be given him." "Stop!" said his mother sharply. "Why should you make so vile a statement? Donald, you never know me to present shabby treatment to anyone, do you?" At this juncture I saw where Donald was placed in a muddy spot. So I said, "You see, Mam, I at one time worked for the Otchins." "Hold it," said she, "are you George that I have been hearing of for all these years? Mrs Otchin always speaks so nicely of you. And I am used to the hearing of some of my boys gabbing of how strong and brave

CHAPTER TWENTY-THREE

you are. Son, you are free to call here at any time." "Thank you, Mam," said I, with a bow tipping my hat slightly. Donald then said, "Come, George, let's go inside."

What a plush house it was for those days. My eyes and mind photoed everything without being observed. As we sat, he said to me, "Well, boy, George, I am thinking very seriously of joining the service." Inquiringly I looked at him. "Yes," said he, "and my choice is the RAF" (Donald Bain was among the first local to join the Royal Air Force.) Said he, "I have not yet discussed this matter with anyone. But I am thinking of the effect it will have on Popo. Next, work is now slowed terribly in the building department. It is a fact that I would be transferred to another department. But that is not all life holds. There is a more positive purpose."

I strongly felt at this point he read my concern. "Don't you worry yourself, George; should I really be leaving, I shall see to it that you first get another job." He then went to the fridge and filled two glasses of lemonade. He handed one to me and made a short toast; as we raised our glasses, said he, "Top secrecy."

As if by magic the days sped. And we do know some sunny skies can be darkened in a moment. It was a Friday morning when Donald came downstairs. I was in the warehouse, rearranging it with the two porters, Fred and John. "Hi, George." "Yes, Mr Bain," I answered. "Will you meet me at your office?" "Yes, sir." I then gave some quick instructions to both men, and off I went to join him.

"Well, boy," said he, "the final decision has been made at a meeting. Our building department would be closed down temporarily. And I am now definitely going to join the R.A.F. Management wants to induce me to another department. But I am standing firmly on my decision. And don't you worry, I have already spoken to Mr Randolph, who heads the hardware department, for your transfer. There is only one hitch to that work, however. Your salary would now be $6.00 a week." My heart skipped with joy instead of sadness, all for the fact that I would be yet employed. Fred and John would be sent as hired hands to other departments. "By the way," said Donald, "Yourland told me last night that he wanted to see you. I think it would be good if you can call on him this evening after work." "What is it all about, do you know?" "Yes, I do, but it is better that you hear it from him." "OK, OK," said I as we both laughed.

I did call to see Yourland after work that evening. He himself had been employed with one of the county government's newly formed departments, the Control Board. "Well," said he, "George, we have not seen each other for quite a while. And I do think I have some good and bad news for you. Which will you rather hear first?" "Of course, the good news," said I. "Well," said he, "I am giving to you all my clothes, shoes, bicycle, and some books and other belongings for $10.00. I am giving you a receipt so that no one or any member of my family can arrest you for same." "Yourland," said I, "are you feeling sick?" "No, George." He smilingly looked at me. Again said I to him, "Then you are going cuckoo." "Not yet," he seriously replied. "And for the sad news, I am leaving for Canada next week. I am joining the army. And don't you say any more about the subject unless you do not want the offer of my bargain. My friend Noble and I are moving together. You can have every thread that I have of which you well deserve. If you do not have the money, still come tomorrow, and you shall yet have the receipt for same." I kept silent while he spoke; it will seem that I am the one sick. Donald had given to me my pay envelope that evening, so I had enough money to pay the bargain.

Yourland and I were sitting in the enclosed porch while we spoke. At that very moment Mr Otchin called him. "Hold on a minute, George," said he to me as he quickly left. As he left, I quickly counted the $10.00 and put it under a sports magazine on the centre table that was there. When he returned, he was followed by his mother and grandmother. "Good evening, George," they both said. "Why don't you come and look for us," said Mrs Otchin. "You have grown much more refined," said Mrs Stedy. "You do not even come to see Laura. She left not quite half an hour ago," said Mrs Otchin. "Mam," said I, "I will gladly come, but when I remember the rude treatment meted out by Mr Otchin to

CHAPTER TWENTY-THREE

Osco Older[1] when he once came here to Yourland, I do know that he would treat me even worse. So for that reason I rather not come." "Oh, George, you must stop remembering dead things," said Mrs Otchin. "He since has changed." (You may wash the leopard clean but not its spots.) "Mam," I said to her phrase, "tell Miss Laura I do inquire for her from my cousin, and I shall see her soon." Mrs Stedy then spoke again. "Keep it up, George, you are an honest, hard-working and ambitious young man, and you shall succeed in life." "Thank you, Mam," I replied. Mrs Otchin with a smile said, "We have been keeping track on your activities."

To that I shyly grinned. There were no other members of the family around. As we spoke, Yourland went inside. When he returned he gave me the receipt covering the $10.00. I then pointed to him the cash beneath the sports magazine on the table. "George," said he, "you are still a son of a gun," he said, laughing. "Look, you know what, as you are here this evening, take all you can upon the bike, and tomorrow you can take the others." The bicycle carried a carrier to the back of it. And I knew well how to manoeuvre it. And so I rode home that evening with an astonishing load.

The next day being Saturday, I told Donald all of what took place. Said he, "Did I not tell you that I knew what it was all about? But I did not want to tell you so as to rob you of the excitement. I tell you what, take time off this morning as we are not busy, and gather the other things while Mr Otchin is at work." I was very glad for that because I wanted to evade Mr Otchin all I could.

When I got to the house, Mrs Otchin and Miss Laura were chatting in the kitchen. "Oh, goodness," said Mrs Otchin. "George, you are here. You just missed Yourland." Miss Laura then said, "George, you would live long. Madam and I have just been speaking about you. Tell me, George, what have I done you that you don't come and look for me?" "Well, well . . ." "Don't worry with that 'well, well' business. Because if

---

[1] Osco Older is George's disguised name for Boscoe Holder, a well-known Trinidadian artist.

not here, you can come at your cousin Vera's home. However, as Madam said, we have all been checking on your welfare, and we are satisfied."

I was then invited into the living room, not as a hired servant but as a visitor. At that moment came Mrs Stedy. As I kept standing, "Sit down, George," said Mrs Otchin. I then timidly sat, and they both advised me on a lot that I had never heard before. Miss Laura, who was standing and leaning slightly with a straw broom, said, "Now you have heard what Madam and Mrs Stedy have told you; all you have now to do is restrain from your hot temper, and you would be alright." I thanked the three for their parental advice. Mrs Otchin then presented me two cartons of gent's raiment which were left by Yourland. Of these I kept two pair of trousers and a blazer. The others I sent to my old school chum Horace in Toco.

Chapter 24

A stormy time for George: he is demoted at work and evicted from his house, and Theo leaves Trinidad

Our building department did close down, and I was transferred to the hardware department, which was really managed by Mr Randolph. I found no challenge in the work whatever. It was just to know your stock and where they were to readily serve the customer. And the entire department was well staffed.

I had not long to wait before I was faced with one of life's storms. One evening as I got home, there was Mr Williams awaiting me. Sadly he told me that the owner of the house had to come back into town because the Yanks had taken over where they now live in Rio Claro. This was indeed a forceful blow, considering first, the inconvenience for Mother; second, the money that was spent and the loss of material and labour; third, a family separation.

I told Donald of what was now taking place in my life, as I was given a month to quit the premises. Two days later he called me at the hardware store. "Look, George," said he, "would you like to stay temporarily in a boarding house until you can get yourself a suitable place to live?" I had no choice because at that time renting was fast becoming a problem because of the mean act of a cash reward offered by people (who were mostly foreigners). "How much will it be?" I asked. "I do not know," he said, "but I shall speak to the landlady and get the price much suited to your pocket. But it shall be for you alone." "I do know that," said I.

Well, we had now to face the sad split. Mother went back to Toco, and Georgiana stayed where she worked. The furnitures were all rudely divided. I kept four pieces to remember the little old lady, Mrs Luguido. And so we left the owner of the house with a well-fenced property and a well-organized out-kitchen, as well as a sty and a chicken pen, both not yet used.

My new home was on Murray Street, Woodbrook. Donald took me to the landlady who was of English Latin descent. She was very pretty and the mother of six lovely children, three boys and three girls. They had been living in England, but when the Nazis began their bombing expedition, she returned to Trinidad where she once lived. Her husband, who was an army captain, died, and she was left alone with these lovely kids.

Donald explained to her all my problems with the house and what was my present salary. She looked at me and said, "You will have to pay me $4.00 weekly. You won't be getting an independent room of your own. You shall share room with my sons, which is outside in the adjoining annex. And remember, young man, I am only doing this for you through the very strong recommendation of Mr Bain. Next, the policy here, of course: you pay first and live after. Does that suit you?" "Yes, Mam, and I hope never to let you both down."

Now no meals were included in this, our verbal contract. "When do you want to start?" the mother asked sharply. "From Saturday, Mam, if God spares life." She then gave me an inquiring look. At this point Donald said, "For his beginning, I shall pay the first week." She again looked at me. "How old are you?" she asked. "I am twenty years old, Mam." "You are one year older than my eldest daughter." Donald then handed her the four dollars from his billfold. "OK," said she, "I would be seeing you on Saturday." "Yes, Mam," said I. I bade good day and left them speaking.

As I sat upon my bicycle and rode off that evening, I wondered was it worth it all. What has life in store for me? After putting out so much, look what very little I have received. Now I will no longer be able to put money in my savings other than a few pennies. It is a fact the bank was called the Penny Bank. But at no time ever had I deposited pennies. But the dark shadows clearly pointed that I would now have to.

CHAPTER TWENTY-FOUR

Come Saturday, needless to mention, good old Mr Williams transported me to Murray Street with my scanty belongings: my trunk and clothing, the four mentioned pieces of furniture, and my bicycle. When we arrived, the landlady's sons were playing in the yard. They immediately stopped and came to help us offload. They took the light things, as Mr Williams and I followed with the more cumbersome. We were led to a room with three beds, so I decided to sling my hammock to save space. I had also four pieces of carpentry tools in my desk drawer which I used in my former home. I then asked the boys for their mother. "Oh," said they, "Mother is out. She told us that you were coming and to be on the lookout for you."

Now the boys seemed to have had various chores laid out for them. But boys in the absence of their parent will first have their fun. When we brought in my belongings, I observed that the yard needed cleaning and that there were two brooms leaning on the garage gate. So, without wasting time, I took one and immediately began sweeping the yard while they looked on with amazement. The eldest then said, "You don't have to do that. If is for us to do." "Never mind," said I, "while I am around, I shall share in your chores." He then took the other broom, and we both swept the yard front and back while the other two brothers picked up the waste. I also scrubbed and washed the drains, and so the whole yard was cleaned in about ninety minutes. No sooner had we finished in came their mother and sisters. I heard her calling so I hurried to the room. I now wondered must I go to her, yet I felt that I should not. And so I stayed seated in the room.

As the evening grew late, I overheard the voices of men and women in the house, and I guessed they were boarders. The boys did not return. After being alone for about two hours, I decided to go out some place and get something to eat. As I was about to leave, the eldest son came to me and said, "Mammy would like to know if you would eat with us in the kitchen." I looked at him and asked, "With who?" "We," the three boys said. "Will you follow me," he said. When I got there, his mother said, "You may join the boys. I am very busy now. I shall speak to you later." There was a makeshift table, and we four sat and ate. While eating with a puzzled mind, I thought that the $4.00 could not include meals. "Eat," said the boys, "there are lots more." Suddenly a thought came to me. When I left Donald speaking to her that day, he must have told her fully of my situation.

That night, as we four turned into our room, I lay in my hammock, and the three boys told me quite a lot of stories about England, its soldiers, and the many air attacks by the Germans. To be truthful, coming from boys, some stories sounded true while others sounded tall. I then lay on my back, prayed and fell asleep.

On Sunday morning I arose early. I was not quite sure of my situation, so I sat and pondered. I then decided to pay a visit to the Roman Catholic Cathedral. It is a fact that I could not understand what was said by the priest, but there was no seating discrimination as the Anglicans. After the Mass I went to Mr Williams to let him know how things were going because when he left me on Saturday he was a worried man. As I got off the bus, there was Lidia walking from across the RC churchyard to where they lived. And behold, what wonder to my sight, I saw that following her was no one else but Theo. It was truly a surprise for us both because we had not planned a meeting for this Sunday. And, as Lidia said, she knew not where I had moved to, and therefore could not notify me. Theo then said, "Don't you worry. I prayed while I was in church with Lidia, and here we are." As she looked at me smiling, we embraced. Lidia was also given an unmeaningful hug as we laughed.

When we entered the house, it was 8:30 a.m. Very strange but true, Mr Williams and Bob were yet asleep. Lidia said, "We will not wake them because they returned very late last night from doing a job." She then turned to Theo and said, "Let me fix breakfast alone, and not as we had planned. You two can sit in that room and chat only, nothing else!" said she with a concealed smile. "What do you mean nothing else?" I asked. "Man," said she, "your head hard or what? I mean no necking, just simple talking."

Theo and I then chose to sit in the dining room near the kitchen. Theo could have seen into Bob's room should his door be opened, and I could have seen into Mr Williams'. Theo, holding my hand, said, "Well,

CHAPTER TWENTY-FOUR

George, I have heard that you swept into bitter disappointment with your home and relatives. My goodness, money is so very hard to come by, and after you had spent so much, you have now to lose it all. What a blow is it now to Tant Plum." (That's how everyone familiarly called my mother.) "Well," I said, "it certainly will not be the end of my line because you are yet around." "No, no, George," she sadly said. With those two words of two letters, I felt as though something left from my stomach into my mouth as blood. "What! What do you mean, 'no'?" I then tried to calm the pitch of my voice as I searched for words. She then held both my hands gently upon the table. "George, George," said she. "I have never told you this because since I met you, my attitude to life became changed, and I was hoping that this event will not mature. My paternal grandparents who reside in the United States of America for the past thirty years are sending for me to do nursing at Tuskegee Institute in Alabama. All my papers are made up, and I will be leaving in a fortnight. That's my chief reason for coming to town today, so that you may know. And only to be met with this shocking news of yourself."

Sorrowfully with tear-filled eyes we both said, "This will not be the end of the line." "I am sure," Theo said, "we would again meet some day. Don't you worry, George," said she, "I am going there to become a nurse. And I shall save every penny I can to send for you. Just do not let me down." "And how about your sincerity towards me?" said I. She then got promptly up from her chair and took my right hand, as I myself stood up and rested it upon her bare bosom as she said, "I swear to this, that I shall always remain faithful and true to you, ever as I am." It was then the closest nearest physical contact of that nature that was ever made by us both in that home. Lidia looked and sadly shook her head as we again sat in our seats.

No sooner were we seated, Mr Williams's room door opened. "Oh, my goodness, George," said he, "you are here. How are you settling in?" "I cannot just yet say for, as you know, today is just my second day, and here I am." "That true," said he, "but I am thinking of your weekly fees without meals." He then went on to say, "In homes and places of that standard, it's just a favour granted when housed." "Oh, don't you worry yourself about that. Yesterday she made me sit at the table with her three sons." "What! Did she?" "And will you believe those youngsters encouraged me to eat! I do not know what will happen today." "You do not have to worry about today for you are here with us." "Oh no," said I. "I just happened to attend Mass at the Roman Catholic Cathedral this morning. And being so near I thought of paying you a visit, only to meet this lovely niece of yours here." "I won't believe it," said he. "Was this not planned?" "No, Pappy," said Lidia. "Well," said he, shaking his head, "things do happen in a remarkable way at times."

After breakfast, Bob started his morning chores, so I entered his room to change. He bolted in as I kicked my shoes off. "Listen, man, George, I have been keeping my eyes upon you – No, no, not today, you are not coming out there to help me one bit. Why the hell don't you take the girl out for a drive? It could be Toco for that matter. Be alone and have a good chat with her. You both may not see each other again for quite a while." "But . . ." "But what?" said he. "Don't be such an ass." I looked at him in wonder, for never had we accosted each other in that way. "Do you think she will agree to that?" "Why the hell, man, ask! Just ask!" "OK," said I and walked out of the room.

I put my shoes on again and went out to Theo, who with an apron on was about to wash the breakfast dishes with Lidia. As I brought the suggestion up, Lidia was very supportive of the idea and thought that we should leave right away. It was only then did I perceive that there was an emptiness upon Theo's heart and that we should be by ourselves. I then asked her once more, "Do you agree?" There was an assured yes with the sparkles in her dark eyes. "OK, hold on a minute," said I. I hurried across to Mr Williams, who was himself very busy attending to a horse. I asked his permission. "Sure, George," said he, "just make sure that she is back for dinner."

We went out and hailed a passing cab. "Oh no, George, what are you doing, why not a bus?" "No," said I, "what I have in mind will be inconvenient with a bus." "Well, go ahead," said she, "if you so desire. I will pay." "We will see who will when the time comes," said I. By

CHAPTER TWENTY-FOUR

this time the cab had made its turn and come to us. The driver was of Oriental descent.

I then asked the driver to travel along Ariapita Avenue. On nearing Murray Street I asked that he should proceed slowly around Adam Smith Square. When we turned into Murray Street, I pointed out the house to Theo where I am staying. No one then expected to see me in a taxi at that time of day. The landlady, two of her sons, and two of her daughters were standing at the front of the house chatting with an army man clad in US uniform. Theo loved the area and said, "It's only the elites lives around here." "Yes, Miss, rong here is only big shots,"[1] said the cab man. To my amazement he drove around not once but three times with us. "Oh," said I, "do not worry to go around the Savannah." "Let dat not worry you," he said. "I sal take you der. Jus gee me one shance to zee my family at Bossiss Vilege. Since I leff home zis morning five o'clock, I not see dem nah."[2] "Surely," said I, "that's no problem at all."

He then headed by way of St James and took the Long Circular Road exit. As he drove slowly, he pointed to us the homes of merchants, businessmen and professional men whose names I had only heard of or seen in the media. There were also two places of interest which he pointed to us. They were the St James Police Barracks and the Country Club. As we journeyed through Boissière Village, he stopped at a parlour and bade us in. We entered and stood up in the public section. "Oh no," said he, "come inside and meet my family." He then lifted a section of the counter and opened a small door that we may enter. We met his family of five: three boys, one girl, and his wife. We were then offered Lipton tea; we drank and felt refreshed. Then in came a poodle with its long curly hair, wagging its tail. Theo was afraid, but our host bade her be calm. As he came wagging his tail and licking my hands as though he knew me, I in turn stroked and patted his head. We then left for our trip around the Savannah. He finally took us to Nelson Street. On

---

1 'Yes, Miss, around here there are only big shots.'
2 'Don't worry about that,' he said. 'I shall take you there. Just give me one chance to see my family at Boissière Village. I haven't seen them since I left home this morning at five o'clock.'

nearing the home of Aunt Bertrice, we both handed a $1.00 each to him. "Oh no," said he, "$1.00 only." "No, no," we both insisted, "please take $2.00." "Many thanks," said he, as he dropped us to the house.

When I knocked on the door, I heard Aunt Bertrice say, "Here comes George. Go open, Lou, and let him in." As he came to the door, he yelled as if shocked, "Oh goodness, Mother! Not only George, but come and see who is with him." Before we could have entered the living room, there was Ren hurrying from his room. Excitedly he said, "Theo! George!" As he hugged Theo, life's solitude swept over me. He observed, "Don't you worry, little cousin, she is so cute and lovely. My approach is that of a family and meaningless." Then came Aunt Bertrice, wiping her hands on her apron. She also hugged and greeted us both. Said she, "Will you believe this, George? As I was preparing the salad, you came fully into my thoughts." Lou then laughing said, "Well, well, just look at this. I did the letting in and had not been rewarded, not even with a left-hand shake." "Oh, I am so sorry," said I, as I firmly shook his hand. And Theo hugged and kissed him on the cheek. No one was seated except Lou, who sat upon a dining-room chair facing backwards in a prostrate manner. As we stood chatting, Ren said, "Mother, something is burning." She hurried from the scene. Ren bade us to be seated, and we four chatted. I shall not now go into details, but we had a meal which only Aunt Bertrice in all the family could prepare.

Aunt Bertrice did accompany us back to Mr Williams's home. As they chatted, Bob said to me, "Boy, George, I have to run to San Juan." Lidia said that she was tired and suggested that we then go into her room. As we entered, she unbolted the door which linked her room and Bob's, and said, "Should Pappy call, just wake me over here," as she closed the door behind her. Theo looked at me and said, "Well, well, look at that smarty." We were now left fully alone. We again went over her going to the United States, my present situation and other matters. We hugged and kissed but were mindful to respect each other just as we did that Sunday at my house. And she fell asleep. I also pretended to be asleep, as I rested my hand upon her bosom.

We were now by ourselves for a good hour and a half. Lidia tapped

CHAPTER TWENTY-FOUR

upon the door, and then there was a knock – Bob, sporting a broad grin. It was only then did I realize that our meeting was a fixed programme by Lidia and himself. As we four talked, there was a heavy rap on the door. It was Mr Williams himself. He told Lidia how about preparing some iced mauby and condensed milk for everyone, which she did.

As the evening shadows fell, with a sad heart Theo and I bade farewell to each other. Aunt and I then boarded a bus. We shared the same seat, and she began to prattle. "Well, well, young man – I saw when you three smart scoundrels slipped into the room, so I thought of holding the big bad wolf at bay for a good while. I gave him a real interesting talk. I took the right track of bringing some unionism between Aunt Rache and himself, providing that she is willing to comply with his side of the bargain." "Aunt," said I, "it's no wonder why Hilda sticks so closely to you. Believe me, you are a real sport. I thank you very much for your support." "Chile," said she, "don't mind people with their old talk in using their remark 'ee go live at eee aunt' – boy, dat is jazz talk – send them by me." And we both laughed. She said how sorry she was about Theo and myself. Mr Williams had told her all about it. "But you don't seem worried." "Oh no, not at all," I replied. "For we have agreed that I shall join her soon. We shall both save our money and have a quiet wedding." "That sounds very good," said Aunt Bertrice. At that very moment our bus drove into the station and halted. As we disembarked, she said, "Tell you what, George, should you have some time tomorrow or any other day this week, let me see you." "OK," said I, and we parted.

I took a tram and got off at Murray Street and Ariapita Avenue corner. The time was 7:55 p.m. As I entered the gate, someone asked, "Are you looking for somebody?" "No," said I. "Good evening to you." And I continued my walk inside. (The enquirer was an American boarder.) As I got to the room, the eldest boy was lying on his back reading a comic. "Hello," said I. He looked up and saw me. "Oh my goodness," he exclaimed, "where you been all day? Mammy must have inquired over one hundred times." With those words he sprang from the bed and was off to the main building before I could have made him a reply to his question. I then sat at my small table with my hand propping my chin when the landlady came up, followed by two daughters and the son who called her. I stood to my feet and said, "Good evening, mam." "Good evening," she sharply replied. "Where have you been all day? I thought you left for church this morning, but I expected you to return for breakfast. Also, after lunch, Mr Bain came over, and he waited for quite an hour. But you did not show up. Next you were not home for supper. Let me know what you are doing because food is far too expensive to waste. I have noticed that quite a lot of that practice is done among the people out there." As she spoke the children listened as though they were hired witnesses to hear what was being said. I stayed mute. "Well, aren't you going to say something?" she calmly said.

"Well, mam, I did come back after church, but when I got here, you and four of the children were speaking to an American serviceman. I then went twice around the square. But you were yet in conversation. I did not want to enter for my own reason, so I left." She then gave a doubtful look as to what I was saying. "Yes, Mammy, can't you remember us being out there in the front this morning speaking to that Marine officer who wants to come and stay here with his wife?" "Oh yes," she replied, "but then why did you not come in?" Again she looked at me and strongly said, "Let me tell you something, young man, this is my property, and I have admitted you here, and I want no inferiority complex with you or anyone, do you understand?" "Yes, mam, I do understand." "The boys have already eaten; you shall now have to eat by yourself." "No thanks, mam, not tonight. I had already eaten at my relatives." "Alright," said she, "but never let it happen this way again." And they all left me.

As they got to the main building, I hurried and took a shower in an outdoor bathroom. And before one could have uttered the words "Jack Robinson," I was lying in my hammock upon my back after praying. Vivid thoughts came over me that night about Theo's parting, Donald's enlistment, the big disappointment and liquidated home with Mother, the huge withdrawal from my bank savings which failed, and now the new home and style of living.

Chapter 25

Mrs Bell becomes his "Mammy"; bitter news about Theo and about Yourland; a new job as a cash collector; a stay in Mayaro where he meets May

I was up at 5:00 a.m. the next day. After giving thanks to God, I went out, took the yard broom, and was off to the front yard, sweeping up the many cigarette butts and their wrappings. I washed the drains, cleaned up the backyard and took the garbage out. It was all done by 6:30 a.m. When the boys got out of bed, they greeted me and hurried for their shower upstairs. I made busy myself to the outdoor shower. As I walked across, I observed the landlady, two of her daughters, and a maid busying themselves in the kitchen. After my shower I tidied myself for my work, when all three boys bursting with laughter came into the room. "Thank you! Thank you!" said they. "When did you do it all?" asked the youngest. "While you all were asleep," I replied. I then heard someone calling, "Boys, it's getting late, come and have your breakfast." I pretended not to hear but was watchful as to know whether the call was meant for me also. Then the eldest of the three hurried back and said to me, "Come on, man, George." I was truly caught by surprise at this, for I knew not their names and neither had I thought they knew mine for never had we been introduced. We were all four joined at the table. After our breakfast we cleaned, washed and put away the wares in their places. I then hopped upon my bicycle and was off for my work.

At work I met Donald and truthfully told him all that took place on Sunday. I also told him that I knew not the landlady's name. He was truly surprised at this but claimed that it was all his fault for not letting me know earlier. "She is Mrs Hilda Bell," said he. He then wrote her name and the names of all the children, according to their ages and places in the family, and gave them to me. He also said that when he got home on Saturday, he received a phone call about his departure to Canada the next Tuesday. That's why he came to see me on Sunday, but I was out.

The next morning I was up very early. I said to myself that I will not begin the sweeping exercise as it could cause an unrestful sound to the boarders. There was then a light in the living room. And I saw Mrs Bell hurrying through the passageway with a market basket. I walked across and cut her off. "Good morning, mam," said I. "Where are you going?" "To the market," she replied. "May I come with you?" "Oh, I will be delighted," she replied. As I turned to hurry back to the room, she then asked, "Where are you going?" "To get some travelling money, mam." "No need for that, I have enough."

We apparently got the first tram that morning on the avenue, which was headed to Charlotte Street. As we entered the Eastern Market, Mrs Bell busily visited various stalls, buying only vegetable items, while I toted the basket as it gradually increased in its weight. She then said, "I do think we have gotten everything, George. Come, let's go home." We were back home at 5:45 a.m. When we got back, her three daughters and two maids were busily preparing breakfast. I made an attempt to wash the yard. "No, no," said Mrs Bell, "leave that alone." I told her that I yet had time before preparing for my work. She shrugged her shoulders. So I cleaned up speedily.

I was glad to return home that evening to see what response was there for me. As I parked my cycle, a maid said to me, "Madam said should you come in before five o'clock to call her." "Very well," said I. "Then could you please tell her that I am here." As she turned away, I wondered what could it be.

Within minutes Mrs Bell came. "Oh, George," said she, "none of the children are here, and I have not sufficient coffee for tomorrow morning. Could you ride over to Allums and buy me a large tin?"

CHAPTER TWENTY-FIVE

"Yes, mam, that's no problem," and off I went. On my return she said to me, "Oh my goodness, you have certainly saved the situation." That evening when the boys came in, I again joined in washing the dishes and tidying the kitchen. We were almost finished when their sisters came up. "Oh, you smarties," said the eldest boy. "You gauge when the work is all done to show yourselves up." "Nonsense," said the second eldest girl. "Where is Mammy?" asked the youngest. "In her room," said the second boy. At that time came this shuffle of footsteps, as Mrs Bell walked into the kitchen. "Well, why are you so late?" she sternly asked. "Transportation, Mother," came an answer quickly. I then walked off from the family discussion. "Come here, George," said Mrs Bell, "let me officially introduce you to my children. You have already been with the boys, Alfred, Charlie and Billy. These are my daughters, Hazel, May and Violet. Now my children all seem to like you, so please let it stay that way." I welcomed not her last remark. Nevertheless, I humbly lent a deaf ear and replied not. Mrs Bell then went on to say, "Should you at any time be dissatisfied about anything, don't be hesitant to let me know. I shall do my best to have all matters rectified." "Thank you, mam," I replied.

Thursday and Saturday of that week we again visited the market. On the evening of the Saturday, however, when I came in from work, I placed my boarder's fee of $4.00 into an envelope. As I entered the kitchen, Mrs Bell was busy with the seasoning of some meats. She took it not from me but motioned me to rest it on the kitchen counter. The boys were all out so I got into my hammock with a book, and I soon fell asleep. I was awakened by Charlie, who said, "Mammy asked if you can come; she is in the sewing room." When I got there, to my wonder, Mrs Bell handed me back the envelope opened with the $4.00 and said to me, "You are helping me very much more than this. I want no money from you." "But..." I stuttered. "Young man," said she firmly, "will you leave with your 'buts'." I left the room in wonderment. When I got to my shared room, Charlie asked, "Have you spoken to Mammy?" "Yes," said I, seating myself upon a chair. As I sat thinking, my thoughts snapped back to Aunt Bertrice, who told me to let her see me that week whenever there is time. And so I thought now was an excellent moment to do so.

When I got there, I made sure to lock my bicycle because I intended not to lend it to anyone. As I knocked at the door, a voice responded, "Come in, George." It was Aunt Bertrice. "Oh, my child," said she, "I am so happy to see you. I have been praying for you. Tell me, how are things moving with your life? I am so sad about your recent experiences, but always remember, child, as my mother used to say, 'no cross, no crown'. Let me fix us a drink that you would like. Ren is on an evening shift, and Lou has gone to the cinema as usual." "Hold it, Aunt, do not prepare anything. I have come to discuss something with you." "What is it?" she inquiringly asked. I then showed the envelope of $4.00 and related to her the full story of my work. She said to me, "Boy, I have said this to you. And I do know that you are annoyed at times. But I will maintain my idea that the good Lord and your father's spirit are with you." I said, "Aunt Bertrice, the good Lord, yes. But my father's spirit, no." "You may have it as you want it, sonny," said she. "But one thing I will advise: always keep close to that type of people." I knew not what she meant then, but as I grew older I found out.

Very soon I was treated as part of the Bell family. Mrs Bell very often will entrust me with cash to pay the Building and Loan Association and other monthly bills. Occasionally, I will make the market, taking with me either Alfred or Charlie. Many times at my work I would be called to the phone by her to pick up some small or needed item on my way home. And never to my knowledge had she ever checked my bills. All the boarders respected me. And she also stopped me from calling her "mam," but to say "Mammy" instead, as her children did.

During this period Theo never failed me with her correspondence. She did attend Tuskegee Institute in Alabama. Her grandparents then made her take up medicine instead of the nursing career. She worked at it exceptionally well, which pleased "Doctah" (Doctor Carver) as he remarked on her work and studies. But, behold, there came a bitter winter that year, and she fell a fatal victim to pneumonia. (Please, Reader, let me not say more on the subject.)

I also received a letter and postcard from Yourland. I could not reply

CHAPTER TWENTY-FIVE

because he was constantly on the move from one base to the other. I learned also that he had got married, but while yet in service he died. I never knew what was his complaint. Donald never failed to write me, as he enclosed pictures and clippings at times of some wintry Canadian scenery.

Through jealousy from others, I became faced with some bitter experiences on my job. But I was strong enough to fight them off. I did my best, as Aunt Bertrice had advised, to stay close to certain people, which debarred me from trouble. For example, a shipment of corrugated asbestos and galvanize roofing was imported from Canada and apparently had been stored on deck. On arrival, the galvanize sheets were partly damaged by sea blast and sea water. I approached the hardware manager for a bargain on the fifty ten-foot sheets to cover Tanty's house that was still thatched. He decided to give me a bargain price of $65.00 for my fifty sheets. The news did circulate, and the head porter selected the most worthless sheets for me. It happened thus before I could have removed them. A friend of the very porter also wanted fifty sheets. I need not now say how they were assorted. I need not say that my transportation was to be done by Mr Williams. The day in question when he came, the manager went over to the warehouse. What for, no one knew, for it was not his practice of going into that portion of damaged cement and other material. I pointed out my fifty sheets that were placed in a corner for Mr Williams. As he backed his cart and was about to load the sheets, the manager said, "Wait, hold a minute, carter." He then turned to the porter who was there to witness the removal. "How many sheets are there, Joe?" asked the manager. "Fifty-six," Joe timidly replied. "Ok, carter, you may load this fifty instead." I was astonished, as the porter stood dumbfounded. And to crown it all, while we were yet loading, the porter's friend called for his. He was then directed to take my first batch of fifty. Throughout the loading process, the manager just stood there and will not move. Folks, I then recalled the doing of wicked Haman found in the Book of Esther 5:14, 7–10. I sent them all to Tanty with four forty-gallon oil paint drums and two damaged buckets.

Tanty was able to cover her house and outdoor kitchen and toilet. And the remainder of the sheets she gave to a religious group. I felt elated doing so because it was a problem which had burdened my mind for years. After that episode I kept very far away from that porter. I had but one friend in that department. His name was Clive Clayton Coggins, who later turned out to be the godfather of my second son, Michael. I shall be speaking of him a little later.

One day the assistant manager asked me if I would like doing the job of cash collector. "What do you mean?" I asked. "Well," said he, "you would be going out to collect unpaid cash bills from various homes, individuals, and in many cases you will have to call at business places for outstanding bills and old accounts." At the moment, I thought it was all to do with the hardware department. But he corrected my wild thoughts by letting me know that it was to do with the largest drug establishment of the country, Messrs W. Serious. He then went on to say that he has a friend there who needs a tidy, honest and hard-working young man who respects and cares about people. And he thinks that I would be ideal for such a job. The pay would be $7.00 a week, and I would be getting all my personal drugs and medicines at a discount. Although saddened to leave my present employment and my good friend Clive, I was, however, glad to take up the challenge. "Can I give you a definite answer tomorrow, sir?" "Yes, George," said he.

That morning I went home and discussed the matter with Mammy, who told me it is a wonderful idea because she personally knows that I possessed the qualities for such a post. And should references be needed, she would not only write but she will also go to them in person. She also said that the manager of that firm and her late husband were very good friends. I became now strengthened to accept the job. So the next morning I went to my assistant manager's office and told him I have decided to accept the job. "Good," said he, "let me ring my friend." On those spoken words I stepped out of his office. About five minutes later he called me back and said that the job was all mine. That day in question was a Thursday, and I was told that I must start the Monday of the next week. The Friday at noon I was paid. Both the manager and

CHAPTER TWENTY-FIVE

the assistant manager gave me a parental talk, which they ended by saying to me that I can have the evening and Saturday off as a bonus. I was also given a sealed note to take to my new employer. I told Clive what was taking place and no one else.

I took up my new employment that Monday morning. Very sad to say, my new boss, Mr Perez, suffered from the same complaint as did President Franklin Roosevelt of the USA, infantile paralysis. My new boss seemed a very kind man in his mannerism to me. Carefully, he laid out my duties to me. And I perfectly understood the simple way in which he put it. I set out that Monday morning with a prayer on my maiden trip and the determination to win. That day I collected $8.00. On the completion of my week, I collected $75.00. Mr Perez congratulated me. He said that the collection was very good. Jokingly he said, "What have you used upon some of these people?" To this question I only smiled. (But I had been loaned a book by a boarder months before I even dreamed of getting a job like this. It was titled *How to Win Friends and Influence People*. Its author was Dale Carnegie. Some of its passages were of great help.) "I am going to show this to the manager, Mr Williams," he said. My goal was now set to collect $100.00 for a single week. But the closest I could reach was $97.00, and that I did on the third week. Mr Perez then said outright to me that some of the debts I collected were about to be written off for they were very old.

On the fourth week of my employment, I was met with the wonder of wonders of my then life. Mr Williams, the manager, was going to Mayaro on vacation with his family for a month. He wanted a porter to accompany the driver who drove the van from his home on Long Circular Road, mainly to help load and unload the vehicle. (At this time, labour was difficult to hire because of the war, and an American firm by the name of Walsh and Driscoll, contracted to the US Army service, then employed quite a lot of labourers, skilled and unskilled men, and this caused a lot of commercial businesses to be crippled for labour.) Mr Williams then asked me if I will not mind assisting the driver for just one day. "Not at all, sir," said I. "But please let me first tell Mr Perez." "No, no," said he, "I shall speak to him myself."

Mr Williams then took me to his home on Long Circular Road, where the driver was at work all by himself. I quickly summed up that they were a family of five: two little boys, a baby, his wife, and himself. He left me to work along with the driver, whose name was Andrew, and he went back to the pharmacy. We both packed everything that was given to us in the van. Mr Williams then said to Andrew, "OK, you all may leave." Just then the nursemaid came and peeped in the van. She was indeed a very attractive person, and she reminded me very much of Miss Laura in looks and mannerism. I softly said to her, "Why don't you send along the baby's crib? Room can be made for it." Mrs Williams saw me whispering but heard not what was said. She then walked to us in a fury and said, "What has this man said to you?" The maid then told her my suggestion of taking the baby's crib. "Oh my goodness," said she, looking at me and shamefully squeezing her forehead. "I had quite forgotten it. Thank you," she shyly said. To this I made no reply.

We packed the crib with its contents, which also included some toys for the two boys. As we drove off, I asked Andrew to pass home with me so that I can tell Mammy of my late-coming that evening. As we left the Murray Street home, Andrew said, "Boy, I have to look at you differently from now on." I kept my silence and asked him not what he meant.

As we drove along the way, we spoke, but I allowed him to do most of the talking because Tanty always said that whenever you are with strangers, "Be a good listener and let your accomplice talk." May I also add to this, Mr Abe Lincoln once said on one of his many harangues, "It is better to remain silent and be thought a fool than to speak and remove all doubts." Andrew was a man in his late thirties, early forties, and I respected him. As we drove along the way, he realized I knew not the areas and their villages, and so he pointed them all out to me.

Suddenly he said to me, "Boy, George, I do love May very much." "Who is May?" I asked, thinking then of Mammy's daughters. "The maid," said he. "She is a Martiniquan, and anyone can see that she has class. Yes, man," said he as if speaking to himself, "plenty of class." "Well, why don't you tell her?" said I. "Boy, the trouble is I am much

CHAPTER TWENTY-FIVE

older than her. And whenever I try to speak to her, I become choked for words." "Well," said I, "you have no worry." "What do you mean I have no worry?" he asked. "Because, Andrew, you do know your problem." He gave a quick glance at me. "Well, Andrew," said I, "you have said that you are older than her, and cannot speak. Therefore, your problem is solved." "Boy oh boy," said he, "I really has to watch you because you are so smart."

That evening as we got to Mayaro, he made a delivery to the village drugstore, after which we drove to a locked beach house. The building was built about ten feet off the ground, with a small storeroom and parking space to accommodate two large vehicles. "Well," said he, "this is the place in which they would be staying for the month." As we waited, the evening sun shone very much upon us. "Andrew," said I, "why don't you park under the house?" And he did so. Then, said he, "Let's go by the beach. The boss and they won't be here before 5:00 p.m., I am sure." The thoughts of Sans Souci and its beach that I had not seen for a very long time confronted me. And so I needed no persuasion. He locked the van, and as we set off, it was like someone said to me, "George, you better not go." I turned to him and said, "Andrew, let's not worry to go there now." "Why not?" he asked. "Because I no longer feel like going." "Well, I am," he said, and continued walking.

I went back and sat on the steps, and being faced with the sea breeze, I fell asleep. I was awakened by the heavy engine beat of a vehicle. As I looked, there was Mr Williams driving with his family, accompanied by the maid. He was Scottish, and he spoke with an accent. "Whe es Andrew?" "He has just walked up to the beach, sir," I replied. "Goooo get em." Now as I got to the beach, I knew not what direction he went, but having said he went up, I made a right turn with the hope of seeing him. I had just walked about 150 yards when I saw Andrew astride and fast asleep on the bent trunk of a coconut palm. "Hi, wake up, they are here." "Already," said he, rubbing his eyes as he jumped up. "Oh meh gosh," said he, "I have the keys for the van which must be unpacked." As we got there, without an apology he opened the van, and we both began unpacking. The crib was the first item to be taken out. Mrs

Williams muttered something to Mr Williams. And from the corner of my eye they both looked pleasingly at me. We offloaded all the stout articles and took them up to the upstairs floor, while the small items were laid at the bottom of the stairs. Andrew said, "George, let's hurry" (although I was very much faster than he was). "I want to be in Port of Spain by seven." But, in spite of what he said, I took articles up according to their seeming importance. I could have seen that Andrew was not quite pleased at this.

Mr Williams then came down and said, "Well, fellars, you are about to leave now. But, Wright, can you stay on with us until tomorrow morning and I shall drop you up? It's no obligation." "That would be no problem, sir, because before we leave today, I passed home to let them know that I may be very late in getting back." "You did? Oh, oh boy, that's great. OK then, Andrew, you can leave, many thanks for all your help. By the way . . . hold it, Andrew. Wright, have you a phone that Andrew can call when he reaches town?" "Yes, sir," and I gave the number to him. Quickly he scribbled the number and handed it to Andrew. "When you get into town, pass by the Night Dispensary. I do think that Mr Lyndon is on duty tonight. Ask him to allow you to make this call. And please let them know that Wright will be up tomorrow. Thanks again, Andrew, and drive safely," said Mr Williams. I also bade him bon voyage as he slowly drove off. I knew well the art of handling domestic matters, especially that of dealing with children, all of which I learned from the Otchins. And now to create an impression, I displayed it. For here was I now with my boss and his family while working with his company for just a month.

I did work earnestly that evening, and it will seem as though I was thinking ahead of them in all that I did. I even washed the baby's diapers. (In those days Pampers were not yet introduced.) I went down to the garage where the car was parked. I tore down some old marlin lines, came up and washed them. And in the porch I tied some lines facing the sea, where I displayed my laundry. (I after learned how deeply impressed were the Williamses. My action also pointed out to them how wrong they were in granting leave to their other maid.)

CHAPTER TWENTY-FIVE

The supper that evening, though rough, was enough. I then sat in a room facing the sea. I was somewhat saddened because, had I known this would have worked out this way, I would have walked with some reading matter and a pair of pyjamas. However, I prayed and laid on my back with the intent of counting sheep while fanned by the cool sea breeze. And then came the wild idea: instead of counting sheep, why not count ships instead? It is a fact their bright lights could not be seen on the coast and beach of Toco because of the war. Yet one could have seen enough light to discern a passing craft. So I counted sails of easterly and westerly direction. I did, yes, I did. I do know that I had as I fell asleep.

Morning came, and before anyone woke up, I thanked my Lord and rushed to the sea for a quick bath. The water was very warm. What a pity I could not go in even knee high. However, I did enjoy the way in which I was having the bath. When I was satisfied, I went back to the house, and there, in an outdoor freshwater shower, I re-bathed as I washed the sand from my skin. There were several scales of dry soap lying on the ledges. I combined a few pieces, then soaped and washed myself. By the time the first adult awoke, I had already the kettle whistling and was busy sweeping the floor. Mrs Williams was now out of her room holding her infant babe in one arm and preparing a feeding bottle with the other. I looked at her and was doubtful as to whether I should ask her to let me hold the baby. She looked at me and said, "Do you want to hold her?" "Yes, mam," said I with delight. And so she gave her to me. Having learned from Mrs Otchin how a baby must be held, I had no problem. Mrs Williams, however, seemed quite surprised to see the way in which I held the babe. When she had prepared the feed, she thanked me for the boiling of the kettle and holding her babe, then went into her room. The maid came to me and asked if I had a family of my own. "No," said I, "but why do you ask that?" "Just from the way in which you act," she replied. "Well, I don't, but I do know a little about the nursery." I then quickly sensed that a conversation was going to arrive, so I avoided it through reasons of my own.

At 7:30 a.m. Mr Williams called me. "George," said he, "it is entirely left to you to make your own decision. We shall both be leaving for Port of Spain in an hour's time. The challenge is left open to you. If you want, you can go home and have a change of raiment, taking along with you your swimsuit, personal toilets, and maybe some extra clothes in case it should rain and you get wet. You can then join me at the Dispensary at 2:00 p.m. and come and spend the weekend. I shall take you up on Monday morning. Or you can stay when you go home today. Just think about it. You do not now have to give a ready answer."

As he turned to go, "Sir," said I, "I will be delighted to be back for the weekend. I have not been exposed to this type of sea scenery for many years, and it now brings me fond memories of my home." "Where you from?" he asked. "Toco, sir." "Then you do know the Bishops' house?" "Yes, sir, it is on top of the hill in the Palm Tree area." "That's right," said he, "I have visited there on two occasions, and I do agree the beach with its swaying coconut palms and the rolling waves are similar to here. And what of your folks? Will they agree?" "Yes, sir."

We left on our journey to Port of Spain at 8:25 a.m. Unlike Andrew, who spoke on many subjects on our way to Mayaro, Mr Williams said nothing. His eyes were set on the road. After about twenty-five minutes of steady driving, I pondered in my mind what can I say to be of interest and not be deemed a fool. "Sir," said I, "do you think the Allies can win this war?" "Yes," said he, "under the present leadership of Mr Winston Churchill as prime minister, they could. But never could they under the leadership of Mr Neville Chamberlain." And so he kept on talking of many events that I had never before heard of. He then said, "Wright, the English and Scots are a very brave and fearless people when it comes to warfare." And so he talked of many wars that they fought and were victorious.

Now, not to be knowledgeably defeated, I said to him, "Yes, sir, and you must also remember that the very English once faced defeat at the hands of your ancestors. The then leader was the Spider King, as he was called by the lower class. His real name was Robert Bruce. He fought and defeated Edward the Second's army in the battle of Bannockburn in June of 1314." Mr Williams slowed down, almost bringing the car

CHAPTER TWENTY-FIVE

to a standstill. As if perplexed, he looked at me and said, "Yes, Wright, you are quite right. I had almost forgotten that. But you must remember that wars in those days were not fought as they are today." And so he went on and on. I found him to be a great conversationalist.

He was a fast but careful driver. And so we were at the pharmacy at 11:25 a.m. I then boarded a tram and was at home at 11:50 a.m. Mammy and the boys were quite happy to see me back. She had received the phone call from Andrew at 8:16 p.m., just when she had begun to be concerned of my late homecoming. I then told her of what was now afoot. Off she went into her room and brought me out a small suitcase. "What time are you to meet Mr Williams?" "At noon, Mammy." "Well," said she, "pack three changes of clothing, two pairs of pyjamas, a large towel, two wash rags, a change of light footwear, your toothbrush, toothpaste, and light soap, some talc powder, and your shaving set." "But I shall be down on Monday." "Just do as I say," she snapped. "And do take some money with you also."

I did as I was told, not forgetting my swimsuit and three changes of undergarments, my prayer book, two up-to-date newspapers, which were given me by an American boarder, and $2.00. I then bade Mammy and the boys goodbye. As I was leaving, Mammy asked, "How much money have you, George?" "$2.00, Mammy," I replied. "Wait," said she, as she returned to her room and came to me with a small torchlight and $10.00. I thanked her and was off.

Having known that I was really to meet Mr Williams at 2:00 p.m., my watch showed me that I was 50 minutes ahead of time, so I went over to Aunt Bertrice to let her know what was taking place so that she can relay the news to concerned relatives. She again began, "George, I do know you do not . . ." "Please, Aunt, not any more of my father's stuff." "OK, son," said she, "no hard feelings. By the way, how about a quick bite before you leave? It is now lunchtime, and you probably may be long before eating something." I looked at my watch and saw I had yet twenty minutes. The menu was chicken pelau*. I bolted a fair portion, bade her goodbye and left.

I was at the pharmacy at 1:58 p.m. I espied Mr Williams moving around in a lackadaisical manner. Someone then spoke to him. He then looked at his watch and in my direction. "You are here on time, laddie," he said, and with a quick look at my suitcase, he asked, "Have you taken your swimsuit?" "Yes, sir," I replied. He laughed as he shook his head from side to side. We left at 2:10 p.m. Mr Williams drove by way of Sangre Grande. When we got to Sangre Grande, he went into the market and purchased some nice cuts of beef and mutton, along with a fair amount of plant seasoning, and we were off again. Like Andrew, he realized that I knew not the district, so he named the villages and every estate to me as we drove along. "I do hope that ferry is working," said he, "or else we would be kept back." However, the ferry was no problem; it worked out nicely. We chatted along the way. I was careful not to mention to him anything about my work or where I lived, but we spoke widely on other matters.

We were at the beach house at 4:55 p.m. There were two pedlars with fruits who came and asked him if he was interested. "No, no," he said. I was tempted to buy some oranges and bananas, but my inner thoughts said no to me. When we got upstairs, anyone could have seen a great change that was done in rearranging of the house. I was again shown the very room for my weekend, not with a cot but a nicely made sofa made up and covered with a white linen sheet, a pillow in a crochet case, and a blanket. There was also a chair and a rudely made-up table neatly covered.

That night I was given some lovely steamed fish and vegetables for supper. After supper I went to the kitchen and washed all the dishes, pots and pans. I then took all leftovers for two stray dogs that were outside. I sat on a treader of a step and fed the hungry canines. As I fed the animals, there began a musical concert of night creatures: the croaking toad, the whistling tree frog, the hooting owl, the chirping cricket, the mosquito with its witch-like hum, as fire bugs and glow worms radiated their lights beneath the growth of the dancing coconut palm, not for a moment forgetting the roaring waves, with the hissing wind conducting. What a pantomime of Nature! (1 Chronicles 16:32–33: "Let the sea roar and the fullness thereof. Let the fields rejoice, and all

CHAPTER TWENTY-FIVE

that is therein. Then shall the trees of the wood sing out at the presence of the Lord because He cometh to judge the Earth.")

I had not washed myself, so I got to it. When all was done, I scanned the day's *Gazette*, prayed, and got into bed with my window open, and being now fanned by the sea breeze, I fell asleep. I was up very early that Sunday morning, and as there was no church to attend, I prayed and sang three hymns from my Anglican hymn book. Later I went to put the kettle on and laid the dining table for breakfast. Mrs Williams first came out, and one could have read the surprised look on her countenance. She was thankful that I had the water all boiled, so she prepared the baby's food right away.

I then went to the beach to look at the rolling waves breaking upon the sandy shore. To my surprise there were scores of people just bathing and having fun. Some youths were even beating bottles with spoons for merriment. I said to myself there may be war elsewhere but certainly not in Trinidad. I went back to the beach house. And being now tortured by not having something to do, I cut some shrubs with my combination penknife, made a broom, and so I began sweeping some dried leaves and paper blown by the wind. As I set myself upon this task, my mind strayed to a campfire. Upstairs in the kitchen was a very sharp cutlass; I took it and cleared a spot nearest a pool of darkish water which was alive with hundreds of tadpoles. I cut fallen, dried branches of coconut palm and, gathering four bags of both wet and dry coconut shells along with some driftwood, I made a huge pile, which was all in readiness for a campfire. Mr Williams came and looked at it. "Oh, George," he said, "me lads will be very excited bout that. Let's hope it does not rain."

After lunch I sat by my window facing the beach, and I saw a score of people digging in the sand. I looked and wondered what were they doing. So I inquired from May if she knew. "Oh yes," said she, "what moon is it?" I could not answer her question, yet she continued to talk. "Oh yes!" she said. "They are looking for chip-chips*. Come, let's go and get some," said she. "We do not have those in Toco," said I. "To the contrary, all I ever knew of chip-chips was an old calypso which goes like this: 'If you want your body to keep in order, wash yourself with some chip-chip water'." To this May laughed.

We then armed ourselves with a shopping bag and the very cutlass with which I prepared the pile for the campfire. As we got on the beach, May said, "Let's join them." "No," said I, "not so quickly." I really cared not for the maddened crowd. As we gazed on, a couple came by. Being alert, I overheard the gent saying to his partner, "Those are too small. Let's go higher up." I said to May, "We shall follow them." We were about sixty yards away from the crowd when our couple started digging with a rake-like tool and really getting some large ones. We then went about twelve feet away from them, where we found quite a lot as I dug with the cutlass. Very quickly our bag was filled. The young man came to us and said, "Man, you are a boss, you sure know how to find them. You all are not like the people down there." I smiled and said to myself, you do not know how much you have helped us. May said not a word. When we got back to the house, there were visitors with the Williams family. They were all surprised at our large catch and more so of the very large ones. I then went and fetched two pails of sea water. Everyone helped in washing them; even the children helped in the fun. After washing our catch twice, I decided to quit the scene, being allergic to all shellfish if eaten.

As the evening shadows cast, the darkness fell fast. It was time that the fire be started and so, while the folks were speaking, May brought me a box of matches and a bottle of kerosene. I did not need the kerosene. "If I can get some old used paper, the job can be done at a lower cost." "OK," said she, and upstairs she went and was soon back holding some discarded paper and the kitchen bin, followed by the two boys. Taking the papers, I went to the heap as the boys came after me. In two minutes the heap was lighted, and in ten minutes it was aglow with flames leaping to the skies. The wild growth and palm trees began dancing. And it seemed that a message was radioed around the neighbourhood because people came around, warming themselves. The movement went on for fully an hour. As the flames and intense heat died, grown-ups and children were roasting fish and sausages on

CHAPTER TWENTY-FIVE

the red coal. I also saw two young men roasting a dried coconut in its husk and shell. I had not to put the fire out myself. At 11:00 p.m. the water from the pool with its many tadpoles was thrown upon it by the campers for its quenching.

I finally went upstairs and packed my belongings for home the next day. When I was finished, I sat on the veranda facing the sea, looking for passing ships. I was seated just about five minutes when Mr Williams came and said, "George, you have made everyone happy tonight with your campfire. My friends who were here said it was the largest they had ever seen. Mrs Williams, Rich and Chris really loved it – even May was happy. We do make them in Scotland; I remember as a boy visiting one at Perth on the grounds of a demolished palace. It was not immense because we could not spare the material, but I was reminded of it tonight." I kept a silent listener as he spoke. He then paused. I said, "Thank you, sir. When the Boy Scouts held their camp in Toco, they made larger ones while they sang and made jokes to entertain the crowd."

"Oh me gosh," said he. "George, tell me how long can you stay with us? When are you to report home?" "Staying with you is as long as you wish, sir, for my relatives all know that I am with you all. So they will not at all worry themselves." "Well, that suits me fine," said he, "because I really did not feel like driving to Port of Spain tomorrow. Well, good night," said he as he walked towards the living room. I could not believe it all. I remembered Mammy's sternness when she told me to pack the many items in the suitcase. I then went into my room and sat upon my bed thinking of the long conglomeration of experiences of the past day. I then prayed and fell asleep.

At 1:10 a.m. I was awakened by a heavy downpour which beat heavily upon the galvanize roof. The entire building was unsealed, so in no way could the noise be less deafening. There were flashes of lightning followed by thunder. I then recalled that evening in Toco and my child-like experience. As I looked across at the window pane, I could have seen on the beach flashlights and hurricane lanterns. They were those of fishermen pulling their boats to safety. I then realized that there was a rainstorm out at sea. As I peered through the pane, I wondered if there was anyone else awake in the house. Must I alert the Williamses, or must I call May, having seen a leak in the living room which was quite heavy? The water was flowing towards some suitcases and cartons Andrew and I had brought in the van from their home. I dashed to the kitchen, grabbed two pails and four kitchen towels, for I could not then locate the mop. I was back to the leak, where I placed one pail under the heavy leakage and set myself to the task of sapping up the running water with the towels. I had sapped about six pints of water off the floor when I heard a movement, then a light was turned on. It was Mr Williams. "Oh my goodness, what's the matter?" as he seemed somewhat shocked. I pointed the heavy leak to him; by then the pail was almost filled. He took it and quickly emptied it in the kitchen sink, while I kept on drying the floor. I told him I knew not where the mop was, which was why I am using the kitchen towels. "Forget about that, you could have used some clothing for that matter," said he. "For you have saved a lot of things from being ruined." By then the rain had ceased; there were also fewer flashes of lightning and the rolling of thunder. And so we retired into our rooms. I flung myself upon my bed and fell into a sound sleep.

I awoke at 8:00 a.m. and was very much alarmed to see everyone was up. I quickly prayed and scampered downstairs for my bath. On my way down, I met May coming up the steps with a kerosene tin. "Good morning," said I, "why didn't you wake me?" "I would have, but Mr Williams said not to because you were up all night with him securing things from the storm. He himself got up at 7:30 a.m. because of the hard romping of the children." "Thank you, however," said I as I made for the bathroom. As the sun became warmer Mr Williams made no delay. We both drove to the village Chinese shop, and he bought a small container of putty and a pint of linseed oil. When we got back, I mixed a good portion of it and climbed up a nearby tree which overhung the roof and stopped that dangerous leak along with a few smaller ones.

Needless to say, as the days passed by, May and I grew to be very good friends. She told me she was originally from Guadeloupe. While there, she got married to a Frenchman who left France and came there

CHAPTER TWENTY-FIVE

to reside. They were doing well with a winery and a small commercial business of their own, plus some investments made in a thriving dry goods store. But when the horrid war broke out, he was conscripted back to France and was drafted into the French First Army. He quickly attained the rank of sergeant. But as fate would have it, he fell victim following the fall of France to the Germans. When the sad news reached her, she almost went out of her mind. She then turned the businesses to be managed by her relations and thought of migrating to either Puerto Rico or Trinidad. Trinidad was chosen because an uncle of hers who was a lawyer and an aunt of Mrs Williams who was also a lawyer had some ties. And so she came here to work with the Williams family. I questioned her no further on the matter because it was not my concern. But I felt sorry for her on hearing of her plight.

For two weeks I then displayed all the skill and knowledge I had gained at the Otchins under the tutorship of Miss Laura: washing, cooking, cleaning, ironing and even that of childcare. This helped not only May but also Mrs Williams, who was herself a very active person. After work was done on evenings, May and I would take a long walk on the beach. Either catching crabs, a sport that I knew well, or selecting strange-looking objects washed ashore by the waters. Fresh fish was always available. Most of the catches were done by seine. As you helped the fishermen to pull to the shore their catch, you may be rewarded with a fish or two, which was always welcome in the house. Both Mr Williams and myself loved fish. Now, although I had with me but little clothing, I was always clean, for as you wash and hung on the lines, the sea breeze will dry day or night as fast as our modern-day clothes dryer.

One day Mr Williams went into Port of Spain with his elder son, Rich, who was six years old. A hunter came by with a fawn. It was cute and tame. He had a leather collar around its neck held by a vine-made cord. "Madam," said he, "would you buy him for your children? I am now selling him for $6.00." Mrs Williams looked at the quadruped; it walked straight to her and rubbed its nose on her skirt as if to say, "Please buy me." Little Chris, who was four years and made not the trip with his father, came scampering down the stairs with a bit of bread. The little deer just went and gently helped itself to it.

We all laughed, being astonished at the action of the beast. "Yes, Madam," said the hunter, "it is all yours." "No," said she. "And, furthermore, my husband is not here at the moment." "When will he be back?" asked the hunter. "Late this evening," she replied. "By then I am afraid you would lose the bargain because I am sure that your neighbour will buy it. Look, you know what? Give me one pound and ten pence, and take him." (I smiled at the fellow's wits as I wondered if he was also an ardent reader of Dale Carnegie's book.) "I have no money," Mrs Williams firmly replied. "Ok, Madam," and he turned away. I could have seen Mrs Williams really loved the animal. Meanwhile, Chris was pleading that she buy it. I told May to ask her if she would not mind borrowing the $5.00 from me. "But why did you not tell her that yourself?" "No," said I, "that may be bad manners to her." May looked at me and sadly shook her head, and went and spoke to Mrs Williams. "Yes!" said Mrs Williams to me, "you get the money while I call back the man." I quickly went up to my room and was back. I handed Mrs Williams the $5.00. The smiling man came back with his merchandise and was paid. I took the little creature upstairs, followed closely by Chris. I made him hold the leash as I went for an unused press that was in May's room. With it, I blocked the end of the gallery and put the little creature in. When Mr Williams and little Rich came in that evening, Rich was all excited over their friend and so was Mr Williams of its purchase. He handed me my 1.0.10 sterling in currency and so the animal became fully their property.

The month passed with joy and lifelong memories. One Saturday morning at 7:00 a.m. Andrew came with the van to transport us back again into town. "Well, boy, how was it?" he cunningly asked. "Very tough," said I. "I am dying to be back home from this month of imprisonment. Tell me, Andrew, how are things moving in the city?" "Good enough," said he, "with the exception of some flooding a few weeks ago in the lower Dry River area." Now I had already told May about his interest in her, and should he ever come to take us back that

CHAPTER TWENTY-FIVE

day, we must have but very little communication. The suggestion was well taken, and it worked beautifully because he displayed not his lazy attitude, but willingly helped in taking the things downstairs along with the packing of the van. He was very good in doing the latter. When everything was placed in both vehicles, there remained but one problem. That was seating space for the added passenger. How was he to be carried? The van was packed, and there remained no space. And there was a risk with the heat. Nor could he be placed in the trunk of the car, which also had some smaller items, which will then lead to suffocation. Mrs Williams then suggested that the boys drive down with us in the van, and May will sit at the backseat of the car with the fawn. "No, no," cried Chris, "I want to be with Rescue" (that was the name given to the fawn). "So do I," said Rich. "Hold, hold it," said Mr Williams, "let me handle this matter." He then leaned against a coconut tree laughing and passing his fingers through his hair. At that very moment, an idea came to me of what could be done, but I thought it was best not to speak unless I was asked.

So I went to Mrs Williams and asked if I should go up and recheck the rooms should anything be left. "That's a good idea," said she. So off I went. I found one side of her bedroom slipper under their bed, a pair of socks, Mr Williams's umbrella leaning against the doorway, and a cloth tied with some things that felt and sounded as shells in May's room. I then checked my room, but there was nothing left with the exception that I had forgotten to close my window. So I reported back to Mrs Williams with the forgotten articles. Everyone was surprised of my findings. I then reminded Mr Williams that the door was not locked.

I then asked Andrew if they had come to a final decision. "In a way," said he. "But yet they seemed not happy about it." "What is it?" I asked. "Well, Mr Williams will drive the van himself with Mrs Williams, the baby, and May. I shall drive the car with the boys, you, and the deer." I smiled and walked off. Mr Williams must have had his eyes set upon me. He called me and asked, "Has Andrew told you how we are travelling?" "Yes, sir," said I. "And what do you think?" (Now as I had already solved the problem my way, I had then a ready answer.) "Sir, don't you think it would be nice to travel in your car with your family? Let Mam and the baby sit with you to the front with the infant necessaries. Rich and Chris to back seat with the fawn on the floor. Andrew, May and myself in the van. We take the lead, and you follow." "Good idea," said he, clapping me on my shoulder. "Except one thing – I will take the lead, and you shall follow." He spoke to Mrs Williams, who seemed happy. He called Andrew and said, "Andrew, you shall drive the van with George and May, and I will lead." One could have seen the joy on Andrew's face as he said, "Alright, sir."

A riddle for my reader: I went to Mayaro a boy, but on leaving there in one month's time, no doubt I was man. You may hold your answer.

Chapter 26

Mr Isiaha begins his harassment of George; Mammy visits him at work

We left that beach house, and I have never again visited there. When we got to the village, Mr Williams passed in at the village drugstore and handed the keys of the house to the proprietor. He then came to the van to see if we were settled, and he also asked if we wanted anything. "No, sir," we all said. "May," said he, "you are in the middle." "Yes, sir," she laughed, "a thorn between two roses." And we all shared her joke.

Once again we began our journey, with Mr Williams in the lead. The weather was beautiful. Before we left the beach house, I had asked May to direct all her conversation if possible to Andrew. And she certainly was making a beautiful job of it, as Andrew beamed with joy. Mr Williams again took the Sangre Grande route. As we got into the town he again stopped by a drugstore. I got out and walked to the car to see how the children were doing with their playmate. Mrs Williams had the baby fast asleep upon her lap. "George," said she, "see, they are a happy bunch at the back." As I looked, the fawn was laying on the floor while Chris and Rich gently stroked him. Mr Williams, on his return to the car, stopped by a fruit vendor. He called me; as I went, he said, "Take some fruits for you all." Seeing that I was hesitant of what to take, he said to the vendor, "Please, let me have a large paper bag." "Yes, Sar-Boss," said the delighted vendor. Mr Williams then chose twelve lovely oranges and a lovely hand of Gros Michel bananas. He then slipped the vendor a coin, and the man seemed to be very satisfied as he exclaimed, "Oh,

Boss, thank you very much." When we moved off, Mr Williams said, "I know you have a penknife." Then he suddenly said to me, "Oh me goodness, I took none for myself." So he again bought a similar amount of fruit. And so we left for Port of Spain with him still at the lead.

Andrew and May ate bananas. She peeled for him as we drove along, while I peeled and sucked of the oranges. They were very sweet. I said nothing because I would have then to peel for three of us. When we got into St Augustine, Mr Williams turned right into Scott Street. Andrew followed as the car drove into a large yard. They all got out, leaving the fawn rubbing its nose on the partly turned up windows of the car. The occupants of the house came out to them as they exchanged greetings of "Hello, Daisy, hello, Bill." They then shouted to the Williamses. "How are the children? Oh my goodness, look at this little girl. In just a month she has added so much weight! And the boys have grown also. Please tell us how was your holiday?" I yet could not hear the Williamses' reply. They went inside with little Mariann. But Rich and Chris stood in the porch looking at their pet, Rescue. We kept our seats in the van. Andrew, who seemed tired, leaned his head upon the steering and was soon asleep. It was now getting into noon, and the van was growing hot. As May and I decided on getting out, Mrs Williams came out with her baby, followed to the car by her family and the lady, who stroked the head of the fawn as she made comments.

We were again off, and this was our final leg, for this time Mr Williams stopped not until we got to their Long Circular Road home. "Close the gate and set him free," said Mr Williams to the boys as we busily unpacked the van. When we were finished, I bade goodbye and set off with Andrew for my Murray Street home. On my arrival I was very much surprised at the welcome I received. I was hailed as though I was Britain's Black Prince Edward.[1] The boys were all happy to see me home again, and so were the girls and the boarders. Mammy said

---

[1] Edward of Woodstock (1330–76) was known as the Black Prince and hailed by his contemporaries as one of the greatest knights of his age. The origins of the name are uncertain. The name is used by William Shakespeare in his plays *Richard II* (Act 2, scene 3) and *Henry V* (Act 2 Scene 4).

CHAPTER TWENTY-SIX

had I not come down today, she was arranging a special trip tomorrow to get me up. I was truly delighted, for never could I dream that I was so recognized among them.

The Sunday morning I was up at 5:00 a.m. I prayed, took a quick shower, dressed, and was off to church. I visited Trinity Cathedral, but this time I was very careful in selecting my seating place. By 7:15 a.m. I was at Aunt Bertrice's home to let her know that I was back in town, for I knew fully well that by her knowing, the news will be relayed to my other relations. I also told her that I could not stay for breakfast but will join her another time. I was back at Murray Street at 8:15 a.m. Everyone thought I had slipped away again. So I explained the cause of my early absence. The boys and I had breakfast. When we were finished, I set myself to work. There were mossy and clogged drains, a grassy sidewalk, an unruly growth of the hedge, and not forgetting the state of our room. I ganged and directed the boys. By noonday we were all through with our allotted tasks. I gave Mammy almost all the beach treasures I collected. And everyone who saw them was fascinated and thought them to be curious.

Then came Monday morning. When I appeared on the job, I was happy about one thing. I had not to discuss my month's absence with anyone. For beside now knowing Andrew, I had made no friends among the employers during my first month's stay. I had only to report to Mr Perez, the gent who hired me. And he it was that Mr Williams spoke to that Friday of my going to help Andrew. Mr Perez was very happy to see me back. With a smile he asked if there were many mosquitoes and jiggers*. I had not to give ready answers to his question, for they were asked only to be nice. He then added, "There is quite a workload awaiting you. Will you go upstairs to Mr Linsed and let him know that I have sent you. After that, you will come back to me." "Very well, sir," I replied.

Now Mr Perez had not an enclosed office due to his illness and so he could see or be seen by anyone. As I left his office and was making my way through the customers' thoroughfare, I was rudely summoned by someone. As I looked around, it was the assistant manager of the pharmacy. "Oh, good morning, sir," said I. He returned not the compliment but went on to say, "Well, you are the man that has worked for one month and has gotten one month's leave." Before I could have made him a reply, he said, "Don't you know that you are to report to me?" "No, sir, but I have reported to Mr Perez, who has now sent me up to Mr Linsed. However, sir, I am sorry about that." He looked at me narrowly. "Where are you from?" "Toco, sir." He then scratched his partially bald head and said, "Toco! Oh, so you are not one of Toco's stupidees*, but you are a 'smart man*'," said he with disdain.

I was very much ashamed in the presence of three clerks and some customers. But again I said, "Sir, I am very sorry." "Where are you off to now?" I again said, "To Mr Linsed office." Just then came Mr Williams. "Mr Isiaha," he said, "I have been looking for you." Mr Isiaha then turned to me with a smile and said, "Alright, sonny, you may go to Mr Linsed." As I walked off, I breathed a sigh of relief, as strange thoughts and questions came to my mind. I took not the lift but walked up to the second floor to Mr Linsed's office, as I pondered on Mr Isiaha's attack and wondered what will it be now with Mr Linsed. "Good morning, sir," said I as I entered, giving my smart salute. He raised his head, peering through a pair of tortoiseshell-framed glasses. "Good morning," he replied. "What can I do for you?" "I am the collector, sir. Mr Perez sent me up to see you." "Oh goodness," said he, "please excuse my manners of forgetfulness. I did not recognize you." (My downcast spirit was immediately uplifted.) "How was your stay with Mr Williams and his family?" "Very good, sir. I could not have desired better." "That's very nice to hear. For many folks resent his mannerism. But for me, I do like him, and we get along fine. Oh my goodness, I should not be saying this to you." "Never mind about that, sir, although I now speak, yet I am a mute." He looked at me for about three seconds and smiled.

"Well, let's get down to some business," said he. He took a ledger from his drawer and began checking. There were bills that accumulated over the past month and quite a few outstanding old ones. He gave them both to me and said, "Try your best to collect the new ones because we do not want them to fall in the file of the old."

CHAPTER TWENTY-SIX

"Very well, sir, I shall do my best," and so I went back to Mr Perez to let him know what was afoot. "You had not to come back, just go ahead. By the way, has he given you a receipt book?" "No, sir, the last one I used, I left with you." "With me," said he, somewhat doubtful. "Yes, sir, you placed it in that bottom drawer." He looked, and there it was. "Oh my gosh," said he. "I am glad that you have remembered." He then gave a quick check on the originals and handed it to me. And so I was off on my bicycle. As I rode along, I asked the good Lord to help guide, shield, and protect me, and to give to me the right approach to the debtors.

Then the thoughts came to me as follows: (1) The customers who have already paid off their old debts: Collect whatever you can from them on the new. (2) Those who owe old debts and part: Pay off all parts, and begin the old no matter how small. (3) Those who owe both old and new: Pay off all old with a promise to pay off the new ones shortly. The strategy worked well, for at the end of my first week I had collected $158.85. Mr Linsed and Mr Perez were so pleased that Mr Perez rewarded me with two dented tins of Tono (a nutritious chocolate drink). The following week I collected $90.00, the third week $70.96, but on the fourth week, which was the end of the month, I collected a bumper amount of $212.80. As it now stands, the only old debts that were now outstanding were those of individuals who had fled the country or were deceased. Mr Linsed jokingly said to me, "You should get another month's holiday!"

Now may I say, for reasons of his own, Mr Isiaha never ceased in persecuting me. This gent seemed just not to like me. So I kept out of his way as much as possible. Now that my workload was controlled, Mr Perez told me whenever I get in early from my collections on evenings to assist the clerks on the floor. I am not to write any bills but give my sale to any clerk without prejudice. And this I did. For some strange reason, however, many times customers will bypass official salesclerks and come to me. May I say, however, I had never changed from the attire of my prospector's outfit which I had forged from Mr Advance, wearing both khaki and white outfits. And so I felt the presentation of my attire helped very much in the wooing of customers. I tried to avoid floor sales and will station myself at the door which led to the druggist for prescriptions. I will escort the customers to the druggist on duty, not send them as other folks did.

I remember on one such occasion Mr Isiaha approached and said to me, "You are no druggist; you are not even a clerk. Why are you holding that prescription?" "Sir," said I, "I am just leading the customer to the pharmacist." He impolitely pulled the writ from my hand and, with a smile, looked at it and said to the customer, "Sir, will you please come with me." The gentleman then said, "Is this not the very service the young man was performing? Whatever your position may be here, you must first show courtesy to them, and they in turn shall learn from you. Then, and only then, will they be able to serve John Public wisely. But should you be arrogant, as I have now seen, they will in turn display same. Always remember, Mr Whoever-you-may-be, good manners begin at home and spread their delicious aroma in business places as well as in society." The customer then ended vigorously by saying, "Give me now my prescription back. There is a pharmacy across the street. I shall now rather have it filled there!" Standing a mere two yards away from the event and hearing were two clerks, two customers, a porter and a vial washer. With a trembling hand Mr Isiaha gave the prescription to the gentleman and quickly moved away without saying a word.

Mr Isiaha never seemed inclined to give me an easy moment. He just pounced on me whenever he could. One morning after checking out with Mr Perez, I had then to meet a customer at Alexandra Street, St Clair, at 9:15 a.m. As I got to the door and was about to step on the pavement, I was tapped on the shoulder by a porter who said, "Look, Mr Isiaha is calling you." "Oh my goodness," I muttered to myself. "I shall be late to meet this customer." "Where are you to, young man, in such a hurry?" I then told him the nature of my haste. "Let me see your bag." I handed it to him. "No, no, open it upon the counter." The morning was not yet busy, and there were a few clerks looking on. Vehemently I emptied the bag. "What's in that paper bag?" he asked. I opened it and showed him two sandwiches and a flask of cocoa. There was also

CHAPTER TWENTY-SIX

my receipt book, a bodice-type raincoat, a Cadbury Milk chocolate, a pocket dictionary, a copy of the New Testament, and $5.00 in change that was given to me to travel with. All eyes were set upon the items. By then there were about three customers at the desk. The senior druggist, Mr Lyndon, came and said, "Mr Perez will like to know what is this young man still doing here. He has sent him out in a hurry about ten minutes ago." I said not a word. And Mr Isiaha just cleared the scene without mentioning a word. A female clerk said, "This is ridiculous. I have witnessed this young man being persecuted by Mr Isiaha. But this certainly is the extreme." I carelessly flung everything into my bag and was off.

I got to that home three minutes ahead of time. The gent, who was an English lawyer, looked at his watch, smiled, and said, "You are on time. For that I shall give you a reward. I shall pay off the whole bill." The amount was $10.75. He handed me $11.00. I made him his receipt and handed both receipt and change to him. "You may keep the change, sonny," said he. Now being so very near to St James, I went to a pharmacy there and collected $3.00 and returned to Mr Perez's office. As I got there Mr Perez asked, "Were you on time?" "Yes, sir," said I, "with three minutes to spare."

On one occasion there was plenty of rain that day, and sales had dropped considerably. There were a few people sheltering, and almost all eyes were set on the heavy waters, on which floated empty cartons and other debris as they sailed down the street. There were flashes of lightning and peals of thunder. Mr Isiaha also was looking on with interest. Then said he, "Come, gentlemen, line up, I have a question. How many are you here?" I then tried to sneak my way out from among them. "Hold it, Wright, this also includes you." There were nine of us there from various departments. His question was based on the elements. As we all stood somewhat lackadaisically in line, my position was fourth as he filed his question. The first man seemed to answer quite intelligently to me. The second, an assistant druggist by name of Bitson, who hailed from our sister island Tobago, gave a straightforward answer, which I taped in my mind. He asked the third, who seemed somewhat related to him. That chap also gave a very high explanation. Then came my turn. I very calmly replied as Bitson had. I observed Mr Isiaha twitched his eyes. And so on he went to the others, who all gave different answers. He finally came to Mr Lyndon. He asked not authoritatively as he did to us, but simply said, "What do you think, Lyndon?" "I am quite in agreement with Bitson and Wright." Oh boy, I felt an indescribable warmth of satisfaction glowed from within as Mr Isiaha just walked away without saying another word. I now realized myself living in two worlds: at home, where I was kindly treated by Mammy, and on my job, where I had to avoid getting into constant struggle with the second in authority.

When the rain ceased that day, I went to Mr Perez to see if anything had been programmed for me. For I just wanted to be out. He handed me two bills: one for a St Joseph Road client, the other for a Boissière Village client. "Watch the weather," said Mr Perez as he handed me the bills. "Very well, sir," I replied. I hurried to St Joseph Road, and I collected $6.00, which was half the amount of the bill. My thoughts were now all set for Boissière Village. As I got to the corner of St Joseph Road and Piccadilly Street, there was a vendor selling pigeon peas upon the pavement at six cents a heap; they were full and lovely. I bought two heaps, which he stuffed into a stout paper bag. I hurried over to Aunt Bertrice. She was out, but Ren was at home. He had by then quit the police force and was now employed as a sanitary inspector with the City Council. I told him of my early morning experience with Mr Isiaha and my forged answer. "Good boy," said he. "That scamp wanted to make an open ridicule of you, but you made it of him instead."

During our conversation Aunt Bertrice came. She made no comment on the matter but served us both with a glass of lemonade. As I was leaving, "Look!" said she. "You are forgetting your parcel." "No, no, Aunt, it is for you." "Oh, thank you for whatever it is. Be careful with the weather," she said. I then hurried back to the vendor. "Have you a salt bag?" "Yes, sir," he replied. "Put four heaps in it for me." "Look, man," said he, "I have seven heaps and a little bit. Give me thirty-six cents and take all because yuh buy from me already." "What about the

CHAPTER TWENTY-SIX

worms?" I jokingly said. "Nah, man," said he, "not a worm. I planted dem peas three days after the full moon." He then stuffed the salt bag; I paid him and hastened to Murray Street. As I placed it upon the kitchen floor, I wondered if I should still proceed to Boissière Village; an answer came, "No!" As I was about to relax, another thought came: if for some reason Mr Perez would ring them about something or vice versa. And so I was off again. When I got there, I was paid the full amount of the bill, $9.00. I then went back home and joined the pea-shelling crew. And the next morning I went in with the cash of $15.00.

There was an occasion I was taking some instructions from Mr Perez when Mr Williams came and said, "George, your mother is at the front." My heart leapt as I wondered what could have brought her down from Toco. Is something wrong? Was she nicely dressed and looking as smart as Aunt Bertrice would do should she come to see me? My good Lord, what was now her problem? As I hurried to the front, I was consoled with the fact that it was Mr Williams who met her and not Mr Isiaha. And so I went out looking for Mother. But to my surprise, who was there waiting for me? It was Mammy. Many eyes were set upon us as she spoke to me. Even Mr Isiaha came and stood at the doorway with an air of authority. He could then say nothing to me because not too far off was Mr Williams standing. Mammy then walked slowly with me across to where Mr Williams stood with his back turned to us. As we got to him, she said, "Hello, Bill." He turned around, and they began chatting. I left them both, and I went back to Mr Perez.

In an hour's time I was summoned to Mr Williams's office. "Sit down, George," he said to me. He for the first time ever asked how was my work going. He also said he was informed by Mr Linsed that all old debts were cleared with the exception of those debtors who had fled the country or deceased. "That's a damn good job, George. Keep it up," said he. "Thank you, sir," said I. He then added, "Is everything working good with you around here?" "Well, sir," said I, "someone once told me that I must not worry because worries kill. And I am too young to die." He laughed jolly at my reply. "By the way, George, is that lady really your mother?" "No, sir, she is my adopted mother." "I knew her husband," said he. "He was an Englishman. We both served in the army in the First World War; out here we met again. He was once a director of Stephens Ltd. But it is the first time I have met his wife. George," he said to me, "I am removing from where I now live to Scott Street, St Augustine, and Madam will like you to help us very much that weekend. But will you like then to assist us?" "That shall be no problem at all, sir, should life permit and I am well." He smiled. "One thing more, George, tell it to no one here because I have not publicized it." "Sir," said I, "I have no friends around here, not even Andrew." "I do know that," he said.

When I returned downstairs, Mr Williams was standing in the public section and looking into a showcase. "Come, George," he called to me. As I went to him, he rested one hand upon my left shoulder, bending his head low to my ears. Said he, "Can you make it this weekend?" "Certainly, sir." "Good!" said he, partly aloud, "you may go." Mr Isiaha heard the latter part of his statement. And so I thought of pranking. I went into Mr Perez's office, took up my bag without even searching it, and walked out without saying a word to anyone. I had a bill for a very good customer in lower Henry Street. The amount was $10.00. I went, collected the amount, and was off to Aunt Bertrice.

There I met Sister Hilda, whom I had not seen for quite a while. She was pregnant and seemed slowed down a bit from her wits. I left them both speaking and walked over to Mongoose Store. From there I bought two towels, half a dozen baby's diapers, a blue baby's blanket, and two White Rose and Cucumber toilet soaps. I then went over to the market and bought some green mangoes and went back to the house. I knocked but entered without being called in. Aunt said, "Watch him, you can see he is up to some mischief; he is just as his father." I then displayed the items upon the dining table. They both said, "Boy, you can waste money!" Hilda said, "I really felt like having some mango chow for two days now. Come, let's make some." "Not *let's* make some," said Aunt, "*you* make some." And we three laughed. Then Aunt made it for her.

They both were pleased with the purchased merchandise. But yet I was reminded of my spending. "Remember, money does not grow on

CHAPTER TWENTY-SIX

trees," said Aunt Bertrice. "Waste not today and go wanting tomorrow." I returned not to the pharmacy that day but proceeded to Murray Street. I told Mammy of all that took place after she left. She said that she was awaiting for Mr Isiaha's presumptuous approach had he made one. And she had a hearty laugh at Mr Williams's inquiry into her motherhood.

Chapter 27

George helps his boss's family to move house and brings May a vase of roses; she proposes marriage and leaves for Guadeloupe

That night there was a siren warning, and all bright lights were to be put out. So we had then to do everything by way of shaded candles. The serving of dinner to the boarders was somewhat difficult. However, I was told to move around like a professional chef, for this was an occasion when a high-ranking US officer and his wife called in for dinner. That evening the children, both maids, and myself worked as a team while Mammy supervised. I wore my toxicedo* and braided black pants and was told that the visitors were quite impressed. Very quickly we got through with the dinner without the help of electricity or powered lights.

The weekend did come for Mr Williams and his family to remove from their Long Circular home to their residence in Scott Street, St Augustine. They hired two mule-drawn wagons from Messrs Haynes Clark and, with the van driven by Andrew, everything was in their Scott Street home by 3:00 p.m. that Saturday. Andrew pulled well his weight after the mule train left. When we were finished and about to leave, Mrs Williams came and thanked us for what she described as a splendid job well done. She then handed an envelope to Andrew, which he immediately tore open. I saw from the corner of my eyes currency notes, which he tucked into his shirt pocket. She then turned and asked me if I do not mind staying an extra hour with Mr Williams, and he shall drop me home when he goes into town later. "Not at all, mam,"

CHAPTER TWENTY-SEVEN

said I. So Andrew left alone, while I followed Mrs Williams back to the house once more.

Now there were two ladies helping Mrs Williams, assisted by May. And those four women worked at a non-stop rate together. Rich and Chris were busy sweeping the floors. "That's to keep them occupied," said their father. Mr Williams and I moved the heavy and bulky items around as directed by his wife. It was 5:00 p.m. when Mrs Williams and friends flung themselves upon a bed laughing. Mr Williams and I had just moved a heavy press into that very room. "I think we have made it," said Mrs Williams to Mr Williams, all laughing. "Yes," he replied. Turning to me, he said, "This fellow has just begun; he is as fresh as ever. I am now going to have a bath and relax a little before going into town."

Mrs Williams asked me if I won't mind giving May a hand to fix the annex, which was to be her room. "Not at all, mam," said I. Next came Mr Williams into the room with a bottle of Limacol*. He applied some upon May's head, and she was again calm and smiling. When May and I got to the annex, there was hardly anything to be done. The floors were cleaned and bright, the walls seemed newly painted. I passed my fingers between the jealousies and louvres, which were all dust free. Neither were there any cobwebs. I knew May was tired of her day, so I bade her sit and direct me as to how she wanted her furniture placed. "No, no, George," said she, "why must you do this?" "OK," said I, "I am leaving, for you need no help." (I was truly bluffing.) "Oh no," said she, "will you please stay?"

I very quickly assembled her bed and stored an old-fashioned wardrobe in a corner, a cedar clothes press with see-your-whole-self looking glass inserted upon the door, a dressing table made exactly as the one I had, an antique couch, and a collapsible bridge table with four chairs. She made me place all in various positions. She herself covered the table with a satin-like material. When this was all done, I went across to the main building. There I found a milk bottle; I washed it and filled it with water. I gathered some pink and red roses along with some buds that will soon be opened. As I walked past the washhouse, there was an Oxford

Blue cube upon a shelf. I broke it and dissolved it in the water, making it a light blue in the bottle. I placed the roses into it, and there I had a lovely vase of roses of which neither England nor Holland could boast.

When I returned to the annex, there was May laying and snoring on the couch. Poor thing, I knew that she was tired and fatigued over some days of hard work at Long Circular preparing for today. (Pardon me, dear Reader, although I had not mentioned this outright, but after our Mayaro trip, May and I grew to be very close. The only one who knew of our relationship was Horace. We made our dates by phone whenever she was off duty.) I placed the vase of flowers on the table without disturbing her. I came out and began pulling weeds around the base of the annex. It was 6:10 p.m. when Mrs Williams brought us some food. The sun was just sinking on the horizon. "Oh my goodness," said she, "where is May, George?" "She is inside, mam," said I. As she entered, I followed close behind her because May had not yet seen the flowers, and I did not want her now to proclaim a remark of surprise about it. "Whaw!" said Mrs Williams and May awoke. I pressed my finger upon my lips, giving May a sign not to speak. "Look," said Mrs Williams to May, "I have brought you all something to eat. But your room looks lovely. And I do envy your vase of roses. There should be a screen someplace to bring privacy to your bed. And there are curtains for your doors and windows up in the house." "I shall get those tomorrow," said May. "Come to eat, George." "Alright, Mam, but first let me wash my hands." I headed for the washroom and left them speaking. When I returned I was greeted with hugs and kisses for the vase of roses, which, as May exclaimed, gave the room a lift. "Nothing more was spoken on it by Mrs Williams," said she, "but she commented on your weeding around the annex." May then left to get washed, and upon her return we both had our dinner.

After our dinner that evening, May said to me, "George, I have some sad and happy news to give you. I received a letter from Guadeloupe on Thursday." (As she spoke, the memory of Theo came to me.) "My grandmother, who was 69 years, passed away. She was very wealthy, and she has left for me a tidy sum. I am now urged to return home." She continued, "George, as I had already told you, after the tragic death of

CHAPTER TWENTY-SEVEN

my husband, I tried to hide by coming to Trinidad, leaving a blossoming business. What I am now doing is not my life's calling. I am here with these people, and I am treated with respect by them and their friends. I am also paid $8.00 per month, a wage that is very much higher than the average domestic gets in Long Circular. I have spent but very little of it. And now I am blessed with everything, including you," she said laughing. "And as I have told you while in Mayaro, I do not want a franc from you. Should I go back to Guadeloupe, with the money grande-mere leave, I can turn some of it into the business, which I was told is doing remarkably well. And bank the other portion. I will then send for you, and we will get married, or rather let it be done here without pomp before I leave. It can easily be done by a Father Priest* at Woodbrook. I know he shall do it all for us at a very low cost. And you know something, George, I have never said this to you, but Mrs Williams one day said to me while we was having a woman-to-woman conversation that she regretted speaking to you that day in the way that she did when we were packing the van for Mayaro. She said that you would make an ideal husband for any woman, especially if you should be privileged to attend a school and choose a profession of your own. Well, boy, for that you have no worry, for I shall be sending you to a French school in Martinique. Tell not a word of what I am now saying to you to anyone because I do not yet want it to get to the knowledge of the Williamses. For, in confidence, Mrs Williams told me that they shall be going later this year to Scotland. What a daring risk. I will be left with her aunt Daisy B, who in fact have got her own servants. George, George! Come on, George! Will you please say something. I have been speaking for the past fifteen minutes to you, and you have kept your silence. Is something wrong? What do you advise?"

I was truly dumbfounded by what May told me. Was she honestly speaking her mind? Was she now setting for me a goal, and if so, am I not privileged to make a choice? "Will you please give me a week to think about it? I shall phone and let you know." "OK, honey," said she. We then went on speaking on other matters when we heard heavy footsteps coming towards the annex. It was Mr Williams, who came to say that he would be leaving in fifteen minutes. I openly shook May's hand. Although it was dark, I saw her fighting a tear as we were off to the city.

I made sure that I was early on the job come the Monday morning of that week. As the entrance door was opened by Mr James, I was the third person to enter. I stood at a position that I must be seen by Mr Williams should he arrive early. I was not wrong in my calculation because he was the seventh person to arrive. "Good morning, everyone," said he in his drawling Scottish tongue. "Good morning, sir," we all answered. He looked at me and said, "George, you are here!" "Yes, sir," I replied. I knew that there were members there who were astonished to know that I had been given that attention. For there was Big Pierce, who was Mr Isiaha's real buddy. No one at this time dared question me on the matter except Mr Lyndon, who I esteemed a little in my confidence, second to Mr Linsed. Then came 8:00 a.m. when the doors were all open to the public. I gave a hand to this. The employees all seemed on time, even the porters and vial washers. Then I observed Mr Williams pacing the floor as he wore a grim look and made an occasional glance at his watch. He then came to me and asked, "Have you seen Andrew?" "No, sir." "Should you see him, tell him I want him." I was now partially awaiting Mr Perez to call, and looking out for Andrew.

Andrew came at 8:30 a.m. I told him Mr Williams wanted him. "How did things pass when I left yesterday?" he asked. "Good," said I. At that very moment we were interrupted by a call from Mr Perez, so off I went, avoiding any further questions. That day I visited eight clients, of whom seven paid. I collected $115.86. It was a bumper haul; both Mr Perez and Mr Linsed commended me. Having nothing else to be done that day, I went to assist on the floor. Mr Perez then called me and told me to go home. "You have done more than enough for the day," he said.

Because of World War Two, and Trinidad at the time not being a manufacturing country, we were therefore hard-hit for many things: food, raiment and shelter. Being a British colony, we were fully dependent upon her exports, with the assistance of the United States of America, and Central and South America. It is a fact that we may have had more

CHAPTER TWENTY-SEVEN

wealth than lots of those very countries in our oil and asphalt, but we lacked the skill of technology. There were three shirt factories of renown in the country: one on Richmond Street, one on Queen Street, the other on Park Street. Our local farmers could not supply the ground provision in sufficient quantities. To satisfy the need, chickens, pigs, cattle, etc. were mostly backyard farming. There was also a housing problem. The foreigners were offering exorbitant amounts by cash as a reward to acquire dwellings or business places, which made it difficult for those who could not raise such funds. Boarders were coming and going, especially service individuals. I can vouch that Mammy has never taken a reward from anyone. She termed it a cruel deed, and persons found doing it should be sent to jail. I remember at our home there were six very good boarders of the twelve. They were Mr and Mrs Borring, Mr and Mrs Rice, Mr Mickey Burns, and a Scottish lady. These six were extremely kind to me, and at times they treated me better than they did Mammy's children. With the exception of the Scottish lady, they were all USA citizens and therefore would have visited the commissary* for groceries and other items. Upon such visits, if I am at home, they would take me along with them. Mammy will make a list of all she wanted and will always give me $40.00, and never had I come back with less than $5.00 change.

One evening after I returned from the commissary, Violet told me, "Someone phoned twice for you while you were out. Here please call –" and she handed me a slip of paper with the written number. I knew it to be May's. "Thank you," said I. And so I phoned. Within a single ring, the phone was answered. It seemed that she was just sitting there awaiting my call. I told her I was out shopping for Mammy. "Can you come up at any time this evening?" "Is something wrong?" I asked. "Yes, and no," she said. (May I say she had a way of answering and questioning in that unusual manner.) "OK," said I, "see you in two hours. I just came in and must shower and have dinner before leaving." The time was then 6:30 p.m. The day was yet bright; it was the twenty-first of June, which is the longest day of the year. I took with me two O'Henry bars of chocolate and nuts, and a bottle of cider I had bought at the commissary for the boys and I that evening. I told the boys to go ahead and eat by themselves as I would be out late. And so I left. Very quickly I got a tramcar and soon boarded a bus going to Tunapuna. I then got out at Curepe and was at the house at 7:45 p.m.

May looked lovelier than I had known her to be. Shyly I kissed her and placed the package into her hands. Hefty, the dog, came wagging his tail; he knew me, and I was escorted to her annex. The annex bore a lovely fragrance. On the table was a vase of pink and red roses and our dinner. I looked at her and we both smiled. We then supped. And the cider was just right. After, we sat on the couch. She then rebuked me for never having given her an answer in a week about her matrimonial suggestions she once made. So she again repeated the exact statements as though she was a tape being played over. "Well, tonight will you please give me an answer?" "I am at fault, I do know that," said I. "But from tonight will you give me three days to bring you an assured answer?" She fixed me in the eyes with a determined look. "OK, Christopher," she calmly said. I left at 4:00 a.m. the next morning, having missed the last bus that night.

The next day I went over to Aunt Bertrice. Lou was at home so I discussed not my affair. She apparently sensed that there was something wrong, came and softly asked, "Do you want to speak to me?" "Yes," said I, "but I shall return another time." "Eh, eh," said she. She then called Lou and gave him some money to buy her something, as she said to him smiling, "Bring me back my change." As Lou was all ready to leave, Ren came in. I was all very happy about that, and as Lou walked out, I related to them the entire love story of May and myself. Aunt said, "When does she want this wedding fixed?" "Tonight, if possible," said I. "No, honey, the banns* will first have to be set up in the Red House or the Warden's Office before that can be done." Ren then said, "George, that would be a very good move in your life."

"Hold it!" said Aunt, "can you speak French?" "No," said I, laughing. "Then how about patois*?" "No," said I once more. "Well, child, as far as I know we have no relatives across there. And as wealthy as this creature may perhaps turn out to be, her kindred may not like you as much as

CHAPTER TWENTY-SEVEN

she does love you. Then all hell will break loose. And my little nephew will find himself again in childhood days even worst than that of Toco. So please do not even think of doing this. I remember you once said that you are going to Chaguanas to choose a girl there and be married and live among her people. I shall rather that by far. But not Martinique." "Mother, mother," said Ren, "it is Guadeloupe." "It matters not, they are both French islands," said she. "You stay here, and the good Lord shall send you a helpmate. Here's what I shall now advise so as not to break her heart, being a woman myself. Let her know that you are fully interested, but she must first go home to her people and lay her cards on the table of the interest you both hold for each other. And also let them know that you are a poor church rat and you have not even a fundamental education. Should they consent to your romance, you shall then pay two visits among them. With a third, you can fully join them." Cousin Ren fully agreed to all that was said. And so I thanked her for her advice and left. I met May the next night and told her of my ready plan, to which she fully agreed.

The time had come for the Williamses to leave for Scotland, and so May left for Guadeloupe. May on her arrival wrote me three letters which were registered. The first exclaimed how truly the business was prospering and that she thinks herself to be financially better off than the Williamses; how everyone loved my photograph, and that all but her eldest brother, who is shouldering the business, seemed not to care. She said she shall also be sending me my ticket when I got my passport and other papers fixed to be able to travel on the French line. To this I made no reply. Then came a second letter, followed quickly by a third. And never again did I hear from her.

Chapter 28

*George's loneliness is short-lived; he meets Petronilla,
the love of his life, and buys a property in Laventille*

I then worked without interest after Mr Williams left for his leave. To crown it all, Mr Linsed also took his vacation and went to Guyana (then Demerara). Mr Perez, being unable to move around, could do but very little to help me due to his handicap. So once more Mr Isiaha began to give me a hard time. I told Mammy, and she wanted to go and have a chat with him. I advised her not to. I had then no one to speak with as a personal friend. Aunt Bertrice said, "George, don't you push." And so I worked and saved.

I then, however, suffered moments of loneliness. Many were the occasions that I began writing to May, but when I remembered all her relatives accepted my picture except her elder brother, I knew too well that trouble can start between us with a capital "T". And as Aunt Bertrice remarked, I may again fall into the Toco of my young life. I was encouraged by the letter in which she mentioned that the business was booming and that she would like me to come especially to communicate with the English-speaking servicemen. But yet I had then to learn the French language and, as Aunt Bertrice rightly said, I could not even speak patois. I then decisively made up my mind not to reply or harbour the thought of going to Guadeloupe.

Let me now, dear Reader, turn to my life's most important and greatest issue. First, let me quote Genesis 2:18, "And the Lord said that it is not good that man should be alone, I will make him a helpmate for him."

CHAPTER TWENTY-EIGHT

And so I found the real helpmate of my life. Should I venture to write of our meeting, it would entail an additional book in this, my biography. So shall I write a sonnet? No, that would not be enough to describe this wonderful gift of which the good Lord has truly blessed me with for over fifty years of my life. Then may I present her in a poem? Yes, I think I should. And now, dear Reader, in GRANDEUR I present my helpmate "Marm" in a poem.

MARM

Verse 1
Well, this is how it first began,
The year was nineteen twenty-one
T'was on a blessed February morn
That the babe Petronilla Margarita Bruce was born.

Verse 2
Before going further it is wise that you know
The district was the ward of Toco.
There lies a fishing village to which none compare
Shores washed by great waves, O Grande Rivière.

Verse 3
Her childhood days were full of fun.
Senior villagers claimed her to be number one.
Some folks also said that she was pretty.
Because of life's swiftness, entire family moved to the city.

Verse 4
Although she found this way of life to be quite confusing,
Certainly at times it was most amusing.
Then came the time that she must seek employment
Where all earnings were for her own enjoyment.

Verse 5
It happened thus one Sunday eve she boarded a tramcar
Intending to take a jolly ride around the Savannah
When a smartly attired youngster also boarded the car.
Although there were vacant seats, he sat down beside her.

Verse 6
He paused, she paused, they exchanged smiles.
Steadily she braced herself, content to listen to his lies.
However, the subject of his conversation caught her by surprise
Queen's Royal clock rang out their future with its chimes.

Verse 7
Before he disembarked, he asked for her home address.
Reluctantly she gave him, wondering if it was best.
Now without force or arms it surely was a truce
Which eventually changed her maiden name evermore from Bruce.

Verse 8
For no sooner was she home that night
There was a caller, one Mr Wright.
He was the very conversationalist on the tramcar.
Entreatingly he kindly asked her out for dinner.

Verse 9
Their association grew very fast and soon.
They both decided they must face St Margaret's Canon Ramkissoon.
Few were the folks who knew they were engaged
And even fewer of their eventual marriage.

Verse 10
This meek and beauteous damsel once glowing in her charms
Very soon became to be known as Marm.
Five boys, one girl, the world can see
Their names are all written in the family tree.

When we met, I had then over $700.00 in my savings, which was quite a tidy sum for someone of my standard in those days, many thanks to Miss Laura and Mammy. We then lived on Cipriani Boulevard, and I was still employed with Messrs W. Serious. My lifestyle was then adjusted differently. I hinted to Petronilla of my intention to resign and do vending of ground provisions, which was a promising outfield for a beginner in those war-torn days. But let me now use her own words: "George," she said, "that will be too laborious for you."

One day as I was out on my cash collection, I ran into Mr Williams,

CHAPTER TWENTY-EIGHT

my uncle-in-law. We had not seen each other for quite a while, so our conversation was lengthy. We spoke widely of the problems of land and housing. Mr Williams then told me of a parcel of land which he once owned along the Eastern Main Road, and would willingly have accepted $150.00 for same. He very recently sold it for $500.00. "So," said he, "I must have my mind fully made up to acquire a parcel of my own before it became worse." I then asked that he be on the lookout for me, and he assured me he would.

Early one morning before I went on my beat at the pharmacy, Mr Williams came to see me. He told me of a plot of land that was owned by a friend of his while they were both in the Police Service. He also said that the gent was a Barbadian. (May I now say, in the early colonial days, applicants for the Police Service of Trinidad and Tobago were selected from the island of Barbados, St Vincent, or Grenada, but they were chiefly conscripted from Barbados. Trinidadians, especially should you be of East Indian descent, found it very difficult to enlist.)

Mr Williams, however, said the Barbadian began building and ran into difficulty; he could not then continue and so he had decided to quit the idea, pack up, and return to his homeland. But the site still remained a very good one. The gent wanted $50.00 for the debris; he was not actually selling the parcel of land because the land was rented. Its owner was a prominent citizen who owned the entire area as a coconut plantation for many years. But now that crop has extensively failed, so he had decided to rent the lands in plots of 100' x 50' for building purposes. In the areas that were easily accessible, the plots were $3.00 monthly, while less accessible plots were $2.00 monthly. "The piece I am getting for you would be $3.00," he said.

"Where is this place?" I asked. He was a bit hesitant in his reply, then said he, "It is on the eastern end of Parris Boulevard where you rented and had then to leave for Murray Street." "But are you sure that I will not be once more faced with similar occurrence?" "No, not at all, for this time you shall be dealing direct with your kind of people," as he laughed. I told him that I had not now that sort of money, but I shall call to see him the next day.

A BRANCH TO REST ON

After supper that evening, Petro (as she was then called by me) and I leisurely walked up to the Savannah and seated ourselves on a park bench as we watched folks who busied themselves by walking, trotting and skipping. As we settled ourselves, I asked how would she like going to Success Village, Laventille, to live. "No!" she promptly said. "Not that mosquito-, malaria-infested area. And, furthermore, now with a baby on its way, not at all." It was the very first time she had bluntly refused me a suggestion. And her point was well taken and respected. So I said not another word on the subject.

But what shall I tell Mr Williams tomorrow, seeing how interested he was in the matter. Just at that very moment an old Chinese pedlar nicknamed Mile-a-Minute* passed, selling peanuts. I handed him a threepence for two packages: one salted, the other fresh. He handed me back my change of one pence. We then left, munching our way back home, she eating the salted, I the fresh. When we got home, we showered because the evening was hot, prayed, and got into our bed. I pretended to have fallen asleep – an enticement that she would also sleep. Very quickly the lovely ball of charm cuddled into my arm and was sound asleep. I then very gently removed my hand, turned on my back, and began wondering what was I to do. I decided I will not leave the job, and I was also going to give Mr Williams the $50.00 the next day so that I can hold the rights of the piece of land without her knowledge.

The following day I withdrew the $50.00 from my savings. As I left the bank I stood on the pavement and wondered to myself whether I was doing the right thing. Should I not let Petro know what I am doing? Now, good Reader, will you believe just a few yards from where I stood, there was a couple speaking, and the woman at the very moment said to the man, "You go ahead now and do exactly as you now feel. Your plans are good." I could not truly believe what I heard. For it will seem as though the woman was speaking to me.

Being now encouraged, I hurried to the cart-stand to meet Mr Williams. I handed him the cash. Later, I visited him at his home. He went to his table drawer and retrieved two bits of paper. "Here are your receipts. I have also paid three months' land rent in advance so

CHAPTER TWENTY-EIGHT

that your mind can be at ease until you are ready to start." "Waw! I did not walk with any cash to pay that." "Oh no," said he, laughing, "that's my contribution towards the venture. If that was not paid, the owner could then rent the land to another client." "Oh, thank you so much," said I. "Young fellar," said he, "are you not going to see where the spot is?" "I really came not for that; it was just to see you." "Seeing me is one thing, but should I die tonight, how would you know how to find the spot? Come, young fellow, let's go now."

We left Church Street, where he lived, and headed by walking to Parris Boulevard West where I once lived for a short while. "Let's brisk it," said he, "for it seems as it will rain. It lies at the far end of this street," said he. We did get there. As we stood at the corner of Parris Boulevard and Leotaud Street, I looked in wonder. "Here we are, young fellar," said he. "There is your place." He then pointed to an area fully covered with entwined vines, wild trees and shrubs, two coconut palms and three very tall bois cano trees. There was no visible remains of a structure. I did not want him to read my disappointment, but I was indeed. "Let's go under the growth," said he. "Sure," I bravely answered.

The land was so structured that not even the neighbours on both sides could have thrown their garbage on it. On a little mound stood two concrete columns and a few pieces of rotted woodwork. "Well," said Mr Williams, "you have quite a job here of cleaning, young fellar." "This is nothing," I replied. "Don't you know that Port of Spain was once covered with dense forest?" He laughed and said, "Boy, what would they do with you?"

I told Vernon, one of my few friends whom I had helped financially and labour-wise when he built his house at St James. I also told Horace, who had now joined the army and was doing well. Vernon did not hesitate. He quickly organized a team of young men, and the entire lot was cleared completely in three weekends. The cost: three cases of sweet drinks ($1.08), twelve pieces of ice (twenty-four cents), one bottle of Angostura aromatic bitters (twenty-four cents), twelve packs of Anchor (Push) cigarettes (seventy-two cents), three pots of chicken and beef pelau, of which I knew not the cost because he had that prepared himself, plus old talk. In the process I handled the post of fireman, a duty I controlled well even as a boy at Toco. I made a coal pit where I burned eight and a half sacks of charcoal. Now that the lot was cleared, it was in readiness for the laying of a foundation. I then bought the necessary tools for excavating from my former workplace Trinidad Trading Co.: two forks, two pickaxes, two shovels, one cutlass, one rake, one spade, one hoe and one crowbar.

The foundation was begun with a crew of four men whom Vernon termed as "groundhogs". But may I say, unlike the ones who cleared the forest, these were some lazy bastards. They worked five days at $1.75 each man per day. I paid them their $15.00 and discontinued their services. As they left, I saw them headed their way to a Portuguese rum shop at the corner lower down the street. Said I to myself, "Easy come, easy go." I had now to decide how the foundation must be dug. After a few minutes of contemplation, I decided to have it dug by myself on Saturdays after work. That Friday evening I asked Mr Perez for the Saturday off, which he granted. But when I got to the site the next day, the tools were all spirited away. What a catastrophe! I then hurried down to the hardware store and told my plight to my good friend Coggins. I had but three dollars. He gave me a fork, a shovel, a cutlass, a pickaxe, and a crowbar, and charged them to himself. And as I had been able to pay it all the Monday, he was given an employee's discount.

I began the excavation from where the four culprits left off the Monday evening. I worked from 5:00 to 6:30 p.m. and was pleased with my hour-and-a-half work. I said to myself, if I can put in each day when it is convenient and on weekends a day and a half, the entire job can be completed in two months. I could not now suffer the loss of any more tools, so I asked the nearest neighbour to allow me to leave them at his home that evening when I was leaving. I met Petro standing at the gate, waiting for me to show up. I had evaded the truth from her. I greeted her in the usual manner. "You do smell sweaty, and your face is all covered with dirt," said she. "How come?" I looked at her. "Come on," said she, "what were you doing?" "I shall tell you about that later," I replied. "Now!" said she. "No!" said I, "I am sticky and hungry, please let

CHAPTER TWENTY-EIGHT

me bathe and eat." "OK," said she sharply. I looked at her, and we both laughed. I rolled my bicycle in its place and hurried off to get my wash.

While having my bath I said to myself, "Well, this is it. I might as well come forward with the truth before it is told to her by someone else." I waited not until bedtime, but while we were having our dinner, I told her. "Well," said she, "you are yet going along in spite of my telling you of the health hazard entailed in that area. Well, I shall tell you, sir, this is one time I shall not support you." "OK," said I, "that's no problem. And don't you worry yourself; just allow me this one chance." "Chance! Chance!" said she. "Do you realize this involves a lifetime?" At that very moment I heard the gate squeak followed by heavy footsteps. As we both looked, there was Horace all clad in his army uniform. "Well, look who is here! What wind blew you here?" I asked excitedly. "Good night, folks," said he. "Well, I am on fall-off[1] for one month. So I came to let you know." "Fall-off," said Petro, "let it not be fall-out with us!" Horace then looked quite amazed at her remark. "Yes, smartie, you came to notify so that you can both go digging the place together." "Place! What place?" he replied. "Don't you now pretend," said Petro, "you do know very well of what I am speaking." Before Horace could have given an answer, "Horace! Horace!" I interrupted "She knows; I told her all about it ten minutes ago." "Yes, yes, you two scamps," she angrily said. "Anything that is hidden in the darkness would be brought to the light, especially when sweat and dirt are involved." Her wisecrack had us three laughing. "Get yourself a plate," she said to Horace. "I am not getting up. There is sufficient here, help yourself." As we slowly ate and talked, Horace said that he would not be staying any length of time because he has to meet someone. However, I shall see him at 4:30 p.m. the next day. I accompanied him to the gate where he hopped upon his bicycle and was off. When I got inside, I was poked in the sides; I only laughed, washed my mouth, prayed and slumped into bed.

The following day I cheated half-day on the job. And this is how it came about. There was a bill that had been marked off for six years.

---

1 Furlough.

A BRANCH TO REST ON

The debtor, who was a medical doctor, sailed to England in May 1939 for medical school. On September 3, 1939, Britain and France declared war on Germany. The young man was now caught in a fury and could not then return home. His brother, who had always been cooperative with me in settling their pharmacy bills, could do nothing about this bill, which amounted to $28.20, due to the lack of evidence. However, the young man did return to Trinidad, he acknowledged the debt, and so I was handed the $28.80 in cash that day. I then said to myself, this calls for a celebration. So being now spurred with the thought of digging the foundation, I took the half-day.

The next day I was the second employee standing on the pavement awaiting the pharmacy to be open. Mr Williams, who had the keys, came about fifteen minutes later. There were then about eight of us standing by when Mr Williams opened the main entrance. As we entered, there was Mr Perez taking the rear as he slowly hobbled in. When he settled at his desk, I went to him. I had not been able to complete the sentence of "Good morning, sir" to him when Mr Williams quickly came by. I then felt the guilt of my absence, as I wondered whether they knew. I, however, tried to be brave by again saying, "Good morning, sir." "Good morning," they both pleasantly replied. Immediately I was released of my guilt. I then stood aside so that Mr Williams could have his say. "Oh, no, no, George," said he, "you go right ahead. Because I may be lengthy, and you have to be on the road."

"Come, Wright," said Mr Perez. "Good or bad news from yesterday?" he asked with a smile. "I think I have some good news, sir," said I. "That written-off amount of Dr Roland's, I collected it all yesterday." With a fixed brow he looked at me. "Are you joking?" "No, sir, here is it." And so I handed the $28.80 to him. He again looked at me with astonishment. Mr Williams then asked what was it all about. Mr Perez told him of the case. "Oh, I do remember that just too well," he said. He then reached into his hip pocket, took out his wallet and handed me a $2.00 note. It was almost new, bearing its scenery with the words "Columbus landing in the New World". "Take that and have all the day off as a reward," said Mr Williams. "Thank you, sir," said I. I then

CHAPTER TWENTY-EIGHT

hesitated as I looked at Mr Perez. "Go ahead, Wright," said he, "you more than deserved it."

That weekend Horace and I worked to 10:00 p.m. each night. The entire neighbourhood was illuminated by a bright moon. And with the lights of four bull-de-flair* and lighted stumps of trees to ward off the horrid mosquitoes and other stinging flies, we lacked not daylight. The neighbour by whom we left the tools was also a builder and contractor. He said never in his life had he seen two young men work with such cooperation. We dug and filled the spots that were necessary. And by Sunday night we barrowed out and made a large mound on the side of the road.

Vernon did turn up the following weekend as promised. He was accompanied by two burly men. He stood aghast on seeing what was done. "Who did all of this?" he asked. "Horace and I," said I. He then turned to one of the men and, pointing to the dug soil, said, "This is mostly waratal*, not sand," said he as he walked off, scratching his head. He then called me aside and said, "George, boy, as it now stands you are faced with one problem." "What is it?" I asked. "You see, that loose earth on the side of the road will have to be removed before the rain falls and bind it." "I never thought of that." "Yes," said he, "that is the nature of this soil when it catches water." He again walked a few steps, scratching his head. "Give me a chance," said he, "don't you worry. Just organize with the fellows to barrow out whatever loose earth that is there." And he left.

It was under two hours when Vernon was back with a truck and its driver. The mound of earth at this time had grown much larger. Vernon then said to me that the owner of the vehicle will truck away the earth at one dollar per load starting at the very moment. Only one hitch: he does not have a loader. I bluntly said to him, "How come you are charging so very little?" "Oh that." He smiled. "Oh well, I am selling it to someone at Barataria for filling, and the run is less than three-quarters mile away for $5.00 per load. And next, when you are building, I do know you shall use my truck for the transportation of your materials." "Well," said Vernon, "well, one hand can't clap."

A BRANCH TO REST ON

When I got home, Petro said to me, "You are overworking yourself and also encouraging Horace into same, which is not fair. Remember well that he is on vacation and should be freely enjoying it, not working as you both are apparently doing." "We do work to our own free will. However, your point is well taken," I assured her.

CHAPTER 29

Marm does not care for Laventille but is persuaded
by her mother to obey her husband

The next day at work I was called by Mr Isiaha in a most impolite manner. As I went to him, he said to me, "When you are not on the road, you must sell over the counter, and you are to make no bills but pass all your sales to Miss Lego." "Sir," said I, "I have been doing that all along and have been sharing sales not only to Miss Lego but also with the other clerks." He frowned and said to me, "Am I speaking Chinese? Just do as I say." "Very well, sir," said I. At that moment Mr Perez called me. He was sending me to Maraval to collect a bill. From the corner of my eye I saw Mr Isiaha looking at me, so I allowed Mr Perez to do all the talking. I took the bill and went upstairs to Mr Linsed's office. And there I told him what had been said to me. "Listen, George," said he, "this thing has been going on for far too long. Enough is enough. Why not tell Mr Williams outright of what is going on? He shall stop the nonsense." "No, sir, he shall get fried in his own fat." "OK, OK, you are one young man whose opinion I respect to a point," said he, laughing.

I did collect the full amount of the bill and was back in the pharmacy by noon. Most of the staff had gone on their lunch break, including Miss Lego. Mr Perez, who took his lunch on the job, said to me, "Boy, you are something else. I try to summarize what is the influence you have on these people, but cannot do so."

That evening I gave fifteen sales to Miss Lego; the other clerks were disgruntled. The next morning I was asked by Mr Perez to take a small package to a St James pharmacy on COD¹ terms. I did and collected the amount of $28.00. On my return I went to the floor and, it will seem as through some unforeseen force, customers were just coming to me. Some with prescriptions, whom I will lead to the druggist, others for assorted items from behind the counter shelves or showcases. As I attended to them, I directed them to Miss Lego to have their bills made. At the beginning, all worked well. But very soon there was a line-up, which caused murmurings. This aroused the attention of Mr Williams, who came walking across the floor. He inquired what was taking place. I made no comment while I kept my focus upon Mr Isiaha, who headed quickly to the back. Dear Reader, he was certainly fried in his own fat, don't you think? Mr Williams then directed the waiting customers to other clerks.

At 3:30 p.m. that day, I asked Mr Perez if I can leave. "You go right ahead," said he. I was at the site at 3:58 p.m. to be exact; traffic was busy. Horace was digging a hole with a vest stuck to his skin with perspiration. I called aloud. "Oh boy," said he, "is it four already?" "One minute to," said I, laughing, and before saying another word, I told him Mr Perez had given me the extra half hour. As I looked around, there were three more holes left to be dug. I quickly changed and joined in the task. In spite of stinging insects, we got through by 7:00 p.m. that evening.

The weekend seemed to have come very quickly. That Saturday evening we got to the site at 1:30 p.m., but Vernon was already there with the very two men to dig the holes we had already dug. He looked at us and scratched his head. The neighbour at whose house we left the tools came, and as had earlier mentioned, he was himself a builder and contractor. On looking at the dug holes, he said to Vernon, "You have no problem from what I can now see here. All you have to do is get your materials on the job, select yourself a good tradesman and two handy labourers, and with the help of these two gentlemen, this work can easily be done on weekends."

---

1   Cash on Delivery(E).

CHAPTER TWENTY-NINE

"But, by the way, have you submitted a plan at St Joseph Health Centre?" "No, not as yet," said Vernon. "Well, you better act quickly on that because they are getting strict with it nowadays. Before, one could have taken the chance to first build and then submit a drawing, but the present-day rules are your plan must be first submitted and approved." He went on to say, "There is a very nice sanitary inspector there whose name is Mr Peter Sen; he will get someone to draw it for you if you cannot get it done."

Vernon was a shipwright and not a builder, although he acquired lots of knowledge in the building field. He then worked out roughly with the help of my neighbour, whose name was Mr John, two loads of gravel, two loads of sand, one load of boulders, twenty bags of cement, twenty lengths of quarter-inch steel rods round, twenty-five pounds mixed PP nails (Paris Point nails), two shovels, two cement-size buckets, and two drums for water. Vernon said that he had quite a lot of boxing boards at his home. Turning to me, Vernon said, "What do you think, George?" I said, "You can get the truck for the sand and boulders. But Mr Williams will be carting all the other items." Mr John then said, "You have made no decision about the plan." "Oh, I shall have that all drawn up and submitted," said Vernon. He also added that he shall get Marksman, the very fellow who assisted him when he built his house at St James. That Saturday morning, no manual work was done, only old talk. We left at 2:30 p.m. Vernon promised to be there with Marksman at 10:00 a.m. the Sunday.

On our way home, Horace and I stopped at Mr Williams, and I told him what was going to take place and I shall need him to transport materials. He in turn asked me what was the contract deal. "What contract deal?" I asked. "Why, are you not going to sign an agreement of how your money would be spent in the payment of labour and otherwise?" "No sir," said I. "I really thought that was only applicable for the building of schools and other business places." Mr Williams had a hearty laugh as he said, "Well, George, this is town, not Toco where people get together for the building of a house freely helping in whatever way they can." "But when he built his house, I helped him financially and labour-wise." "That may be so, George, but that's not the way it really works. When they should come tomorrow, let them know that you will like to know what will be the cost for labour. But in no way let them know that you have the ready cash. Tell them that you have got to borrow the money from your relatives or perhaps from your kind of people." (In that he meant good-natured aristocrats.) "For goodness sakes," he warned, "avoid strange deals and bargains from individuals. Be sure and get a bill or receipt for everything, and keep it. Let every man feed himself. Avoid strong drinks being used when work is going on the job. You are at no time to buy cigarettes or strong drinks for anyone. Should they purchase it for themselves, smile but join them not in its usage. And, George, I mean not even with a sweet drink. Now, George, there are times that you shall get genuine free labour offered you; accept it in good faith; don't ever turn it down. But at all times keep a level head and do nothing stupid. Should you at any time be doubtful of something, come to me. If I do not know, I shall enquire for you."

The Sunday morning Vernon really showed up with Marksman at 10:00 a.m. as proposed. I then spoke to Vernon outright in the manner advised by Mr Williams. "George," said he, "man, you making joke. You aren't serious. How can I ever charge a fellow like you who stuck by my side, better than my own brother had, when I was building my house. Man, what style is that you making, we don't live so." "Well," said I to him, "our friendship still remains, partner. But the house-building deal is closed. I shall speak to Mr John for an estimate." "OK, OK, but let me first talk to Marksman before you make any move." That day again Horace and I did nothing. Vernon and Marksman measured and marked off while we stood like dummies. When they were finished, Vernon, who loved clowning, said to Horace and myself, "Come on, fellars, down sail, oars in hand, let's go home." And so we all four left on our bicycles at noon. It was Horace's last day of his vacation because he had to be in office the next day.

The Monday morning Vernon came to my work and told me Marksman said to give him $95. He promised to work on some evenings

CHAPTER TWENTY-NINE

when he could, also every weekend and most of the public holidays with his own labour. "As for myself," said Vernon, "I would be getting all your boxing boards up today by the truck. I shall be speaking to the driver also to drop the gravel, sand, and boulders the quickest possible time. You don't worry about those costs: I shall handle that; you go ahead and handle all the other materials." "Good," said I. By evening all the essentials from me were safely stored under Mr John's house. Notwithstanding, Vernon had two loads of gravel on the side of the road and a stack of boxing boards.

The Tuesday evening when I got there, I was met with a big surprise: the sand and boulders were there, and four boxing frames all ready for casting were erected. I met no one there and so I left for Horace's home to let him up to the knowledge of how things were moving. He told me he was himself set upon a shift from 7:00 a.m. to 5:00 p.m., filling the extra two hours for a colleague that was on leave. We spoke at length on the matter of the building of the house. In speaking, Horace suggested this point. Said he, "George, since all the materials are on spot as required, and they have made a start, let us not go there until the end of the week, which will give them a chance to work freely by themselves. Plus, I do know Petro will be very delighted to have you home." We both laughed at his last remark.

The structure did move fast. The truck-man never failed to bring the best materials. I know that through the experience I had while I worked in the building department of my former workplace. At its third weekend, we had then to surround. I was now asked to choose the material to be used. There was nogging*, a mixture of gravel, sand, and cement, which was used by the upper class. There was tapia*, a mixture of mud and grass used by the lower class, especially those living in rural districts. Hollow clay blocks were used, but with doubt in the mind of the layman. They were sold at one penny each, and as I have said, persons were just sceptical at its first introduction. I, however, chose its use for the entire surrounding of the house.

Now the building was roofed. One half was covered with corrugated galvanize and the other with corrugated asbestos. The house was now floored and covered; also all inside walls were plastered. Yet doors and windows were needed, and my funds were almost exhausted. Petro, who by this time had borne our first two children, Lincoln and Michael, was now no longer called "Petro" by me but was given the glorified name "Marm" up to this day. She had never for all this time visited the site, being very strong-willed in her say about the malaria-infested area.

I went over to Sister Hilda, and I told her of the situation. (At this time Aunt Bertrice had migrated to Venezuela.) She advised that I get Marm in a pleasant mood and point out our financial status to her. Show her how difficult it was to be paying an exorbitant rent and have a partially finished unoccupied house of your own, doing nothing. But she warned me make not a quarrel about the matter.

One Sunday we decided to visit Mar (Marm's mother), who at this time was nursing our␣Lincoln with a heavy nasal cold. I grasped the opportunity and then I related to Mar fully what was taking place. Mar, who was very kind and an ardent peacemaker, told her daughter she was wrong in her attitude. Even though the district may not be as where she is now, she will be going to her own place and obeying her husband. "Furthermore," said Mar, "right now or when you get home, you read Genesis 12:1–20." Now we all loved and respected Mar and so Marm dared not back off from what Mar said. When we got home that evening, my heart was filled with joy. Marm looked at me and said, "So, smartie, you have worked on me." I made no verbal reply, but smiled, and then changed and washed Michael. We than washed ourselves, prayed and got into bed.

The next day I saw Horace, who had now a family of his own, his wife and a beautiful little girl. I told him of what went on with Mar. "Boy, George," said he, laughing, "you certainly do know how to burrow your way out from the rubble." The following evening we both went to the unfinished structure. We had made two hammocks from empty jute sacks, which we hung upstairs. We got into them and began talking. Our topic was centred upon the unfinished doors, windows, and outside walls that were yet to be plastered.

CHAPTER TWENTY-NINE

Vernon, who had got himself into a very good boatbuilding contract, left for Venezuela. Now, although I had already reasoned this out by myself, I felt elated when Horace said, "George, boy, it will seem that you would have to ask Mr John for an estimate to complete the house." "Boy, Horace, you've struck the nail with the hammer. For what's to be done, we know not A from Bullfoot*." "That's a fact," said Horace. At that very moment there were movements outside. Horace promptly got off his hammock. "It's Mr John," said he. "Well, young men, I saw your bicycles outside, and I knew that you were here." I at once brought the suggestion to him. He assured me that he could handle same. He at once took the measurements of the doors and windows, of which he said he made not himself but gave to a woodwork factory. "The cost of those will be $25.00 without glass. You have more than enough plastering sand on the ground that can be sifted. With that you may need ten sacks of cement to start with the plastering of the walls outside. For your partitions, use the asbestos flat sheets, it gives a nice finish as a plastered wall. Right now," said he, "I am using some at a house in St Clair. You also have more than enough gravel for drains around the house, although you may yet have to get another truckload for the casting of your downstairs floor. That, as you know, has now gone to $9.00. Now, for myself, what can I tell you? You would be my neighbour, and the very first one to call upon in case of sickness. Ah-ah, let me see," said he as he made a mental cipher. "With the help of you both labour-wise..." He pulled at his nose, which gave a sniff-like sound. "Look, man, give me $25.00. That will also cover all labour cost that I shall hire." Before I could have made a reply, Horace said, "That sounds quite good."

On our way home, we passed at Mr Williams, and I brought him up to date of what was taking place. He agreed solidly to Mr John's proposals. Mr John did push the work to the finish with the exception of the doors and windows not in. And this could not be done due to a breakdown of the factory. Being satisfied of the work done, I paid him fully the $25.00. For I had then enough confidence that he would handle the doors and windows when they were finished. Marm and

I had then a mutual understanding of the house, and she visited the premises three times and seemed somewhat satisfied.

Now the following is a burden which laid upon my heart and was then to be released. Horace after his marriage had been living at his in-laws with his family. And although he never once complained, one could have seen that he was not all that happy. I had said to Marm that we were going to use the downstairs as living room and kitchen, upstairs as bed and utility rooms. But I had now in consideration to change such a plan by having Horace join us. In so doing we will use downstairs as planned. Upstairs we shall occupy two rooms as bedrooms and let Horace have the other two with his family. In it they shall have their own privacy because all partitions were up. And the interior doors were made by Mr John himself and fitted. Together he and I can build an outdoor kitchen together because we were no longer novices. And outdoor kitchens were widely used, even in the plush aristocratic homes.

I laid my proposals to Marm, who readily agreed. "Have you made the suggestion to him as yet?" she asked. "No, not as yet, for I first wanted your opinion." "Well," said she, "although it is a very thoughtful gesture, I shall advise that you first tell him before venturing on your own idea." The following evening Horace joined me from his work, and we rode up to the house. Though rustic, yet it certainly looked good even with its missing doors and windows. I told him of what Marm and I brewed in our minds. He held me and wept upon my shoulder as he gladly accepted the offer. Came that very month-end Mr Williams made two trips from Cipriani Boulevard where we lived, as we bade farewell to the city.

Chapter 30

*Vegetables, fruit and chickens: George is a part-time
market vendor and runs afoul of the law*

Now in our new home there was no electricity nor pipe-borne water. Added to this inconvenience, sacks were hung for doors and windows. Yet with it all Marm adjusted herself in such a beautiful manner that I fully blamed myself for wasted years. Mr Williams brought me two cartloads of used lumber and galvanize. Horace's kitchen was erected and an outdoor bathroom and privy plus a general washroom for the wives, which was nicknamed the laundry. Horace and his family joined us three weeks after we were at our new home. The unionism of both wives and children moved perfectly, for which we their husbands were happy.

The idea of vending into the ground provision business, of which Marm had earlier on objected, still dawned on me. And now, having only the sum of $186.00 left in the bank, I decided to quit my job in spite of Marm's entreaty not to do so. I must admit, however, that I was very stupid in so doing because I made no survey of this, my venture. Neither had I consulted with Mr Williams or Sister Hilda. (I was becoming very frustrated, for Mr Isiaha had been acting up again.) Only to Horace did I voice my opinion, of which he himself was also a dummy in that field.

I went ahead and had some cards printed and decided to take orders to sell and deliver to the aristocrats on weekends, figuring to use the very influence that I used as cash collector, while I looked forward to the patronage of my district neighbourhood during the week, which turned out to be very poor. There was one good, however: there was always excess food in the house. I got quite a lot of support from Horace, who at this time was faced with demobilization from the army. For World War Two was now fully over (1945), yet forces were kept in strategic places, and Trinidad happened to be one of them. The final for Horace's dismissal was delayed for quite some time. Being now post-war, his service was used some weeks on, some weeks off. With his off weeks, we would both travel to Toco and buy vegetables, fruits, citrus, eggs and fowls. This was quite an advantage because we were always given articles under the wholesale prices.

Gradually, sales improved within the neighbourhood. And this is how it started. I began giving to children all fruits that had not very long to go, whenever by chance they came to buy. The word of this deed got around, and whenever they were sent to buy elsewhere by their parents, they would come to us. Marm adjusted herself fittingly to this way of life without a complaint. Horace one Saturday jokingly said that Marm and I are likened to Antonio and Shylock, the characters described in *The Merchant of Venice* by William Shakespeare. He classified me to be Antonio, always ready to give a little more. Marm was Shylock, being always exact on the weights. I could however safely have done that because I did quite a bit of backyard farming, which helped to defray cost and loss.

Reader, I once got seriously entangled with the law, which was very stupid of me, and all of being too hasty and hot-tempered. Horace and I went to the Eastern Market to purchase a few items from the wholesale department. We needed not many things because we were at Toco the previous week. A pedlar approached us with an open handbag of sive*. "Buy me out," said he, holding a very large and lovely bundle as he hurriedly spoke. Said he, "I am going now at ten cents a bundle." "How many heads are there in the bundle?" I asked. "Man," said he, "yuh want de sive or not?" "OK," said I, "let me have a bundle." "Ef yuh is only buying one, dat is twelve cents. Fram two up, ten cents." As I have said, the bundles were large. So I handed him a twelve-cent coin. I gave

CHAPTER THIRTY

it to Horace, who had some other items in his care. I told him to wait there while I went to another section to purchase some dasheen bush.

On my return there was a mob around Horace, and I pushed my way through to him. "What is happening?" I asked. "That woman there," said he, pointing at an apparent vendor, "she said that the sive is hers." "What do you mean? What?" said I. "Have we not now purchased it from –" Before I could have finished my sentence, an elderly man among the crowd said, "Hold it, let's hear what this fellow has to say and see if his story fits with this man's." I then completed the sentence. "Well," said the old man, "it is just what that fellow there has said to you, lady." "Well, is way de man garn wid de other bundle dem?"¹ said she. "How am I to know? Just check around. There may be other people who may have bought as I have." At that very moment a big burly guy grabbed our bundle and exclaimed, "Well, ah taking dis wan!" Without hesitation, WHAM! went my hundred and twenty pounds of solid fist, which anchored between nose and eyes as he sank to the floor holding his face, groaning.

Police arrest. I was charged $25.00 that very morning by a magistrate. Lucky for me, Horace had been holding some money drawn from a susu* for his mother. With what I then had, the amount was made to pay the fine. I was then so very scared that I never again set my feet at the Eastern Market, at least not until years after when the market was relocated to the Beetham Highway. I therefore decided to close down the shop completely, a tremendous blow to me. What was I now to do for a livelihood in the support of my family? (1) I had not a trade or skill of any kind. (2) Through pride, I was not going back to the pharmacy to face the hostility of Mr Isiaha, although Mr Perez and Mr Linsed, whose home I supplied on weekends, had said to me, should my business fail me at any time, return back to my job. (3) Nor was I again going to be a gardener or yard boy.

Now I had a very good friend of whom I made mention while I lived at Murray Street. She was Scottish, proudly answered to the name

---

1   'Well, where has the man gone with the other bundles?'

of Miss Cope, and would with pride speak of her fatherland and her forefathers who were Highlanders. She knew quite a lot of Scottish history, and we would at times sit while I discussed the little I knew about the Caribbean as she elaborated on Scotland. She would speak with the same national pride as Mr Williams did when we had travelled from Mayaro. Miss Cope became married and also left our Murray Street home, so we lost track of each other for quite a while.

Mammy, on one of my visits, told me where she lived. I paid her a visit and told her of my woe. She pointed out to me that it can be a great setback and tarnish my life's career. So I now firmly decided not only to close down the shop but to quit peddling entirely and seek employment elsewhere. But again I was faced with the mammoth question: what was I now to do? My savings were now under one hundred dollars. Had I a driver's licence, I could have then made a quick leap to success, for there was then a demand for that profession. I became very forlorn and downcast. Horace of course knew that I was going no further with the business and soundly agreed with me. I told Marm that our losses were outweighing our gain, so I am closing down shop. Her reply to me was, "George, it must! Because you are a Father Christmas all year through!"

Now Mammy's father carried on a fine tailoring establishment on Tragarete Road of which he was the sole proprietor. "George," said he, "I would have liked you to work with me as an apprentice. But I cannot now pay you a salary whereby you can maintain your family. But I know a gentleman who owns a blacksmith's shop in St James. I would ask him if he can hire you so that you can learn a quick trade also. You would not get a big salary. But I do know that you would be paid something decent. And should you apply yourself in the forge, welding, you shall very soon have a paying trade of your own." To this I readily agreed.

The following day he gave me the address and said the smith also lived on the premises. I thanked him and wasted no time as I hastened to St James. I found the place quite easily. I spoke to the proprietor, who said that he shall hire me at three shillings (seventy-two cents) a week, which was merely passage, but I had my bicycle. I agreed to his bargain. He then said, "You can start right now if you wish." "Yes, sir, I

CHAPTER THIRTY

will." And so it was did I start on a job with the hope of learning a trade.

I was then directed to a heap of rusted junk iron and steel to assort these lengths and shapes. This exercise I did for three days, as I destroyed mounds of ants and secreted hideouts of centipedes. The smith had a son who was about my own age. He would at times come and speak kindly to me if his father was not around. At times he would even lend me a helping hand. There was also three other employees working there. I observed that they were building gates and had other wrought-iron skills.

As I formerly said, they lived on the premises. On my fourth day of assorting the junks, I was told by the mother that I must come and eat each day with her son, whose name was Phillip. And so he and I became good friends even up to now in our old age. His father kept me employed as a labour hand only. But if he was not around, Phillip and the men will call and show me skills whose operation I took notes for. Meanwhile, I had then to make small withdrawals from the bank each weekend to help my salary of three shillings. May I say many thanks to Marm, who unknowingly to me had pushed aside a few shillings while we were in the vegetable business.

One evening on my arrival home, Horace met me at the gate. "Well, boy, George," said he, "the final has come. I was fully discharged from the army today." Although saddened, we both knew that it was coming, being only a matter of time because many of his colleagues had already been sent home. "But now," with a sudden grin and smile upon his face, said he, "the captain, an Englishman, has secured me a local job. He apparently had been working on it for a good while unknown to me," said Horace. "Good boy," said I, "but where? And when will you be starting?" "Hold it, George, for you may not like to hear this. But it is in Caroni." "Caroni! What is wrong with Caroni? Is it not there that our best quality cane sugar comes from?" "Yes," said he. "And will you believe it, George, I am going there to do some clerical work on one of those very sugar cane estates. I am also granted living quarters. And I am charged to take up duty in fifteen days' time." I was now myself glad but sad. "Well, boy," said I to him, "let's look at it this way. One door has been closed upon you, but another has been immediately opened."

A BRANCH TO REST ON

When we got in, both wives and children were in the "laundry". The story was then retold by Horace to them in the hearing of the children. Turning to me once more, he said, "Boy, George, who knows, I may be able to get you a job there as an overseer later. And then move you from that work that you are now doing." Our wives were really sad indeed to hear the news of their separation, while the children accepted it as that of a vacation.

The time did come, and Horace with his family moved to their Caroni home. I was left struggling, for I really missed his moral support. For there are those things that you can discuss with a man and be comforted as a friend, while with the implication of feelings you would in no way share with a woman. And may I say throughout our lives I have always tried not to implicate Marm unnecessarily on any matter. We were then approached by individuals to rent the vacant rooms of Horace. And although we were faced with great straits financially, we did not rent the rooms.

It happened this one Monday morning, while riding along Tragarete Road to my work, I was honked by a car. As I pulled to the side, who could it be but my Scottish friend, Miss Cope, now Mrs Kingsley. "Oh, George," said she, "for months I have been looking for you. Not even Mammy seems to know how to get in touch with you. After speaking to you that evening, when my husband came in from his work, I made mention of you to him and your situation. He works with a very large bauxite and shipping company out here, and holds a very responsible position. He asked what can you do. I told him you are skilled in hard work. He said that he can get you a place with the trimmers on the barge. He also said that it is a paying position. One can make $30.00 weekly. And with overtime it can even reach $60.00." My eyes popped on hearing the figures, which then all sounded as a Cinderella world of fantasy. "But where and what is the nature of the work?" I asked, for I knew not then of bauxite. Neither did I then know or hear of a trimmer except in the art of cultivation. She switched her engine off and gave me a brief explanation of how she thinks it is all operated on an anchored barge at sea. Said she, "You leave port at 6:00 a.m. and

CHAPTER THIRTY

return at 7:00 p.m. or even 11:00 p.m. at times. One thing," said she, "the job is a very dusty and filthy one. But knowing you as I do, I am sure you won't mind giving it a try for even one month." I again was wooed by the encouraging way in which she spoke, plus the thought of the wage it can bring.

That morning, instead of continuing my journey to work at the smith's shop, I went back home and told Marm of my expectation. "What do you think?" she asked. "Can you work at sea? Remember you cannot swim." "I will be on a boat," I told her bravely. "Please be careful, George, and think well of what you are going to do before making a decision." "As it now stands, Marm, there is absolutely nothing to think about. Look, dear," said I, "on a Sunday morning when I go to the lime tree and pick those limes, peel and divide one each to Lincoln and Michael, as I would proudly hold one up for myself, saying to them, 'Come on, boys, let's have our full supply of vitamin C.' And thus we three will suck. Why? Well, it's because I cannot afford to buy four oranges for six cents. Look, Marm, as it now stands, our savings are exhausted, while I am daily robbed of my labour. And if I was given a fair chance of learning something, it will later compensate. But he shows me nothing. Only if he should step out by chance, Phillip or one of the men will call and show me something. Marm, if he would just pay me six shillings and leave me open that I can learn something in the machine shop, I do know later it shall pay off. But I am given no such opportunity. Marm, as it now stands, anything that I can get to do which will involve honest sweat and blood in labour, I shall do in the support of you all. What I have now said to you, through reason of my own, I really never told you. But deep within me it really hurts." "The work of which you now speak, what are the hours involved?" "I really for a fact cannot say to you." "Well, that you must find out." I knew well the hours involved, but purposely lied because I did not want to make her upset with a burdensome thought.

That very evening I went to the home of Mrs Kingsley, my Scottish friend, to speak fully on the matter with her husband. I was indeed very lucky to meet them, for they were both leaving for the Yacht Club.

He was a strongly built and elderly gentleman. He spoke quite kindly to me. He told me to be at the customs port for 6:55 a.m. the next day, as the launch will be sailing out at 7:00 a.m. sharp. "Do not walk with any 'grub,' for that would be provided out there. Some days you may get ashore at 3:00 p.m., and there are times you would not get to shore before 11:00 p.m. It all depends of how quickly the hatches empty, plus with the docking time of ships. Should you work and do not fall in with slackness with the gang, you shall be able to do it." Mrs Kingsley said, "Honey, you made no mention of wage to him." "Oh, I am really sorry. I've forgotten all about that. Well, George, with a normal week you would take home a pay package of $30.00, and with overtime you can take $60.00 to $70.00. It all depends on the docking and departure of ships."

I left the Kingsleys' home feeling quite elated that evening. I thought of going to St James to let Phillip know what was going to take place. But on the other hand, his father may be there, and I did not want him to know one jot of my affairs. So I headed back home. When I arrived, Marm was by the washtub. We greeted each other with her soap-sud hands. I told her I went and had Mrs Kingsley's statement confirmed by her husband, and I shall be starting to work tomorrow. With tear-filled eyes, said she, "Remember, George, you cannot swim. I do know that you are striving at this to prevent poverty in our home." "But, Marm, you speak of poverty. We are not poor." "What are you talking," said she with a light frown. "Well, Marm, at least not as long as you are around." "What do you mean?" she asked with concern. "Well, dear," said I, hugging her, "Mr Abe Lincoln once said, 'No man is poor who has a godly mother.' But I shall also add a little to his remark by saying 'No man is poor who has a praying mother and wife.'" She again embraced me as we both laughed.

Chapter 31

*George goes to sea; long hours lead to financial blessings;
he paints Mr Higman's house*

The next morning I decided to follow the time first told to me by Mrs Kingsley. So I left home at 5:45 a.m. I rode down slowly and was at the customs pier before 6:00 a.m., which had me placed one hour ahead of the time given to me by Mr Kingsley. Then I met a friendly customs guard who showed me where to lock my bicycle for safety. As we both chatted, he told me that I would not be back that evening until late because he was himself going to be on duty on the very barge for customs purposes. He also gave me a quick rundown of what my duties would be like.

At 6:15 a.m. Mr Kingsley and five other gentlemen rode up in a jeep. I perceived a surprised look upon his countenance when he saw me and beckoned me to come. As I went over to him, he introduced me to one of the men, who he said was the foreman of the operating crews. He also said, "George, you shall live long because I have been concerned of the time which I told you to be here. I am so glad that you have made an earlier move. For late last night, a call came from the ship that is now loading bauxite. It must sail tonight at 7:15 p.m. instead of scheduled 3:45 p.m. tomorrow. So we have now to leave here earlier this morning." When it was 6:25 a.m., six other men came. And we sailed from the pier at 6:30 a.m.

I once had a sail as a boy. It was upon a St Peter's Day when my uncle and three other men took quite a few kids in a rowboat out to sea. There

I got sick, and they were forced to return back to land. Since then, I had never again sailed upon the sea. But here was I now in a motored launch ripping through the water with great speed. I sat in the cabin, not braving the deck as did the other men.

As the launch sped along, I called to mind the poet who wrote the poem, "Spanish waters, Spanish waters, you are ringing in my ears,"[1] and I wondered had he then a similar experience or was it only a great imagination of his. Then the launch slowed as she encircled a huge brown barge covered with bauxite dust. We were all then standing upon the open deck of the launch when it made a quick turn. I, being inexperienced, almost got my head licked* off by an iron ladder which was suspended there for boarding the barge. I was pulled away by someone. Being so very scared, I never found out who was that good Samaritan.

The foreman told me that I am to work only with the shovel. And I am at no time to let any of the men know who recommended me. "Just work with the shovel," he again said, "and at no time must you venture to use the scoop, for it is a dangerous contraption if you are an inexperienced person." At 7:10 a.m., operations started for the loading of a ship that was moored alongside the barge. I was now at school and had then to learn very fast. I got myself close to one of the other men who looked strong and healthy, and also held a composed look as to what he was about. We had then to shovel bauxite from the barge's hatch into the ship, using a crane. I worked alongside this guy as he shovelled away with such skill. I then recalled the good old days at Bishop's, where I worked alongside Evasily. However, this fellow, though strong, had lacked art. For apparently he had in mind to "burn me out," but he did evil to himself, for he had not the art of resting on the shovel, a trick Evasily had taught me.

---

[1] A reference to John Masefield's "Spanish Waters" (1918):
Spanish waters, Spanish waters, you are ringing in my ears,
Like a slow sweet piece of music from the grey forgotten years;
Telling tales, and beating tunes, and bringing weary thoughts to me
Of the sandy beach at Muertos, where I would that I could be.

CHAPTER THIRTY-ONE

Later in the day when we had our lunch break, he asked, "Are you a Trinidadian?" To this, I answered not, but looked at him and smiled. I gave the best I can that day because I also learned that we were short on labour hands by sixteen men who did not arrive on the pier this morning due to the sudden change of time that came about. Operation halted at 6:00 p.m. As we got out from the "hole" (the barge's hatch), we looked like seven strange beasts on deck. As I looked across the horizon, there was the setting sun in all its splendour. Truly it was one of the most beautiful scenes I had beheld up to then, as it glittered upon the waters far beyond my reason to describe.

We cleaned ourselves with sea water, which came gushing from a pump. We after had a quick rinse with fresh water from an open shower, dressed, and were all ready to leave for shore by 7:00 p.m. I had really enjoyed my day, with the exception of my close experience with the ship's iron ladder. As we sailed back to the mainland, I occupied a seat all by myself. The foreman joined me and said to me, "Now, young man, I do not ever say this to any of my workers, but you certainly have satisfied me today. Just keep it up, and your pick shall always be secured." I felt elated and thanked him for his compliment. When we arrived at the pier, it was 7:40 p.m. I then grabbed my bicycle and was off for home.

When I got home, Marm and our three children were anxiously awaiting me, being my first day ever out so late at work, and it was Tuesday of that week. She inquired most excitedly of the nature of my work and how my day was spent, what had I to eat, and a barrage of other questions before I could have properly answered one.

When we sat around our dinner table that night, the children, who had all eaten earlier, listened with curious interest, especially our two sons, to what was said and done. I then explained to Marm that the work was not at all a difficult one, except being very dirty and its long hours. I said to her it was one of the easiest jobs that I had encountered so far. And so I gave her fully the day's happening, while being mindful not to mention a word of my close contact with the ship's ladder. I also told her that the men swore quite a lot for every and anything. "Put your finger in your ears," she smiled, "and pay no heed to what may be said."

And so was the rest of my work passed to Friday. No work was done on Saturday. Now learning from my first-day experience, I made sure to be on the pier no later than 6:00 a.m. And, with the exception of my first morning, the next three days following, no less than twenty men were selected for the barge. And so it was that I fully knew the foreman's terminology when he said to me the first day that "my pick is secured."

Then came the Friday evening of this, my first work. There came a very loud cry. "The launch! The launch!!" The men all scampered as a herd of wild beasts from the hatch, as they made their way hurriedly to the deck. That call was meant for wages. I was the last to be on deck. Names were seemingly called alphabetically, for mine was the very last to be called. I afterward learned that who did not then collect their wages could on Saturday morning to collect same at the company's office. As the men received their pay envelopes, they with excitement broke them open immediately, while the strong wind blew the torn bits of paper across the deck like miniature kites into the open sea.

I folded and tucked mine into my fobs, as I wondered what was next to be done. "Come on! Come on!!" barked the foreman, "down the hole! I want that mound level." As I turned to join the swearing crew, he tapped me on the shoulder. "Not you," said he. "Stay up here and clean up the deck," as he handed me a heavy bass broom. Very quickly I was finished. "Alright," said he sharply. "You go bathe, for we shall soon be going ashore." Glancing at his watch, he said, "In the next three quarters of an hour's time." My shower was quick, for I used fresh water only. As I lazed and gazed at the open sea, I saw him on two occasions looking at his watch. On the third occasion, he strode to the hatch and shouted, "All aboard!!" I, on hearing that command, moved up to forward deck and sat beside a huge coil of rope.

Very quickly my associates were all on deck washing themselves. The time was 3:15 p.m. At 3:25 p.m., the launch pulled up alongside. I then joined the crew of trimmers. And we were all aboard the launch by 3:35 p.m. in readiness for the shore. Within the very short time of our sail back to shore, it was most astonishing to hear and see how the

CHAPTER THIRTY-ONE

crew of trimmers swore and gambled before we touched the shore at 4:05 p.m. I sat and wondered at their behaviour.

I raced for home and was there at 4:20 p.m. that Friday evening. Needless to mention, my family as usual were all happy to see me. I with pride retrieved the pay envelope and handed it to Marm. Said I to her, "Please open it, and let's see together what is my week's pay." Very carefully, as only Marm would do, she opened it with a sword-shaped letter opener (one that we still have). I went looking through a window as I said to her, "Count and tell me what it is." "Oh, George! They have paid you $40.00, which includes Monday according to this attached slip," said she with excitement. I could not believe it. For never in my then life had I ever earned so much money in so short a time. I wept for joy. Then said Marm with concern, "Why should they pay you, George, for Monday when you did not work? It is a mistake. How can you check on it?" I really did not know how was I then to handle the matter. "Let's wait for Monday," said I.

Came Saturday morning as I had not to work, Marm gave me $10.00 and sent me to make* the groceries. On my way I thought it best to go and thank the Kingsleys for getting me the job. And also to let Mr Kingsley know of the mistake made in overpayment to me. "Oh," said he, "George, the foreman gave an excellent report about you, which led to you getting Monday's pay. Just do not let me down, Wright," he said earnestly to me. "Have no fear, Bobby," Mrs Kingsley interrupted. "He won't."

I did make the groceries, not in a housewife fashion but in a child's delight. Marm had a good laugh, as she helped herself to a bar of Nestle's Fruit and Nut Chocolate. In all I spent $6.88, and I handed her the change of $3.12. "OK," said she, "you must go again." So she handed me a list of all she needed for the next week and again gave me $10.00, sternly warning me that I am not to repeat a single item that I had already bought.

In my second errand I spent $7.70. On handing her the change of $2.30, "You know what?" said Marm. "Hold this forty cents in your pocket. Should the bicycle fail you on your way to work one morning, you can park it up and take transportation. I shall take care of this $25.00," said she. I looked at our children, who seemed quite happy as they feasted themselves upon a tin of Bermudez cheese biscuits. To this I laughed. Marm said, "Now don't you start breeding them into bad habits! I know you."

At 6:00 p.m. that evening, Phillip and his father drove up in the jeep. "George," said his father, "I did not see you out this week. I thought that you were ill? Madam insisted that we come and see what was wrong." (Madam was his wife and Phillip's mother.) "No, sir, not at all," I replied. I then proceeded to tell him my former savings are all exhausted. "Where I am now with you? I am only doing underpaid labour, without being given a chance to learn something to compensate in filling the gap. And with a family comprising five, I must seek some other avenue of employment to fulfil our needs." "Have you found anything?" "Well, sir, I have met very good prospects. I am now keeping my fingers crossed." "You might as well forget about this crazy idea and come out on Monday. I shall pay you $5.00 per week, and you shall work alongside Phillip." "Thank you, sir, but let me first think it over."

As he with interest surveyed the yard, looking at my plants, I hastily told Phillip that should he get a chance tomorrow after church, he should come up, and we would talk. "OK," said he softly.

When they drove off, Marm asked, "Why did you do that? Suppose the children were around and hear you, especially Lincoln, who is quick to catch things. He would have heard you lying! Why did you not tell him plainly the truth?" "Marm," said I, "it is like this. First, he was not true to me. Because when he saw my willingness, he could have paid me $2.50 per week even as a handyman. And I would have been satisfied until I was taught the skill in handling the machinery as a tradesman. Look, Marm, I have never told this to you; neither have I spoken about it with anyone else. He would at times take me up to Laventille Road to houses that he owns around that area to clean their surroundings. Or I may be taken to jack up a house in his presence to make it higher for a dugout room. I would at times be faced with frogs, rats, centipedes, plus the stench of human urine and other waste matter. For this he will

CHAPTER THIRTY-ONE

at no time hand to me an extra penny. Had it not been for the kindness of Phillip's mom, who would make sure that I eat with Phillip, I would go starved. Look, for instance, he came, and for principle he could yet have given me the paltry three shillings. It would have been left to me to say 'no thanks' to him. But did he do that?" "OK, alright," said Marm. "You have missed your vocation. You ought to be a lawyer."

The Sunday evening, Phillip did come as promised. And I related to him truly everything. "George," said he to me, "always remember that hymn Mother taught us to sing after meals: 'Safe am I, safe am I, in the hollow of his hands, etc.'" I then shared to him some dinner mints from my free spending on Saturday and so he said goodbye to the family and left. In my now new job, we became financially blessed. My then and only inconvenience was the time involved, of long hours from home, because the children hardly ever saw me during the week before sunset.

Our house was all complete and painted by a professional painter. Marm now knew fully the nature of my work and requested that I take a daily supply of Seven Seas cod liver oil, a purge of Andrews liver salts each weekend, plus a bottle of Buckley's Mixture should I cough. To these, her suggestions, I did comply. It happened one day there was a crew of sixteen of us. We were supposed to clean the corners of a hatch where the scoop and crane could not reach. (Now may I say that I spoke kindly to everyone, but I had not a friend among them. It is a fact that we toiled in the same field, but our domestic lifestyles were entirely different.)

On this day the foreman was apparently summoned to the ship's office and got delayed, and it would seem that the gang perceived this. They all then, as little irresponsible boys, stopped working and began to throw picongs* to one another, as they swore with every uttered sentence. Two fellows even went to sleep, resting their heads upon their shovels as pillows. I was alone working. I was no less than twenty minutes shovelling away when the foreman yelled from on the deck, "Hey! What the hell is happening down there?" The men all scampered in a wild dash and began shovelling. Within seconds the foreman was down and was himself swearing his tongue out. "What the blankety-blank! You fellows wants me to lose my far-fetched job or what! I was in the barge office when the superintendent passed three times and saw one man working for half an hour. I could not believe that. I looked down and see the same from up there. This is no far-fetch feather in the cap for me. So before I should be forced to join into your rank, I shall have to do something drastic about it. Before something is being done to *me*!" he screeched.

That evening when I got home, I told Marm of the happenings that day. "George," said she, "do be careful. Remember the Bible story of Cain and Abel, Saul and David. They were both connected with the sin of jealousy. Plus, nowadays people do get jealous if one should say a polite good morning to another." "Don't you go worrying yourself about that, Marm. I am now a seasoned workman among them. There is no one there to match me with the shovel. It's only the scoop I cannot handle good enough; only a few of us can handle. And I was warned by the foreman not to use it."

That week it happened that my pay envelope was $30.00, for we worked flat hours. The following week on Monday morning, the foreman told me Mr Kingsley wants to see me. "Go to him," said he, "tomorrow morning at head office." "Alright, sir," I assured, as I wondered what could it be all about. The following morning I left home at the usual time and was at the pier. But I joined not the crew but stood afar, unnoticed. When the launch sped off, I began a survey of the anchored schooners and jetty.

At 7:30 a.m. I went over to the head office to see Mr Kingsley, as I was told by the foreman. "Oh, George," said he, smiling, "sit down." I now wondered even more what could it be. "Someday last week," said he, "the superintendent visited the barge. As he looked down the hatch that was working, he saw one man alone shovelling away, while the others were resting. On investigation it was found that man to be you. George, I truly felt proud when I openly could have said that 'you were my finding'." At this I blushed, and with bowed head I said, "Thank you, sir." "Now, George," said he, "tell me how much do you know

CHAPTER THIRTY-ONE

about painting?" "Not very much, sir, but I can daub. And should I try, I would be able to mix a few colours. Although, as you may know, nowadays house painters are fast moving out of the era of blending and mixing hues. For nowadays when one go to the hardware store, you are given or shown a chart to choose the colour and shade you want at the counter." "You are right, George, that is a fact," said he. "Now, George," said he, "the superintendent has got a house in Maraval, and he wants you to supervise the painting job. How about you choosing three men from the gang?" "No, no, sir. Why not tell that to the gang foreman and let him choose the three most experienced men in that field and send them along with me to the house?" "Good idea," said Mr Kingsley.

That was done, and we were sent to the superintendent's Maraval house. It was unoccupied. A low-built house was it, so we needed no scaffolding. We were supplied with two ladders and planks for same, two ten-foot stepladders, and a fourteen-foot one. The colours that were to be used were cream on all walls in and out with Hall's Distemper; the eaves, bashboards*, windows, and rails in white with fast-drying oil paints, while all doors were to be covered with mahogany varnish, and the entire roof in green paint, with a carton of paint brushes of various sizes. There was nothing to be mixed or colours to be blended.

Before I set the fellows to work that morning, I briefed them in letting them know we are four men and not boys, and I am looking forward to manly duties. Should I not be satisfied, surely I would send them back to the barge and get other men. I told them to first prepare the surface of the walls before priming. I spoke authoritatively as though I knew professionally what was to be done. All three were much older men than I and hailed from other Caribbean islands. I was the lone Trinidadian, and they seemed quite aware of what I stood for. On the barge they saw how relentlessly I worked and shared not in their fun, so they knew very well what I demanded of them.

I took a gallon of green paint and the fourteen-foot ladder, and made for the roof. At noon I climbed down, having used the entire gallon of paint. I had forgotten the men had not lunch with them. For this I made an apology. As they all had money I told them to find themselves a parlour in the village. As they left I surveyed the work that they had done and was quite satisfied. Taking another gallon of green paint, I was again on the roof daubing away. When they returned from their lunch, one man climbed up to the roof. "Oh me gash! Man, youh have a spray gun or wot?" I made no reply, as he descended the ladder back to his colleagues. I then murmured to myself many thanks to old Otchins. He made me do all his painting and other manuals, which seemed very cruel at the time. But here I am today proudly sharing in some of the benefits.

Now as we four worked on the barge from Monday to Friday as regulars, I told the guys that we must work on Saturdays to repay a missing day. To this they readily agreed. No one came to check on us during our hours of work, which we performed from 8:00 a.m. to 4:00 p.m. On the Friday, however, the superintendent himself (who I had met but once) and another gent came. I was yet again occupied upon the roof, finishing a second coat, while the other men were busy in various sections of the building. Being high up, I saw the car, but pretended not to see it. That did I for my own reason.

I was then called down from the roof, where I met a smiling superintendent who seemed quite happy with the work done by us. As I was again going to the roof to fetch the can of paint and brush, which was to create an even greater impact upon them, the superintendent called and handed me four envelopes. Said he to me, "You can pay the fellows." He also outright said that he was quite satisfied of the work done by us. I in turn told him of our intention for Saturday. "Oh no, no," said he, "leave that for next week." I said to him, "Sir, we have already decided on that." "Alright," said he with a twitch of smile, "my wife is very anxious to move in, and she would really welcome that news." And so I called the men in their presence and handed them their wage.

As the car drove off, one, a Dominican, among us tore open his envelope and yelled, "Oh me gash, dem boys wuck two evenings late." His action was quickly followed by the other two who endorsed his statement. They all had their $40.00 each. As usual, I did not open mine. That Friday afternoon, however, we wound up at 5:30 p.m. The

CHAPTER THIRTY-ONE

Dominican said, "Fellars, why can't we be here at 6:30 a.m. tomorrow morning and work to 1:00 p.m." One of the other two, a Grenadian, said, "Dat ent no problem wid me. Becausen de man is a nice man. Watch how nice he talk to us." The other, a Vincentian, said, "Fellars, I was tinking so oll along becorse de wedder is moch cooler den."[2] So we all four agreed to start at 6:30 a.m. the next day.

That Saturday morning, I was on the premises at 6:00 a.m. because I held the key for the back entrance, only to meet those three men awaiting me. I thought that I would have been there before them, but they all beat me to it. By 6:15 a.m. noiseless paintbrushes were daubing the walls, doors, windows and roof. The roof, though wet with dew, was dried with my rag as I worked along. By 9:00 a.m. the entire roof was completed with its second coating of paint. At 9:05 a.m. I joined the guys. I told them that I shall start preparing the fence and gate at the front. This, however, entailed but very little to be done because it was not an old wall. I took along with me the Vincentian, who worked like a "Speedy Collins."[3] He primed the wall while I worked on the wrought-iron work of the gate and rails with green paint. By 12:30 noon it was all done with the exception of the utility gate. I told the fellows, "Let's wind up and leave."

As we were about to leave at 1:00 p.m., the superintendent, two ladies, and a gent came. The gent, I afterwards learned from my colleagues, was the general manager of the entire operation of both barge and office. The two ladies I presumed were their wives. I told the superintendent we were there from 6:00 a.m. "I have no reason to doubt," said he, "from what I am now seeing, for the doors, windows and fence are far advanced to how I left them yesterday. Do you all want me to drop you into town?" he asked. "No, sir, we all have bicycles," I replied. As I joined the fellows to ride off, he called me back. "What's your name?" he asked. "George Wright, sir," I proudly answered. "Oh yes, Mr Kingsley's

---

2   'I was thinking so all along because the weather is much cooler then.'
3   J.H. "Speedy" Collins, a famous American football, basketball, and track star and coach, active 1920–64.

real buddy." I was somewhat alarmed at his remark but said nothing. "Well, George, take this $10.00 for yourself," and then he handed me three extra $5.00 notes. Said he, "Give one each to the other fellows." I looked at him inquiringly. The gentleman who came along with him said to me, "Yes, you all are doing a fine job. Go buy some flowers, and take them home for your wives." He knew not whether we were married or not. "Thank you, sir," said I with a bow. I tucked my $10.00 into my shirt pocket and gave the fellows their $5.00 each.

When we rode to the corner, the Dominican, who was likened to St Peter among us – he was always the first to suggest something – said, "Lisen nar, man, lea we come out from Monday at 6:00 a.m., nah an we shore can finish every ting by Thursday. Becarse it look like dey really anxious to move in."[4] To this we all readily agreed. The next week we did work as planned, and on the Wednesday at 5:30 p.m. the entire job was completed. I told the men to be there on Thursday. Should they be there before me, leap the fence, and start a general cleaning of the surroundings.

They did get there on Thursday morning before me. I met them cleaning the yard. The Grenadian had improvised himself a broom of palm leaves, the Vincentian had brought with him a machete from his home, and the Dominican made a rudely made cutlass from an old barrel hoop. And so they were hacking, chopping, and sweeping. I joined in the exercise with an improvised mop from a piece of sack that was laying in the outdoor sink. And so in that way we four had the place cleaned up indoors and outdoors to the eyes' satisfaction.

At 11:00 a.m. sharp, the superintendent drove up alone. He looked surprised and seemed pleased of what he was now seeing. "Well," said he, clapping the Grenadian, who was nearest to him, on the back, "you guys come tomorrow at the office at noon. I shall leave word with the cashier to pay you all." Turning to me, he said, "Wright, if it would not be

---

4   'Listen, man, let us come out from Monday at 6:00 a.m., and we're sure we can finish everything by Thursday. Because it looks like they are really anxious to move in.'

CHAPTER THIRTY-ONE

inconvenient for you, could you meet me here at 4:30 p.m. tomorrow?" "Very well, sir," I assured him.

Turning to me, the Dominican said, "Don't you forget to show the boss the paint remaining in the lobby." "Oh, thank you," said I. Now I had arranged the stacking of all the empty paint cans by themselves. All that had some or very little used were stacked together. And all unused cans together. They were all stacked in a grocery-like fashion. The superintendent was very pleased seeing their formation. "Well," said he again to me, "do not forget at 4:30 p.m. tomorrow, Wright." "No, sir," said I. "I shall be here, should life be spared." As he drove off, the Dominican said, "If the company have yet another house to be painted, don't forget us." "Yes, man," said the Vincentian, "it is nice working with you." I made no reply to either, although I knew this to be rude. But I've always acted that way whenever I sensed a familiar conversation will arise.

The Friday I collected not my wage from the cashier, as we were told, because I felt the men may all be there awaiting me to form a conversation. One thing I was partially sure about is that they all knew that I should not be there any later than 4:00 p.m. to collect my wage, because they heard me promise the superintendent to meet him at the house at 4:30 p.m. I left my home at 3:00 p.m. and arrived at the Maraval house at 3:30 p.m. I was very much surprised to meet the superintendent and the very gentleman who accompanied him the first day when we were paid. They seemingly had been overlooking the painting work that was done.

"Oh, well, Wright, you are here? Would you like to have the loose used paint and brushes and five gallons of the full cans of any colour?" I made not an answer of gratitude but stood confused. The gent presumably observed my hesitation to speak. Asked what was the matter, I told him that, although I was indeed grateful for the gift, I had no means of transportation by which to convey same. To this he smiled and said, "Don't you worry yourself about that. The van shall take you to your home with it." At this juncture the superintendent reminded me not to forget about the used paint brushes because they would stay and become ruined. "Oh, thank you, gentlemen," I bowed. The van did come that afternoon, and the gent told the driver to first take me to my house with my bicycle and bounty before going to the warehouse with the remaining unused cans. Before we drove off, the superintendent said to me, "George, will you like to make yourself some extra cash tomorrow?" "I will not mind that at all, sir." "Then will you meet me here at 8:00 a.m.?" "Very well, sir," I assured.

Marm was very much astonished when I arrived in the shipping company van. I quickly unloaded my belongings with the help of my two sons, whom I taught well to use their hands. When we were finished I gave the driver, who stood glum while the boys and I hastened ourselves, a two-dollar bill. On receiving it, his countenance immediately became brighter, and he drove off. I was then arrested by Marm. "Why did you do that?" "What, Marm?" "Why give that money to the driver? You said he was told to bring you here. Therefore, you owes him nothing." I gave a wince as I shrugged my shoulders. "George," said she, "you have to stop this Father Christmas way you have about you. For instance, that man stood there with his tall, lanky, lazy self, offered not a little finger to move an empty can, and has now driven off fat with $2.00. Why?" I smiled with no remorse. Then I told her of my hired service for the next day.

The Saturday morning I was at the house at 7:00 a.m. The superintendent drove up twelve minutes later. "Well, well," said he, "George, you are here. I really expected you at 8:00 a.m. I am so glad that you have made it earlier. Will you then help me to unpack the car and its trunk." As I gazed into the car, there was seating space only for him. The vehicle was packed to its roof with what seemed to be personal items. He carefully parked the car close to the front door. We took all the items into a single room, and he locked it. I then turned over the key which I had for the back door. When we were finished, we both mopped the floor and passageway which led to that room. At 9:00 a.m. two trucks and the very van which took me home arrived loaded with furniture and domestic electrical appliances of all description. There were four loaders with the trucks. The van had not a loader. I then

CHAPTER THIRTY-ONE

recalled Marm's observation and remark used at home yesterday and therefore wondered whether I should go to his assistance or not. Then jokingly I said to myself, "I am Wright. And two wrongs could never make one right. Plus here stands the golden rule: 'Render evil not to evil'." So I went across to his assistance, for which he was very glad.

At 9:30 a.m. three ladies drove up in a Ford car. One gave instructions where she wanted the items placed. The furnitures were all modern and the best I had seen. When all were cleared from the vehicles, the superintendent called the men and gave them money from his billfold. They seemed all happy as they left. The three ladies, he, and myself worked together. They all seemed astonished as to how I managed in the handling of things. At one point the ladies were all exhausted. Even the superintendent himself showed some sign of fatigue. It was now more or less a one-man team, with me putting things in their seemingly rightful position. It is a fact that most of the heavy and bulky items were placed in rooms by the truck men as ordered earlier. Then came a meal break. There were cakes, sandwiches, coffee and root beers. I shared in the cakes and root beers, and was satisfied. We halted work at a little past 3:00 p.m. The lady who gave the orders around asked me my name. "George Wright, mam." "Oh yes, that's you. I've heard my husband mentioned your name before. Well, you do look right and work right, Mr Wright." The other two ladies laughed at her wit. She then addressed the superintendent and said to him, "Oh goodness, Fredrick, can we borrow him again next week?" "I don't see why not if you need him." The elder of the two ladies said, "He seemed quite knowledgeable about house arrangement." The superintendent then asked me if I was willing to work there yet another week. "Yes, sir," I assuredly answered. "Then you may take this," said he, as he handed to me a $20.00 note. "Thank you, sir," said I with a bow. And so I bade their company good evening and left.

As I rode home, my thoughts went wild. If only the stores were opened at the time, I could have spent it all on Marm and the children. Because here was I now with real extra cash. And I had not yet collected my week's pay. I rode home in high spirits that evening. Just to think that so much would be coming our way in one week's time, while I evaded the bauxite dust and the hearing of blasphemous words. Added to this, I was also assured that I would not be out on the "stream" for yet another week.

May I now say I had not been to church for quite some time. And I had then no objection going to any Christian church to pray and give thanks unto God for His mercies and kindness by which He has now blessed us. I shared the thought with Marm, and to this she readily agreed. But to my amazement, said she, "Let's attend a full gospel church." At this I looked inquiringly at her. For when I first knew Marm she was a staunch Roman Catholic, although I wooed her into marriage under Anglican rites. Now I always loved and respected her and will at all times try to comply with most of her requests. "Have you then," I asked, "a particular place in view?" "Yes," said she, "let's go to San Juan. There is a little chapel on Hunt Road. Let's go there." "Very well," said I, "if that's your wish, then let's go." Came Sunday morning we prepared ourselves and the children, and left.

We were warmly welcomed by the members of the chapel, who prayed and sang rejoicing hymns together, some of which I knew. A woman ministered the Word, which really made an impact upon my heart. Dear Reader, that chapel today is a branch of the AME (African Methodist Episcopal) Church in Hunt Road, San Juan, with over fifty years of service to the nation. That female pastor, now deceased, has gone to be with her Lord Jesus Christ. Her name: Rita Burkett.

I then spent the balance of that evening weeding and cleaning around the yard, while Marm busied herself with the boys and their schoolwork. "For," said she, "I do not want them to become men and be doing the same laborious work as you do." I replied, "There is no disgrace in honest labour, Marm."

Came the Monday morning I was at the Maraval house at 6:00 a.m. Mr Higman, the superintendent, was taking a bin of garbage to the gate. I was somewhat surprised at this. For I knew not that he and his wife had moved in on the weekend. "Well, George, you are here quite early. You truly are an early man," said he with a smile. "I am indeed

CHAPTER THIRTY-ONE

happy about that. Please come and let me show you around at a few things that I would like to have done." And so he took me around the yard, pointing out to me his desire but not with an assured feeling. I, sensing his incompetence, said, "Sir, can I use my own initiative while carrying out the assigned duties?" He looked me squarely in the eyes. "George," said he, "you go ahead from 'bow to stern'. You are in full command." "Ay ay, sir," said I with a smart salute. To this he smiled and went into the house. He was back out to me in about eight minutes. "Oh, George, it slipped me to tell you Mrs Higman, my wife, may also call you to help her inside." "That will be no problem, sir," said I. So now I was more assured that the folks with whom I work were called Higman.

Now Marm for me had prepared two thermoses that morning: the smaller with porridge and the larger wide-open mouth with soup. So meal-wise I was quite prepared for the day. Mr Higman showed me his tool cupboard, which was placed under the eave of a window with an assortment of tools. Said I to myself and in agreement with the old proverb, "Bring me the tools and the job is done," bringing to my mind old Otchin.

I made an imaginary sketch of everything before starting my chores that morning. First, I gathered up all the loose stones around the yard, plus a few big rocks that were found in a dry creek just bounding the property. These I formed into a mound indicating a rock garden, which only needed plants to complete same. I raked all the withered shrubs and fallen leaves to the root of the very tree which shaded me from the sun when I painted the roof. This I covered with loose earth to plant anthurium lilies.

At 11:00 a.m. came Mrs Higman to see me. "Good morning," said she. Politely, I returned the compliment. "Oh my goodness," said she (in awe), "who is working with you?" "I am alone today, Mam." Staring at the mound, said she, "I cannot believe my eyes of what I am seeing. Did Fredrick –" and as though correcting herself, she said, "Did Mr Higman instruct you on this?" "Yes, mam, he did, to a point." With a brisk turn she went back to the house looking very pleased.

At 11:45 a.m. I heard Mr Higman's car, so off I went to open the gate. When he parked the vehicle, he inquired of me how my morning went. "Fair, sir," said I. To this he only smiled. He then with quick steps walked straight up to the backyard, with me trailing. On reaching the piled rock and laid stones, he clasped his hand to each side of his head in wonderment, declaring, "George! George! This looks good." He immediately without another word went inside.

"By the way, George," asked he, "have you eaten?" "Not as yet, sir." "Oh no," said he, "break off and come have some lunch." "Thank you, sir, but my wife prepared me lunch this morning before I left home." Mrs Higman said, "You can still have a cold Coke or a root beer. Whatever you wish." I accepted and helped myself to the root beer. The day sped on, and I was myself fully satisfied with what I had done. At 3:00 p.m. Mrs Higman came and said to me, "You have done enough for the day. You go home to your family until tomorrow."

The following day I prepared a few vegetable garden beds with drains and furrows. On the third day, one of the very ladies who accompanied her the first time drove up with a female domestic. I was challenged that day to work indoors with them and was openly asked my opinion on many matters. And so did I work in and out of door on to Saturday without being sent back to the barge. And so did I for weeks keep working in and out of doors, doing anything applicable in the domestic field, all of which I knew.

One evening they proposed to hold their very first party at the house. Mr Higman asked me if I knew of anyone who could assist as a waiter. I told him that I knew no one (which was the truth). He said that they were hoping to have over some of the city's dignitaries, including Mr Dell, the company's manager, who was also sending him a bartender. "But," said Mr Higman, "I also wanted another person to assist with the maid as a waiter." "Sir," said I, "why not try the Queen's Park Hotel? There you are likely to get a professional waiter who may be off duty and will be very happy doing an odd job like this for the evening." "Good idea, George. I did not think about that. And I do know that we would be having quite a crowd."

I hurried home that evening, and I told Marm of what would be taking

CHAPTER THIRTY-ONE

place within the next few hours and that I am going to assist. "What will you wear?" said she. "Your toxicedo is not prepared." I checked my clothes closet. My black braided pants only needed some fuzzing off. But looking at my white coat it was a bit crimpled and could very well do with some ironing. With my white stiff-bosom shirt and black bow tie, the toxicedo will not be at all missed. "OK," said Marm, "you go fix yourself. I shall take care of these."

Now these very clothes I had when I lived at Mammy Bell, for she kept numerous parties for her boarders. It was at her home I gained a pretty good knowledge of bar tendering from her English background, plus what little I had gained from the Otchins, so I had then no problem. Most beautiful Marm had taken care of my raiment that evening. They lacked not the professional laundry finish. And so, taking my raincoat, I set off for the home of the Higmans.

When I arrived there that evening, there were only six guests. The Higmans were spellbound of my appearance. Mr Higman raised his hands and clasped both sides of his head (a habit had he whenever excited). As he looked pleasingly at me, "Oh, George," said he, "you do look smart. I followed your advice and had been able to get the bartender from Queen's Park Hotel. I am now awaiting his arrival, plus that of the other bartender from the company's manager, Mr Dell."

There were two maids, and one seemed to be quite knowledgeable of what was to be done. So with her leadership we arranged the bar. Both bartenders arrived within minutes of each other. (They seemed to have known each other by their greetings.) Mrs Higman at once arranged that they work on the drinks, relishes, and ices, while both maids and myself served the guests. It was a packed house seemingly really only of the elite citizens. To my surprise, and to theirs also, was my former employer and Mrs Williams. The elder of the maids said, "Look at the head druggist of W. Serious waving to you." "No," said I to her, "he is not a druggist, his wife is," as I acknowledged the wave.

It will appear that my presentation impressed many of the guests that evening, for I was approached by quite a few to work should they be having parties. But to these I politely turned their requests down. May

A BRANCH TO REST ON

I say the party seemed to be quite a success, for everyone looked quite happy with smiling faces. In the midst of it all, a gent, who seemed quite a boozer, stood up in the lobby and shouted to me, "Hey! Rochester,[5] come here!" To this I saw both Mr Higman and Dell quickly walk over to him with stern looks on their faces as they said something to him. And may I also say there were some generous folks who gave tips among them. When I got home at 3:30 a.m. and emptied my pockets on the settee, Marm counted $56.88. What a packet!

On leaving that morning I was told by Mrs Higman not to return until the next Monday. And from then on I became a perfect "landlubber" and was no more seen on the pier or barge. In the entire neighbourhood their plot of land was kept the finest, with grass lawn, rock garden, lime hedge at front, a flower and vegetable garden, not at all forgetting a rudely made aquarium in the centre of the grass lawn. Whenever visitors or friends called, the outdoor ground was surveyed with pride for its unique presentation by a joyful Mrs Higman.

May I now say that I became not only a favourite domestic helper of the Higmans but a friend. Occasionally they would pay a visit to my home. Mr Higman would openly show his interest of how I landscape my small plot of land and its utility. Mrs Higman loved Marm and our children, and would at times send or bring gifts to them. What an open couple were they when speaking to us.

Months passed on of my being of service to them. And one evening as I was pruning the hedge, Mr Higman came to me and asked how would I like to work on one of the barges that ploughed the sea transporting bauxite from Suriname to Trinidad. In astonishment I looked at him. Then said he, "You see, George, Pat and I are going to the United States on vacation, more so to settle some domestic affairs. And Mr Dell and I shall rather have you working on one of those crafts. There would be a hitch in the difference of your pay, which shall be instead of you being

---

5   The role of Rochester van Jones, usually known simply as Rochester, the valet of Jack Benny on the television series *The Jack Benny Program*, was played by Black actor Edmund Lincoln Anderson.

CHAPTER THIRTY-ONE

paid weekly as you are now, you shall be receiving a monthly wage." "That would be fine with me, sir. But let me first talk it over with Marm tonight, and I would let you know decisively tomorrow, God spare life." "I do hope she agrees," said he.

I laid the suggestive proposal to Marm that evening, and she also thought it to be good. So the next day I gave Mr Higman an assured "yes!" "Well," said he, laughing, "George, you shall be a jolly sailor in a fortnight." And so it was I really did become a sailor in two weeks.

Chapter 32

*George at sea: he helps to save Bozo the dog, risks his life,
and meets the river people of Suriname*

Our craft comprised a crew of ten men, myself included: the captain, an engineer, a cook, a bosun*, a storekeeper, and five deckhands. Our greyed captain was a Caymanite, the engineer a Colombian. They were two kind gentlemen. They held the responsibility of our barge. However, the barge was powered by a tug and not its own steam.

On this, my maiden sail, I decided to do some fishing when off duty. So on the advice of my good friend Coggins, I bought two sets of nylon lines and some assorted sizes of fishing hooks. On the barge I was sent to work with the engineer. I told him frankly that I had not the slightest idea on mechanics. "Don't you worry about that," said he. "I do admire your frankness. While here, you would learn what is to be done. I began as you are today, fifteen years ago." As he spoke he pointed to the tug roughly five hundred feet away from us. Said he, "Without that tug, we shall go drifting aimlessly upon the ocean because we have no sailing power of our own. All we now do is to set course with her, and we are safe."

Down in the engine room where he took me were lots of valves of various sizes, some of which he turned off or on. On occasion he would briskly step across to some electrical switches, turning them on or off amidst the continuous beat of a huge engine on which he would on occasion turn off a hissing valve. "Don't you worry yourself," said Mr Roberts, "you shall soon get into it."

CHAPTER THIRTY-TWO

We were on our journey far out at sea that day when an accident occurred. The captain had a lovely fox terrier he called Bozo. The little creature fell overboard. A yell came loudly from someone, "Dog! Dog!! Overboard!" No one could then think of a way to rescue the poor beast. There were no nets, and the grapple hook was too short. Someone suggested that the tug be signalled to stop and lower down a lifeboat for its rescue. I then remembered the hook and line that I had brought to fish. I told a deckhand of my having same. "Bring it," said he. This shipmate was a very tall man. (I was after told that he was a Vincentian and a very strong swimmer.) He made quickly a contraption with the grapple pole and the seventy-five-pound-strain nylon cord and a few hooks.

The little animal was strong, and he kept swimming alongside the rocking barge. The mate then dangled the hook-lined contraption about its legs. Then one of the large hooks caught the beast on its left hind leg. The animal, which was about thirty-five pounds, was hauled aboard in pain and fright, trembling without a bark, with the hook sunk deeply into its flesh. With his long shaving razor, the captain gashed the wound, causing yet a larger wound, to get the hook freed from the flesh of the animal. He then sapped the bleeding wound with warm salt water and cotton wool. He had a crew member burn some cotton wool for him, which he mixed with mercurochrome and iodine; he stuffed it into the wound. He then bandaged the wound as an authorized nurse. But up to this day I could not understand why he poured a drink of brandy into the stomach of the animal.

Slim (as the fellow who rescued the dog was called) came in for high praises, for his venture was very risky and brave. I was also given some recognition for having had the gear aboard. As we sailed on, the waters became choppy, and when we entered into nightfall it became rough. It was so very rough that the barge began rolling heavily. The captain then ordered all deckhands into their cabins. The bosun, an elderly man of Spanish descent who also was familiarly called Pop, remarked it was the roughest water he has encountered along this course for a very long time. As the men made their way into their cabins, they prattled frightful stories, which made my heart pulsate fearfully as I thought of Marm and the children back home. The engineer and myself proceeded down to the engine room. There was a watch on the bridge, steering. The engineer and I were down at the engine room for about half an hour when he said to me, "Let's take a look on deck to see what's taking place."

We were just in time to receive a radio call from the tug which said that our starboard light was blown. This aroused great concern because at a time like this it was very difficult to get there. The walk was a good sixty feet away, and with a rolling boat, disaster can be imminent. Our captain seemed greatly worried. "I can do that," said I. He looked at me with amazement. "Can you, son?" "Yes, sir," said I. At this point, one could have seen through a bright moonlight, as the boats rode the waves with the strong cable that connected them both gashing the waters and beating as a huge whip.

"If someone will go with me, we can carry the bulb to be replaced tied with a piece of twine. This would be clutched between my toes. I shall then climb the pole and have it replaced." Very quickly the engineer got both bulb and twine. At this time two deckhands came from their cabins. I overheard one saying, "I hope nothing try to pass between us because that would be fatal." Those words, though frightening, gave strength to my courage.

The captain and I then inched our way, as we clutched onto the sides of the hatch. When we got to the pole, he said something I did not understand because of the very strong winds. I then climbed the swaying pole, pulled out the dead bulb, and inserted the new, once more restoring light. During this action, my eyes were closed as I thought of Marm and our children. As I opened them, I saw as though I was taken up to the highest heaven and quickly lowered back to the lowest hell. I closed them quickly and slid down the pole. Once more the captain said something, but it was again stolen by the wind. We then inched our way back to the quarters. By then everyone was there with the exception of the man on the bridge. We all gathered in the mess room, where I was openly congratulated. The captain also said that the

CHAPTER THIRTY-TWO

deed would be recorded in his log. One fellow said, "Supposed you had lost your grip and tossed off?" I quickly replied, "Well, I would have had to swim for it." (Throughout my then career, I never at no time let anyone know that I could not swim.)

As we turned into our shared cabin that night, Pop (the bosun) and I had a chat. Actually he did most of the talking while I listened. Because I knew listening was a way of learning. He had knowledge of the sea, I had none. He then shared with me some sound advice of the sea, and we fell asleep. The next morning the water was as calm as though it could be walked upon. We were then towed by another tug into the harbour of Suriname, then taken by yet a smaller tug up a large river called the Mungo. The morning felt very crisp and dry.

As we were towed up the river, a few miles up its stream, I observed it to be densely forested on both banks. One sees and hears parrots, macaws, and many other tropical birds fluttering and ringing out their tunes among the forest trees. One's attention is also drawn to the howls of monkeys as they swing with agility from branch to branch. Occasionally you may see an alligator or two laying on the mudbanks. The water appears to be brown and greenish at times. As we were towed further up the river, there you may find a few patches of cleared forest trees. Standing in their place are some rudely made ajoupas on tall poles. They form a little village (perhaps like what Rajah James Brooke described of the Borneo villagers).[1] The inhabitants are of an Oriental cast, who look at you with an independent air. As we were towed further upstream, there we met another group of people that were of African descent, sailing on the waters in small dugout canoes. They paddled quickly along the river and were poorly dressed; the men wore loinclothes, with exposed buttocks, the women with both fronts and buttocks covered and breasts bare. The few children I saw were boys, and they were all naked. I was told by a Surinamese native who joined us when the barges were changed that these people were the

---

[1] James Brooke (1830–68), a British soldier and adventurer, and founder of the Raj of Sarawak in Borneo.

descendants of runaway African slaves who came and settled beneath the forest green many years ago. He also said that they were all good swimmers. They held a ritual; as babes were born, they were taken to the river and laid upon its waters to make friends with it, because their livelihood depended upon it in many respects. These people are known as the Talkie Talkie[2] tribe. They are short and strongly built, and they are solemn-faced beggars. They beg chiefly for used clothing, soap, tobacco and alcohol. They care but very little about money.

I said to myself, on my next trip, God permit, I will bring all the old clothes and rags that I can lay hands on from home. As we sailed further upstream, the cook came and said to me, "Do you want to see something?" "Yes," said I. "Then lend me one of your lines and a large hook." I again brought the seventy-five-pound-strain cord with a large hook. He then strung the ribbed portion of a cattle he claimed was frostbitten and had now been in the cold storage for over a year. The weight was roughly thirty pounds. It was then lowered down to the water. With a splash did it hit the water that now seemed to be turning yellow. In about three minutes there were ripples in the water. He then gradually raised the line. To my surprise there were hundreds of small fishes feeding ravenously upon the carcass. They looked ferocious. "What kind of fishes are these?" I asked. "Piranha," said he. "They are also known as freshwater sharks." In about twenty-five minutes, just bare bone was left. What a wonder was that to me.

We arrived at the plant for the loading of our bauxite. At the large berth alongside the quay, there were gigantic cranes and many other apparatuses, the which I have never seen on our pier. There were also huge mounds of bauxite between twenty-five to fifty feet high. With the exception of the bosun and myself, everyone went ashore. I retired to my cabin to read the conclusion of a book titled *Mein Kampf*, which was written by Adolf Hitler,[3] but I fell asleep while reading.

---

2   Suriname's lingua franca, Sranan Tongo, was once known as talkee-talkee; it is an English Creole language.

3   *Mein Kampf* is the 1925 autobiographical manifesto by Nazi Party leader Adolf Hitler. Ralph Manheim did the first English-language translation in 1943.

CHAPTER THIRTY-TWO

I was, however, awakened by the strong barking of Bozo. I looked out and, behold, there was an intruder. I asked him what he wanted. He replied to me in Dutch, which I could not understand, so I called loudly to Pop, who was then sharpening the end of a piece of wood up forward. The stranger quickly left. "That's a thief," said Pop. "There aren't many of them, but you have to be watchful for many a time when they strike, they do strike big."

We were then loaded. All supervision and labour were carried out by the natives, a people who all seemed very interested in the execution of their post and duty held. With cranes and other skills, the empty hatches of our barge were filled without a sign of fretfulness among them. When they were finished, the barge was hosed down from bow to stern. There was no bauxite dust visible. It was a job well done. And so we left for Trinidad on the evening of the next day.

Our sail back to Trinidad was a very smooth one. The waters were all calm, and the barge was fully loaded and rolled not with the calm sea. When we arrived in the stream, we anchored, and there was a launch in readiness to take us ashore to the customs pier. I was exceedingly anxious to rejoin Marm and the children, for this was my first trip out and, as one may know, a sailor's story is usually a tall one. But here in my case, I had not to tell a "tall one" but imparted true facts and experiences to my boys. It was indeed nice to be home to give a general clean-up outdoors. I weeded and pruned the plants for my absent days at sea and shared greetings with my lads when they came from school on evenings.

For my second voyage I was well equipped with used clothing, rags and soap to be given to the Talkie Talkie people. I again took my fishing tackle with an additional line and a few more hooks. Marm also baked me a cake and some fudge. The following week, I bade my family goodbye. We were told to be at the pier at 6:00 p.m. for we again had a night sailing. At 5:30 p.m. I was at the pier, only to be told due to some delay the launch was not leaving before 7:00 p.m. I felt hurt because I could have spent at least an hour more with my family without being there now awaiting and guarding my packages.

We boarded the launch at 7:05 p.m., and at 7:45 p.m. we were all aboard our barge in readiness for our sail to Suriname. The entire trip was a calm sail and a sportsman's paradise. Although it was night, no one seemed interested in sleep and so every man tried his hand with the fishing lines. The result was a catch of five sharks (total weight 196 pounds), two dolphins (sixty pounds), four kingfish (sixty-five pounds), and as we neared the coast of Suriname, forty-eight catfishes were caught and were not weighed. These gillbackers, as they are called in Suriname, are a delicacy among the natives. Our cook had all this packed into his cold storage. He also said that the kingfish and dolphins we shall use, but the other catches will be given away.

The same exercise was again carried out on our barge, as we were towed into the mouth of the Mungo River. I once again placed myself on the lookout for birds, animals and friends. As I watched eagerly, I was called by our captain. As I got to him, he pointed to the right bank. "Look over there," said he. As I watched, there were no fewer than twelve alligators lying like driftwood on the muddy riverbank. Most of these reptiles with open mouths were catching flies. As we sailed further up the river, he showed me a manatee*, also called sea cow, feeding ravenously upon some water weeds. Although it is said that some of these mammals live in certain rivers of Trinidad, I had never seen one. This was my first and only time that I had been able to do so. To me they look very much like the seal whose picture we do see in books. Then flew past, going in a straight line up the stream, a flock of toucans making an awkward tune. The captain said that never had he seen so many at one time before. There were many monkeys scampering among the branches of the trees. Parrots and other birds were hovering over the barge from one side to the other. I curiously looked for snakes, but I saw none.

Again, as we sailed past the village of our Oriental friends, with the exception of the smiling expression on the faces of the little children, the adults showed no sign of interest whatever in our sail. Slowly but steadily, we sailed up the river. We then came into the waters of our Talkie Talkie friends, who came canoeing with such skill alongside

CHAPTER THIRTY-TWO

the barge as they gesticulated with shouts and begging signs. Our cook threw overboard a frozen shark; it had no chance to sink but was retrieved by someone who, like an anxious butcher, cut it into pieces, and it was divided among them. They showed no sign of gratitude to anyone. There was a native guide on board. He joined us from a launch just before we left the sweetwater (where the river water reaches the sea waters, it is often referred by sailors as being sweet) and entered into the river. It was said that he spoke English, French, Dutch and Spanish, and he also mastered the tongue of the Indians whom I call Orients, and that of the Talkie Talkie people. A linguist was he in his own right. He was a friendly man, and he appeared to be in his early forties.

Our captain then said to the cook, "Bring the unwanted catch and have it distributed to each canoe." The idea was welcomed by all aboard. The fishes were then brought from the cold storage. The guide then asked if he can be given two gillbackers. He was allowed to have his choice. Before they were lowered, I asked for the largest gillbacker of the lot. The crew laughed and joked, "Are you taking that home to Trinidad?" said they. The guide then spoke to someone among them, and the fishes were lowered and peacefully divided.

In the midst of this all, the barge kept sailing. I had observed a canoe paddled by two women, a young man, and a child who kept themselves far away from the others. Neither did they share in the bounty. I asked the guide what was the reason. "They belong to another tribe," said he, "and they will mix themselves with no other. Occasionally you do meet it that way on the river," he said. "But don't they fight?" "Oh no, never on the river will they do that. A fugitive is always safe on the water until he sets his foot on land."

I told him to ask them if they would sell or barter with me for an oar and a canoe. He looked at me in wonder. "Are you serious?" "Yes," said I earnestly to him. He then called and spoke to them. He said to me that they live very far up the river, and the distance was too far for them to swim with the child, and now with the full moon, the piranhas are gluttonous. However, if I do wish, they can barter an oar that they take with them as a spare for two cakes of soap and an old pants or any other used clothing. I told him to tell them it's a deal.

As the barge sailed, they followed, and so I went to my cabin and fetched two cakes of Sunlight soap and a large Palmolive soap and all the used clothing and rags that I had brought, along with the huge catfish that I was joked on. They were all lowered over the side to them. They in turn attached the oar to the cord. (I have the oar in my collection to this day.) I have never seen those people again nor had I been able to get the canoe on my other trips, but the dear love and memory of my primitive friends remained with me.

Now Bozo became fully better. The wound healed very nicely, leaving a distinct scar upon the leg. But besides the captain, the little creature just took a fancy to me. The engineer would say, "When you want to know where Wright is, look for Bozo." Should I be down in the engine room, he would wait for me at the top of the spiral stairway. The captain said that he was very glad to know Bozo had a friend because he was now due leave and was going to Grand Cayman, and he was quite sure that Bozo would be cared for. The captain did go on his holiday, and I was left in charge of Bozo. Owing to the laws of quarantine, he could not be brought ashore, so he was always left on the barge until my return.

Our new captain was a Norwegian. He was not as friendly to the crew. But one good thing about him: he was thorough with his rules. Very often he would quote Lord Nelson when he gave an order to us by saying he expected every man to perform his duty in the best way. I was shaded from his sight most of the time by being down in the engine room with the engineer. Our new captain also befriended Bozo. Very often he would go on the bridge and steer for long hours, taking Bozo with him. He tried, however, to be friendly when he observed that members of the crew avoided him on their break time.

Six trips were made with the captain, during which time there was no fishing or sightseeing on the riverbanks. He loved, however, the game of draughts, and he whipped everyone except the cook and myself. The fact was I knew not the game and did not play, but our cook was

CHAPTER THIRTY-TWO

an expert at it. Our regular captain returned from his short holiday. For that we were all happy. He remembered every crew member as he presented a small token to us. Even for Bozo he bought a lovely studded leather collar.

We had made two trips with Captain Carson after he returned from his leave. On completion of the second trip, I was told to report at head office the very morning we arrived in the stream and tied up alongside a ship for unloading. This message was given to me by our captain, who seemed very much concerned as he spoke to me in the presence of the engineer.

Chapter 33

*George is in a mess of trouble; Marm is a source of strength;
his life turns around when he meets Mr Mac*

When we got ashore, I hurried to the company's office. I was taken to a large room and made to sit by a large, polished mahogany wooden table. As I sat wondering what it was all about, in came the manager (whom I knew) followed by three gents (one of whom I had seen before) and a lady. As they came to the table, I stood up. "No, sit down," said one gent calmly to me. The manager then said, "You are George Wright?" "Yes, sir." I found it odd because he knew me. "Well, Wright," said he, "I would like you to tell us of your connection with Mr Higman, when you worked and what you did. Also right now, what is your duty with the company?" I sat in the chair, and hundreds of thoughts came flowing through my mind while he waited upon me to speak.

I then asked where was Mr Higman. They all looked at me in silence. Then one gent said, "As you can see, he is not here." I then asked, "Is this an interrogation, gentlemen?" In amazement, all four men looked directly at me. Even the lady, who was then writing, looked up under her glasses with a wry smile upon her countenance. The manager then answered, "Yes, it is." I turned to him and said, "Sir, I find this to be rather unethical because you do know as well as I do. For you were at their home on many occasions, and I showed your wife and yourself around the building with its variety garden that you always highly commended. Today, why is it in the absence of Mr Higman you sit

CHAPTER THIRTY-THREE

here as the big and great Gulliver seemingly to slay me, a Lilliputian?"[1] (Reader, I spoke those words deep within with unseen fright but with outward boldness for him to lose his balance and cool. And it did work.) He sprang to his feet and was coming towards me when two of the gents held him back. I smiled. He looked at me furiously and bellowed, "You are fired fully from this moment, you damn nig...," but he did not complete the sentence. I smiled again and said, "Sir, can I collect my wage?" Then the gent who up to this moment had said nothing said to me, "Alright, alright, son, go out and wait by the cashier's cage." I bowed and said, "Alright, sir."

As I walked out of that hall, a feeling of sadness crept over me, for I knew that I was once again exposed to a world without an education, a trade, or a job, and had now a family to take care of. Hundreds of weird thoughts came streaming in my mind as I walked that short distance to the cashier's cage. When I got there, there were two other persons awaiting attendance, sitting upon a long bench, while she attended to a third person at the cage window. I sat upon the far end of the bench as though cast upon a rock by a storm, hoping to be rescued. I saw not the gent who spoke kindly to me nor any other persons who were at the meeting.

The persons whom I met at the cashier were attended to and discharged, and I was left alone. After a short while, the cashier then asked me if I was waiting on someone. "Yes, mam," said I. Half an hour then passed, and then three quarters of an hour. I again began to wonder whether I had been skulled* and purposely left to see if I would blow my temper. I was just about to leave for home when the cashier said, "George Wright." I stood up. "Are you George Wright?" "Yes, mam." She looked narrowly at me. "But I can't ever remember seeing you here before." "No, mam, my salary is usually brought to me." She looked at me again with an inquiring look. "OK," said she, "please sign on this line." As I placed my signature, "Me oh my," said

---

1   George is referring to *Gulliver's Travels* (1726) by Jonathan Swift, in which the protagonist is shipwrecked in the country of Lilliput. The Lilliputians are six inches in height.

she, "you have a signature of that of a doctor or lawyer. Will you please sign your name in block letters below." This I did. (Reader, as I am on the subject of signature, may I brief you of how mine came about. Mr Otchin, with whom I worked when a boy, had a very outstanding signature, and very often when his friends came to visit, you may hear a remark used with dignity, "Boy, Orman, you do have an outstanding signature." I then began watching how he wrote when he had the cause to sign anything in my presence, and in that way I practised mine.)

The cashier then handed me an envelope; it was stout, but I did not break it to check its contents. With a very sad heart I walked down the stairway, wondering to myself how was I now to face Marm and tell her of my calamity.

When I arrived at home, the boys were already at school and our daughter was fussing over a rag doll which Marm had made for her. We greeted each other. "I expected you much earlier," said she. "What happen, you all docked late?" "No, no," said I, "we were on schedule." "Then what kept you so very long to get here?" I looked at her, and without a verbal answer, I hugged her and burst into tears. "Stop," said she, "do not let Vin see that you are crying." She then reached for the candy bottle and handed Vin a lollipop as she pulled the door behind us. "What happen," she asked again, "have you lost your money?" "No," said I, "how I wish to heaven it was that." I then gave to her the envelope. "Then what can it be?" she asked. "I am as to this day fired." "Fired! Fired! Fired!" she kept on repeating as though she was a record that had been stuck. She then looked at me and calmly said, "Come on, George, cheer up. If a door is now closed, another would be open. And our God never made a bird without a branch for it to rest upon. Have you forgotten that you once said you do not like the sea life because the children are growing without you? Well then, today if the end has come, then let it be, and don't you lament about it. Just remember, behind each dark cloud there is a silver lining." I looked at her and said, "Marm, I am not educated, what must I do? Am I to go out there now and burn and sell charcoal? Where will I find something to do with integrity, something for the upliftment of the children and yourself?"

CHAPTER THIRTY-THREE

"Nonsense," she replied, "was not Whittington made Lord Mayor of London?" She then opened the door, and there was Vin fast asleep with the half-sucked candy. Marm took her up and laid her upon our bed.

"Now listen, George, you have struggled all along without having to beg of anyone for anything, and we are much respected in the neighbourhood. Just bear in mind the same God who kept us yesterday will keep us today and tomorrow. We just have to believe and trust Him for all." I looked at her and said, "Marm, your courage has certainly shamed my fear" (as I hugged her). "Man tramples on his brother man, but God is ever near" (words quoted from the writer of the poem "William Tell"[2]). "Look," said Marm, "I asked Uncle West to buy me a cow-heel, and I going to make you a soup for lunch. Why not go and sleep near to Vin until I am finish." I took no note of the time. I slept very soundly.

I was awakened by Marm's soft hands being gently played over my cheek. "Get up," said she softly, "you has visitors." "What, what, visitors? Who is it?" I asked sleepily as I rubbed my eyes. "Your captain and the engineer. They are downstairs." A glimmer of hope sparked within me as I stumbled out of bed. As I hurried to the stairs, I was met by my two sons (Lincoln and Michael) who had just came in from school. I hugged and kissed them both. As I looked at my watch, it was 3:45 p.m. I then was going to say something further to them, but Marm pulled me and said, "Have you forgotten the gents are awaiting you downstairs?" "Oh, yes," said I. I first got the smell of tobacco and so I knew for sure that "Cap" was there. He was a heavy pipe smoker of Raleigh tobacco. I greeted them. As we shook hands, it will seem as though we had not seen each other for months. A sympathetic feeling could have been perceived on their faces.

"Well, George, me boy," said Captain Carson with a hoarse voice, "we got the news." "Yes," said Mr Roberts, the engineer. "Tell us what happened, for no explanation has yet been given to us as to your

---

2 Rev. J.H. Gurney (1802–62) was an Anglican clergyman and hymnist. George no doubt read this poem/hymn, "William Tell", in his Anglican hymn book.

dismissal." I then told them fully in the presence of Marm, for the story had not been told to her of what took place that morning. They both appeared to be very sorry about the matter. Captain Carson then asked, "What about your seaman's paper?" Bewildered, I told him that I had never heard of that. Mr Roberts then said that my being with them was my first experience out at sea. "I won't believe that!" the captain replied. "Yes, sir," said Marm, "he had never sailed the sea before." Captain Carson then looked astonished. "OK, OK," said he, "I shall now see to it that you get that. By the way, Robbie, what I spoke to you about, perhaps he can be drafted into it." "That would be an excellent idea," Mr Roberts replied, "for it ran through my mind when I first heard of this, but I said to myself, let you have the first say." "What is that?" Marm asked. "Well, madam," said Captain Carson, "this is very confidential, and it must not yet be spoken of. I have an offer to master a boat with the Dutch KSN Line which will ply from Aruba to Texas, then to England via Norway, and back to Aruba." "How long will a trip like that take?" Marm asked. "Roughly five months, madam." She smiled and looked at me. I felt an approval was written on her face with that smile. I then felt very happy for I once again will be employed. And it will not be on a barge towed by a tug but on a swift and stately liner that can touch the East and tell the West (as a poet puts it).[3] Deep within, I felt myself as a floating bubble in the air. "What do you think, George?" asked Marm. From the now enquiring tone of her voice, my bubble burst, as I sensed disapproval. I promptly replied, "Whatever you agree to, that will I do."

She then turned to the two gentlemen and said how well she appreciated their deep concern about us, but would rather that I now end my sea life. She went on to say, "Right now the children are growing without hardly seeing him sufficiently. It is a fact that they are yet small and can be controlled by a single parent, but there comes a time when it may be difficult to do so by myself, especially with boys. Next, as you have said, the boat will be docked in Aruba. From there he shall have to travel by air or some swift craft to Trinidad, which may be only for

---

[3] George is probably referring to Rudyard Kipling: "East is East and West is West and never the twain shall meet."

CHAPTER THIRTY-THREE

a couple of days, during which, of course, I cannot then be weighing him down with domestic complaints."

They both agreed with her. Mr Roberts said right now he is faced with the very problem at his home in Colombia. Captain Carson said nevertheless he shall still keep in touch, should there be a change of decision. Before saying farewell they handed me $100.00 in twenty-dollar bills, saying, "Hold on to that." To this Marm very strongly resented my accepting. "No, no, gentlemen," said she, "we have money. Things are financially good with us." She then added, "See here, the envelope which he handed me is not yet broken." She then reached for it on the safe. Mr Roberts looked puzzled at Captain Carson. (I believe it was due to their rejected offer.) Marm then tore open the envelope in a manner I had never before seen her open one. It contained $360.00, which was very much more than my wage. We were all very happy about it. They then bade us both goodbye and left. We accompanied them to the gate, as they walked down the street talking. I saw the smoke coming from the captain's pipe winding into thin air. When they got to the main road, they waved us goodbye. We returned the compliment, and never have we met again.

As we walked back to the house, she held my hand and we entered in silence. It was a customary habit of mine after each trip to buy from my pocket money something nice for Marm and candies for the children but due to my abrupt dismissal, this was not done. I tried to make an apology. "You worry yourself too much," said she. "There is yet some Nestle chocolate with almonds from your last trip. You can hand them each a bar, as they do love almonds." She then looked at me with dreamy eyes and said, "You may give me a kiss as my booty." When we got upstairs the boys were playing, but my daughter was asleep with her thumb in her mouth. The boys came to me as I sat upon the sofa, and each wanted to speak at the same time. I then handed to them their chocolate bar, charging them to leave a small piece for their sister when she gets up. Although the sun was fast sinking west, I changed my clothing, and with a broom and cutlass, I went to the backyard, chopping and sweeping as I secretly nursed the thought which rested upon my mind. What now must I do for a livelihood in the support of my family?

Marm soon came to me. "You don't have to do that now," she said. "Why not leave that for tomorrow?" She then withdrew the cutlass, which I had stuck on a log. "OK," said I, "but first let me pick this heap up." She quickly went and fetched the shovel and an old bucket. I cleared the stuff, had a bath, and changed into a pair of short pants and an armless vest. As we sat speaking, up came Uncle Weston, my brother. I had charged him to give the family a look as often as he can, and he never failed to do so. "Must I tell him now?" I whispered to her. "Suit yourself," said she. "I rather not," was my quick reply. We then greeted Uncle West and spoke on other matters, the chief of which was the country's hard-hit recession. We then had supper, and he left.

The following morning I prepared breakfast, bathed the boys, and Marm had them dressed for school. They attended the village school, which was then the Success RC, and were doing fine with their lessons, especially Lincoln. We saw them off, and I again went to the back and resumed the task of cleaning where I left off last evening.

It was 1:30 when I was called to lunch. "I am not hungry," said I. "That's not strange news," she replied. "I have been hearing that cry for many years now. But today you shall lay aside those tools and come to eat!" I looked at her and out came my answer: "Alright, Tanty Pet," as we both laughed. Very quickly I washed my hands and face. As I got to the table, before me was my favourite dish of codfish buljol, fried bake and lemon juice. It was really the first meal I enjoyed for the past seventy-two hours. When I was finished, I said grace and was about to resume my work. "Hold it," she said somewhat sternly. "You are not going back out there, at least not today." Inquiringly I looked at her. "Don't you think that we should talk over something?" I was again in my mind confronted with my saddened thoughts. I raised my head, looked her in the face, and said, "Yes, whenever you are ready." "How about right now?" said she. "OK," I sheepishly replied. "Well then, will you start?" said she. "Oh no," said I, "ladies first." "Very well, smarty, but remember, in the game of draughts, the knob moves first." "I cannot play the game," said I as we both laughed.

CHAPTER THIRTY-THREE

"Well, let me first start with an apology that's long overdue, for I cannot remember ever making it to you. And even if I did, it is no harm repeating it again. I was hurt," said she, "to leave the aristocratic site of Cipriani Boulevard to come into this mosquito-infested area, Success Village, Laventille, to settle. Had it not been for your determination, right now we would have been still renting from the good Lord knows who. Neither had I given you my moral support when it was most needed." "Hold it! Hold it! Is it that why we are here?" "No," she replied. "I am just trying to bring clear a point to express my personal feelings today." I looked at her. "OK, go on," said I to her. "You have made me lose track of what I wanted to say," said she. "However, let me put it in a nutshell. Had it not been for your determination, today we would not be owning our own home and would be paying an exorbitant rent to someone or perhaps be cast into the streets. But thank God, today we have our own home." "Well," said I, "it is the duty of a husband to provide for his family. I do think that or something of the sort is written in the Bible. And at the same time let us not forget Horace with his physical and moral support." "That's also very true," said she. "But let me say also that you must pray, or rather may I say that *we* must pray, that the good Lord leads you into a better job." "Better!" said I. "Yes, better," she replied. "Hem," I sighed. She then went on to say, "Do you know last night while you snored I got up to check our savings? Including the $360.00 that you received yesterday, it all amounted to $1,112.98." "Is that right?" said I. "I then went to my steel trunk and took my piggy bank out, for in it I put my pocket money, which I hardly ever spend. I felt sad to break it, yet I did. In it was $492.77. My goodness," said she, "George, we are rich. Look we now have $1,605.75, and I know that there is yet about $15.00 elsewhere in the house." I then unhung my trousers. I had in my fobs $4.00 and $1.60 in my other pockets. Then came the feeling of new hope.

"Marm," said I, "how about us starting a parlour with $500.00? I can make an earthen oven in which we can bake our own bread and cakes, plus some of those delicious pies whose recipe I learned from Uncle West. And you make fine fruit juices. Should all go well, we can buy ourselves a delivery bike, and I go selling on the wayside and on the premises of some firms, especially on peak and break time." Marm was silent for a moment. And then halfway lifting her hands, she said, "George, that's a most brilliant idea, but we shall have to employ someone to do the selling, and it will be somewhat difficult to do so at the beginning." "But Marm," said I. "Will you please give me a chance to speak?" said she. "You spoke without my interruption." "OK," said I, "go right ahead." "You see, George, you cannot go into business, especially the food business, without hiring someone to do the actual selling. Should you do it yourself, everything will be given away. Can't you remember when we tried the vegetable shop how much you actually had been giving away?" "Yes, Marm, but it was better to give those things away than to see them rot." "Yes," said she, "I do agree, but do you know that there are people who will just hang around to get their freeness? They also knows the weak spot you has towards little children, and you would be whipped with that. I would again say, George, that your idea is an excellent one, but the business will soon go to ruin through your sympathetic heart."

Weeks passed, and I had around our yard so well kept, better than any yard in St Clair or Woodbrook. Marm being an excellent economizer, there was always enough while very little was spent. In our backyard I grew lettuce, tomatoes, spinaches (both English and local), salad, and string beans, and a hedge with a row of melongene*, while our front yard was brightened with flowers and shrubs (crotons, etc.) which caught the eyes of passers-by. The name of our house was "Bushy Shanty", and it sported a lovely sign on the front gate.

The thought of being at home and spending without an income coming in began to take an effect on me mentally. So I decided to visit a few good friends of the Higmans: to mow their lawn, trim their hedges, lay out garden beds, and at times wax and polish their floors. This plan worked beautifully. Sometimes I took home no less than $7.00 each week, which I considered not at all bad. Since I had not an overseer, I left home when I wanted and returned to my own leisure.

CHAPTER THIRTY-THREE

George in his backyard with his dog

The time for the Higmans' return seemed long overdue, but for reason of my own, I asked none of their friends about them. Mrs Higman had a very good and trusted friend who was a garment designer. Sometimes when I got to her home, she would fit a dress pattern on me to see how it looked. I hid that secret from Marm. I was made to understand that this designer hailed from a very prominent US family. Her grandfather, it is said, was chiefly responsible for a particular function on motor vehicles as they are today.

One evening when I got home, Marm told me that Mr Higman had paid a visit. He had quit the bauxite company here and was now employed with one of the largest steel companies in the USA with whom he once worked at an earlier age. He was now paid three and a half times the salary he was paid out here. He also sent me US$250. (In those days, not much emphasis was stressed upon the dollar exchange as it is done today.) They were having a sale of the household furnitures. The house itself was the estate of the bauxite company, but all its contents were theirs. Whatever was not sold was to be given to me. They also had a very good friend in the firm of Charles McEnearney and Company whose name was Burton. This gent I knew very well, for he always visited their home. Mr Higman told me to seek him out that I may get employment.

I did get in touch with Mr Higman to confirm what Marm told me. And so I went to see Mr Burton, who was the son of the very Charles McEnearney.[4] Mr Mac, as he was familiarly called, told me he had seen and spoken to Mr Higman. He was aware that I had no mechanical experience, neither was I a chauffeur, but he shall try to find me some place. Let me call the next Monday at 7:00 a.m. to see him.

Up to then I think it was the fastest I had ever ridden. I got home and broke the news to Marm. "What work will you be doing?" she asked. "I do not know, not even Mr Mac himself knows where he can fit me because of my incapability, but he assured me that he will try to have me fit somewhere." She then left and went upstairs, but was down again in about five minutes. "How about going to church on Sunday morning in thankfulness to God for whatever your duty might be?" "I will be delighted," said I.

Then came the Monday morn. I was awakened out of bed by Marm. She said to me, "I do know that you would like to wet your plants before leaving home, so you better pray and get started. Remember you said you has to be there for 7:00 a.m." "Yes," said I. "Well, George, you ought to be there no later than 6:45 a.m. each day." "What time is it now?" I asked. "Exactly two minutes past 5:00 a.m.," she replied. I then hurried, prayed, wet five garden beds, took a quick shower, bolted some tea, got on my bicycle, and was off.

---

4   The young Irish American Charles McEnearney, a purchasing agent for coconuts, established the Ford car dealership in Trinidad in 1919.

CHAPTER 34

George joins the McEnearney company, plots to catch a thief, and becomes a trusted employee

That Monday morning, everything worked as Marm and I had planned for being on the site. As I got there, being a stranger, I had then to wait. Mr Mac was not yet there, so I waited on the pavement. On the other side of the street, there was an elderly man standing with a dignified look. He seemed to claim the respect of everyone that passed, as abasements were made to him with uttered words like "Good morning, Pop." I kept a steady gaze in his direction. Suddenly he looked towards me, and I made him a smart salute which he immediately returned. As 7:00 a.m. grew closer, the surroundings grew more alive with folks moving to and fro. At 7:15 a.m. he crossed and came to me. "Good morning," said he with a Barbadian accent. "Good morning, sir," I replied. "I seem to know you," said he. "Maybe, sir." He then looked at me and asked, "Have you ever worked at Sam's Garage?" "That's my brother," I replied. "Oh boy, you both do resemble," said he. "Are you waiting for someone?" he asked. "Mr McEnearney told me to be here at 7:00 a.m. for employment." "He won't be here so early," said he, "for he generally comes in at 8:00 a.m. You don't mind me asking, are you a driver or a mechanic?" "Neither," I replied. (At this my pride hurt deep within.) He then scratched his head slightly. "Come with me," said he. "Let me check Phillips or Santos to see if your name is booked." He then took me to a caged portion of the garage. He addressed both gentlemen and said to them he saw me standing upon the pavement since about 6:50 a.m. We spoke and I told him Mr Mac said that I am to check in this morning for work. Will they check to see if my name is down for work so that I can join the work crew? I then gave them my name. They checked, but mine was not there. I felt sad deep within and foolishly wondered in my thoughts. Mr Phillips then said, "Hold on, son, he would be here no later than 8:15 a.m." Pop quickly endorsed that statement and bade me to follow him. He took me to an area where some cars were parked. He then pointed to a vacant area. "There is where he generally parks his car," said he. "Don't you move, just wait here, he shall soon come." And with that help, Pop left me, for he was himself to take up duty.

Promptly at 8:00 a.m. Mr Mac drove up. I went to him. "Oh my goodness," said he, "Wright, I clean forgot about you. Nevertheless, come with me to the Firestone building." As we entered the ground floor, he said, "Wait here. I shall be back in a moment," and he hurried up the stairs. I said good morning to the folks that were around and began an eye search of the floor. The building seemed a new one.

At 8:30 a.m. Mr Mac came downstairs, and he took me to the manager of the ground floor. "This is the young man of whom I spoke on Friday. Wright," he said, "this is Mr de . . ." (I caught not the full name). "Good morning, sir," said I again to him. "Oh yes, Burton," the gentleman said, "he has already said good morning to me." "Now, Wright," said Mr Mac to me as he tapped his cheek softly with his pen. (These words I shall always remember.) "I know that you are a family man and an unskilled worker in this field. For beginners, we pay a boy's wage of $4.00 per week, but I will see that you get $9.00. You shall be listed as janitor of the Firestone department. And you shall also help in the tyre warehouse whenever there is a shipment of tyres cleared from the docks. You shall work as directed by Mr de . . ." (again I caught not the name) "down here at all times. Should anything better arise that you are capable of handling, I shall fit you in. But should you at any time get something better to do, without obligation you are free to quit." (Those were the words that morning, which came from the mouth of the man, my mentor, who made me proud of my tomorrow.) With

CHAPTER THIRTY-FOUR

sadness he spoke kindly to me. But, dear Reader, for myself I felt as though floating on cloud nine.

He then took me upstairs for the maid to show me around; it appeared that he had already spoken to her. She gave me a broom, a duster and a dustpan. I then set myself to work to the task, to which I was no stranger. To me there was not much to be done. The maid then spoke to Mr Mac. "OK, Wright, you may go downstairs to Mr de Sousa" (I finally caught the name of the manager).

Downstairs there were three fellows rolling and packing tyres around, displaying at the same time other accessories. "Join them," the manager said to me. And so I did, giving a general help. At 3:30, the manager called me and asked, "Where did you work before?" I told him where. He then smiled with a look at me as though being knowledgeable about something. "Come early in the morning," he said to me. "The door will be closed. Just push it and go upstairs. Angelia will be there, and she shall show you what she wants done. When you are thoroughly through, come down and clean up here. You are at no time to go to the back; there is a workforce out there. Try and pull your hand fast upstairs so as not to be in the way of the office staff when they take up duty at 8:00 a.m. Should you follow and take instructions, your job will not be at all a difficult one." "Very well, sir," said I. The office was promptly closed at 4:00 p.m., and by 4:15 p.m. I was at home. (In those days vehicular traffic did not command roads as it does today.)

When I got home that evening, Marm was in tears of happiness to see me. "How was the day?" she asked while the children followed around inquiringly. I do recall that evening also Lincoln and Michael fussing around my bike with rag, soap, and water, while daughter Vinneth looked on. As I sat down there, son Nunice came as he hurried to me with an apparent damp diaper. "Tell me," Marm said, "what is the nature of your work?" I was silent for a moment. And then I told her I shall be the building janitor and storeroom assistant, and will be paid $9.00 a week. "Thank God," said she as she clasped her hands and looked towards heaven. "I do know," said she, "that you can handle that." After telling her how my day was passed, we had then a family altar. Marm summoned that we offer a prayer of thanks unto God. I held Nunice, as she lead in prayer. After that I busied myself with my plants and other chores. I then got washed, and we both had dinner. (She never let the children wait upon us to eat due to my irregularity.) After our dinner I helped the boys with their homework, and we retired.

    The next morning I was on the premises at 6:30 a.m. Mr Santos came along with Angelia. He opened and locked the door, leaving us both inside. (So Mr de Sousa was wrong when he told me that I can push the door and enter.) We went upstairs. Angelia then asked, "What's your name?" "George," said I. "Now, George, I had not sufficient time to show you fully your duties yesterday morning. But as we are early today, let me show you everything." She then showed me both toilets and baths. "These are to be cleaned each day," said she. "The windows and ledge: due to the movement of the vehicles, lots of dust rises, so they must be given a quick run-over. All waste-paper baskets must be emptied into the waste crate downstairs. Do not shift anything on desk when cleaning, just wipe around them. Give all chairs a quick dusting, then sweep the floor. I shall tell you when it is to be mopped. Follow me," said she. She then took me into the tea room. "Leave here for last each day." She then looked at me and said, "Well, you ought to know what must be done in a kitchen, I am not to tell you." And using almost the very words of Mr de Sousa to me: "Pull your hands fast, especially in the office, so as not to be in the way of the clerical staff when they get here." "Very well, Miss," said I to her.

    Now may I repeat myself, being an old pro in domestic cleaning and arranging, it was all a simple matter to me. May I also add that the office and its utilities were all well kept. So my job was in no way a tedious one to me. And so I quickly went over it. When I was finished, I went downstairs. I swept the floor, dusted the outside of the cashier's cage, and wiped the manager's desk and chair. I had just began cleaning a shelf when I heard a click at the front door. As I took a look, the door was opened by a gent who came in followed by about fourteen people. I said, "Good morning," but no one answered. I continued what I was doing. Then the manager, the cashier, and three chaps entered. I did not say good morning because I felt maybe I would be treated with the

CHAPTER THIRTY-FOUR

said scant courtesy once more. I then moved my hands a little faster without looking in their direction. I then heard, "Good morning, are you finished with upstairs?" I looked around, and there I was face to face with Mr Mac. "Yes, sir," said I, "everything that was showed to me to do." Then the floor manager walked across. "Good," said he, "I was hoping to set you upon these very shelves cleaning today."

I did clean all the shelves; they were all very dusty and stacked with an assortment of vehicular tubes and other items. I also swept and mopped an unused stairway, which seemed as though it never has been cleaned for months. In this way I worked through the entire week with no haste, as I tried to be nice and friendly with those whom I met.

Then came the big day, Friday. Mr Mac was truly a man to his word, for I was paid $9.00. I got home and presented it to Marm. "Don't you worry," said she smilingly, "this will stretch a very long way." Now Saturday being half-day's work, I was then home before 1:00 p.m. And so I had a very busy weekend with my backyard garden. The lettuce was doing fine, and I plucked some for our lunch. I also gathered tomatoes from some of the old vines, plus a few melongene. That Sunday, Marm took the children to worship. I stayed at home with our toddler, Nunice. I also washed, cooked and helped with other chores.

Unaware that I was being watched, I worked for one month on the job. However, I realized that I was not made to clock in like the other workers, and my pay envelope was given to me by our department cashier. Then one Saturday morning Mr Mac told me, "Wright, as from Monday of next week, you must clock in at Mr Phillip's desk, and your wages will be paid to you from upstairs." He went on to say that this had not been done before because management did not know whether I would have stayed on or not. And so far the staff are pleased with my work. "Thank you, sir," said I.

I paid quite a lot of interest to my work and got through so very quickly with upstairs on mornings that smart Angelia, with the exception of three desks, will leave the other eleven for me to clean. It mattered not, however, because I was always in time with downstairs before they were open to the public.

Now throughout my life I have always tried not to say thank you easily. I will not, however, say to anyone that I am doing this for what you have done for me, but I will labour and put more interest into same. I have tried not to cheat, envy or covet.

After lunch one day I was called upon by Mr Mac and Mr de Sousa to write a bill for a wholesale customer. Now up to then, no one was allowed to make bills except Mr de Sousa himself or the cashier. I saw and learned how he made them, so it was no problem. While I made the bill, Mr de Sousa said to me, "Take your time, Wright." I felt assured by those four-letter words. When I was finished, they both checked it. Its amount was $87.90; it was found to be alright with the exception of my missing out the date. After which they both spoke, and Mr Mac went upstairs smiling.

I always carried with me a duster cloth in my hip pocket. So whenever there was no pressing work to be done, I would dust or wipe somewhere. Three other male hands were there, two salesmen and a porter. Although they made no bills, I could see they knew their work well. Especially the porter: he could stand at any distance and tell you the correct size of a tyre on any vehicle. I was then determined to prove my usefulness with what I knew, which was keeping a place clean and the manner in which to speak to someone. One morning after cleaning both floors, the hours seemed dull. A customer then came and went to Mr de Sousa, who called me and said, "Wright, this gentleman is interested in some tyres. Attend to him." I then approached the gentleman politely and asked him what size of tyre he wanted. "500-16," he replied, "for my Prefect car. I want two good recaps with very good casings." I chuckled on the inside. I, however, was able to let that gentleman buy himself four used tyres instead of his two recaps. After the customer left, Mr de Sousa said, "I had been listening closely to you, Wright; you have sales talk. I will give you a bill book. You will in the future make bills, and I shall check and sign them. If I am out, pass it to the cashier, and should she be busy, then take it upstairs."

When I got home that evening, as usual I told Marm all that went on and added that I may get a raise of salary. Disdainfully she looked

CHAPTER THIRTY-FOUR

at me and said, "I am very much surprised to hear such a statement coming from the lips of my husband. Just apply yourself to the job, and by God's grace, the wage increases will follow. Just remember the words in 1 Corinthians 3:6, which says 'I have planted, Apollos watered, but God gave the increase'." Very shyly I walked off, feeling very stupid.

The next morning, however, I was the first to clock in. I walked over with Mr Santos because Angelia was off that day. I quickly covered both floors in readiness for the staff. Mr de Sousa then called me by his desk and said to me, "As from today you would be the junior clerk on the ground floor. Go steady and be confident of yourself." With his encouragement and remembering the words of Marm who said to apply myself to the job, I found my work an easy one in approaching customers and the making of bills.

This practice went on for two months, after which I was paid $15.00 a week. Someone else was also hired to do the job of janitor. However, this altered not my way of getting to work. I would get in and clean downstairs, and would even give a lending hand sometimes upstairs. (Some folks thought me very foolish to do that, but I felt not that way. And thank God that I did, for it really paid off.)

It then happened that there was quite a lot of departmental stealing rocking the firm and which struck very heavily the Firestone department, for it was there the recapping of tyres were done and new tyres warehoused. A watch was set, and six chaps from the recapping section were caught. But yet the onslaught went on in the sales showroom where I worked. Tyres, tubes, and other accessories were just spirited away. I began to feel quite discomfited about the matter. Marm one evening said to me, "George, you are taking on an unnecessary worry. Do nothing. Fear nothing." "That's very true," said I, "but how about those who are daily doing wrong and cannot be caught, while their wicked deeds reflect upon others?" "Oh yes, I have seen your point," said she. "Alright, you hold on, George, and with faith I shall bend my knees, and no weapon that is formed against you shall prosper." "Yes," said I to her, "but how long will that take? I am sure Mr Mac and Mr de Sousa are watching me." "Don't be foolish, George, if they are, that's good, for you are being protected by their eyes. And should anything be wrong, then they must see."

One day my little friend whom I helped with the janitor's work came and said to me, "Mr Wright, ah see de tief." "What thief?" I asked. "Don't talk so loud," said he. "De one who tiefin de tyres and all dem tings." I looked at him in amazement. "Yes," said he, "Sookie is de colprick. He doing his business wid de wholesale dealer who does come here often." I stood perplexed. "Boy, are you sure?" I asked. "Yes, Mr Wright, ah marking dem for a long time now, but ah did'ent want to break de mark before ah was sure, sure, sure!" (Dear Reader, as I now pause, let me say this. Sookie is the porter of whom I made mention earlier, who could stand at a distance and tell you the correct size of any tyre.) "Who is the dealer?" "I ent go tell you yet; you go see him yourself. As ah tell you, ah was long watching they move, and today I more dan sure."[1] Now Mr de Sousa had quite a lot of confidence in Sookie. I do think it was as much as he had in our cashier, so I could not approach him with this matter. "By the way," I asked, "have you mentioned this to anyone else?" "Only to my mudder," he said, "an she tell me ah mus tell you." The name of my little friend was Vinch. "Vinch, say nothing to anyone, just wait until tomorrow, God's will, and I shall tell you what move shall be made."

---

1   'The one who stole the tyres and all those things.' I looked at him in amazement. 'Yes,' said he, 'Sookie is the culprit. He is doing his business with the wholesale dealer who comes here often.' I stood perplexed. 'Boy, are you sure?' I asked. 'Yes, Mr Wright, I have been watching them for a long time now, but I didn't want to break the watch before I was sure, sure, sure!' 'Who is the dealer?' 'I won't tell you that yet; you will see him yourself. As I've told you, I was long watching their move, and today I am more than sure.'

Chapter 35

Sookie is caught; George finds a briefcase in a ditch, and Marm makes sure he does the right thing; he loses his temper at work

The next morning I went down early, as I usually do, and as Vinch cleaned upstairs, I did downstairs. It so happened Mr Mac came in very early that morning. I told him that I would like to speak with him. Jokingly he said, "Why, are you going to start doing the cleaning again?" "No, sir," said I, "I am only helping Vinch out." "OK, you may come now," said he. I was glad for the opportunity, for none of the office staff was yet in. Only Angelia and Vinch himself, and they were busy on their chores. I then told him all that Vinch had said to me. He then called Vinch, who in turn told him of all he knew. "OK," said Mr Mac, "go to your post and say nothing whatever to anyone." And he emphasized, "Do you both understand that?" "Yes, sir," we replied in agreement.

At ten o'clock in came a well-known wholesale buyer. Vinch, who was then going to display some accessories, apparently dropped by accident a quart of tyre solution. I hurried across to pick it up. "Mr Wright," said he to me, "dat is he," as he whispered in a low voice. Now Sookie never made me make a bill for him since I was given all the authority to do so. He will go to Mr de Sousa or to the cashier, if Mr de Sousa was out of his desk. Honestly, I cared not about that. Sookie then went with the gent to Mr de Sousa. Vinch then said to me, "Watch close the action." While Mr de Sousa made the bill, Sookie quickly took four tyres into the customer's vehicle. As Mr de Sousa completed the bill in readiness for payment, the customer counted the cash on Mr de

Sousa's desk, walked to the cashier, paid the bill, and rolled out four tyres into his Jeep and was off. I then went and told all that I knew to Mr Mac. "Good," said he, "say nothing to anyone. Any time he should come again, just let me know. Do not wait for any transaction to take place. And be unobserved. Just keep far away." "Very well, sir," said I.

At two o'clock that very day, the dealer was back again. But before he entered, Vinch said to me he saw Sookie moving two recaps to the back of the service station, which he took from off the rack. Immediately I went upstairs to Mr Mac, and I gave him the number of the Jeep. "OK," said he, "go down and clean a shelf or do something. Just don't be moving around closely. Also send Vinch upstairs; he is wanted in the tea room." The very exercise was then repeated with the exception that this time he rolled the tyres out with the bill held between his lips. Our friend Sookie was nowhere to be seen.

Now there was a very talented police officer who hailed from British Guiana. His parents were English Canadians in that country, and there he had crime controlled. And he was now doing a very fine job in Trinidad. Mr Mac alerted him of the happenings. He set his men up, and the culprits were brought to justice. I shall therefore not go into details of the crime. But I shall say it was the end of such offence which took place in that showroom department.

Mr Mac said to me, "Wright, I am so glad that the thieves were caught because I have been given hell for promoting you downstairs as a clerk." "I thank you, sir, but had it not been for Vinch and his keen observation, that onslaught would have taken a very long time to be discovered." In the department there was sadness and gladness with the salesmen and cashier, while Mr de Sousa lamented Sookie's rascality.

Let me in a nutshell describe Mr Mac. He spoke fast, and somewhat from his nose. One could hardly understand what he says sometime. On many occasions I would read his lips or catch a word or two of what is being said. On one occasion he said to me, "That hand tool is for Mr de Pass." I then thought he told me, "Tell Abdul go to Mr de Pass." The poor chap did go, but Mr de Pass did not know what it was all about, so he

CHAPTER THIRTY-FIVE

457

passed. But let me say it was the end of the existence of such crime in our department.

Mr Mac said to me Wright I am so glad that the thieves were caught. Because I am given ___ for promoting you down stairs as a Clerk. Thank you sir. But had it not been for Vinch and his keen observation. That onslaught would have taken a very long time to be discovered.

In the department there was sadness and joy with the Sales Men and Cashier. While Mr de Sou_ lamented at Sookie's rascality.

Let me now in a nut shell describe the "Man" Mr Mac. He was truly a Christian and delight_ in helping the underprivilege and those who really needed help regardless of rank or social class. He in no wise helps slackers. If ~~your~~ you are doubtful of your ability he would bring the good qualities out of you. A lover of Children. A man of keen buisness insight. He spoke very fast and somewhat _understands_ from his nose. One could hardly what he says at sometime. A lover of sports especially Golfing and delights in making ___ jokes.

In the early while at the Higmans I read his lip_ And now being employed by him I would at least catch in his sentences a few words and arrive at its meaning. Which of course I was never always right. Here is an ex_ ample. On one occasion he said to me "That hand too is for Mr de Pass". — I instead thought he said to me. "Te_ Abdool go to Mr de Pass". — The poor chap did go. 63_ Mr de Pass knew not what it was all about. He phoned Mr Mac only to be told that it was all a mistake. There was something most gentlemanly about him. He never will rebuke you or made you feel ashamed in the presence of others. On one occasion I was sum_ moned to his desk for making a silly mistake or

Facsimile page from George Wright's first draft. Note the changes he made in the final version

phoned Mr Mac, only to be told it was a mistake. There was something most gentlemanly about him. He never pulled you down or made you feel ashamed in the presence of others. One day I was summoned to his desk. "Wright," he said to me, "do you know that you are a damn fool?" "Yes, sir," I replied. With a wince he looked at me. "Oh boy," said he, "I do not know between Cumberbatch and yourself who is more damn foolish." (Cumberbatch was Pop, the Barbadian agent I met on the first day.) "I do not know, sir," I replied. He then scratched the top of his head which was slightly bald. "You may go," said he. To this day I am yet to know what that scolding was about. He was a good Christian, and he never failed to give alms or help the unfortunate. He would give a listening ear to the highly qualified financial accountant as well as to the lowly janitor in his employment. A real businessman was he, with acute foresight. And a great lover of sport, especially that of golfing.

Time passed swiftly by. Our children were growing, and as each year passed us, life was becoming rougher financially. So I then started the rearing of pigs in our backyard. At first I started with two animals while they were piglets. At that stage they were all fun. But as they grew into hogs, they then needed more attention and were somewhat ignored by my family. I then became very stern with my two eldest sons in giving their help. Patient feeding was not then widely known to the layman farmer. I gathered husk from the marketplaces, along with cast-out junk fish, which resulted in an excellent job of feeding. Added to this, I gave them much grass as roughage, which also helped in controlling the smell. In a very short time I had twelve lovely hogs in my backyard.

Now in no way am I challenging the experts, but I will like to say that should pigs be kept clean, they would stay clean. I once reared as many as twenty-five hogs in my backyard. And should you as a stranger call at my home during daylight, you would not detect them unless you are being told.

(Dear Reader, as I am on livestock, may I mention that I have tried my hands on the rearing of various livestock to offset my financial needs, i.e., pigs, sheep, goats, chickens, turkeys, ducks. To date I have yet six sheep that I keep for the fun of it, plus ten dogs for the protection of

CHAPTER THIRTY-FIVE

our home. May I also thank Dr Bennett and Dr Kanhai, two veterinary surgeons who freely advised me with their knowledge.)

One morning as customary at 4:00 a.m., I set out to gather the jelly of coconuts that were cast off by the coconut vendors in their shells on the wayside. Although an unhealthy practice, it was most profitable to me. For me, that morning, everything seemed to move right. I very soon found a heap with small kernels. And so I quickly got a bucket filled with two nuts that had slipped the vendor's attention. As I rode a little way towards another heap, I stumbled upon a briefcase that lay upon the shoulder of the road. I immediately dismounted. Now although it was yet dark, I looked quickly to see if there was anyone around. Hastily, I picked it up and stuffed it into the bucket that had the two jelly nuts. I left one nut on the roadside and placed the other in a way to help conceal the briefcase, and covered it with some of the kernels from the filled bucket. I then made my way home. As I rode for home, I gave an occasional look to see if I had been followed.

When I got home, excitedly I called Marm. She knew very well whenever I found a jelly nut that was unnoticed by the vendors, I would bring and cut it up for her to drink its delicious beverage. She was at the time preparing breakfast. "Is there anyone here?" I asked her softly. "How do you mean?" she replied. I then realized I was wrong in my approach. So, taking the bucket with the briefcase, I went into the kitchen, followed by her. I took out the whole nut and pulled out the briefcase from the covered jelly and proudly said to her, "Look what I have found." With that saying I quickly emptied its contents on the kitchen counter. In it there were many scraps of paper, bills with other documents that held no importance to me. From a pocket, some coins came falling out. But, lo and behold, from a compartment were some packed notes. Excitedly I checked. Its amount was $375. Boy oh boy, was I happy. I looked at her to see how happy she was, but she stood dormant and said not a word. "What's wrong?" "I am wondering to who does this belong," was her reply. "To some rich person," said I. "Well, what are your intentions?" "How do you mean? I am keeping the money." "And what of these documents and loose papers?" "They will be laid to rest in the cesspit; no one will know they are there."

A BRANCH TO REST ON

She then lowered the stove, and turning around, she fixed me in the face and said: "You do not sound, George, as the husband I know you to be." "Well, what do you want me to do?" "Find the owner! Let's look through the papers. We may find some sort of clue to its owner, or you can take it to the police or *Guardian**." "Do you really mean that?" "Yes, I do," she replied. Reader, I felt as though I was thrown into a bathtub of cold water with shame before her. "Alright, alright, but first let me hurry and wash the animals because I am late."

I then got myself ready and was off to work with the briefcase and all of its contents nicely wrapped in newspaper. On my way down I began to reshuffle my thoughts. Must it be the police or the *Guardian*? Which was the better of the two to hand over my findings? And to stop now for either of them will make me late. So I went right to work and clocked in as I held tightly to my prize. As I entered the door, there was Mr Mac speaking to the cashier. I said good morning to them and made for the tractor-tube shelf, where I rested my parcel. When they were finished speaking, I said to Mr Mac, "Sir, I will like to talk to you." "Come upstairs in fifteen," said he, looking at his time. Mr de Sousa was not then at his desk, so I asked the cashier to allow me to rest my parcel in her cage. In about twelve minutes Mr Mac sent Vinch to call me. I took my parcel from the cashier's cage and went to him. "Well, what is now on your mind?" he asked. I then told him everything with the exception of my wanting to keep the money for myself. "OK," said he, "leave it with me and go back to your work."

At 10:00 a.m. he summoned me upstairs. "Well, Wright," said he, "you would be sure surprised to know whose briefcase you found." As he spoke, his eyes were fixed on me. With head bowed, I said, "I do not know, sir." "Make one guess," said he with a smile. "Someone from the bauxite company," said I. "No, Wright, it belongs to the boss of my brother-in-law, Mr Gwyn." Reader, earlier I felt as though thrown into a bathtub in front of Marm with shame. Now I felt as though standing in the midday sun and being fanned with a gentle breeze with pride.

Mr Gwyn was married to Miss Theresa, Mr Mac's sister and a very good friend of Mrs Higman. She was also a dress designer in company

CHAPTER THIRTY-FIVE

with the one who tried those dresses on me. (What a small world.) Mr Mac spoke by phone to Mr Gwyn, who then got on to the owner of the briefcase. This gent was apparently a high-ranking person at U.B.O.T. (United British Oilfields Trinidad). He had come to a meeting in Port of Spain. Thieves broke into his car, stealing groceries and other articles, but he had then his briefcase with him. He did not know what happened to cause it to be lost. "What I personally feel, Wright, he had a few drinks and found himself like a child throwing things through windows." I looked at him. "Yes," said he, "Mr Gwyn agrees with me on this." I smiled and said, "Do you want to know how it got there, sir?" "Yes, Wright, we are all concerned about that." "Sir, judging from what you have said, this is what may have taken place. After having had his drinks, on his way home he may have found himself wanting to urinate. The time being night time, he stopped the car and lazily pulled his backside on the seat. This action dragged the briefcase and so it fell on the shoulder of the road, where it remained unseen by anyone until I stumbled upon it."

Mr Gwyn, who by then had come over to collect the briefcase, said, "Burton, this young man is doing the wrong work. Why not ask Leaslie[1] to give him a break? He would make good in that field." "Yes, I've found that out, Ted, not only now. But I'd rather keep him for myself." And they both laughed. Mr Gwyn then gave me $75.00 with such encouraging words of thanks in a way that can come only from the lips of an Englishman. And so I left them both.

On my job it was not at all smooth sailing. I was nettled by some rough and indiscreet handling by some folks at the time who were in authority. I do believe it was due to Mr Mac's humane way in which he handled me. That may have created a feeling of jealousy. Even Mr de Sousa would say to me at times, "Wright, keep out of the way of such and such a person," without telling me why. And, of course, Marm would say to me, "Never lose your temper with anyone. Remember you are the child of a king who has an army that can defeat any pharaoh,

---

[1] Police Officer.

Alexander, Caesar, or even the modern-day Hitler's army put together in a moment. And don't you forget I use my knees daily."

It happened, however, that Mr Mac went on a three-month vacation, and one of those very gentlemen took his chair. I was then not given an easy chance from the very week he left. I was called upon many a time to do the menial part of the janitor's duties. I sometimes swept around the island and driveway of the gas station, helped in the painting of the boiler room and toilets, and also the offloading of tyres from trucks, even though they had their loaders. At all times, I was kept busy along with my regular clerk duties and paint-room supplying for vehicles. And every two weeks Mr de Sousa wanted an inventory of all tyres and tubes in the showroom. He was very unhappy with what was going on. But I said, "Sir, don't you worry, I can handle it all." Vinch was a very clever lad; he looked after all the paint stocks and other accessories for me. I can freely say we worked hand in hand.

One morning, however, at 11:00 a.m. a workman was found rolling a tyre away from the recapping plant. For this, our new boss was summoned. He was so arrogant and blasphemous about the matter that it caused a few staff members, customers, and neighbours to gather on the scene. Vinch and I stood in the doorway. The activity was roughly about thirty feet away from us. I then said to Vinch, "Boy, we miss Mr Mac, eh? Had it been him and he had to call the police, he would without anyone knowing. Or if he was going to fire him, he would have done so, but not this scene." All Vinch replied to me was, "Yeah, boy."

Perman was the name of the new boss conducting the matter. He then left the crowd and came straight across to me. "You! You!" he yelled. "What the hell did you say? I heard you." "Nothing, Mr Perman, I was just talking to Vinch." And so I slowly backed inside the showroom. "I shall see that you get fired on this very day," he bellowed. As he went upstairs, Mr de Sousa called me and asked what was taking place. I told him what I said to Vinch, and I went on to say not even the cashier who was about four feet away from us could have heard. "Boy," said Mr de Sousa to me, "you too dam harden*. I warned you to keep away from those people. Most probably he read your lips." "No, sir, my back was turned to that direction." He then called Vinch and asked him what

CHAPTER THIRTY-FIVE

did I say to him. Vinch gave him the very story. Just then a customer came for four tubes, so I was sent to get them from the storeroom. I was very glad for the opportunity, for I was curious to know what Mr Perman was doing about me.

As I got into the storeroom, hardly had I a chance to take down the carton of tubes when he bolted in at me with a spasm of abusive language. I dropped the carton of tubes and quickly scampered. I pulled a tyre lever from a nearby carton. He was a big and heavyset man. I shoved him off with a force that he stumbled and fell. As I have mentioned earlier, I was taught never to strike my fallen foe. I said to him, "Get up." As he stood up, I held him by the collar, with the tyre lever raised in the other. I saw that he was very scared; he showed no fight in him. I told him (and I did use some very hard and rotten language to him) that should I lose my job, I shall maim him for life. I then pushed him off and unlocked the door; he quickly made his way out.

When I got downstairs, Mr de Sousa asked, "What kept you so long?" "I was speaking to Mr Perman, sir," said I. "Boy, for your own good I am again telling you to keep far away from that fellow." Then the lunch break came, the day passed, and so I heard no more from Mr Perman. The chap concerned with the tyre incident was sent home; it was said that he could not be prosecuted by law, for he was yet on the premises.

When I got home after dinner that evening, Marm said, "You just don't seem to be yourself, George. Is something wrong?" "Why have you said that?" I asked. "You played not with the children as you always do. Even Lincoln said that you do not seem pleased about something." "We shall speak about it after I have fed the animals." "Oh no, now," said she. I then related truthfully the matter to her. "George," said she, "I thought you promised me to get rid of that temper. Remember, we have four children. Who would take care of them should something sad happen to you? Or should you be locked behind bars, would we not be left to the mercies of the ungodly? Would it not be better that we suck salt and drink water and be happy together? Just remember the devil is very busy, George." Unobserved by the children I pressed her hand tightly and wept.

Chapter 36

George is fired for the last time; Mr Mac starts a string of new businesses, George is entrusted with the keys, and becomes a licensed customs clerk and a general man of business.

I continued working for six weeks unmolested by Mr Perman. I was always on time on the job and never consciously stole a minute. And I was extremely polite to everyone with whom I made contact. One day Mr de Sousa said to me, "Wright, you don't have to be so polite; had you been in the army, guys will take advantage of you." "Maybe they would try, sir, but I can take care in many respects if the time do arrive, sir." Now I have never told Mr de Sousa or even Vinch what had taken place in the storeroom that day. And it would appear Mr Perman may have spoken about it only with the top brass, for I observed I was no longer shabbily treated by him or any other.

One evening Marm said to me, "George, be on the watch, it can happen any time now." "What do you mean?" I asked. "Your dismissal," said she. "I just don't want you to be taken unawares." I look inquiringly at her. "Yes," she said, "it will happen. They are just playing for time. So be a Boy Scout: be prepared and don't be taken unawares." She also said from now on only $5.00 must be spent per week in this house, and that must cover everything. Ten dollars must be soundly put aside. "With the few eggs and vegetables gathered around the yard, we shall make it. Do you agree?" "Yes," said I.

One day Mr de Sousa said to me, "Mr Mac will be here in less than

CHAPTER THIRTY-SIX

two weeks." That very evening a gentleman who worked as a grievance officer (although up to then there was not a union representing the workers of that company) called me aside and said to me, "Do not say to anyone what am I now telling you, for I shall then be looking for a job myself. But I have overheard that they will be sending you off next week." "Thank you very much, sir," said I, "but I do know that already." "Who told you?" he asked. "My wife," said I. He then looked quite amazed and said not another word.

Then came the Friday evening. I was then called by the financial secretary, who spoke to me very kindly. He said that they were overstaffed downstairs, and I will have to be laid off for the moment. He then handed me two envelopes as he spoke very softly, "You are a good worker and I wish you success." In turn, very calmly, I said to him, "Sir, the stick that stays the door from slamming will be used for striking the black dog as well as the white." He looked inquiringly at me. I smiled and said, "Good day, sir." As I walked away, I came face to face with a smiling Mr Perman. When I came downstairs, I headed for the paint room, took my raincoat and cap, and so I left without telling Mr de Sousa, an act which haunted me for months.

When I got home that evening, in the presence of the children I said to Marm, "Well, it has finally happened. I was fired today." My second son, Michael, asked, "What do you mean, Dad?" I looked at him, and as I tried to explain, I became choked for words. "Hold it," said Marm, "I shall tell them about it a little later. Leave Daddy and I alone for a while," and they scampered off. "Well," said she, "it has finally happened. Remember I told you so. However, let us thank the good Lord that it have happen that way." I told her not of what I said to the secretary, fearing that it might have made her upset. I handed her the two envelopes. She first opened my pay packet of $15.00 as she gave a wry smile and looked at me. The other envelope was stouter. She then opened it carefully, as only Marm can do. In it there were a number of notes. "What is this all about?" said she. "I do not know," I replied. "He had said something when he handed it to me, but all I can remember him saying was 'I wish you success.'" She then counted the bills, $1.00 and $5.00 bills which all added to $75.00. "They have paid you five weeks extra, OK," said she, tucking both envelopes into her bosom. "Whenever you are ready, let's have our dinner."

After dinner she said, "George, we have put away $587.00. With what you have brought, make it $677.00. Added to this I am sure there is no less than $25.00 here and there." I told her, "Ever since I destroyed my piggy bank, it has never been replaced, but I have no less than $200.00 in the Penny Bank." I then told her as from Monday next week, no money must be kept in the house except a few cents for emergency. To this she readily agreed. "Our ship can safely sail now until we get to another port," she said. "By the way," she asked, "have you heard anything of Mr Mac?" "Yes, I was told that he was expected back; he should be here next week." "Well," said she, "don't you make any move until he gets here. You shall then go to his home and truthfully tell him the whole story." (I said to myself, will he ever believe me?) "OK, Marm, I will, but right now I do feel like packing and going back to Toco." "George! George!" she said. "Are you going out of your senses? What can we do then with four children. Please blot that thought out of your mind immediately and do some constructive thinking." "OK, OK," I said.

The days passed very quickly, and may I say, dear Reader, with twelve hogs, eight pigs, thirty-six chickens fully grown, twenty-four ducks, and two goats, it cost me a mere twenty-four cents a day for their upkeep. I cannot now go into details for that's the story of George Washington Carver.[1] One good thing, my eggs were bringing me seventy-two cents a dozen. I would sell a suckling pig for $3.00 while the market price was $5.00. When I could have sold two market pigs to a butcher and be happy with $40.00, another farmer will be selling for $60.00. I had no problem when livestock was to be marketed. For me it was a quick sale to make space, which was a disadvantage.

It happened thus one evening my daughter came running to me in the backyard. Breathless, she stammered, "Daddy, Daddy, there is a

---

[1] George Washington Carver (d. 1943) was a prominent agricultural scientist of the early twentieth century. In 1941, *Time* magazine named Carver a "Black Leonardo."

CHAPTER THIRTY-SIX

mister outside asking for you." "Hold it," I told her. "Remember Marm and I have told you, don't get yourself all emotional whenever you see strangers. Does Marm know?" "No, Dad." "Then will you call her for me, please." Marm did come, and I asked her to see who was at the gate as I could not then leave. Very quickly she returned. "It is Mr Mac. I told him that you were washing down, and you would be with him in a moment." Immediately I dropped the broom, washed my hands, and was going off to see him. I had spoken to Vinneth two minutes before of being too emotional, and here was I doing the very thing. Marm said, "Good Lord, you are not going out to him in that condition." "What else can I do?" Lincoln who was helping said, "Daddy, why not let him come in? He probably might even give us a sale." Marm looked inquiringly at me. "Yes," said I. "Bring him in. I shall pen up the dogs."

Mr Mac joined us at the back very quickly. "Oh my, Wright," said he, "what a set-up you have here." "Good evening, sir," said I. "Good evening," he replied. "I am so sorry I could not meet you at the front door and that you had to come to the back to me." "Nonsense," he replied, "I am happy that it has happened this way, for never would I have thought an activity of this sort could ever be taking place in a backyard in Trinidad adjacent to the city outskirts." Marm stood a little way off, while Vin held tightly to her skirt with one hand as she sucked the thumb of the other.

Michael at that moment was at the home of his class teacher taking lessons, while Nunice was asleep inside. Lincoln was then washing the sty that I had left off. Mr Mac then said, "Can I look around?" "No, sir. I will show you around," said I. I then called Lincoln and said, "This is Mr McEnearney." Very boldly he said, "Good day, I am Lincoln Wright." "I am Burton," Mr Mac replied. "Please excuse me," said Lincoln, "I am helping my dad." "Go right on," said Mr Mac with a smile. I felt very pleased with Lincoln's approach. "You have quite a young man there," said Mr Mac to me.

I quickly showed him the other animals and birds, while I pondered deeply in my mind what was his mission. I also showed him my vegetable garden. Marm seemingly for her own reason kept not abreast with us but trailed behind with Vinneth. "Mrs Wright," he turned around and said to Marm, "had your husband more land, he would create wonders." She smiled, shaking her head approvingly. As we came to the back steps, he sat with no sign of prejudice. Marm gave a quick glance and moved quickly in fetching a chair. "Oh, thank you very much, Mrs Wright," said he, "but I am very comfortable this way."

"Well, young man, what are your plans?" he asked me, without an introduction to his subject. Marm then turned to leave, as I held her back. I began to tell him what took place that led to my dismissal. "Hold it, hold it," he said, "I do not want to hear any more of that nonsense. Mr de Sousa has already explained everything to me. All I want to know is what you intend to do from here on." Before I could reply, Marm said, "Mr Mac, he was waiting on your return." "Well," said he, "I myself shall be leaving the firm in one month's time. I am launching into a business on my own, and I would very much like to have you, should you not have any plans." "I would be very happy to be with you, sir," I replied. I saw Marm smiling. It was that smile of thankfulness she wore when she was happy. "Well, if you will, as from next Monday you are employed, which will be at the beginning of the workweek and, incidentally, that of the month that I shall yet be with them." I was somewhat puzzled at his statement. So I asked, "Am I to go back to Firestone, sir?" "No," he laughed, "you are staying right here during that month. Your pay shall be $20.00 per week, which will be your salary when you begin to work outright with me. Meanwhile, you shall now be paid while still at home, and this will be treated as a one-month vacation with pay. Tell no one about it; let it be confidential. I have not yet located my office site. What you can do is check with me at my home on a Saturday morning early or in the evening, whichever suits you best." He then left.

I then returned to the sty where I left off. Lincoln had already cleaned it along with the others and was more than halfway through the feeding. I said to him, "Link, you gave me very good advice when you suggested to let Mr Mac come in." "Oh, yes," said Marm. I did not know that she had crept up behind me. "And do you know something?" said she. "There are quite often eggs upon the rack; we could have offered some to him."

CHAPTER THIRTY-SIX

"He might not have taken it," said I. "He seemed quite down to earth, and to make us happy, he may have accepted them," said Marm. "Or maybe he might have given us a dollar for them," said Lincoln. "Oh, oh, Lincoln," said Marm.

The days passed quickly into weeks. I did check at Mr Mac's home at the end of the second week. The office, I was then told, will be on Chacon Street North. It was an upstairs building, and we shall be occupying the top floor. I felt a sense of independence when he used the term "we". The next day, from his given directions, I journeyed into town just to make sure I found the correct place, and I did.

Then came the day that we moved into the office. The staff comprised just three persons: Mr McEnearney, Mrs McEnearney and myself. I knew not the name or function of the business on the first week of my active employment. I made sure each morning I was there at 7:45 a.m. at the foot of the stairs awaiting their arrival. And they both arrived precisely at 8:00 a.m. each day. Mrs Mac would then be at the typewriter. Mr Mac would head to his desk to write or make phone calls, while I cleaned or was sent out on errands. Although very keen to know what the business was about, I asked no questions but was on the go like a human robot. Sometimes Marm would ask, "Have you yet found out the name of your firm?" "Not yet," I would reply, and she would laugh.

The office was closed each day at 2:00 p.m., and by 2:15 p.m. for the very latest I would be at home. I became concerned because we were not buying nor were we selling anything. One evening Marm said, "Worry not yourself about that. All we must do is pray that whatever the venture, it turns out to be prosperous."

Then came the second week. That Monday morning, the clouds were dark, and it appeared as though it was going to rain. I hustled through my chores at home and was off. I got to the office at 7:00 a.m. instead of 7:45 a.m. Then came a heavy downpour of rain. As I sat at the foot of the stairs, there came Mr Mac (it was then 7:10 a.m.) with his dripping closed umbrella and a parcel in his hand. "Good morning, Wright," he said to me. "I am so very glad that you are here at this time. I am going to San Fernando, and this will help me with an early start." He handed me the key to open the door. We were then greeted with a foul air. A rat had died over the weekend in the office, and its carcass roused an offensive odour. I quickly cleaned it up and proceeded with my general cleaning. He then handed me the key again. "Hold this," he said, "Mrs Mac will not be here before 10:00 a.m. She has a key of her own, but in case she forgot it at home, mine can be used. When she comes, go over to the locksmith and have one cut for yourself." He handed me a dollar, and at 7:30 a.m. he was off. When it was 10:00 a.m. I was complete with the office cleaning. So I hurried to the locksmith and had my duplicate key made. The cost was forty-eight cents. I was back to our office at 8:50 a.m. and full of excitement to see how will my key work. It worked perfectly. I placed the bill and change upon his desk. I had then nothing to do, so I went across the street at a small bookshop, and will you believe I came upon that very book again: *How to Win Friends and Influence People*. My first owned book was spirited away, so without hesitation I seized the one upon the shelf. It was then like the meeting of two old friends. Its price was now $1.00. On meeting the cashier, the proprietor came and said to her, "Give him for ninety-six cents." That money was my allowance for the week, but I did not spend last week's, so I yet had $1.04. I then hurried back to the office and sat at a little table provided for me, as I scanned through the book as a refresher course.

Precisely at 10:00 a.m. Mrs Mac came in. "Good morning, Wright." "Good morning, Mam," I returned. "My goodness, I thought there was a flood in town; there is so much rain in Maracas." "There was, Mam, but it ceased about two hours ago." "Did Mr Mac tell you anything to tell me?" "No, Mam." "OK, never mind, there is a note here." She then sat at her typewriter. In less than ten minutes she called me. "Wright," she said, "do you know where the Registrar's office is?" "No, Mam." "It is in the Red House," she said. "Take this letter there to Mr What's-his-name; if he is not there, you can leave it with his secretary. Should he be there, wait and he shall give you a reply." When I got there, the gent was there. I handed him the letter, which he read. "Please sit over there on that bench. I shall call you," he said.

CHAPTER THIRTY-SIX

The wait was a very long one. There were also other people sharing the bench. How I regret not walking with my book, I thought to myself, this shall never happen again. At 11:50 a.m. I was called and handed a large brown envelope marked on the back in bold large print, "On Her Majesty's Service", with an address to our Chacon Street office. I hurried to the office. Mr Mac was also there. "Oh, Wright!" He sprang from his chair, excitedly taking the envelope from my hand. As he was about to tear it open, "Oh, no, Burton," said Mrs Mac, "here's an opener." "Oh thank you, Babs," said he. And then he shouted, "Babs! We have got it! We have got it!" And he handed the large paper to her, which she read with a smiling face.

The next day as we three sat, Mr Mac asked me, "Do you know the name of the company for which you now work?" "No, sir," and they both laughed. "Well, Wright," he said, "you now work with the firm of Bayshore Enterprises Ltd." I wondered why Bayshore, and what commercial business can he be doing. (He most probably read my concern.) "Yes, Wright, we shall be starting the very first drive-in cinema in Trinidad, in fact, for that matter, in the West Indies." I again became more concerned. So he explained to me in a nutshell all its functions, not forgetting to say once more that it will be the first of its kind in the West Indies. He then dipped into one of his desk drawers and gave me a magazine and a brochure. "Take these home with you, Wright, and show them to your family. Stocks are limited so you may bring them back whenever you are through looking at them."

Both Marm and I have never been interested in the movies, so it really did not create an impact, and even had we been, we had not a vehicle of our own. But I was happy to know that I now worked with a firm that will launch so great a venture. The very next morning I returned the magazine and brochure. "Oh, Wright, I forgot to tell you the name of our drive-in will be the 'Starlite Drive-In Cinema' and will be situated on a parcel of land in the Diego Martin area. Do you remember Mr MacMillan?" "Yes, sir, I do." "Well," said Mr Mac, "he will be my business partner. Come sit down, Wright," said he. "You see Mr MacMillan is a Canadian, and he is involved in various businesses

L - r: John Sellier, Douglas Krogh, Burton McEnearney, Eric de Verteuil, Everard Scott, Ralph Gibson, John Mair

Burton McEnearney signing a business deal

about which you shall know more later." He also told me that I shall soon be very busy because he intends starting an agency by the name of Bank Hall Shipping Service, and this would involve the clearance of domestic items shipped to individuals in the USA. "That shall be a stepping stone to introduce you to the customs and port." I looked inquiringly. "Don't you worry yourself. I shall be getting someone who knows the field to come over and guide you on evenings with the handling of invoices and other documents in the shipping and clearance of cargo. As I have said, he will not be a full-time but a part-time worker, because he already has a job." The plan did work well. I cleared my first shipment. We were now in the month of December, so I had quite an experience with the customs, port, and my new job.

At this junction may I now say that this job was the real beginning of my life's career, and may I also add that I worked in that field for over thirty-five years as a customs clerk, which was then a glorified messenger to that of a professional broker. I am the holder of License 0026. I state this not as a boast, God forbid, but for an inspiration to

CHAPTER THIRTY-SIX

encourage many a young man who may perhaps find himself employed in a job he may not quite like. But should you have a family, please try and stick it out for their sake. As I have said before, let the word "menial" be used with dignity. Do not go stepping stones without an assurance, lest you leap upon the wrong stone and slip, where you may then find yourself blindly falling into the murk of life.

The Bank Hall Agency proved to be an unwelcome agent, and it fell through in this way: Their customers packed very large cylinder-shaped cartons (known as barrels) with domestic items and took same to Bank Hall warehouse. In it some of them packed unwarranted cargo, which could have caused trouble for us because it was undeclared to customs. So Mr Mac wisely gave up on that agency. May I say, however, I gained quite a lot of knowledge in that field, especially that of classification.

Very soon, he gave up the Chacon Street office and moved into his own office warehouse on Tamarind Square. We were now no longer an office of three but a firm of nine. Mrs McEnearney no longer came to work. There was now a full-time secretary from 8:00 a.m. to 4:00 p.m. Without delay, Mr Mac began the importation of tyre equipment for sale, and he made a rapid stride in the recapping industry island-wide. He also set up a plant for himself.

Let me deviate a bit for this most important subject. A company of business personnel, of whom Mr Mac was one, began the first-ever Caribbean football pool. It was the first of its kind in the country. The office was situated on Broadway above Trestrail's Hardware. It was managed by an English gent. The most amazing thing about this man: he could have added four digits at a time vertically; a human computer was he in memorizing. He took kindly to me and would pick me up at my home at 4:00 every Saturday morning, and we then travelled into the deep South and oil-belt area, placing our betting boxes at strategic business places, and would then collect them on the following Saturday. Needless to say, the takings for so new a venture were quite favourable when checked in the office. And may I also say it was through this exercise I got to know many of the towns and chief villages in Trinidad. In those days, you were not hijacked by rampaging thieves as happens today. But, alas, a sudden end came to this golden enterprise. Certain characters were getting the results of games played in England before us through telegraph transmission. And so they were wiped out of business with only the passing tribute of a sigh.[2]

Mr Mac was now fully in the tyre machinery and recapping business. He was also responsible for the introduction of General Tire in the Caribbean, a fine brand of tyres about which he hardly ever got a major complaint. To be precise, most of the complaints were due really through the fault of customers in driving into ditches or curb walls, or at times driving for distances on flat tyres or perhaps riding on rubble patches.

May I now again be allowed to use the term "we" in some cases, instead of "Mr Mac" or "he". Very soon, the staff grew to twenty souls. Mr MacMillan was a travelling partner and a businessman-at-large. Mr Mac certainly had need for someone to support him, and this help was found in a vibrant intelligent young man by name of Everard Scott. He took office as a director and company salesman. He truly deserved the title given him, for he would have sold a box of matches in hell to Satan or a plain snowball in Greenland. He was also blessed with a working spirit, for in the day we both worked to our calling, and in the evenings, we were down at the Starlite cinema that was now open and doing fine. He worked as a supervisor, and I selling tickets and in the cafeteria. It is interesting to know that the name of the first picture that was shown on the screen was called *My Sister Eileen*. It proved a sell-out that night at $2.00 a carload. Gates taken was $420.00. It could have been very much more, but over one hundred complimentary tickets were given out.

The cafeteria held great interest for me. On leaving the office on evenings, there was no time to get home, so the operator, who also

---

2   See 'Elegy Written in a Country Churchyard', Thomas Gray, Verse 20:
    Yet ev'n these bones from insult to protect,
      Some frail memorial still erected nigh,
    With uncouth rhymes and shapeless sculpture deck'd,
      Implores the passing tribute of a sigh.

CHAPTER THIRTY-SIX

worked at recapping, and myself would travel down to the cinema together. A fine hard-working young man was he, called Roy, who worked for the company, and through our lives he became one of my most trusted friends. Our appetites were similar. And so Mr Scott would tell us to eat and drink all we can; just do not waste. I would then make the largest of hamburgers or double hot dogs. There were two fountains flowing – one filled with root beer, the other with soft drinks – and so we had our fill. Added to this I was paid an extra $40.00 each month for my cinema work.

They then hired a young woman by the name of Hazel Mosca. All that can now be said is that pens would run dry to describe her ability and contribution to the firm. And I was now fully in charge of all customs handling. Shipping bills and invoices were just handed over to me, and they were all attended to suit the arrival of their ships. Now all entries and other documents were handscript by me, which involved much time. And I being the only person in my department, I was constantly on the go. Very soon, Mrs Mosca recognized this and volunteered to do all my typing, which was a very great help. The following may seem quite unethical to many. But let me state this: Mr Mac or Scott would give me a signed blank cheque of their own, with the authority to go into any government or private enterprise to pay their bills if they were not quite sure of the amount to be paid.

Mr Scott for quite a while had been trying to get the contract of a certain company to do their recapping. But, try as he may, he could not make a breakthrough because there was another firm doing recaps. Now, Mr Scott was a very persistent person who never accepted "no" as his answer. He continued going to their office. Alas, one day he was told that should he be able to recap fifty 900-20 carcasses for them in eight days, they would consider giving some of their work to him.

He did take up the challenge, although the time for their delivery sounded impossible. Why? Because we had our own regular customers to supply on a weekly basis. I observed his plight, and being now faced with the challenge of his dream, the job had to be done. So I said to Mr Scott, "There is no problem. It can all be done."

"Wright," said he, "a drowning man will cling to a straw. Let me hear your idea." "Well, you said the tyres must be done and delivered in eight days, then that should be eight working days." "Yes, go on, I am listening to you." "Well, let's say you gather them on Friday and promise that they will be delivered to them on the week after Tuesday, because you do not do your moulds and boiler on a weekend. You will then select the strong fellows that can run a night shift, and I will do the supervision. Let the day shift prepare the carcasses, and the night shift camelback and mould. We shall then work Saturday and Sunday, which will then be giving you two full days' extra time. Should this be done, you can more than cover their demand." He then looked at me, and with a big smile on his face, he said, "Boy, Wright, you are a damn crook. Thank you, that's just what I am going to work on," said he with a smile.

I also said to him, "While they are doing the run" (term for the labour work done in recapping shops) "I shall prepare my customs work for the next day." "OK," said he, "but let me first talk to Mr Mac about the matter." He really did speak to Mr Mac, and they both had a meeting with Alexander, the recapping shop foreman. This gent knew his work as the palm of his hand. (He once discovered a function by which to operate the tyre moulds more speedily.) "That would be no problem," he told them. "I was awaiting that breakthrough for quite a while now; just bring them."

The tyres were brought in, and all fifty were delivered in six days. And so we began to get a regular flow of work from that company. And this was then the beginning of a regular night shift from 4:00 p.m. to 10:00 p.m., or at times we may go to 11:00 p.m. The work was not a burden to me because many a time when I had no papers to be made up, I would enter the shop about 6:30 p.m., look around, then get back into the office and sit at my desk and sleep for no less than two hours. The work was done by a gang of three men only. And so I arranged that each man had a one-and-a-half-hour sleep, according to the situation.

Time sped on, and Bayshore Enterprises boomed in business. Everyone pulled his or her weight and at times willingly helped the

CHAPTER THIRTY-SIX

weaker to get through with his task. This I think was a blessing to the firm. This true unison flowed from Mr McEneaney down to Mr Goodman, the janitor. For instance, the same enthusiasm Goodman showed in washing and polishing the directors' cars, the same he showed for foreman Mr Alexander's car.

With the exception of the cinema, for thirty-five years I held duplicate keys for every office, warehouse, and even for the P.O. box owned by Mr Mac. I remember one Christmas morning a customer phoned at my home, asking that I come to release him his car tyres that were recapped by us. With the busy season he failed to collect them. He had then visitors to take to the country that very evening, and what he had on was not dependable for the run. And so I went down to his rescue. A friendship was then born and lasted until I heard from him no more.

Mr Mac without delay decided to take up fully the agency for recapping machinery, for at that time tyre shops and recapping plants were springing up like mushrooms all over the country. Now, with the exception of one firm who had their equipment from the UK, all other recapping shops used US equipment. Mr Mac kept then as his staff Mrs Mosca and myself and opened his business under the name of Burmac Ltd. (Burmac really being short for Burton McEnearney.) He then imported whatever part or machine the customer wanted and had same delivered at his business door. Mrs Mosca handled all things clerical, and I customs and delivery. Our office then was lower Pembroke Street. It had a setting similar to our first Chacon Street office.

I could have then gone to any cabinet to check on any file for my own information without having to wait or ask anyone. Both Mr Mac and Mrs Mosca coached me into writing business letters to Customs and the then Control Board. There was a rise and fall of equipment sales, but we struggled along. Mrs Mosca and myself both received $200 per month. And Mr Mac did not draw a month's salary for two years. At Christmas, however, we all had a very good cash package. Mrs Mosca and I worked not only with the understanding of helping each other but also with that of building the firm. I do remember Mrs Mosca one day said to me, "Wright, whenever we get out of this, I will sleep for one month. I do not understand at times how you do make it. Your courage do give strength to my weakness." I said to her, "My courage is strengthened through your cooperation and ability in helping me with all typing and processing of documents. By that my workload is cut short and so I am able to make it." Then said she, "What of Mr Mac?" "Oh, let's just not worry about him." "What do you mean?" She looked at me in surprise. "Do you really want an answer?" I asked. "Yes, I do." "Well, let me put it this way. Lowly now lay down, uneasy lies the head that wears the crown. He who sows in sorrow, shall reap in joy." "OK, OK, William Shakespeare," she said, laughing. "Not all of it." I smiled.

One morning as Mr Mac went out, Mrs Mosca said to me, "Don't you notice something, Wright?" "What?" I asked. "Mr Mac seems to be very busy these days, even more than normal." I really made no notice of him, for I myself was constantly on the go in the Customs Control Board and Port Services, deliveries of postal packages to the post office, visits to banks, and general office-boy tasks. The janitor work was shared without prejudice between us both. So I really did not observe. "No," I said to her. "Maybe as you are indoors all the time, it seems that way to you." "Well, maybe," she said.

Then one midday Mr Mac summoned us both to his desk and told us that he would be vacating this building in about a month's time. "We shall be going into our own leased property on Tragarete Road East. There we shall be having our own warehouse and office and an additional staff of six," said he, shaking his head from side to side as he said so. He also said, "The area is a very large one, and Mr Scott shall be renting from us for a while." Oh how we welcomed that news! That day as he left, we both celebrated with an Oriental lunch at the office.

We did remove to Tragarete Road where our sign BURMAC LTD. was proudly displayed in front of our office. There was also that of Mr Scott on the far side (TROPICAL TYRES LTD.), and yet another for an optician's office. All three companies were on the same compound. Our new staff were no strangers to us. We again had Alexander, our old foreman; Roy Lazare, who worked as operator at the Starlite Drive-in; and two other chaps who all worked at Bayshore Enterprises Ltd.,

CHAPTER THIRTY-SIX

the liquidated firm. These four were in the shop and storeroom. In the office with us was Mrs Ingrid Harrison. One could not meet a nicer person to work with. She was also a neighbour of Mr Mac, who was now living at Bayshore. He had sold his house in Maracas Valley and came to reside next to his parents at Bayshore.

Business brightened very quickly, and he again ventured into the cinema field. From this the Highway Drive-in was born. Once again Roy and I worked there on evenings. However, it was short-lived in Mr Mac's possession, for when the takings were good, he sold it at its financial peak.

Mr Everard Scott, our friend and neighbour, one day said to me, "Boy, Wright, Tropical Tyres is doing good, but I do miss the company of you all. Don't be too surprised to see me again once more with you all." I was not at all too surprised to hear this. For he seemed to lack the leadership of Mr Mac. He eventually sold Tropical Tyres and was back with us, as we welcomed his return. Alexander was now made a salesman and maintenance operator to the various tyre shops. The reason for this was that Burmac now monopolized the sales and purchase of equipment of at least 85 per cent of the country's tyre shops.

Mr Mac also went into the field of commercial arts signs and advertisement. To be candid, he entered into this field purposely to give employment to my third son, Nunice, who had successfully done the course with International Correspondence Schools. It made a booming start, but due to bad management of those in charge, it was also sold. But before so doing, Mr Mac made sure that Nunice was placed with another firm who needed his skill.

We had been on Tragarete Road for a while when Mr Mac sold his lease rights and moved west into Mucurapo Road. (It was the very day the good president J.F. Kennedy was assassinated, Friday, 22 November, 1963.) Although a much smaller compound, it held all properties and assets that formed the company.

Mr Mac and Scott began to interest other businessmen of the Caribbean in the retreading of tyres with its low cost. And so they did monopolize the agency of Lodi for the Caribbean. They, with the

George Wright, the man of business

CHAPTER THIRTY-SIX

Oriental partner, set up a plant in the island of Barbados. Alexander was then sent there as its general foreman.

Speaking of myself and the customs department, I had no space in which to breathe. But many thanks again to Mrs Mosca, who at this time was very much acquainted with the classification of basic items, and that again pulled me through immensely. Of course, we were both described as work jumbies*.

By this time I had completely closed down my backyard farming commercially. Burton and Oswald were not as tough as Lincoln and Michael had been. Nunice was now working at the sports firm where Mr Mac had sent him, doing displays and arts in advertising, a position that he held until he joined his brother Michael in Canada. However, I then decided to keep two piglets as scavengers because there was always leftovers and other husks. I still maintain my backyard garden with chores being done on evenings and weekends. My chief means of transportation was then motorcycling, a feat I performed until the age of sixty-nine years, when I was abruptly stopped by Marm and Vin.

Very soon the growing business dwarfed our Mucurapo site, and we again moved. This time we went into the district of Maraval in the liquidated building of the once thriving Bergerac Hotel, which was famous then for its Crab Hole entertainment. There we had a very large office, and double warehouse. Its location was very much to Mr Mac's advantage, for he was now living at Rookery Nook, which was walking distance from the office. We were at Bergerac just about a year when Mr Mac's only son, Charles, who had been working with us, got into a vehicular accident which sent him home to be with his Lord. Yet with all this tragedy, through hard and dedicated work from Mr Scott, the business climbed its way up like Jack's beanstalk.

A fishing trawler by the name of *Amber Jack* was bought. It was fully geared with modern-day nets. All fishing was supposed to be done in the Gulf of Paria and the North Coast. At first the bringing-home catches were great, but it was short-lived, for very soon it was discovered that major catches were all sold out at sea. So it was relinquished.

Mr Mac then ventured into the cattle-farming business at Mausica. This he did without seeking expert advice. However, by the time he was given free advice by a notable vet, he abandoned the whole idea. The result: it was short-lived. He simply just could not be idle in business ventures. And so he got into the Circle (B) Ranch and the Ortinola Estates Ltd. They were syndicates. I shall not go into details through time, but, may I say, I was kept active on the Ortinola Estates by its kind shareholders into a good old age. This was not because of financial problems in my life; it all kept my health aglow.

His attention was again drawn to Tragarete Road, and this time further west. This shop was purposely opened on August 30, as August 31 was observed as Independence Day of Trinidad and Tobago. And Mr Mac had a bumper sale to attract customers; all tyres were sold, even the new General types of assorted sizes that were in stock. Then spoke the wizard Everard Scott, "There is but one regret." "What's that?" I asked in wonder. "We just had not enough."

We seemed blessed in this location, as business boomed. Alexander was brought back from Barbados to take over, so the full responsibility of the shop's operation was now fully laid on him. Our staff now increased to eighteen souls. One midday, Mr Scott said to me, "Boy, Wright, you don't ever seem to be tired." "Why do you say that?" I asked. "Well, with all this endless running around you are doing to Customs, the Control Board, banking, the post office, the Red House, the City Council..." As he paused, I said, "Since you are naming, don't you forget Port Services!" "Oh yes, you are right," said he. "Well, partner," said I, "have you heard that Satan finds mischief for idle hands? Well, I am one man who if not kept on the go will be very mischievous." We both laughed. He then said, "Come on, Wright, let's get serious." I then stopped joking to give him a listening ear. "Now, Wright, you do know as well as I do that trade is brightening with Burmac, and I have always said that you are one person that I shall go all out in helping, and I think that this is the most appropriate time to do so. I have already hinted to Mr Mac, and he told me to do what pleases me best." He then looked at me smiling as I listened attentively. "I am giving you your own office, and

CHAPTER THIRTY-SIX

you have the choice to have it built downstairs or upstairs. And that's not all. I want you to choose for yourself a staff of three. You shall stay in your office and supervise, let your assistants do the running around, or whatever suits you best. But, partner, let them work!" There was a silence. "What do you say?" "Let me first think about it," I told him. "When will I know?" he asked. "Well, today being Friday, how about Monday?" "That will do," said he.

I then discussed the matter that very evening with Mrs Mosca, who advised that my office should be built upstairs. As regards the other matters, she left them to my own discretion. After supper that night I told Marm the whole story. She agreed and said that it all sounded very good. "But is to get honest, hard-working people would be the problem." "Well," said I, "let's put the matter to the Lord."

I was at that time associated with a Christian prayer group, about fifty of us who gathered ourselves on the Queen's Park Savannah in a portion of its grounds known as the Hollows. There we met under the divine leadership of Shirley Chatee of the Open Bible Assembly every Saturday and Sunday evening to thank God for His blessing bestowed to us for the past week. (Such work is still carried on there and is known as the Garden Church.) I spoke of the matter with our group leader, who also agreed that the subject be placed before the Lord in prayer for an answer by Sunday evening.

There was a young man in our group who readily accepted the challenge that Sunday evening. He was always there with us at any meeting and giving his strong support. Yet there was another young man who showed up occasionally, but due to his mother's consistency and seeming devotion to our Lord Jesus Christ, I said I shall give him a try. I looked not for a third person because I thought it much easier to handle two than three.

The Monday morning I told Mr Scott, without him asking me, that I would rather have my office built upstairs and insisted that instead of three helpers, I would rather start with two. "OK, boy, Wright," he said. He also promised to have the carpenter working that very week on its building.

May I now also clarify a term used by Mr Scott when addressing any male whom he befriended and had confidence in. Even at his home you may hear him say, "Boy, Donald," or "Boy, Jimmy" in speaking to his two sons. In my case, whenever the term "Boy, Wright" is used, he means no personal insult. My office was now completed and furnished with a new desk, a swivel chair, a filing cabinet, a fan and other necessities. There was hardly a difference to his and Mr Mac's offices.

Both young men came, and it was made clear to them by Mr Mac that I was authorized to hire and also fire. Reader, I will not now go into detail but will make it clear that they proved more than worthy of their hire. I treated them as my sons, and they in turn regarded me as their father. It shall take too long to describe these two young men and their devotion to their duties. Today they are both happily married and living in the United States of America with families of their own.

CHAPTER 37

George digresses and ruminates on his growing family

During the business boom in Trinidad, Marm gave birth to twins, a boy and a girl. Due to profuse bleeding, the girl died the very day. She was named Lilly. The boy, who was premature, weighed only four pounds, and is our Burton today. We then had our last child, our baby son Oswald. A blue baby was he at birth and weighed twelve pounds. The nurse-midwife thought he was dead. Today he is alive and an intelligent young man holding a degree in agriculture. He also holds certificates for house wiring, welding, motor mechanics, straightening and painting, accounts, and he is at present doing a computer course. He is sometimes referred to as the family brain. "Studying is just a hobby," he would calmly say. He is an unassuming young man who would do all that he can for his mother and siblings.

Through it all, with a low profile, I held on to my backyard farming and kitchen garden. Should I now be asked how was it done, my answer would be by my two sons, Lincoln and Michael. We did quite well with our backyard farming and kitchen garden. What could not be planted on the ground due to space was planted in pots that were placed on the top of the sties.

Lincoln's report form was very encouraging in all his subjects, especially in that of maths, chemistry and English. I once was told at a parent-teacher meeting at Fatima College where he attended that I should do my best and let him pursue his career in the medical field.

A BRANCH TO REST ON

George, Petronilla, and their family of six

But that was not to be. It was a thought that haunted me throughout my life like a fever dream. After finishing college, he was to have entered university. I was told that his hands had far too many corns, which is apt to hinder his sensitivity of feelings and touching of the organs. Marm, poor thing, was grieved for quite a while. Yet she passed not the grudge upon me. He was blessed, however, to hold a very good job with our country's government. And may I repeat the words of Toussaint L'Ouverture of Haiti, "His roots are deep and still alive and they shall sprout again."

Michael, the most rugged yet the most tender-hearted of our six

CHAPTER THIRTY-SEVEN

children, took to the mechanical field. Even from the tender age of six, he would take any of his toys apart and reassemble them. He was in no way academically acclaimed as brother "Link". Having observed this quite early, I gave him an overseas course through the International Correspondence Schools of the USA. And may I say that the fees for this entire course were paid for by our old friends the Higmans. He did very good in the motor mechanic and diesel field. But, for reasons of his own, he flouted the idea and became a nurse while he lived in Canada.

Nunice, my third son, was the most tidy of the children. He was the Mister There-is-a-place-for-everything, therefore everything must be in its place. His raiment and toys lasted the longest. You were always satisfied to give him something. Like brother Mike, he was not academically acclaimed, but he showed skill in lettering and watercolour paintings. I grabbed at that opportunity and decided to give him an overseas course in the field of commercial arts with the International Correspondence Schools of America. He did excel in that field. Today he is a small businessman and his own boss.

I had already mentioned son Burton's relationship earlier with the family. But may I also suggest that he suffered severe illness which retarded his progress. However, he never gave up and kept on fighting with the will to win. Today he is government-employed and has also entered the electronic field as a hobby. He also has the National Examination Certificate (N.E.C.), a goal that many a scholar will be happy to achieve. He moves very unassuming with it. If questioned, he will say with a smile, "No rush. The time will come when it will be used."

I may now be eagerly asked the question: tell us about Vinneth or Auntie "Vin", or you may yet hear the familiar call of "Sister Vinneth" by her associates. I remember asking Marm one day to help me with some writing. "Why not ask Vin?" she said to me. Whenever any one of the grands or their friends wants something, they seek for no one but "Auntie Vin". You may be standing speaking with her, and you may hear "honk honk" by a passing vehicle and the call, "Sister Vinneth." Now let me present her in my rhyme.

Never a scholar, yet never a dunce,
Should a mistake be made twill only be once.
Her friends are many yet so few.
Now I bow my head and bid adieu.

She is also government-employed and an active church worker. At any meetings her views are respected. She is the captain of Trinidad & Tobago Girls' Brigade, and a good globetrotter. She spends all that she can get from her father. However, of the six children she is ever mindful of him. Here is a little illustration of that statement. I was once in Montreal at Michael's spending a month vacation. During that very month she visited Dublin. One evening there came an overseas call for Michael. It happened to be from her asking her brother Michael to treat me good. Just imagine making a request like that to Michael above all persons. Well, that's the character that spells Vinneth.

Chapter 38

George goes on holiday, and while gathering leaves in a Montreal park, meets the La Rivieres; he is robbed on the way to the bank

Now I may at this point say this: Mrs Mosca and I, from the time we began to work as far back as the days of Bayshore Enterprises, had never taken a holiday. It was not that we were ever denied it by management, but we always felt that our work standard might be thrown off, which will cause us much more worry on our return from a holiday. And for this cause she had not in twelve years, and I fifteen. We had no regret, for, as the firm's prosperous years grew, we were well paid. Eventually, however, we were persuaded that it is a must that we take same. And, as it is universally known, no one is indispensable for their services. We therefore bowed. Mrs Harrison was quite capable, and with the added staff, Mrs Mosca's format was followed, and her workload was conquered. She was then given a trip to the United Kingdom at the company's expense. On her return, the following year I was sent likewise to Canada and the United States of America.

When I went to Canada and the United States of America, I did so not only by myself, but I was also given free passage* and covered expenses for Marm. To this, however, Marm declined. She gave as her reason that we both should not leave the home at the same time with children behind, especially travelling in those man-made contraptions. "Iron afloat is risky enough, but in the air it sounds mad," said she.

So Vinneth was given the trip instead. Our first stay was in Montreal, where we lodged at son Michael and Esther, his wife, who resided there. One evening Sheila, a friend of theirs, came along and asked, "Have you all any plans for the evening?" Vin and I promptly answered, "No." "Then how about us going up to visit Mount Royal St Joseph's Oratory on Queen Mary Road?" "What? Where?" "St Joseph's Basilica," she said. Then Esther, who was standing near to us, said, "The shrine of Brother André."[1]

Then she recalled this holy man who performed wonderful miracles of healing. "Yes, I read of him when I was a youngster, how he healed rich and poor men and women carrying crutches, and he called himself St Joseph's 'little dog'." "Yes," said I as I pulled at Vin's hand. And so we then left. On the way up to the Mount, I gathered leaves of various plants. When we got to the shrine, Sheila said, pointing to me, "Go up that hill; in that little forest, you shall find all the leaves you want. Vinneth and I are touring the building. When you get back, if you do not see us, just go into the cafeteria there and wait for us. Should we finish first, we shall wait there for you."

Reader, it was up in the Mount that we first met the La Rivieres, who became lifelong friends of our family. And this is how it all started. As I gathered my leaves, a gentleman came along. He gave me an astonished but yet friendly look. We then greeted each other. "What are you doing?" he asked. "I am gathering leaves of plants," I replied. "Any particular species?" "No," I replied, "to the contrary, what I have gathered I do not even know their names." "Can I have a look at them?" I handed him the satchel. He began calling a few names to me as he assorted them. When he came to that of the maple, I was overjoyed. Seeing my excitement on this, he began telling me some stories about the plant and the native Indians and its usefulness to produce sugar. Now, not wanting to be left a dumb-dumb, I then recalled an old school song that was taught us by Mr Worrell, our teacher, so I held up the leaf and began singing.

---

1 See chapter 17, footnote 4.

CHAPTER THIRTY-EIGHT

> In days of yore from Britain's shore
> Wolfe the dauntless hero came
> And planted there Britannia's flag
> On Canada's fair domain.
> Come let us be with heart and pride
> Let's join with love together
> The lily thistle shamrock rose entwine
> The maple leaf forever.[2]

This did surprise him, and it drew the attention of other visitors on the hill, which brought me a sense of importance. As they all applauded me, he said he loved it. When we came down, we both went to the cafeteria, and there, to our surprise, were Sheila, Vinneth, and Marian, Mr La Riviere's wife, sitting at a table chatting and helping themselves to some snacks. An introduction was made among us and an exchange of addresses. They belonged to the USA; they were from Ludlow, Springfield, Massachusetts. I remember when we parted Vin saying, "There goes two beautiful people; we shall never see them again." But that was not to be. For one month after our arrival back home, I received a book from them titled *All Trees of America*. I wrote them in acknowledgement of their precious gift, and a pen-pal relationship was born. Two years later they decided to visit Trinidad and Tobago. As they stated in one of their letters, they had an urge to see the wondrous Pitch Lake, legend of Sir Walter Raleigh of England in 1595, and to pay a visit to the isle of Tobago, known as Robinson Crusoe's Isle. And our friends were going to make reservations at the Hilton Hotel in Port of Spain for two weeks in order to celebrate this country's Carnival.

To this Marm objected. Said she to me, "George, if these folks are as Vin and you have said, plus what I have read in some of their letters, they are really down-to-earth, respectable citizens. Why let them spend money that they can save for themselves? Why don't you fix up your room and invite them to stay with us for their vacation, providing they

---

[2] "The Maple Leaf Forever" is a Canadian patriotic song composed by Alexander Muir in 1867, the year of Canada's Confederation. George's version is slightly incorrect.

are not difficult in eating?" "OK, Marm, I shall write and make the suggestion to them in the very words that you have just spoken."

Thus I did, and our invitation to the La Rivieres was accepted. We had, however, one major problem which was overlooked. The government at this time was in real straits with the Water and Sewerage Authority (W.A.S.A.) of the country. They were laying new water lines and were experiencing some union problems. The advice of a relative of mine who then worked there was sought because we were having then a very poor flow, which lasted at times up to two hours for the whole day. He came and said to me that my problem can be easily solved because I was connected to the old main. He then said to me, "Do not be afraid to have the job done quickly," for he had ties with persons in charge of the department with no underhand connections. But the job will have to be done on a Saturday. I told him I did not mind. He then checked and gave me a list of the needed material and a stipulated Saturday morning by which to have them on the spot. Strange as it may seem, that delivery fell on the very Saturday that our friends were due to arrive, and they were coming with a night flight.

I could not then get the usage of the truck and its driver before that very Saturday morning. The Friday evening I informed the office that I would not be out to work that Saturday, and I would be using the truck with its driver very early the next day. I had arranged with the driver to meet me at the office at 8:00 a.m. so that we could pick up the material at Trestrail's Hardware, where I do get a discount for whatever I buy. The Saturday morning I was at the office at 7:45 a.m. Both Mrs Mosca and Mrs Harrison arrived within seconds of each other. "Oh, Wright, I am so glad you came. I remember you saying that you were taking the day off. What happen? Have you changed your mind?" "No, no, not at all, I am waiting for the truck." "Then can you please run over and make the deposit for me? Everything is made up." "Hold on a minute, the truck will soon be here to meet me. I will go with him before going to the hardware store." We waited for fully fifteen minutes, and the truck did not arrive. Mrs Harrison said, "You could have been there and almost ready to return. "OK," I said, "let me run over. Just tell him to hold on a while, then I'll be right back." And so I took off on my motorcycle

CHAPTER THIRTY-EIGHT

for the bank on Park Street. (Our bankers were then the Royal Bank of Canada, 18 Park St., now the Royal Bank of Trinidad and Tobago.)

Let me say there was unity and a unique understanding between Mrs Mosca, Mrs Harrison and myself in the office. We all had the full trust of each other. So I had not to recheck the deposit. As I got to the bank, I rode into the driveway with my briefcase hanging on the handle of my motorcycle with the deposit. This very briefcase was all-purpose, used generally for customs and other offices. As I dismounted, a chap came hastily to me and said, "Mister, mister, look something fall out your shirt pocket, and the breeze blow it under a car." I then slapped my breast pocket hurriedly, leaving the bag hanging on the handle of the motorcycle. I hurried out to see what it was. For I really had some extra money and important papers of my own that morning that I really could have put on any part of my personage or in the bag.

I then went, followed closely by the chap. "It's under that one," he said, pointing to a parked car. I bent down, still feeling my shirt pocket. "Look far below," he said. I then realized that I really had nothing in any of my pockets; everything was in the bag. I hurried back to my motorcycle, but, behold, my bag was gone. It all happened in less than two minutes in my calculation. I stood perplexed. I then asked the gate watchman if he saw anyone from my office come in. "No, no," he said. I again asked him if he saw my bag. "No," he again said to me. I still for some reason felt he was trying a friendly prank on me, for he was a guy with whom I spoke well, and his deceased sister was the second wife of Weston, my brother. But as he assuringly told me he knew nothing whatever about it, I became bewail.[3] I went out on the pavement to see if there was anyone. The kind chap was nowhere to be seen. I looked across the street. There was then a bakery facing the bank. Through their show window a young woman beckoned me to come. As I went, she said, "Mister, you loss something." "Yes, Miss," I anxiously answered, "my bag with all of the deposit." She then turned to another young woman and said, "You see? The same thing ah tell you. Mister, two fellas now gone up the road, and one has it."

---

3   Distressed.

A BRANCH TO REST ON

I then hurried up Park Street to Charlotte Street corner. I was now someone looking for a pin in a haystack. I then hurried to the police headquarters on St Vincent Street opposite the Red House to report the matter. But when asked how much was in the bag, I could not say. All I knew was that I had over $400.00 of my own and some poems composed by me that I wanted to have photostat for my friends, along with some very old coins that I kept and other important matters that I kept for reading, plus a few copies of invoices.

The police clerk at the desk said to me, "Look, man, you sounding jokey." He then went to a sergeant, who came to me followed by a corporal. Several questions were hurled at me. My mind was now in a real state of confusion. For here I was now faced with this crisis. I was to have had all my materials at home for the plumbing by 10:00 a.m. And my friends were expected in by 11:00 p.m. that night. I knew not then what to do. For I now had been interrogated by two police officers in a manner as though I had myself committed the crime. With an uncontrolled tongue, I boldly said, "Listen, man, the damn money is lost, and I don't care one bit about it, for whatever the amount is I can repay, but I have some very important documents in that briefcase that money cannot buy, and that is what I am now concerned about." "Oh, yes," barked the sergeant. "OK, carpral, tek em to dere office, an when you bring em back, report to meh."[4] I said to myself, what does he mean "when you bring him back"? "Come, follow me," said the corporal as we walked across the yard. He entered a jeep and bid me in. "Where is this place?" he asked with a sigh. I directed him; he said not another word to me. But as we drove along he sang a few lines of a calypso. The words were these.

> Sergeant Brown berge Mam whea,
> Berge Mam whea killing people,
> Sergeant Brown Berge mam,
> Berge Mam whea berge mam whea.[5]

---

4   'OK corporal, take them to their office, and when you bring them back, report to me.'
5   Lyrics from "Sergeant Brown – Calinda" by Lord Beginner, sung in patois (French Creole), the language of nineteenth-century calypso (calinda) in Trinidad.

CHAPTER THIRTY-EIGHT

When we got to the office, I got out as he followed closely at my heels. As I entered, both Mrs Mosca and Mrs Harrison were speaking. "What kept you so long?" they both asked. "The driver came just as you left, and Mr Scott sent him out to make a delivery of some tyres. He should have been back already." "I was robbed," I told them, "and I went down to police headquarters to report the matter. These fellows kept me so long asking all sorts of foolish questions. I told them I cared not one damn thing about the money that's lost. But I have some very important documents and old coins in the bag, and that's what I need to recover." "Oh my gosh, no, Wright," they both said with one breath. Just then Mr Mac came from his office, and Mr Scott's head was seen as he climbed the spiral stairway which connected both floors. "What's taking place now?" asked Mr Mac, as he looked at the officer who then had his notebook out with pen holding. I then related everything, trying hard not to forget anything. "How much money was it?" asked Mr Scott. "I do not know, sir, and that's what I told them." "Mrs Mosca, how much money was it?" She then reached for a ledger and said, "$21,934.18." "Wow!" said Mr Mac. I then went on to say that I had over $400.00 of my own to go to the hardware and to do some other shopping. "My goodness," said Mr Scott, "over $22,000.00." Mrs Mosca then said, "It was not all cash: $17,736.12 were in cheques, and $4,198.06 was cash, plus Wright's $400.00." "My Lord, over $4,500.00."

During this investigation, the lawman said not a word. Mr Mac then turned to him and said that he was thankful for his concern. The money was not insured, so the firm will face the loss. But should he be really looking for the thief, do not worry to cast a thought on me. However, what he can do is let me give him a full description of the chap that spoke to me. He can then go over to the bakery and speak to the young woman of whom I spoke, and see how it links.

Mr Scott then asked where was my motorcycle. "Still at the bank, sir," said I. "Then let me take you across to get it." I then asked Mrs Harrison to loan me $200.00 from the vault. As I got downstairs, the driver was waiting. I went with him instead of for my motorcycle. I then hurried to Trestrail's Hardware. It was now almost closing time for a

Saturday opening. I had not then the list, for it was in the stolen bag. Nevertheless, I remembered some of the articles, which were sold to me assisted by the clever clerk who reminded me of some additional fittings. To date I have yet three lengths of the very pipe and some unused fittings because neither the plumber nor my relative showed up for that job.

When I got home I told Marm not a word about the incident, fearing it would make her sick and add to the disappointment of not being able to correct the water problem. Plus she said to me that she received a phone call saying that the flight was delayed and would be in at twelve minutes past midnight.

That suited me fine, as I took my wheelbarrow with a small water drum and six covered buckets. I filled the water tank plus the bathtub and laundry sink. This I finished at exactly 10:00 p.m. Vernon, who was now a taxi driver, was home at 10:10 p.m., all in readiness for the airport. Having been told that our friends were coming in at 11:00 p.m., Marm then said, "Why not take a good nap for an hour? I had the settee made in Burton's room for you. Vernon said he shall be down to St James and would then be back at 11:15 p.m." Marm again said, "I told you to take a nap." I took her advice and really did get a much-needed hour's sleep. Marm woke me up at 11:10 p.m. At 11:20 p.m. Vernon came, and we set off for the airport.

On our way we spoke of the country's political state and general election that was coming. He then gave a joke that only Vernon could. He spoke of a candidate who was seeking a seat. This gent in one of the meetings said to an anxious crowd: "Wen all-yuh was hungry, who gee all-yuh B-R-E-D?" (In so saying, he spelt the word.) One of his supporters said to him, "Man, yuh forget the A." "Oh thank yuh, man," he said. He again turned to the anxious crowd and said, "When oll yuh was hungry, who gee oll yuh B-R-E-D-A." To be truthful, those were the days a personage had not to digest over 30,000 words from a dictionary before he could canvass an election. One could easily have done that if you had large estates and a favourable bank account and living good with the poor man.

CHAPTER THIRTY-EIGHT

We were at the airport before the plane touched down. I was allowed to go into the customs area to welcome my friends. This was then the second time in my manhood that I was clearly lifted off the ground, and it was done by Alfred La Riviere as he greeted me. There was one setback, however: their cases did not arrive until three days later.

When we got home, they were greeted by Vinneth and welcomed by Marm as though she knew them all her life. Burton and Oswald were always shy, so they shared not in the excitement. We were now into Sunday morning. I then right away explained to them our water situation when Marm showed them their room. They adjusted themselves to the way of life much better than many of our local friends or relatives would have done.

Now let me say this: Vernon was not a route taxi driver. He drove tourists only and was an assigned driver of our country's Tourist Board. He had an edge upon his colleagues because he also spoke and wrote fluent English and Spanish. And he knew well the places where to take our friends, who were soon his friends also. At the places of merriment, Marm and I did not join because we were no revellers. But there were the days when Vernon took us out to many places of interest such as the Pitch Lake.

They visited Tobago, where they stayed at the Palm Beach Hotel. They visited the Bird of Paradise Island, but they saw no birds. They, however, saw the cocrico*, which is on this country's coat of arms with the scarlet ibis and hummingbird, plus many other points of interest such as Buccoo Reef. On their return to Trinidad, Mr and Mrs Mac had them for tea one evening, after which they went and played a game of golf.

Our friends the La Rivieres left for the United States, their home, a seemingly happy pair. Before leaving they said, "We will return." The thought of General MacArthur came to me, when under different circumstances he made a similar remark to the Japanese people. I will not go into details, but they did come again, and we were invited to their home. Marm did not join me as she held on to her tradition that we both must not leave home at the same time to travel abroad. I was given elite treatment by my friends. I remember asking Alfred over the phone if he thinks that our families would meet and share in heaven. With that he shouted to his wife, Marian, "Honey! Do you think we could stand to have George in heaven with us?" That's the humorous family we dealt with. Marm phones or has me send cables on their birthdays. How simple life can be. Just to think that this all came about through the simple gathering of some wild leaves.

Chapter 39

Mr Mac moves away from Trinidad; George retires at the age of sixty-eight and writes his autobiography

Mr Mac then visited the United States. On his return, he decided to open a San Fernando branch of the business, which turned out to be a great success. At one time they were doing far more recapping of industrial and truck tyres in San Fernando than in Port of Spain. It is a fact that San Fernando is the chief city of the oil belt of Trinidad and Tobago. And so this industry proved a boom.

I had now quite a lot of running around between both points, for all container rubber and accessories were unstuffed by Customs at the San Fernando end, which took me into the late hours of the night. After that, I motorcycled my way back home with the cold breeze or sometimes rain.

Mr Mac from the kindness of his heart then decided to sell shares at $5.00 each to the entire staff without discrimination. I did well in the buying. And when dividends were paid at the end of each financial year, all who had shares were satisfied. (At least I knew I was.) But for some undisclosed reason, they were forced to join the then Macal Group of Companies. It was then not the policy of this group for individuals to earn shares. And so all our individual shares were bought over by them.

Let me just say this of the man who moulded me. I had been an old drift log from Toco whom Mr Mac took clean and shaped into a piece of furniture that could be used. This business wizard, for handling his own domestic affairs, registered an office in the name of Nortrub Ltd. When asked by his friends, "Why 'Nortrub'?" – with a twitch in his eyes and a smile on his face – he will say, "No trouble at all." But, Reader, the word Nortrub, if spelt backwards, is Burton, which is his name.

The time had come for Mr Mac's retirement. He and his dear wife then left Trinidad and took up residence in Florida. After so many years residing there, we never failed to keep in touch with each other during their visits to this country and by occasional airmail. And throughout the years they have kept me supplied with my *National Geographic* issue each month from January to December without fail.

Let me say it this way. Mr Mac's retirement was like the beginning of a broken family relationship. For one year later, Mrs Mosca decided that she had had enough. She then applied for an early retirement, which was granted, and she migrated to the United Kingdom. In meekness, I wrote two poems to commemorate the retirement of both these stalwarts who began in a humble Pembroke Street office which introduced a firm of what it is today. We were now fully under the leadership of Mr Everard Scott, he now being the governing director of Burmac Ltd. There were also two other directors, a financial secretary who knew well his work, and a chairman.

Under the new management, the Tragarete Road premises were then sold. Burmac was now moved to George Street and South Quay Corner. At the South Quay Building I was again given my own enclosed office with my two amiable assistants who up to then had never failed in the execution of their duties. We three worked with that togetherness in the interest of the firm, and at the same time easing the workload on ourselves. I was told, however, to get myself a typist. But these, my sons (as they were called), assured me that they could handle that arm of duty also (which they did). As I have before mentioned, they were more than worth their hire.

Mr Scott, our governing director, demanded that I still hold duplicate

CHAPTER THIRTY-NINE

keys, as was customary in the seven sites under the leadership of Mr Mac and himself. This was mainly because I worked on the processing of documents for Customs and the Control Board very late or early morn at times, as well as on the unstuffing of containers. That on many occasions would run until 2:00 a.m. of the next day, depending on the merchandise or the availability of an officer to check.

Mr Scott also insisted that I get my driver's license. "Of what use will that be now to me?" I asked. "Never mind," said he. "Right now you can get a driver to run to every call you may desire. But the day may come that you may have a jalopy of your own. Will you then call Tom, Dick and Harry to take you around in it? Come on, man, this doesn't sound like the George I once knew. I will speak to Mr Washam Acall to send a driver from his driving school to start you on that." I was then aged sixty-five years. And through being non-confident in myself about the growing road mishaps, I turned him down. "George Wright," he said to me, "do you realize that you are one of the few men, if there are any others of your age, who are riding from Port of Spain to San Fernando day or night on a motorcycle, sun or rain?" Without me commenting, he said, "Get the license and I shall handle the cost." I did. A vehicle was then given to me. But yet I kept my motorcycle for quick movement in the busy city and for convenient parking.

At age sixty-six years, I retired but was asked by management to give them yet another year, and I gave them two. During this time they decided to move down to Lange Park in Chaguanas, where they intended to move into the tractor and other heavy field equipment business.

Oh may I say that Mr Scott had tendered his resignation a few months earlier. And so I went along with the firm for four months after he left and then called it a day.

My departure from the company was somewhat unique, inspired by "The Burial of Sir John Moore" by the poet Charles Wolfe:

> Not a drum was heard,
> Not an extra funeral note,
> Not a farewell word or adieu.
> Not a glass was raised,

A BRANCH TO REST ON

Not a tear or praise,
Did recall my hectic days.[1]

On my final resignation from Burmac Ltd., I bought both the vehicles which I used from the company. And may I say I rode a motorcycle until I was aged sixty-nine years, when I was stopped by Marm and Vin. And may I now say many thanks to Mr Scott for bullying me into the school of driving, which is now my chief means of transport. Again, many thanks to you, Everard.

I am very happy today to look back upon the years of my life, from whence and how it was all started. When the final end should come, let me be able to say boldly to Mr Death as did Sir Walter Raleigh to his beheaders: "Strike, man, strike."[2]

"What does it matter where the head lies. When the heart is alright. Fear not them which kill the body but are not able to kill the soul" (Mat. 10:28). And in my final words may I say, "Praise God, thank you, Jesus."

Signature of George Wright

30-4-97

The End

---

[1] The original lines in "The Burial of Sir John Moore after Corunna" (1817) by Charles Wolfe:
Not a drum was heard, not a funeral note,
As his corse to the rampart we hurried;
Not a soldier discharged his farewell shot
O'er the grave where our hero we buried'

[2] When Sir Walter Raleigh was beheaded in 1618, he is reputed to have said to his executioner, while waiting for the axe to fall, "Strike, man, strike!"

POSTSCRIPT

"I am the true vine, and my Father is the gardener. He cuts off every branch in me that bears no fruit while every branch that does bear fruit, he prunes so that it will be even more fruitful"
John 15:1–2

Thank you, Grandpa, for having allowed Him to prune you so that His fruit can live on, after you have gone, in your progeny.

I love you, Grandpa.

Sandra Wright
Granddaughter

GLOSSARY

Most of the information in this section is taken from *The Dictionary of the English/Creole of Trinidad and Tobago* (Winer, 2009). This work contains extensive information on history, origins, development, spelling and other aspects of vocabulary in this context. (E) indicates a word used in standard English (AE) American English, (FR) standard French, and (SP) standard Spanish.

Word	Definition
acra, accra, acara	a food made with saltfish mixed with flour, water and seasonings and deep fried
Adam hat	Adam Hats, an American hat maker founded in 1924, and a very popular brand in the 1940s and 1950s
advantageous	taking advantage of people; exploitative
"A from Bullfoot"	not know; very uneducated
agouti	a large rodent, indigenous to Central and South American rainforests; hunted for its meat
ajoupa	a type of dwelling or shelter having a roof thatched with dried palm leaves
alpagatas	traditional sandals with a woven rope sole and woven (usually patterned) or canvas top strap
all-yuh	plural of pronoun *you*
as	equals English "like"; compared to
badjohns	men willing to use violence and who like being known as dangerous

GLOSSARY

bake	a circular, thick flattish bread made of wheat flour, water and baking soda, fried (fry bake), baked in the oven (roast bake) or baked in a pot (roast bake)
barrack rooms	rooms in a low-quality barrack building; a housing system originally for the enslaved, later used for indentured workers
bashboards	small vertical finishing boards on the eaves of a house running along the edge of a gable to conceal rafters and keep out rain (E bargeboards)
bassa-bassa	commotion; trouble; aggression; fussiness
bass broom	a natural wood-backed sweeping broom head used outdoors on rough surfaces
benching	punishment by hitting a child, usually a boy, who is put over a bench and whipped on the buttocks
big-guts	a swollen belly, usually due to malnutrition
bobs	shilling coins
bois cano	bois-cano(n), a medium-sized native deciduous tree, with a cannon-like hollow trunk
bois flot	fruit pods of the bois flot tree containing an abundance of seeds in soft brownish fibre once used for stuffing pillows
bongo	a traditional dance of African origin with very strong vigorous movements, usually performed at wakes by men
bosun	a boatswain, a ship's officer in charge of equipment and the crew's duties
break (l'ecole) biche	avoid attendance at school, deliberately and without legitimate excuse
break stick in yuh ears	to give a blow to the ears with a stick
bull-de-flair	usually bull de fé, bull difay, boule-dife, a torch made by filling a bottle with kerosene, and lighting a rag stuck in its mouth

GLOSSARY

buljol	a dish made from salt cod, oil, onions, tomatoes and pepper, usually eaten for breakfast
bush doctor	a healer who uses traditional folk remedies
bush tea	tea made from wild plants
cacapool	rum of a cheap, raw, inferior kind
calabash	a hollowed-out and dried calabash fruit, with a hole or cut in half, used as a bowl or food container, especially for liquids.
callaloo	a thick soup, made with green (usually dasheen) leaves and ochroes, a cultivated plant bearing edible slimy seed pods. An essential ingredient in callaloo soup.
carat palm	a tall native palm in Trinidad with large drooping fan-shaped leaves used as thatching
Carib	of (partial) Carib Amerindian descent. In Trinidad, people identified in this way are usually a mix of Amerindian, Spanish and African descent.
carite	a medium-sized edible game fish
carterman's sponge	a very heavy, inexpensive cake, usually with thin icing
cartoon	a container for holding goods. The author uses words such as *cartoon*, *carton*, *canister* and *trunk* interchangeably.
cassava	a cultivated perennial shrub of about three metres (ten feet) high. Both bitter (toxic) and sweet (non-toxic) variety of tuber used for food and starch.
chac-chac	a musical percussion rhythm instrument made of something hollow and spherical, such as a small calabash or gourd, containing a number of dried seeds with an attached handle
chip-chip	a small triangular bivalve mollusc, found in the sand, especially on the Eastern beaches

GLOSSARY

	of Trinidad. Folk belief holds that it is an aphrodisiac, particularly for men.
coals	charcoal
cocoa bag	a heavy, loosely woven bag made to hold dry cocoa beans for shipping
cocrico	a large turkey-like native bird; the official bird of Tobago, featured on the Trinidad and Tobago crest
commissary	a store for the sale of food and other goods, especially to soldiers and other military personnel; particularly applicable here to the US military bases in Trinidad
coolie	originally, from the mid-nineteenth century on, a person from India, generally an immigrant indentured labourer; now usually considered negative, insulting and racist
cork hat	a helmet-shaped sun hat, made of the dried pith of several Indian trees, used especially by the British in India and associated with police officers and planters
cornbird	any medium- to large-sized black and yellow bird, possibly so-named because of the corn-like bright yellow colour or from some species eating corn and other grain
corn coocoo	a dish usually made with grated corn (maize), cornmeal, or grated cassava, and boiled with ochroes and butter. Sometimes bits of salt-meat and seasonings are added.
corned fish	dried, cleaned salted fish used to make buljol and other dishes, often referred to as *saltfish*
cow-heel	hoof or foot of a cow, used in making soup
cowitch	any of several plants, usually vines, bearing pods with highly irritant hairs
crapaud	any frog or toad

GLOSSARY

crepesole	a shoe with a rubber sole, usually with canvas uppers
crook	wooden saddle for a donkey with crossed pieces front and back to hang things
Crown land	land owned by the government
cuatroist	someone who plays a *cuatro*, a small four-stringed guitar of Venezuelan origin
cuss	curse, swear
cutlass	a cutting tool with a relatively long metal blade and a wooden handle often bound with wire, usually used by swinging it vertically, horizontally, or at an angle to chop or swipe; a machete
dasheen (bush)	a cultivated plant with edible tubers, stems and leaves; edible when cooked to remove oxalic acid; used in callaloo
école biche	miss attendance at school deliberately and without legitimate excuse (*See break biche*)
ee	he, his
estate	a relatively large landholding usually with hired workers for commercial agricultural production. The term is generally used in Trinidad and Tobago rather than *plantation*, which is commonly used throughout the Caribbean.
evening	the time of the day after noon, or about 4:00 p.m., usually before darkness falls
exhibition winner	winner of a competitive scholarship to a secondary school
extra-strong	an imported flat, white, hard peppermint candy. The words "extra strong" are printed on each candy.
father priest	a Catholic priest
feter	someone who takes an active part in a *fete*, the word commonly used in Trinidad and Tobago for a party

GLOSSARY

fired my job	quit my job
fireside	a support for cooking pots over a wood fire made from small rocks, or a low clay wall
flambeau	a torch, originally a flare made of leaves; then a torch made of wood wrapped in pitch-oil-soaked cloth, later a wick in a bottle of pitch-oil. See *bull-de-flair* above.
float	a fried yeast biscuit that floats while frying, often served with *accra*
fobs	watch pocket in trousers
food carrier	a traditional Indian set of small round metal containers on top of each other in a stack, with a metal hook to keep them altogether. Different dishes are placed in separate containers.
for so	a lot
frontin	forward, pushy, overaggressive
furnitures	furniture; pieces of furniture
gaulin	any heron or large wading bird
Gazette (paper)	a sheet of paper from the *Port of Spain Gazette* newspaper, published between 1825 and 1959; any sheet of newspaper; euphemism for toilet paper
Georgie Porgie	a traditional English nursery rhyme: "Georgie Porgie pudding and pie, kissed the girls and made them cry"
golden apple	a tall native tree with pale yellowish white flowers and edible fruit; also called *pommecythere* or *pomsitay*
grass knife	a small curved sickle-shaped knife with a toothed edge, used to cut grass
green tea	a hot drink made from imported leaves of the tea plant. In English this is "black" tea, slightly fermented before roasting; green tea is roasted immediately after picking.

GLOSSARY

Gros Michel banana	a variety of cultivated and commercially sold banana
ground provision	any edible tuber including yams, sweet potatoes, dasheen, tannia, eddoes, cassava and cush cush
Guardian	*Trinidad and Tobago Guardian*, a major local newspaper that was first published in 1917
harden	unwilling to listen to advice or reason; stubborn
heave!	a cry used to encourage participants in a fight
high woods	land under native timber, either never cleared or fully regrown, with tall trees and little undergrowth
honkey-doh-ray	hunky-dory, fine, without problems (AE)
hops bread	a small round soft-yeast bread, traditionally with a hard flaky crust and an airy, easily torn inside
(to) hot	warm up, usually food
hot piss	an urgent need to urinate
immortelle	a tall cultivated and naturalized tree used to shade young plants, often seen in cocoa estates. When in bloom its red flowers are a very conspicuous part of the vegetation and can be seen for miles.
jealousy flaps	narrow strips of wood used as a window covering that are slanted upwards on the outside to exclude sun and rain, while admitting air and some light; jalousies (FR)
jiggers	blood-sucking fleas; chiggers
jumbies	ghosts; the spirits of dead people
kaiser ball	a hard sweet candy striped in different colours, usually red and yellow, coated in granulated sugar. The candy changes taste as it is eaten due to sweet and sour layers.
kingfish	a marine game fish prized for food
lantern fly	a type of large firefly

GLOSSARY

latro	any low forest, especially previously cultivated fields overtaken by trees and shrubs
lavinee, lavani, lavanie	a vanilla sweet, made from sugar boiled with cream of tartar and vinegar, which is cooled, pulled into a long roll, cut into pieces, and coated with icing sugar
licked off	struck off
licks like peas	a beating with a lot of force
Limacol	a Caribbean mentholated lotion used as an astringent, toilet water, or rub
limer	a person who enjoys *liming*: informal conversational activity, especially someone who often does this in public
lushet, luchette	an agricultural tool with a curved spade-like end used for digging holes
macafouchette	leftovers of a meal
maco	a gossip; busybody; eavesdropper
madbull	a large six-sided kite, having a cocoyea (coconut flex) or stick frame and a cloth tail; makes noise when flying
make a right	to wave
make the groceries	shop for groceries, food
maljo	evil eye; the belief that a conscious or unconscious look of envy or ill will can harm someone
mamaguy	tease; deceive; try to get something by flattery
manatee	a large, slow-moving animal that appears in coastal waters and rivers (E)
mango doodoos	a popular variety of small and sweet cultivated mango
manicou crabs	large dark brown or brownish red crabs which resemble a dead leaf and inhabit mountainous forests. The female carries the eggs and young under the flap of the belly, similar to a *manicou* (opossum).

GLOSSARY

mauby	a drink made from the bark of a tree, somewhat bitter but usually heavily sweetened with sugar
melongene	aubergine, eggplant
millions	a small fresh-or-brackish-water fish known widely as the *guppy*, known locally usually as *millions* from its quick reproduction and large numbers
Mile-a-Minute	a well-known roasted-nuts vendor of Chinese background known for his speed-walking in Port of Spain
monkey say cool breeze	said to counsel patience, that your time will come
more in the mortar beside the pestle	there is more to this than meets the eye; something secretive is going on
noggin	a house, wall, etc., made with bits and pieces such as bricks and woodchips
Nordic	a white person (usage of this word appears to be the author's personal choice)
obeah man/ woman	someone who practises *obeah*, a folk system of magic using supernatural forces to bring about effects such as success in love or business or harming an enemy. Based primarily on West African rituals but incorporating Christian, Indian and other practices
old talk, ole talk	talk designed to entertain, seduce, impress
on the papers	in the newspaper
one time	all at once; immediately; right away, right now
oui	a post-sentence emphatic expression, sometimes indicating surprise or agreement
palet	a sweet ice on a stick, usually containing milk
pan am	upon it/him/her
pannier	a basket, especially a large basket used to transport produce to market, often suspended over the back of a donkey (E)

GLOSSARY

parlour	a small shop, usually a little shed, in front of a house which sells ready-to-eat foods, non-alcoholic beverages, snacks, cigarettes and some staple groceries
passage	money for transport, e.g., for a taxi or bus
patois	Patois was the most widely used language in Trinidad from the late eighteenth to the early twentieth century; mostly French-derived vocabulary, but with grammar and phonology also derived partly from African and other languages.
pelau	a dish of browned meat, usually small pieces of beef or chicken, with rice, and usually pigeon peas
Penny Bank	the Trinidad Co-operative Bank, established in 1914, which accepted deposits as low as a penny at a time
picong(s)	teasing, ridicule, or insult, especially in semi-formal or ritualized exchanges, for example, between calypsonians
pigeon peas	a cultivated upright shrub. Seeds have a high nutrient value, cooked fresh or dried. Probably native to Africa, but widely cultivated in tropical regions
pigin	penis (child use)
pirogue	originally a small boat made from a hollowed-out tree trunk, sometimes having a batwing sail and a jib. Now usually a small boat made from overlapping boards, commonly used in fishing
pitched	asphalted
pitch-oil	fuel oil distilled from petroleum or *pitch* (kerosene)
plantain	large, somewhat angular banana-like fruit; contains less sugar than bananas; cooked before being eaten

GLOSSARY

pommecythere	see *golden apple*
poopah, poopa	father
pull-a-ra	likely a sort of enclosure
puncha creme	an eggnog-like drink usually made at Christmastime, including rum, milk, sugar, nutmeg and essence; *ponche crema* (SP)
put away	decorate or furnish beautifully; of a house: clean, arrange, fix up; usually for a special occasion or festive season
redfish	a marine fish with light, bright red scales; a prized eating fish
right	a greeting of recognition, meeting or departure
roo-coo	a natural red food colouring derived from a cultivated shrub or small tree
safe	a wooden cupboard/box often with a mesh section in which foodstuffs are placed to protect them from insects and vermin
saltfish	dried salted fish (see *corned fish* above) used in many Caribbean dishes; formed part of the food given to the enslaved; now considered a special traditional cultural dish
shilling	a British colonial coin worth twelve pence, equal to twenty-four cents in the Trinidad and Tobago dollar system of currency; a bob
short crop	quick-growing agricultural crop grown for commercial sale, e.g., cabbage
sills	strong horizontal beams used to form a house foundation (E)
silvers	silverware and cutlery
sive	a local chive-like seasoning herb
skulled	tricked or deceived
smart man	conman; someone who cheats or deceives people to get money
souse	dish, usually made of a pig's trotters or head,

GLOSSARY

	marinated in vinegar or lime juice, with hot pepper, onion and cucumber
Spanish, Spaniard	of people originally from Spain and now Latin America, usually of Venezuelan descent, often mixed with African or Amerindian
spirit lash	in folk belief, a physical or spiritual injury, sometimes fatal, resulting from malevolent actions
sponge, sponge cake	a heavy pudding made of stale bread and cakes, also called a *bellyfull*
steups, cheups	make a noise, usually of annoyance or derision, by sucking air and saliva through the teeth, also called suck teeth
stump	strike the toe or foot unexpectedly and painfully against a stone or other hard object (E=stub)
stupidee	stupid person
stupidness	stupidity, stupid actions
susu	a cooperative savings system of African origin in which each person contributes the same fixed amount each week, and the whole amount, or *hand*, is taken by a different member each time
sweetbread	a heavy cake made with flour, grated coconut and sugar; usually with raisins, sometimes candied fruit peel
sweet drink	an aerated or carbonated beverage; flavoured soda; soft drink
sweet-water	a drink made from sugar and water, usually as a food for poor people, especially children
swiper	a scythe-like *cutlass* on a long handle
talkari	an Indian side dish usually of vegetables made with sauce or gravy, to go with rice or roti
tannia	a cultivated plant with edible tubers that are long and thin with rough, hairy dark brown skin and edible white flesh

GLOSSARY

tanty	affectionate term for an aunt, or older woman
tapia	a house-building material made of mud mixed with grass applied to a stick framework
tasso	salted dried beef, usually imported from Venezuela, and used in cooking
tow	give someone a ride on the handlebar or crosspiece of a bicycle; usually illegal
too-too	excrement
toxicedo	tuxedo; spelled *toxicedo* in the manuscript, probably the author's word
utensil	chamber pot
waled	marks or ridges made on the flesh from blows with a stick, belt, whip, etc.
waratal	a reddish grey quartz stone, sharp when broken up, used for *suckaways*, pits filled with small rocks used as a drain
watchicong	rubber-soled canvas shoe
whe-whe	a gambling game of Chinese origin, in which the organizer or banker chooses one number or *mark* from a set of numbers and seals it in an envelope; people then bet on what number it is, traditionally according to dreams
whey, papa!	an expression of surprise, amazement, or emphasis
work jumbies	very ardent workers; thought to be possessed by a demon to work hard
worm grass	a small, bushy native plant, the roots of which have a distinctive unpleasant smell
zagaya	a small crab. In this context, it means to catch crabs to cook with the yam.

www.ingramcontent.com/pod-product-compliance
Lightning Source LLC
Chambersburg PA
CBHW051242300426
44114CB00011B/850